PRAISE FOR *Chained to the Desk in a Hybrid World*

"In this classic masterpiece, Bryan Robinson has written the universal guide on work-life balance, offering proven secrets to heal the chains that shackle us to our catastrophic dependence on achievement along with life-saving techniques."
—Joy Erlichman Miller, psychotherapist and CEO of Resiliency Forums

"Bryan Robinson's groundbreaking book arrives at a crucial time in our history. I know of no other book that better identifies this other pandemic of work addiction that takes a toll on individuals, their families, and the companies that foster it, yet is so revered in our culture."
—Richard Schwartz, author of *No Bad Parts*

"A masterful exploration of the mind of the workaholic that offers creative and powerful practices to build resilience, increase mindfulness, and restore balance in the midst of a speedy and stressful culture."
—Tara Brach, author of *Trusting the Gold* and *Radical Acceptance*

"A lifesaver for anyone who is burnt out and exhausted from working too much. It comprehensively explains the problems, provides science-based solutions, and tells personal stories that make a great read."
—Kristin Neff, author of *Self-Compassion*

"A combination of heart-warming stories, cutting edge science, and transforming skills—all packaged in a true page turner that helps you find an immersive presence and fulfillment in life."
—Amit Sood, MD, Executive Director, Global Center for
    Resiliency and Wellbeing

"Masterfully blends compelling stories with cutting-edge science to provide readers with a new way to think about burnout and science-based tools they can use to manage it. If you've ever found yourself struggling to break free from the incessant demands of work, this beautifully written book is for you."
—Ethan Kross, best-selling author of *Chatter*

"This chillingly confrontational and profound book is about more than addictive behavior. It is about the tragic dimension of the human situation."
—Harville Hendrix and Helen LaKelly Hunt, authors of *Getting the Love You Want*

Chained to the Desk in a Hybrid World

Chained
to the Desk
in a Hybrid
World

A GUIDE TO
WORK-LIFE BALANCE

Bryan E. Robinson, PhD

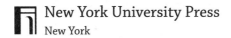

New York University Press
New York

NEW YORK UNIVERSITY PRESS
New York
www.nyupress.org

This book is based on *Chained to the Desk: A Guidebook for Workaholics, Their Partners and Children, and the Clinicians Who Treat Them*, 3rd ed. (2014).

Figure 5.1 by Rhys Davies.

Please contact the Library of Congress for Cataloging-in-Publication data.
ISBN: 9781479818846 (hardback)
ISBN: 9781479818853 (paperback)
ISBN: 9781479818877 (library ebook)
ISBN: 9781479818860 (consumer ebook)

This book is printed on acid-free paper, and its binding materials are chosen for strength and durability. We strive to use environmentally responsible suppliers and materials to the greatest extent possible in publishing our books.

Manufactured in the United States of America

10 9 8 7 6 5 4 3 2 1

Also available as an ebook

This book is dedicated to my dear friends, colleagues, and fellow co-founders of our new company, ComfortZones Digital.

To Steve Glaser, Gina Cruse, Jim Bailey, and Eva Condron-Wells.

It has been an honor to know all of you and a blast to create a new company with such caring people invested in supporting employees coping with work stress.

One of the marvels of the world is
the sight of a soul sitting in prison
with the key in its hand.

—Rumi

Contents

Introduction

Monsters are real, and ghosts are real, too. They live inside us, and sometimes they win.
                    —Stephen King

My Story

As a hard-driving university professor, the thought of a vacation or weekend without work was terrifying, and I structured my life accordingly, just as I did as a boy. One Friday before a long weekend, I left my office with butterflies in my stomach at the thought of facing an unplanned weekend. I grabbed a memo announcing grant proposal deadlines. Suddenly, calm descended over me, and the adrenaline began to flow as I folded the three-inch-thick computer printout under my arm. Like an alcoholic with a bottle, I was assured of plenty "to drink," calmed by the guarantee of having more to do. That guarantee was an anesthetic, a tranquilizer. But after the proposal was written, the feelings of emptiness, unrest, and depression returned.

There were times I needed my work so badly that I hid it from others—the way my alcoholic father needed and hid his bourbon. And just as I once tried to control my father's drinking by pouring out his booze and refilling the bottle with vinegar, the people who loved me sulked, pleaded, and tore their hair out trying to keep me from working all the time. Every summer, for instance, just before we left on vacation, Jamey, my spouse, would search my bags and confiscate any work I planned to smuggle into our rented beach house on the South Carolina shore. But however thoroughly he searched, he would always miss the tightly folded papers covered with work notes that I had bootlegged into the pockets of my jeans.

Later, when Jamey and our close friends invited me to stroll on the beach, I'd say I was tired and wanted to nap. While they were off swimming and playing in the surf—which I considered a big waste of time—I secretly worked in the empty house, bent over a lap desk fashioned from a board. At the sound of their returning footsteps, I'd stuff my papers back into my jeans, hide the board, and stretch out on the bed, pretending to be asleep.

I saw nothing strange about my behavior; it's only in hindsight that I say that I was a workaholic. By this, I mean something quite different from saying that I worked hard. I mean that I used work to defend myself against unwelcome emotional states—to modulate anxiety, sadness, and frustration the way a pothead uses dope and an alcoholic uses booze.

During my tenured professorship at the University of North Carolina at Charlotte, I carried a full teaching load and volunteered for committee assignments, while also writing books, conducting research, and establishing a full clinical practice. Ignoring Jamey's frequent pleas that we "just do something together," I worked in my windowless office in our basement through evenings, weekends, Thanksgivings, and Christmases. I even worked through most of the day of my father's funeral: while my mother and sisters broke bread with old neighbors, I toiled in my university office twenty-five miles away, working on a project so insignificant I no longer remember what it was.

When I stopped thinking of myself as an extraordinarily talented and dedicated professional with a great deal to offer the world and realized how empty my life had become, I hit bottom. Until then I'd been proud of my work addiction and well rewarded for it. Jamey might complain that I was never home— and that when I was, I didn't listen—but my university colleagues called me responsible and conscientious. Jamey might call me controlling, inflexible, and incapable of living in the moment. But the promotions, accolades, and fat paychecks that came my way built an ever-stronger case against his accusations, and I used them to further vilify him: *Why couldn't he pull his own weight? Why couldn't he be more supportive? Why didn't he appreciate my hard work and the creature comforts it provided? Why was he constantly bothering me with problems that distracted me from earning a decent living?*

After nearly fourteen years together, Jamey—who had been trying without success to talk to me about my absence from our relationship and his growing problems with alcohol—told me that he had found someone who *would* listen to him, and he moved out. My first book had been published, and I had two more books and several funded research projects in the works. I was also recovering from surgery for stress-related gastrointestinal problems. My life was crumbling under my feet, and there was nothing I could do about it. I lost weight. I couldn't eat. I didn't care if I lived or died.

I was a chain-smoking, caffeine-drinking work junkie, dogged by self-doubt. I had no close friends. I didn't smile. I thought my colleagues didn't really appreciate my hard work and were breathing down my neck. My memory got so bad that members of my family wondered if I was developing an early onset Alzheimer's. I snapped at colleagues, and they snapped back. I once angrily confronted a university librarian, demanding the name of the irresponsible faculty member who had kept, for three months, a book I needed for research. With a raised brow, she gave me the name: my own. Work had been the one thing that I had always done well, and now even that was turning against me. Yet I couldn't stop working.

In the summer of that year Jamey and I reconciled, and in the fall he checked himself into a treatment center for alcoholism. When I eagerly took part in the family treatment component to "help Jamey with his problem," a facilitator confronted me with my own work addiction. I joined Workaholics Anonymous, entered therapy, and began my climb out of the work pit into a saner life. And Jamey and I started to understand the crack in the foundation of our relationship. Today we celebrate decades together with peace of mind.

Some Things *Never* Change

This books builds on the three editions of my *Chained to the Desk*. The first edition appeared in 1998, the second in 2007, and the third in 2014. During this twenty-four-year span, many societal changes and research advances have yielded fodder for a new work. In 2019, the World Health Organization (WHO) officially classified work burnout, stemming from "chronic workplace stress," as a medical diagnosis and included the condition in the *International Classification of Diseases*, the handbook that guides medical providers in diagnosing diseases. Burnout appears in the handbook's section on problems associated with employment or unemployment. It describes burnout as "a syndrome conceptualized as resulting from chronic workplace stress that has not been successfully managed."

Shortly after the WHO's declaration, a firestorm erupted when Dr. Richard A. Friedman, professor of clinical psychiatry at Weill Cornell Medical College, published an op-ed in the *New York Times* asking, "Is burnout real?" His supposition was that burnout is everywhere and that nearly everyone seems to have suffered from it. Dr. Friedman argued that "when a disorder is reportedly so widespread, it makes me wonder whether we are at risk of medicalizing everyday distress. If everyone suffers from burnout, then no one does, and the concept loses all credibility."[1] Arianna Huffington, founder and CEO of Thrive Global, challenged Friedman's logic: "So it's strange to say, in the face of overwhelming evidence, that a phenomenon can't be real because it's widespread. That's precisely what an epidemic is. Friedman's observation that almost everyone suffers from burnout doesn't refute the existence of a crisis—it makes the case for one."[2]

Friedman's comments were emblematic of the mental health profession's rampant denial of certain forms of mental issues related to work stress. If there's no such thing as burnout, then there's no such thing as work addiction. And clinicians have a history of relegating burnout and workaholism to the pop psychology bookshelves. Having experienced the personal damage of work addiction, hearing people joke about it is painful and cringeworthy. I have spent the greater part of my career exposing the damage overworking causes individuals, families, and businesses. I have treated hundreds, maybe thousands, suffering over broken homes, job losses, and even death because of this invisible illness. To say that the public and media—even the mental health profession—do not take workaholism seriously is an understatement.

When it's not praised, workaholism is dismissed as a joke. One light-hearted portrayal in a newspaper cartoon showed a huge, empty meeting room with a sign posted at the front that reads: "Workaholics Anonymous." The cartoon's caption says, "Everybody had to work overtime." Advertisers bathe workaholism in the same glamorous light that they poured over cigarettes and liquor in the ads of the 1930s. A Lexus ad in the *Wall Street Journal* boasted, "Workaholic? Oh, you flatter us: The relentless pursuit of perfection." A radio commercial for a truck praised the versatility of the "Workaholic 4 by 4." If you tell people you're a workaholic, they usually chuckle.

A 1980 book on workaholics applauded the workaholic lifestyle, presenting it as a virtue, suggesting that workaholics are happy because they are doing what they love.[3] Supporters of work addiction reform have been the targets of ridicule and butts of jokes, as a 1994 commentary from *Fortune* magazine illustrated: "Along with heroin, gambling, sex, and sniffing model airplane glue, work is now taken seriously as something people often get addicted to, in which case they need to get cured. . . . The references to work addiction are instantly psychiatric. The phrase is enveloped in psychobabble about inner insecurities, lives destroyed, and—could it be otherwise?—support groups needed."[4] To add insult to injury, a movement is afoot in this country today to deconstruct the term "work/life balance." Corporate honcho Jeff Bezos, for example, has advised his Amazon employees to stop aiming for work-life balance because it implies a tradeoff between the two. Bezos thereby threatens to erase the work/life boundaries self-professed workaholics have fought so hard to establish.[5]

Psst, Denial Is Not a River in Egypt

Perhaps most alarming of all is the rampant denial among mental health practitioners, as Friedman's op-ed illuminated. In 2012, a professor in the Netherlands who coined the term *engaged workaholics* argued that "if you love what you do, where's the harm in doing too much?" I wonder if that's something anyone would tell an alcoholic, shopaholic, drug addict, overeater, or compulsive gambler.[6] These kinds of comments by fellow professionals reflect ignorance about a condition that wreaks misery and havoc on millions of workers in this country. Obviously, a lot of education is still needed, even for mental health professionals, which brings me to an even more disturbing situation.

Although *workaholism* has become a household word, sadly it has not been accepted into the official psychiatric and psychological nomenclature. The American Psychiatric Association considers it a symptom of obsessive-compulsive personality disorder. Jeffrey Kahn, a consultant for the association's committee on psychiatry in the workplace, insists that "other professionals who think workaholism is an addiction or a diagnosis in and of itself are 'missing the boat.'"[7] It's also shocking that in 2006, a representative of the Priory, Great Britain's high-profile clinic for addiction, charged that "workaholism is just something journalists like to write about."[8]

In the fifth edition of the *Diagnostic and Statistical Manual of Mental Disorders* (DSM-5), the American Psychiatric Association recommended that the addictive diagnostic category include both substance use disorders and non-substance addiction such as gambling. The APA's recognition of behavioral addictions as true addictions is a groundbreaking departure from past actions. But unfortunately, workaholism—or work addiction or overworking—were not included as a nonsubstance addiction in the DSM-5.[9] This oversight occurred even though the association is recommending further study of internet use disorder as an addiction and is recognizing other addictive disorders that are related to the use of caffeine, inhalants, and tobacco.

It comes as no surprise that many in the mental health field continue to assert that job burnout and work addiction are not real. The medical world has a pervasive history of denying the existence of procedures and diagnoses if they're not first identified within its own purview. In the 1970s, we saw this trend with the medical field's initial resistance to consumer demands for prepared childbirth (now accepted and encouraged by physicians because it eases childbirth—a benefit for parents and doctors).

Many clinicians and business leaders—vast numbers of whom are workaholics themselves—still do not recognize workaholism, job burnout, or eighteen-hour pressure-cooker days as a mental health problem. Clinicians often overlook workaholism as a contributing issue in troubled relationships when couples seek psychotherapy. Although workaholism surrounds us daily, many in the professional community still consider it much as caffeine or prescription drug use—as harmless, even beneficial. Clinicians often prescribe work immersion as a solution to a problem instead of the cause. Over the years, I've been appalled at the inability of the professional community to recognize, understand, and treat workaholics. Indeed, I have been shocked and dismayed at the pervasiveness of workaholism among practitioners themselves, and their attendant denial about their own out-of-control work habits. I have also seen misdiagnosis after misdiagnosis because of this lack of awareness among clinicians.

Russell is a case in point. He had a six-week sabbatical from his job in Silicon Valley and decided to see a clinician for his workaholism. After six sessions, he stopped going because the therapist told him there was nothing wrong with him, that it was normal for people to work excessive hours in Silicon Valley. Back at work after his sabbatical, Russell said he felt lost again—he had returned to his old habits of overworking, thinking about work all the time, and reaching for the next recognition like a drug addict searching for the next fix.

Dierdre also struggled with the therapeutic community's blindness about work addiction: "It's bad enough when family and friends don't get it, but it's truly horrifying when the therapist you hire doesn't get it. Nine different clinicians assured me they could help my husband and me, and each failed to notice the monster that eventually crushed our twenty-four-year marriage. The therapist even told me that words like 'addiction' were not helpful to the therapy. But as far as I'm concerned, to not name the monster is to keep it hidden and its power intact. I wish professionals had a full vocabulary and clear understanding to effectively help families struggling with this unidentified monster."

Thirty-seven-year-old Blake agreed to individual counseling for his work addiction. When Marilyn, his wife, was invited for a session, the therapist dispelled all notions of workaholism and told her to stop being "Dr. Marilyn" and stop reading "pop psychology." After only two visits, the therapist told Blake that he was not "marriage material" due to his childhood.

Emma from New Jersey called me in anguish to say that after her husband's successful recovery from alcoholism, he was doing a replay, only this time with workaholism. "It's déjà vu," Emma said. "Same story, different drug, but now it's work addiction that takes up ninety percent of his time. He eats, thinks, and breathes work. My marriage is going down the tubes again, and the therapists are saying, 'So what? He likes his job.'"

In the 2010s, work addiction was rebranded as the "hustle culture" for Millennials and Gen Zers working relentlessly and continuously by taking on side hustles and freelance gigs as a way of life. The harder and longer you work, the cooler you are. Corporate climbers wear the workaholic badge with pride, proclaiming their loyalty on behalf of the company, proudly announcing that they binged for eighteen hours or three days on a project. But rarely do you hear adults boast about being on a three-day drunk or proclaim that they binged on an entire apple pie.

Despite this pervasive massive denial, this book brings good news. Burnout, work stress, and work addiction are being recognized and addressed in the United States and around the world, especially after epidemic rates of job stress and burnout during the pandemic. Workaholics Anonymous has over a thousand members and holds meetings around the world—in Paris, Sydney, London, Reykjavik, and Bangkok.[10]

Historically, social scientists and addiction specialists have generated hundreds of studies on alcoholism, substance abuse, compulsive gambling, and eating disorders, but only a handful on workaholism—a profound omission. In the last few years, however, more social scientists have begun to take work addiction seriously, resulting in published research across the globe which I incorporate throughout this book. On average, I receive several queries a month from researchers and graduate students studying the problem in such countries as Hungary, Poland, Spain, Slovenia, Turkey, Japan, Canada, Australia, the Netherlands, and the United Kingdom.

Pandemic Working: Fast, Furious, and Frenzied

Early in the year 2020, when COVID-19 hit, the landscape of workplaces changed around the world forever. People were forced to work from home, and remote and hybrid working became the new normal. Due to pandemic restrictions, remote workers spent a disproportionate amount of screen time on Zoom to work and connect with families, friends, and colleagues. And studies in 2020 showed that *Zoom burnout* was a real mental health condition.[11]

In 2021 and 2022, the Delta and Omicron variants of the coronavirus led American workers to leave their jobs in droves, creating a context in which people were prompted to take stock of their priorities and triggering what has been called the "Great Resignation." This mass exodus had employees reassessing what mattered most in their careers after a year and a half of working from home, whether that is a more diverse workplace, opportunities for advancement, or an overall healthy workplace culture.

The term "pandemic posture" was coined to refer to the bad posture that people developed from remote working and being slouched over computers in makeshift home offices for extended periods during the quarantine. And people referred to the extra pounds that they gained from stress eating and lack of exercise as the "quarantine fifteen."

In 2021, a Gallup poll found that 45 percent of the workforce said the global pandemic had a negative impact on their work engagement, productivity, and stress levels.[12] Those who were already self-described workaholics found their condition exacerbated. Well into 2022, studies showed that working from home blurred boundaries and led to a surge of people burning the midnight oil and burning themselves out. The new work trend led to 40 percent of American workers identifying themselves as modern-day workaholics, indicating an urgent need to address mental health and well-being in the workplace. A Visier report found that the pandemic created widespread remote work with burnout at epidemic proportions (89 percent).[13] These trends were an indication of how work continued to slither its way into every hour of our day—the "smart phoning" of our lives. But how smart are we, really?

Shortly after the publication of the first edition of *Chained to the Desk*, we entered a new century. A lot happened in terms of work and workaholism by the time the second edition was released in 2007. In the 1990s, "blackberries" were something you consumed, not something that consumed you. If you had a "Bluetooth," you went to the dentist instead of to work. By 2007, the 1990s workday phrase "nine to five" had become a dinosaur, replaced by the "24/7" of the new millennium.

During the years between each of the three editions of *Chained to the Desk*, we worked longer and longer hours. According to *US News and World Report*, the workweek jumped from forty-four hours in 1998 to forty-seven in 2000.[14] And the Organization for Economic Cooperation and Development reported that Americans put in 20 percent more hours in 2012 than in 1970, with sixty-hour workweeks becoming the norm.[15] Along with that time increase, work stress skyrocketed. Studies show that after financial worries, job pressures are the second major cause of stress among Americans. According to the American Psychological Association, 62 percent of Americans said their jobs caused them stress in 2007, but the figure had jumped to 70 percent in 2011 and 71 percent in 2021 in the association's follow-up studies.[16] But not only has the problem of workaholism not gone away, it has worsened. Hence, *Chained to the Desk in a Hybrid World*.

How This Book Will Be Helpful

This book provides an inside look at work stress and addiction, debunking myths, refuting false claims, and setting the record straight with the available clinical research, empirical data, and case studies. Since the first three editions of *Chained to the Desk* appeared, new studies have emerged that provide deeper insights into work stress and the effects work addiction has on the workaholic's family.

From California to the Carolinas, men and women recount their agonizing bouts with work addiction and the devastation left in its wake. It's no accident that personal stories in San Diego resemble the accounts of those in Atlanta. It's no coincidence that patient after patient in Charlotte who grew up with workaholics describe haunting feelings that are strikingly similar to those of children of workaholics in Peoria, St. Louis, and Houston.

It's not a fluke that spouses and partners of workaholics in New York describe experiences that are identical in almost every detail to those of partners in other parts of the country and around the world. These personal accounts are not scientific in the quantitative sense, but they carry their own validity. They document the psychological experiences of individuals affected by work stress and addiction—and the details in so many accounts provide such an uncanny match that the emerging profiles cannot be attributed to chance alone. In this respect we have a qualitative science of work addiction derived from the parallel themes and feelings that clinicians have observed in the field.

This is the only book that reveals the devastating effects of work stress and overworking on the workforce as a whole and on those who live and toil with workaholics—their partners, offspring, and business associates. It contains new and innovative research on the outcomes of adults who carry the legacies of their workaholic parents and the problems this creates in their own adult relationships. As before, each chapter opens with a case study, followed by information assembled from hundreds of case reports and a small body of clinical and empirical research.

In addition to the published research of others, I have drawn on my own personal experiences, the research I've conducted at the University of North Carolina at Charlotte, my vast clinical practice with workaholics and their families, my work as a contributor to *Forbes.com* and *Thrive Global.com*, my position as chief architect officer at ComfortZones Digital, and correspondence from around the world. I bring the information to you in a readable way for workaholics, their families, and clinicians who might be struggling with these issues. I have written for psychologists, social workers, marriage and family therapists, counselors, health educators, the clergy, medical practitioners, teachers, healthcare administrators, heads of corporations, and employee assistance personnel, as well as those struggling with workaholism themselves. *Chained to the Desk in a Hybrid World* reveals the origin and scope of work addiction, its pervasiveness within the family system, and how professionals can diagnose, intervene, and provide treatment for workaholics and their families.

A Makeover for the Hybrid World

If you're familiar with the earlier *Chained to Desk* books, you will notice some significant differences in this one. For starters, it has a new organization: Part I (Work Addiction: The New American Idol) describes the problem of workaholism with updates and revisions. Part II (When Work Addiction Hits Home) explores how work addiction, like all addictions, is a family disease, affecting the entire family. Part III (Risky Business: Invasion of the Balance Snatchers) includes three new chapters that profile societal and corporate trends enabling work addiction. And Part IV (Recovery from Work Addiction) focuses on solutions. I include new information on work stress and job burnout, radical self-care and self-compassion, life balance, how to integrate mindfulness by meditating on the fly throughout the workday with Microchillers—short, quick, and effective stress management exercises of five-minutes or less throughout the workday. In addition, I incorporate a tool on how to heal workaholic tendencies called the Triple-A practice—an offshoot from Dr. Richard Schwartz's Internal Family Systems Therapy.[17]

Each chapter opens with new and updated case studies, many from high-profile personalities in the political, business, and entertainment arenas, to illustrate that no matter how famous or powerful one may be, none of us is immune from work stress, work addiction, or mental health issues. The book includes personal stories from such prominent figures as singer/songwriter and four time Grammy Award winner India.Arie; meditation expert Dr. Tara Brach; environmental advocate Erin Brockovich; CNN anchor Alisyn Camerota; former ABC anchor Dan Harris; founder and CEO of Thrive Global Arianna Huffington; dancer and actress Julianne Hough; singer/songwriter Jewel; psychologist and University of Michigan Professor Dr. Ethan Kross; singer/songwriter and activist MILCK; singer/songwriter Alanis Morissette; U. S. Surgeon General Dr. Vivek Murthy; author and university professor Dr. Kristin Neff; singer/songwriter and actress Rhonda Ross; and political advocate, Gloria Steinem.

Each chapter concludes with revised strategies and tips for clinicians to treat workaholics, their loved ones, and their employers and colleagues in the workplace. I have integrated cutting-edge research on work stress, resilience, remote and hybrid work because of the pandemic, and the debate between work/life balance and work/life integration. Also included are sections called "Recharging Your Batteries," which contain practical recovery steps for workaholics and their families. The reorganized appendix contains information about Workaholics Anonymous, samples of Microchillers, and psychometric information about the Work Addiction Risk Test (WART) that continues to be used worldwide.

Here's what else is new:

❖ Cutting-edge research on work stress, burnout, and work-life balance

❖ The latest information on neuroscience, the workaholic brain, and neuroplasticity, along with the power of perspective expanders

❖ The pros and cons of how the pandemic changed the way we work with remote, hybrid, and in-office arrangements

❖ How the pandemic and the "Great Resignation" forced corporate America to create more humane workplaces

❖ Groundbreaking mindfulness techniques, mindful working, and how to practice Microcare on the fly throughout the workday

❖ How to untangle from your workaholic role and use self-talk to find the onramp to your C-Spot, your stabilizing center

❖ Myths about the virtues of multitasking, overtime, and overworking and the importance of radical self-care and self-compassion

Idle Moments without Imperatives

If you're like most people, you may have heard the adage, "An idle mind is the devil's workshop." For many people, doing is more valued than being, such that the more you do, the greater your worth. But in today's world, that worn out saying no longer holds water. In fact, neuroscience has shown that the opposite is true: intentionally creating an idle mind with present-moment awareness rests and resets your brain, promoting calm, clarity, and creativity and thus, improving work performance, engagement, and effectiveness.

Chained to the Desk in a Hybrid World is for you and anyone you know struggling with work stress and the insidious and misunderstood addiction to work. It aims to provide both counseling and consolation when you cannot find them elsewhere. It shows you how to work hard, find your work resilient zone, be kind and compassionate to yourself, keep a positive attitude, and maintain balance with the three Rs: relaxation, recreation, and relationships.

May this book help you, the reader, find a place in your life where career success and personal and intimate fulfillment reside side by side—where you will know more about special times without imperatives, with idle moments when there's nothing to rush to, fix, or accomplish. And where you can give yourself the gift of being mindfully present in each moment.

Bryan Robinson, October 2022

Part I

Work Addiction

The New American Idol

The Making of a Workaholic

*I advise all the young kids to not over-
work. You can't be out there blowing
hard. You have to pace yourself.*
  —Freddie Hubbard, trumpet player

Alanis Morissette on Her Nervous Breakdown

Alanis Morissette has been working since she was nine years old. The singer/
songwriter and Tony Award and multi-Grammy winner told me she used to
think she was invincible until she burned out and hit bottom. She shared her
story of how childhood work addiction stalked her into adulthood burnout,
nervous breakdowns, and near death.

> I started writing songs when I was nine and started a record company when
> I was ten. That's when I started meeting with lawyers and producers and
> began the active part of my professional life in earnest. I started learning
> what conference calls were, about legal conversations, and what publishing
> meant. These were the first few steps toward a well-honed work addiction.
> I started feeling like my sense of self was best defined through my work.
> There are pros and cons to that. The self-expression aspect is a boon and
> exciting, but the overwork aspect is hard on the nervous system and turns
> into a full-blown addiction. I started going on the road at around fifteen and
> worked with local producers between twelve and eighteen and released two
> records in Canada. In my teens, I did a lot of charity work and entered talent
> contests and performed for twenty dollars an hour.
>
> When my work became more visible back in the 1980s and 1990s, there
> were so many versions of burnout. It was predictable for me. I would burn-
> out and have the equivalent of a nervous breakdown about every three
> months. I would anticipate them. I knew they were coming, and they were
> equally intense. It would give me seventeen minutes of permission to melt-
> down. It's horrifying, but it was as though the illness, or the debilitation

of the burnout was the only time I gave myself permission to rest. That's not the case anymore because I lean on my friends and reach out in relationships, and having my kids pulls me away from work. It's a mandatory integration—it's energy management versus time management and realizing my energy is limited. I used to think I was invincible. I could, in fact, just go and go—that is, until I burned out.

My survival strategy has always been to soldier through things. For me the challenge was, "Can I lean on someone, risk being vulnerable, learn about having needs, open myself up to expressing more than just how resilient I could be in the face of intense circumstances?" It really became about painting a fuller picture of who I was. So, I put controls into place. I render myself accountable by asking people who are my professional partners, as part of their job descriptions, to require me to be accountable for my well-being. Because I can't be trusted, I ask people around me to keep me on my toes in terms of my self-care. It might be me sitting in the garden, getting a massage, or having a friend swing by for a visit. I used to say eventually self-care will get higher on the list, but as you know there is no 'eventually.'

One big question that's been helpful for me is, "What do you really want?" Work addiction has us chasing something. We're chasing a sense of peace, a sense of fulfillment. Instead of thinking that the only means through which we can feel that feeling is through work, the question becomes, "How can I cultivate a sense of peace?" A lot of me was thinking I would arrive somewhere, somehow, someday, and eventually I could rest. The goal all along was to find a sense of balance, but I never knew how to do it. My addictive tendencies were always set in the extreme. One evidence of my maturation is that things are more moderate. I'm having the time of my life. Everything I thought would eventually happen is happening. Some of that has to do with family. It has to do with career being expressed from a serviceable place—a place where self-care must be maintained. I still get to play music. I'm just finishing a record. I'm working on a musical. I'm writing articles and blogs and my book. My husband and I un-school our children. It feels like my life is a match to what I've always valued.

The thing I'm most proud of is that I'm still alive. A lot of my colleagues and peers are not alive. There's a bill of goods that is sold about what fame and notoriety and success will afford someone. There's a big underbelly to it. It's an odd, almost inhuman way of living in the public eye. I realized if I wanted to keep contributing and being of service at the cost of my own body and sense of self, I would drive myself into the ground. With any addiction— and work addiction isn't exempt from this—if we keep going, we die.

There was a juncture a few years ago when I was at this fork, and I could keep going and die. Or I could turn right here and really mean it and surrender. It was then that Chris Cornell, Chester Bennington, and Dolores O'Riordan—shortly after George Michael, whom I respected and loved—died. Their passing was highly resonant and impactful for me. I was at a rock-bottom juncture. I remember thinking, "Okay God, I want to live." So, for me to still be here and to be thriving and to continue to make music and write and still have that fire. It's like my pilot light has never gone out even in the worst moments when it was down to a flicker. I think that flicker is what I'm most grateful for. I had to do an about-face, and so I started down that journey, and that for me was a turning point. I'm so happy I did that.[1]

Work Addiction's Emotional Blueprint

In this chapter, we turn to the workaholic's childhood to get a better understanding of the template that shapes the distorted thinking and exaggerated feelings that enough is never enough. Once grown, children primed for workaholism often have an emotional bond with each other that is stronger than any more obvious demographic characteristics. As is the case with many self-professed workaholics, Alanis Morissette, Gloria Steinem, and I—and perhaps even you—share an early emotional blueprint: isolation, pain, loss, fear, and sometimes embarrassment. We are comrades of the soul bound together by common childhood wounds.

"I Feel Like I Know You"

The first time I spoke with Gloria Steinem, we both said, "I feel like I know you." Although our lives were very different on the outside, the way we experienced them was much the same on the inside. The following childhood accounts of two self-professed workaholics illustrate the parallels that can lead two adults of different genders, ethnic backgrounds, and geographic regions who have never met to say, "I feel like I know you."

MY OWN STORY

I could have been the workaholic poster child, living in an alcoholic home where I was caretaker of a younger sister and overly responsible for the emotional tone of an out-of-control family. Poised against the uncertainties of a scary, unpredictable boyhood, housework, homework, schoolwork, and church work became my sanctuary. It gave me the control, stability, and self-worth that laid the groundwork to my adult work addiction. When a teacher forgot to assign schoolwork over Christmas vacation, I raised my hand to remind her. I became a serious little boy, searching to always brace for the next ax to fall.

My stomach turned as the jolt of my father's drunken outbursts hit me like a jackhammer. I quaked in my bed late at night as I heard him stagger up the porch steps and fumble around for his house keys. Lights came on all over the house, and everyone was in an uproar. I'd jump out of bed to control the scenario, closing doors, windows, and drapes so that neighbors wouldn't see and hear, hiding lamps and breakables so that the house wouldn't be destroyed, and no one would be killed or sent to the hospital. It was not a role I chose; it was one that I took by default, out of necessity and out of a will to survive. I had become the one who ran the show: the protector, the peacemaker, the referee, the judge, the general. I was nine years old.

On many nights, my father abandoned me and my little sister at the movies. And although I was learning to read and write, I still had to get us home. Underneath the big-screen excitement of James Dean and Marilyn Monroe lurked my fear and worry. Sometimes, when we stood in the dark street not knowing what to do, my sister would cry, and, although I wanted to cry too, I had to make her think I was in charge of the situation. I was scared and mad because of the cold and the dark, empty streets. Sometimes the police would take us home, and other times we walked the three-mile trek in the dark, dogs barking and chasing after us.

In high school, I wrote and directed the church Christmas play, single-handedly designed and built the sets, and acted in the lead role. I didn't know it at the time but doing everything gave me immense feeling of control and a sense of stability that served as an anchor to my rocky home life. Paradoxically, accolades from teachers, neighbors, and relatives who admired and rewarded my disguised workaholism only drove me further into misery, feelings of inadequacy, and an addiction to work that would stalk me into adulthood.

Schoolwork helped me feel good about myself, and, later, the working world gave me the same sense of what I thought was fulfillment. It provided an escape so I didn't have to deal with the many feelings I had buried since childhood. I covered my pain with a cheery smile and hard work, both of which concealed the problem, kept me disconnected from people and intimate relationships, and gave me something intimate with which I could connect safely. With the sense of total control that work gave me, I'd found my drug of choice. I transformed my long hours of college study into long hours of career building on weeknights, weekends, and holidays.

By the time I was forty, I hid my work as my father had hidden his bottle. I slept off work highs in my clothes, just as my father slept off his alcoholic binges in his clothes. As an adult, I came to realize that I had cultivated the use of work to conceal emotion and my true self instead of expressing them.

Believing my family's problems were unique and shameful, I strove to gain control and approval by excelling in school and the world outside my home.

GLORIA'S STORY

On the surface, there seemed to be no similarities between Bryan's child-hood and my own. Unlike his father, mine had been a kindhearted and gentle man who took care of me more than my mother did. Because her spirit seemed to have been broken before I was born, she was often a figure lying on the couch, talking to unseen voices, and only able to make clear that she loved me and my sister. There was no violence in my house, and I grew up with the sureness that my parents were treating us as well as they treated themselves. That not only satisfied my need to feel loved and therefore lovable, but also the sense of fairness that seems innate in children.

Nevertheless, as I read Bryan's account of his feelings, I felt deep parallels. He had felt ashamed of his home and parents—and so had I. A house filled with dirty dishes, stacks of unwashed clothes, and a "crazy" mother had made me fantasize about a normal home where I could invite my friends. He had adopted cheerfulness and competence in school as a way of concealing the shame of sad feelings and "differentness"—and so had I.

I realized that Bryan had turned to the more rational and controllable world of first school and then work as a way of escaping emotions he did not want to feel—and so had I. I had even denied my need for vacations and periods of introspection, just as he had done. Though I had been lucky enough to find feminist work that was a direct way of helping myself and other women—and an indirect way of helping my mother—I had sometimes carried on these efforts at the expense of my own writing and as an anesthetic for buried childhood emotions.

Only when I, like Bryan, was forced by one too many episodes of burnout to uncover those childhood sadnesses did I begin to see work as an irreplaceable part of my life, but not the whole of my life. And only then did I begin to focus on what I was uniquely able to do instead of trying to do everything—thus beginning to be far more effective as a worker.[2]

The Breeding of Work Addiction

Studies show that work addiction is generally a consequence of family dysfunction in childhood and that it contributes to continued family dysfunction in adulthood.[3] In childhood, it's natural to try to make sense and order out of your world as you grow, learn, and develop. When everything falls apart on a prolonged and sustained basis, your natural inclination is to stabilize your world by latching onto something predictable and consistent—an anchor to keep you afloat amid the sea of chaos, turmoil, and instability. Out of your confusion and desperation, you begin to seek control wherever and whenever you can find it.

Work addiction develops more frequently in kids who get a roller-coaster ride through childhood than in those whose bounces and jostles are buttressed by steady parental hands. Imagine if you were propelled as a child into the adult world and expected to cope, even though you were unprepared and lacked an adult's emotional and mental resources. This happens with emotional incest when one parent is physically or psychologically absent (because of workaholism, depression, divorce, mental illness, or other factors) and the other parent elevates the child to replace the absent parent emotionally. Lacking the emotional equipment to meet these unrealistic expectations, you instinctively grab onto any life raft you can find to carry you through the storm. You might find security in caretaking, schoolwork, housework, homework, church work, or perfectionism.

Families that breed work addiction operate in the extremes and can be placed into one of two categories: the perfect family on one end of the continuum and the chaotic, imperfect family on the other. They either have rigid rules or hardly any, boundaries that are too thick or too blurred, and lifestyles that are over-organized and perfect or disorganized and confusing. These families are often characterized by open or subtle conflict, poor communication, and lack of nurturance.

In perfect families, looking good and putting up a happy front are unwritten family rules. The message is clear: say and do the right thing, pretend everything is okay even when it isn't, don't talk about your feelings, and don't let people know what you're like on the inside. Being in control, being perfect, and doing what others want are some of the character traits reinforced in workaholic kids from these families.

In imperfect families, inconsistency and unpredictability are often at the root of childhood work addiction. The common theme is a lack of psychological insulation during your vulnerable childhood years. Although no child's life is completely carefree, children have a basic need to receive psychological protection from their caregivers, who keep them safe and separate from the adult world. When your childhood security is breached, you learn that you cannot depend on adults to protect you. You conclude that you must have absolute control over people and situations to survive psychologically and physically. Constant disruptions require you to take charge of a life that feels like it's crumbling under your feet.

Portrait of a Workaholic Child

If you were a workaholic child, you ...

❖ Put more time into schoolwork than playtime

❖ Had few friends and preferred the company of adults to that of other children

❖ Showed signs of health problems related to stress, such as chronic exhaustion, headaches, or stomachaches

❖ Took on such adult responsibilities as keeping the household running smoothly, cooking, cleaning, or caring for a younger sibling

❖ Strove for perfection in most of the things you did

❖ Remained serious much of the time and carried the burden of adult worries on your shoulders

❖ Spent little time relaxing, playing, fantasizing, having fun, or enjoying childhood

❖ Had precocious leadership abilities in the classroom and on the playground

❖ Sought constant social approval from adults by striving to be a good girl or boy

❖ Demonstrated compulsive overachievement in church work, schoolwork, sports, or other extracurricular activities

❖ Got upset or impatient easily with yourself for making even the smallest mistake

❖ Showed more interest in the final result of your work than in the process

❖ Put yourself under self-imposed pressures

❖ Frequently did two or three things at once

❖ Had trouble asking for and receiving help

As a workaholic child, you learn to take control of your surroundings to keep your world from coming unglued, overcompensating for the confusion. And you eventually bring these qualities to your adult job. While your carefree friends played, your childhood was marred by serious, adult problems. Your outward competencies concealed deeper problems of inadequacy and poor self-esteem. Underneath, you were an overly serious child who browbeat yourself into perfectionism, judging yourself unmercifully so you could survive the chaos. See the "Portrait of a Workaholic Child."

Emotional Bombardment and Self-Regulation

Most of the workaholics I've studied in my twenty-five-plus years of research had childhoods characterized by *Global High Intensity Activation (GHIA)*—a condition in which the central nervous system is overwhelmed because of a massive shock to the body and mind.[4] This massive shock can create a sense of disintegration and fragmentation, coupled with intense emotions such as rage and terror. This was true of my own childhood in alcoholism, where the seeds of my work addiction were planted. Looking back, I realize that my writing was a coping strategy to regulate my feelings of anxiety in a chaotic household beyond my control. At age nine, I instinctively fled to my bedroom and wrote stories about characters I made up so I could control the outcomes of their lives—a great comfort to me.

My upbringing is an example of how chronically stressful childhoods are often at the root of workaholism. Incessant working is often the limbic system's red-alert reaction (your stress response) to current work pressures, much as if you were in physical danger. Thus, constant control, while providing the workaholic limbic system with protection and safety, also keeps the *sympathetic nervous system* (your fight-or-flight response) in high arousal, trumping the *parasympathetic nervous system* (your rest-and-digest response). This explains why many off-duty workaholics say it's difficult to relax and do nothing.

For many workaholics, early stress is severe enough or repeated early in development before the parasympathetic nervous system (PNS) is well established, and GHIA consumes the workaholic's response even with minor triggers. Cooper, now a forty-seven-year-old workaholic, recalls his frequent futile attempts as a child to escape his parents' loud, heated yelling matches: "There was no getting away from the shrill voices and harsh tones, so I hid in my bedroom closet, curled up in a corner. The hanging clothes would muffle the yelling, and I would push my fingers into my ears as hard as I could to block out the screaming bouts and fists pounding the kitchen table on the other side of my bedroom wall. Mom would drive off in the car. And Dad would head back into the garage and tinker on a car or lawnmower. I was left physically untouched but injured by the verbal onslaught."

The existence of this GHIA pattern is supported by personality research showing that major traits of Type A people are anxiety, hostility, and anger.[5] That research also supports the evidence that children who grow up in dysfunctional or alcoholic families often latch on to early work (schoolwork, after-school jobs, or housework) as a stabilizing survival strategy. Gloria Steinem, who describes herself as a workaholic, has chronicled her attempts to stabilize her childhood by caring for an invalid mother who alternated between wandering the streets and sitting quietly: "I remember so well the dread of not knowing who I would find when I came home: a mother whose speech was slurred by tranquilizers, a woman wandering in the neighborhood not sure where she was, or a loving and sane woman who asked me about my school day. I, too, created a cheerful front and took refuge in constant reading and afterschool jobs—anything to divert myself (and others) from the realities of life."[6] There's an old saying among neuroscientists that "neurons that fire together, wire together." This is certainly true of workaholics.

Carried into adulthood, the stabilizing force that gave children early control in a roller coaster ride becomes a compulsive stabilizer that they depend on to regulate their lives in the present. In other words, constant working mitigates anxiety, worry, or depression. This relief acts as a reward to the nervous system, causing a dopamine release (an adrenaline high) that creates feelings of safety, enjoyment—even a worker's high—that motivates workaholics to continue overworking. Many workaholics describe the addictive feeling of this neuro-physiological payoff as the sensation of a drug rushing through their veins.

If you're a workaholic, chances are GHIA has been embedded in your nervous system, and you're "stuck on high." It's as if your nervous system is a constant idling engine running inside you. This engine can be triggered into overdrive when you're deprived of constant working. The aftermath of prolonged childhood stress is a lack of safety in your own physical body. To avoid this feeling, you get stuck in future thoughts, are jittery in present situations where you must relax, and unwittingly employ constant overdoing and overworking to regulate a nervous system stuck on high.

Stolen Childhoods: Thirteen Going on Thirty

When the generational lines that insulate children from adults get violated or blurred, children become a parent to their own parents, setting aside their own emotional needs to accommodate and care for the needs and pursuits of another family member. Many workaholics, I have found, grew up in homes dominated by parental alcoholism, mood disorders, or other problems that forced the child to take on adult emotional and practical responsibilities. Children renounce their need for comfort, protection, and reassurance because their best shot at gaining emotional attachment is giving support to a needy parent. They become grave and serious little adults and first forgot how to play when they were still young. We call this precocious induction into adult life *parentification*—parentified kids carry grown-up emotional burdens bigger than they are without the emotional scaffolding to bear them.[7]

If you were parentified, you became a little adult at a young age. You might've been a child caretaker of younger siblings or of an emotionally dependent, alcoholic, or mentally and physically disabled parent. Your role required you to become overly responsible at a young age, before you were fully constructed. It's not unusual for adult family members whose own needs were not met in childhood to turn to you, the chosen child, to satisfy those needs. You might've been a product of emotional incest—made into a confidant or an emotional caretaker or required to live out a parent's dream—even if it went against your desires and best interests.[8]

Sometimes workaholic seeds are sown when you try to keep the family balanced. You establish family justice by providing parents with whatever they didn't get from their own upbringing. Or maybe you were engulfed and molded your identity to fulfill parental needs. Empirical research shows that, "Parentified children take care of their parents in concrete, physical ways by comforting them emotionally, and also by shaping their own personalities to meet the expectations of the parents, thereby increasing the parents' self-esteem."[9]

Parentification can take two routes: you are shaped to be Mom or Dad's "Little Helper" or inducted to live out a "Parent's Dream."[10] If you were the "Little Helper," you developed a caretaking, self-defeating character style, the mode of adaption that offered the best possibility for achieving proximity to your parents.[11] If you were the parent's "Dream Child," you were more likely to forfeit yourself to serve your parent, falling short of self-development, which left you with a narcissistic character style. Either path can lead to careaholism and workaholism, a sacrificing of the self in favor of another person or a task.

At age seven, Carol stood on a chair in the kitchen to make homemade biscuits. She ironed the family's clothes and did most of the housework. She already had learned to write money orders so that the electric bill would get paid. Both her parents were alcoholics. Nobody told her to take on the grownup responsibilities; she did them as an intuitive way of bringing order and security to her young life. At twenty-eight, Carol is a workaholic.

As Carol, Gloria, and I became the family caretakers, we forfeited our childhoods in return for the adult jobs of being over responsible and overdoing. We grew into adults who believed that we couldn't count on anyone else and that our emotional, financial, and physical survival required us to do everything ourselves. These qualities provided us and other workaholics with the psychological insulation of certainty and security that we had to manufacture early to survive childhood.

Paradoxically, the insulation of your parentification becomes your isolation. As an adult, it's difficult for you to become fully involved in an intimate relationship. You're suspicious and unforgiving of people who procrastinate or who fail to follow through on commitments. Having renounced your own early need to be cared for to attend to a family member, you carry the pattern

Nurturing Your Inner Child

The grieving process can help workaholics remove their uptight, inflexible masks and embrace the spontaneous, playful, and joyous child within—the parts of themselves they disowned to cope as children. The practice of self-parenting and nurturing skills are integral parts of the recovery process for workaholics and careaholics (See chapter 15 for a detailed discussion of self-care and self-compassion). Deep within us is a wounded child—sometimes known as an exile—whose needs were forfeited, disowned, or neglected.

Although accessing your deeper feelings might be difficult at first, awareness and practice help cross the barriers your inner system built to protect you from further hurt. Through the self-parenting process, you learn to give to your inner child what you had to give up as a youngster. You think of yourself as a parent, providing your inner child with what was missing by meeting his or her unmet emotional needs. You get in touch with that playful, spontaneous, flexible part of you and learn to relax and play more and have fun. This experience, in turn, sensitizes you to the emotional needs of others and opens you to intimacy from loved ones.

forward into adulthood where you pay the price, subjugating yourself by attending to your work above all else.

Your parentified attachment bonds—causing you to refuse to ask for help or delegate—put you at risk for compulsive caregiving, careaholism, and compassion burnout. "The structure of a person's interactions with the parent is carried forward into adulthood and serves as a template for negotiating current relationships. Deference and subjugation of self to others is assured to be the price exacted by attachment. The compulsive caregiver thus develops affectional ties along old relational lines: playing the role of the caregiver is the vehicle through which relational proximity is sought and maintained."[12]

Even the most righteous and well-intended among us are vulnerable to *care addiction*—workaholism masquerading as caring for others. A Methodist minister and therapist to his flock believed that every person who came into his life was sent by God. Even when he was overloaded with congregation members, hospital visits, and pastoral counseling, he had difficulty saying no because his guilt told him it was God's will that he help every person, even when his phone, mounted on the headboard of his bed, rang in the middle of the night.

At 2:00 one morning, after a full and hectic week, he got a call from one of his parishioners who had lost a family member. He told the caller he would come to the hospital immediately, rolled over for what was to be a brief second, and reawakened at 7:00 a.m. By the time he got to the hospital, the family was furious. Guilt-ridden and overburdened, the pastor took ten years to recover from his feelings of failure and inadequacy (See chapter 15 for more on careaholism as a form of work addiction).

Tips for Clinicians

Workaholic youngsters emotionally escape from their stressful surroundings through their achievements and accomplishments. Or they immerse themselves into caregiving. Along with this self-distancing comes a greater sense of emotional insulation, independence, and a more objective understanding of what's going on around them. Their early family misfortunes, instead of destroying their intellectual and creative potential, help motivate them, and in adulthood they often become high achievers in their careers, as the case of Alanis Morissette illustrates.

DON'T LET THE GAME FACE FOOL YOU

If you're like most clinicians, you might have overlooked workaholic kids because they are high functioning. Exercise caution in labeling high functioning children as invulnerable. Despite the fact that they are functioning better than their siblings, they may, in fact, be in greater need. The invulnerability could be masking deeper feelings of inadequacy, anxiety, or poor self-esteem. As a clinician, you can best help these over-functioning children by making sure that, while developing their talents and skills, they get a chance to add the maximum balance possible to their personal lives.

MOURNING A CHILDHOOD LOST

The workaholic's defenses are strong. The unresolved hurt and pain of a lost childhood are buried under piles of ledgers, sales reports, and computer printouts. Here's where you can employ inner-child work and family-of-origin work. They pinpoint how and why work became a sanctuary from a dangerous world. By introducing self-nurturing techniques, you give clients tools other than overwork to soothe themselves. When this work is done in the presence of the workaholic's partner, it can give the relationship some breathing room, as the spouse sees clearly that the work compulsion has ancient roots and is not a personal rejection.

Once I uncover the childlike vulnerabilities, I teach clients ways to access their own nurturing abilities so that they can consciously protect and nourish the childlike parts that they had to disown. Clinically, we know that psychotherapy organized around the completion of mourning allows clients to master the consequences of role reversal in childhood. You can assist clients in coming to terms with their childhood losses by helping them complete a delayed mourning process. Missing out on a magical and joyful childhood, one that is free of adult concerns, is good reason to grieve. As clients recognize their parents' inability to nurture and emotionally protect them and to provide a strong, wise, and loving model for them, they uncover their internalized feelings of anger, bitterness, sadness, disappointment, and sorrow. As they respond over time to the realization that their childhoods are lost to them forever, they often travel through the predictable stages of grief and loss that parallel the loss experienced by people mourning the death of a loved one.

In a way, the period of mourning, which usually lasts from several months to several years, can be thought of as a grief process for the workaholic's lost childhood. The grief framework of the physician Elisabeth Kübler-Ross can guide your therapy with clients so that they see their progression through the stages of mourning and their emotional movement forward.[13] You can encourage grief work around the loss of the safe and secure childhood, supporting clients as they work out their anger, sadness, and hurt.

PARTICIPATING IN LIFE'S CELEBRATIONS

Many workaholics refuse to break for birthdays, holidays, or even funerals. This pattern has the effect of reinforcing their feelings of inadequacy: "I don't deserve to indulge myself." I suggest helping clients to reestablish the rituals and celebrations in their lives that have fallen by the wayside. Without such rituals, people can feel separate, isolated, and disconnected from life. Taking time to acknowledge rituals helps people realize the passage of time and the markers on the road of life.

Events such as a child's recital or graduation or a loved one's birthday are markers of time that can help workaholics to appreciate the here and now— what it's like now, rather than what it will be. Have clients assess the value they put on the birthdays, graduations, anniversaries, reunions, and weddings in their lives. Then emphasize the importance of taking time to recognize and celebrate their accomplishments and those of their loved ones and friends with present-moment awareness.

FAMILY-OF-ORIGIN WORK

Family-of-origin work is essential for clients to fully understand work addiction and the emotional blueprint they bring to their adult lives. You can help clients identify their childhood family roles (for example, hero, mascot, lost child, or scapegoat) and see how fulfilling these roles functioned as survival behaviors in a dysfunctional family system.[14] By using a family systems approach to treatment, you can help workaholics examine more deeply the family-of-origin wounds that led them into work addiction. It's important to examine the etiology of the depression, anxiety, and anger that often drive the work addiction and then help your clients find constructive outlets for the expression of these feelings. Drawing a *genogram*—a diagram of the family tree—can help clients understand the intergenerational nature of addictions and trace the origins of their own low self-esteem, difficulty with intimacy, perfectionism, and obsessive control patterns.

Bibliotherapy

I often use bibliotherapy with workaholic clients who feel trapped in work addiction. The readings I mention at the end of each chapter match the content and are excellent resources to augment recovery plans. The following readings relate to the content in this chapter:

- ❖ Nancy Chase, *Burdened Children: Theory, Research, and Treatment of Parentification* (Thousand Oaks, CA: Sage Publications, 1999).
- ❖ Patricia Love, *The Emotional Incest Syndrome: What to Do When a Parent's Love Rules Your Life* (New York: Bantam, 1990).
- ❖ Elaine Miller-Karas, *Building Resilience to Trauma* (New York: Routledge, 2023).

2

Who, Me? A Workaholic— Seriously?

This is a man for whom work always came first. Now he can't even remember it.
> —Chris Wallace, journalist, on the final days of his hard-driving *60 Minutes* correspondent father, Mike Wallace, who died in 2012

Margo Discovers One Thing She Can't Fix

I got my first job at fourteen, not out of necessity but out of want. I went to school to finish my senior year in the morning and at noon to work in a grocery store, where I worked for forty hours a week. I bragged about what a great work ethic I had, but little did I know that this was just the beginning. I went to college and found myself studying and usually working a job— always busy, working too many hours.

The real workaholic came out when the pace I kept landed me in my first deep depression. During the day, I was driven to succeed in the wholesale manufacturing firm that I worked for as general manager. It was a $3.5 million company that produced twenty-four hours a day, six days a week. Plus, I enrolled in a university to study business management at night. I had a wonderful husband who supported my efforts and a beautiful baby boy.

I continued this regimen until I graduated with a Bachelor of Science in business management, and then I continued school during the summers. I took two courses while still running the company, which had grown to a $5 million business. The last semester I took three courses while working over forty hours a week. I made almost all As and won the President's Award for the best-managed plant—twice. As you may have noticed, my family hasn't been mentioned. My husband still supported me, and by now my son was ten years old. But my relationship with both suffered because of my not being there. I was constantly working at my job or doing school assignments at the university. I was obviously gone on weekends and many nights during the week.

I thought I was superwoman and succeeded at everything. Although I had a lot of guilt where my son was concerned, I tried to be the best mother I could. In reality, I was on a collision course and didn't have any idea how to relax. I hit a wall at age thirty. Even though I had graduated, I missed college. I was still in the same position, making a lot of money but no longer fulfilled by the job. I felt like I was eighty years old. I hardly listened to the radio for pleasure, read only educational books, and felt miserable if nothing was planned for every second on a weekend. I was used to being busy every second of my life and hated slowing down.

My marriage was suffering, I was having horrible mood swings, and I was angry at everyone and everything. Through therapy I came to realize that I was going through a major depression brought on by years of workaholism. So, what did I do? You guessed it. I went back to work. I enrolled in an MBA program and took two graduate classes each semester. I poured myself back into school and immediately felt better, or so I thought. I was doing what my father had done: when things get tough, work harder. I was withdrawing from my husband more and more and, regrettably, expected perfection from my son, just as I did myself.

In addition to classes during my last year of graduate school, I taught a night class at the local community college and ran the manufacturing plant. I knew I needed to slow down but didn't know how. After I received my master's degree, I found the perfect job. My plan was to slow down, relax, and enjoy. It was hard to leave the company because my employees were my family. I had given my heart and soul to that job for almost twelve years. But I managed to walk out the door for the last time as the "boss."

I knew my life was unmanageable when one Friday afternoon I called a local mental health hospital. Feeling desperate, I was ready to commit myself. I would have done anything to stop this all-too-familiar roller-coaster ride. I cried for two solid weeks for no apparent reason. My life had slowed to a snail's pace, which would have been great for most people but not for a workaholic like me. In desperation, I emergency-beeped my therapist, whom I had not seen for some time. I was now willing to try anything, and I shamefully took the new antidepressants that I had refused to take before. How could I stoop so low? Why couldn't I just work harder and fix everything? I had finally found one thing I couldn't fix.

I Only Work on Days That End with "Y"

Recording artists have always known something about the work world that the American workforce still doesn't get. The Beatles sang, "It's been a hard day's night, and I've been working like a dog." Cyndi Lauper belted: "When the working day is done, girls just wanna have fun." Michael Jackson crooned it in *Off the Wall*: "So tonight gotta leave that nine-to-five upon the shelf and just enjoy yourself." And Dolly Parton warned us about working nine to five: "It'll drive you crazy if you let it."

And Dolly's right. It will *if you let it*. But you don't have to worry about nine to five workdays any more. Since the global pandemic and the "Great Resignation," we have 24/7 workdays, soaring job pressures, and remote and hybrid workplace changes. "It's enough to drive you crazy if you let it." The key is not to let it, but that's easier said than done.

❖ Do you feel like you're tethered to your smart phone?

❖ Are you working far more than forty or fifty hours a week?

❖ Are you eating fast food or vending machine snacks at your desk or skipping lunch altogether?

❖ Do you stay in constant contact with work even on weekends, holidays, and vacations, or forfeit your vacations to keep on working?

❖ Do you get nervous or jittery when you're away from work?

If you answered "yes" to some of these questions, you could be a workaholic. Increasingly, American workers find themselves on a tightrope, trying to hold that line between calm and frantic activity, looking for a way to balance crammed schedules and keep clever work gadgets from infiltrating their personal time. A 2021 study reported that nearly half of remote employees were working past midnight during the pandemic lockdown because they couldn't get everything done.[1]

"Chained to the Desk" is a metaphor for the agonizing work obsessions and stress that haunt you even when you're away from your desk. If you're a workaholic, chances are you openly admit your obsession with work while concealing the darker side of the addiction. Perhaps you testify to your passion for work, your nonstop schedule—all of which present you in a favorable light. But you fail to mention your episodes of depression, anxiety, chronic fatigue, and stress-related illnesses—consequences of working obsessively for days on end.

The Best Dressed Addiction

Workaholism is the best-dressed of all the addictions. It is enabled by our society's dangerous immersion in overwork, which explains why we can't see the water we swim in, and why many clinicians look blank when the spouses of workaholics complain of loneliness and marital dissatisfaction. The term *workaholic* was coined by Wayne Oates in the first book on the subject, *Confessions of a Workaholic*, in which Oates described workaholics as behaving compulsively about work in the same ways that alcoholics do about alcohol.[2] More than fifty years later, no consensus exists among clinicians on how to define or categorize workaholism.

I use the terms *workaholism* and *work addiction* interchangeably throughout this book. I define *workaholism* as *an obsessive-compulsive disorder that manifests itself through self-imposed demands, an inability to regulate work habits, and over-indulgence in work to the exclusion of most other life activities.* The frantic work habits of workaholics activate their stress response, and their neurological systems are on constant red alert. Although workaholism is a form of escape from unresolved emotional issues, the relief it provides has an addictive quality. The addictive nature comes from the fact that workaholics are temporarily delivered from deeper red alert conditions through the distraction of working, as I described in the introduction. But because the deeper issues are not addressed, constant working is necessary to keep the smoldering coals from becoming wildfires.

Glorification of an Illness

In a society based on overwork, Margo's behaviors had plenty of camouflage. Flextime, twenty-four-hour Walmarts, and electronic devices have vaporized the boundaries that once kept work from engulfing the sacred hours of the Sabbath and the family dinnertime. iPhones, iPads, and laptops have blurred the spatial boundaries between workplace and home: you can email a memo at midnight from the kitchen table, bend over a laptop on an island in paradise, or call the office via cellphone from a ski lift. But work performed in exotic environments is still work, however much you tell yourself it's play. And when any place can be a workplace and any hour is work time, you can work yourself to death, just as some people drink themselves to death in a culture in which any hour is cocktail hour. Little in our present culture teaches workaholics when or how to say no.

The line between work and personal time continued to evaporate when the pandemic mandated working from home and many people had trouble setting boundaries around their work schedules. As major corporations batted around the new buzz phrase "work-life integration," recovering workaholics resisted the term because it implies 24/7 connectivity, erasing much-needed boundaries for workaholics. Organizations that routinely provide free electronic devices to employees also have been accused of sending the message that employees must be on call, suggesting that wireless devices force employees to stay connected to their jobs when they try to disconnect.

Along with my research team at the University of North Carolina at Charlotte, I have studied workaholics and their families for twenty years. Although no formal records are kept on the numbers of workaholics, we estimate from our extensive studies that one-quarter of the American population can be classified as workaholic. But as you have seen, for many the concept of workaholism is a hard sell. You might be thinking that some of these trends and statistics apply to you. You work hard and put in long hours because you have a mortgage, two children approaching college, and two car loans. If you don't work hard, how would you stay afloat financially?

Actually, you might not be a workaholic at all. You might be a hard worker. There's a big difference between hard work and workaholism. Hard work put us on the moon, sent Richard Branson and Jeff Bezos into space in 2021, and discovered vaccines for COVID-19. Chances are that from time to time you put more hours and effort into working than into being with loved ones or relaxing. Starting a new business can be an all-consuming affair at first. If you're trying to find a cure for a disease, it can make you single-minded. Or if you're a new employee, you might want to make a good impression as you start your job. These examples are exceptions that most of us encounter at some point, but workaholics routinely operate in this fashion, using their jobs as escape. So, it's possible for you to work long hours, carry a mortgage, send your kids to college, pay for the two cars, and not be a workaholic. Working long hours alone does not make you a workaholic.

Perhaps you're a single parent or someone who must work overtime to make ends meet, and you're thinking, "From morning to night, it's go, go, go. I'm barely scraping by as it is, and now you're saying I have another problem?" This is not necessarily the case. A workaholic is not the single mom who works two jobs to pay mounting bills. Neither is it the tax accountant who works extra-long hours on weekdays and weekends as April 18 approaches. True workaholics are driven by deeper, internal needs, rather than by external ones—not that it's tax season or that baby needs a new pair of shoes but that the process of working satisfies an inner psychological hunger. But if friends or loved ones have accused you of neglect because of your work habits—or if you have used or abused work to escape from intimacy or social relationships—you might want to take a closer look at your life.

The Workaholic Joy Ride: This Century's Cocaine

Overwork is this century's cocaine, its problem without a name. Workweeks of sixty, eighty, and even a hundred hours are commonplace in major law firms and corporations; tribes of modern-day male and female Willy Lomans, manacled to cellphones, trundle through airports at all hours with their rolling luggage; Starbucks is filled with serious young people bent over laptops; young workers at dotcoms are available for work 24/7. Could this be you?

As you saw earlier, some folks wear their workaholic label like a prize, but if you're like most workaholics, the picture is far more subtle. You don't party or stay out late. You don't waste your time or throw money down the drain. You're level-headed and rational. You've been called dedicated, responsible, and conscientious. You work long and hard, and you're always at your desk or available electronically.

At first the accolades and applause, slaps on the back, fat paychecks, and gold plaques make you feel it's all worth the effort. But after a while, the addiction starts to feel like an unwelcome burden. You have a lot on your plate. You've got to do it perfectly. Can you measure up? Will you be able to perform? Or will you let others down? You've got to prove that you can do it. If you fall short, you dig your heels in deeper. You can't let up because everyone's depending on you.

Burrowing itself deeper into your soul, work addiction is like a prisoner's chain that moves with you wherever you go. When you're not at your desk, your compulsive thoughts are still there. They beat you to the office before you begin the day. They stalk you in your sleep, at a party, or while you're hiking with a friend. They loom over your shoulder when you're trying to have an intimate conversation with your partner. You can't stop thinking about, talking about, or engaging in work activities. Like an alcoholic, you have rigid thinking—sometimes called "stinkin' thinking"—patterns that feed your addiction. When you're preoccupied with work, you don't notice signals, such as physical aches and pains or a reduced ability to function, that warn of serious health problems.

Your projects take priority over every aspect of your life. You get soused by overloading yourself with more work tasks than you can possibly complete. You toil around the clock—hurrying, rushing, and multitasking to meet unrealistic deadlines. You might even pull all-nighters, sometimes sleeping off a work binge in your clothes. The uncontrollable work urge engulfs you in a work fog called a brownout, numbing you to anxiety, worry, and stress, as well as to other people. Work highs, reminiscent of an alcoholic euphoria, run a cycle of adrenaline-charged binge working, followed by a downward swing.

Euphoria eventually gives way to work hangovers characterized by withdrawal, depression, irritability, anxiety, and even thoughts of suicide.

The Workaholic High

Many people insist that workaholism is not a legitimate addiction because it doesn't have a physiological basis, as chemical and food addictions do. But the truth is that work addiction is both an activity (overdoing) and a substance (adrenaline) addiction in the same way that cocaine and alcoholism are chemical addictions. Long-standing research shows that workaholics have greater anxiety, anger, depression, and stress than nonworkaholics and that they perceive themselves as having more job stress, perfectionism, more generalized anxiety, more health complaints, and greater unwillingness to delegate job responsibilities than nonworkaholics. Plus, workaholics are at higher risk for burnout—specifically emotional exhaustion and depersonalization.[3]

THE ADRENALINE RUSH

Studies have linked work addiction to the release of adrenaline in the body. Adrenaline—a hormone produced by the body in times of stress—has an effect like that of amphetamines, or "speed." The release of adrenaline, like other drugs, creates physiological changes that lead to highs—in the case of workaholism, "work highs"—that become addictive and may even be fatal.

Workaholics often describe the rush or surge of energy pumping through their veins and the accompanying euphoria as "an adrenaline high." Addicted to adrenaline, workaholics require larger doses to maintain the high that they create by putting themselves and those around them under stress. Some researchers believe workaholics unconsciously put themselves into stressful situations to get the body to pump its fix.

Adrenaline addiction, in effect, creates addictions to crises that lead the body to produce the hormone and give workaholics their drug. On the job, workaholics routinely create and douse crises that require the body's adrenaline flow. Pushing subordinates or themselves to finish designated assignments within unrealistic deadlines is one-way crises are achieved. Another is biting off too much at one time or attempting to accomplish many tasks at once. But while the workaholic gets high, coworkers and subordinates experience stress and burnout and many of the same emotions as children in alcoholic homes do—notably, confusion and frustration caused by unpredictability. The adrenaline flow also boomerangs for the workaholic in the form of physical problems. Too much adrenaline blocks the body's ability to clear dangerous cholesterol from the bloodstream. Elevated cholesterol levels clog arteries, damage their inner lining, and can cause heart attacks.

HITTING BOTTOM

Progressive in nature, your addictive work behaviors are unconscious attempts to resolve unmet psychological needs that have roots in your upbringing. Your work addiction can lead to an unmanageable everyday life, family disintegration, serious health problems, and even death. The Japanese have a name for the ten thousand workers a year in that country who drop dead from putting in sixty-to-seventy-hour workweeks: *karoshi*—death from overwork. We have no comparable term in the English language. Otherwise, healthy Japanese workers keel over at their desks after a long stretch of overtime or after consummating a high-pressure deal, usually from a stroke or heart attack. In the 1990s, *karoshi* among corporate workers in their forties and fifties became so common that the Japanese dubbed the workplace as "a killing field." By 2022, the Karoshi phenomenon had become a worldwide serious health hazard.[4] And some economists in India referred to work addiction as "a poison by slow motion."[5]

In the United States, members of Alcoholics Anonymous often speak of the moment they "hit bottom." The glamour peels off like old varnish, alcohol stops working for them, and they can no longer think of themselves as simply bon vivants or men about town. Workaholics, too, hit bottom: a spouse may threaten divorce; a long-ignored back problem or stress-related illness like psoriasis may become painfully disabling; or valued employees may quit, tired of trying to meet impossible deadlines. Some workaholics hit bottom before they can admit they have a problem and get the help they need. Some become so depressed they cannot get out of bed. They find themselves alone, unable to feel, and cut off from everyone they care about. Marriages crumble, and health problems hit crisis proportions. Breaking through the denial shakes workaholics into facing the truth and getting the help they need.

Many of the workaholics I treat are dragged into therapy kicking and screaming by their spouses or partners; others finally burn out or get tired of being perceived as the impossible boss at work and the tyrannical parent at home. "It finally reached a point that I hit a wall!" Ed said, smacking his right fist into his left palm, "and I couldn't escape it any more. I was either going to deal with it or I was going to die."

Despite longer hours and more determination, your life is falling apart. Your company doesn't appreciate your hard work. Your boss is breathing down your neck. No matter how hard you try, nothing seems to satisfy him. You're impatient and restless at work, your tolerance for slow-moving coworkers lessening. You resent the fact that you get to work earlier and stay longer than anyone else in the office. You feel contempt for colleagues who don't work on weekends or who "goof off" on holidays.

You have a comfortable income, and your family appears to have all the material comforts. Not only does work addiction look good on you, the workaholic, but your family also appears to be thriving from the outside. Behind closed doors, though, you're breaking down inwardly, and your loved ones are suffering in quiet desperation. Your family doesn't appreciate your hard work and the creature comforts it provides. You can't depend on them to handle things at home in your absence, and they're constantly "bothering" you with problems that distract you from earning a decent living. They say you're always working and that when you're not, your mind is off in the clouds. They drag you into their disputes, and your kids are out of control. Sometimes it feels like they're ganging up on you. You're starting to feel like an outsider in your own home. Your old friends don't call any more, and you never seem to have fun.

Work is the one thing you do well, and now even it has soured. If you don't have your job, there's nothing left of you. Still, you keep plugging away, hoping it will get better. Your life has become cold, dark, and lonely—without meaning. You're dogged by self-doubt and failure. You wish you could talk to someone who would understand and help you remove the invisible chains.

If you've reached this point, you might feel as though there's no place to turn. Even the clinicians you seek out may be oblivious to your problem or ignorant of how to treat it. When this happens, you feel even more disconnected from others, lonelier, and more hopeless. It's as if work has stolen your soul.

Could You Just Be a Hard Worker?

In a society where many people work long hours, it's important to make a distinction between hard workers and workaholics. If you're a workaholic, you're likely to prefer working alone, focusing on the details of work. But if you're a hard worker, you can see the bigger picture and work cooperatively with others toward common goals. Like most workaholics, you're apt to look for work to do. But if you're a hard worker, you enjoy your work, often work long hours, and focus on getting the job done efficiently. Plus, you think about and enjoy the task you're engaged in during the present moment. A workaholic mindset, though, drives you to think about working a disproportionate amount of time. Even during social activities or leisure times your mind wanders and you obsess about work.

Hard workers see work as a necessary and sometimes fulfilling obligation, compared to workaholics who see it as a haven in a dangerous, emotionally unpredictable world. Hard workers know when to close the briefcase, mentally switch gears, and be fully present at the celebration of their wedding anniversary or a child's Little League game. But if you're a workaholic, you allow work to engulf other quarters of life: sales reports might litter your dining table; your desk could be covered with dinner plates; you frequently fail to attend to your self-care, spiritual life, and household chores and break your commitments to friends, partners, and children to meet work deadlines.

If you're a workaholic, you seek an emotional and neurophysiological payoff from overwork and, unlike hard workers, you get an adrenaline rush from meeting apparently impossible deadlines. If you're a hard worker, you're able to turn off your work appetite, while workaholics are insatiable. Workaholism keeps you preoccupied with work no matter where you are—walking with someone you love at the seashore, playing catch with a child, or hanging out with a friend. If you're a hard worker, you're in the office looking forward to being on the ski slopes, compared to the workaholic on the ski slopes thinking about being back in the office.

If you're a true workaholic, your relationship with work is the central connection of your life, as compelling as the connection that addicts experience with booze or cocaine. You could be the lawyer who brings his briefcase on family picnics, while his wife carries the picnic basket; the therapist who schedules appointments six days a week, from 8:00 in the morning to 8:00 at night; or the real estate salesperson who cannot have a heart-to-heart talk with her husband without simultaneously watching television, eating dinner, and going over property-assessment reports. In each case, work is a defense against human relationships, and balance is lost.

Workaholism is not a black-and-white matter, however. Just as *alcoholic* refers not only to the bum in the gutter but to the relatively well-functioning professor who gets quietly soused every night, *workaholism* describes a wide spectrum of behaviors. For some people, it takes outwardly bizarre forms, such as working around the clock for three or four days straight and periodically catching a few hours' sleep in sweat clothes. For others, workaholism is subtler: work is the place where life really takes place, the secret repository of drama and emotion. Family and friends are little more than a vague, if pleasant, backdrop.

By now you might be saying, "Fine, I'm a workaholic. It makes me miserable, but I prefer it to having to confront intimacy issues, living without my second home, taking my kids out of private school, and giving up all the other advantages work brings me." So, you've settled on being miserable at work rather than being miserable at home. The belief that you can have happiness only at home or only at work, but not both, is all-or-nothing thinking. Whether you're a workaholic or simply caught up in the workaholic pace of juggling work and

Cultivating Abstinence on the Work High Wire

Recovery from any addiction requires abstinence from the drug of choice. If you're chemically dependent, that means total sobriety because alcohol and drugs are not necessary for the body to sustain itself. But if you're a workaholic, you still must work, just as compulsive overeaters have to eat. Abstinence for you, means that you refrain from COMPULSIVE OVERWORKING and cultivate workaholic abstinence through work moderation and healthy work habits. The key is work-life balance, not sacrifice. You don't have to choose misery in one arena or another to put balance into your life. It's possible to work hard, have all the material advantages that result from your hard work, and still have a full and satisfying personal life outside the office.

Healthy work habits, in contrast to workaholism, help you lead a more balanced life—one with time for social and leisure activities and personal and family pursuits. The payoff is a fresher, more clear-minded approach to your job that makes you more efficient at what you do. Chapter 3 guides you through a work moderation plan that helps you find the proper integration of work and personal time to support you in all areas of your life.

family, this book can help you see that you don't have to give up your lifestyle to change your work habits.

Millions of Americans, although not workaholics in the literal sense, find themselves struggling with work-life balance and caught in work stress and a workaholic lifestyle that gives them some of the same physical and psychological symptoms that workaholics have: Emotional burdens, exhaustion, and suffering from stress and relationship problems caused by the disproportionate amount of time and emotional energy put into work. They are consumed by never-ending, obsessive thoughts about work and work-related functions. Many are unable to be emotionally present with loved ones or engage in meaningful intimate, spiritual, and social relationships. And their partners feel lonely, isolated, and guilty in these empty relationships, questioning their own sanity as friends and employers applaud the workaholics for their accomplishments. If this sounds familiar, keep reading to see if you or someone you care about could be chained to the desk.

Are You Chained to the Desk?

There are different degrees of workaholism. Some people fall in the low to mild ranges, and others fall in the higher ranges. The greater the degree of your workaholism, the more serious your physical and emotional side effects will be. Let's look at your work patterns.

Could you be chained to the desk? Or are you just a hard worker? To find out in a flash, you can take the Work Addiction Risk Test (WART)—a psychometric valid and reliable measure—on my website, www.bryanrobinson-books.com, click "show results," and see your score in seconds. Or you can rate yourself right here using the rating scale of 1 (never true), 2 (sometimes true), 3 (often true) or 4 (always true). Put the number that best describes your work habits in the blank beside each statement. After you have responded to all twenty-five statements, add the numbers in the blanks for your total score. The higher your score (the highest possible is 100), the more likely you are to be a workaholic; the lower your score (the lowest possible is 25), the less likely you are to be a workaholic.[6]

WART scores are divided into three ranges. After you've taken the WART, here's how to interpret your score:

❖ Red light: If you scored in the upper third (67–100), you're chained to the desk. You are highly workaholic with poor work-life balance, and you might be at risk for burnout. In addition, research suggests that your loved ones might be experiencing emotional repercussions as well.

❖ Yellow light: If you scored in the middle range (57–66), you tend to become busy and work to the exclusion of other life events. Your work habits are mildly workaholic. But with modifications, you can find work-life balance and prevent job burnout.

❖ Green light: If you scored in the lowest range (25–56), you're a hard worker instead of a workaholic, and your risk for burnout is low. You have good work-life balance, and your work style isn't a problem for you or others.

Tips for Clinicians

The workaholic's problem is doubly difficult when mental health professionals don't tune their radars to detect workaholism. Here are some tips to help you, the clinician, treat workaholism instead of suggesting that workaholics just cut back on work hours, subtly pressuring the partner to adapt to the workaholic's work obsession, or missing the problem altogether.

The Work Addiction Risk Test (WART)

____ 1. I prefer to do most things instead of asking for help.

____ 2. I get impatient when I must wait for someone or when something takes too long.

____ 3. I seem to be in a hurry, racing against the clock.

____ 4. I get irritated when I'm interrupted while in the middle of something.

____ 5. I stay busy with many irons in the fire.

____ 6. I enjoy multitasking with two or three activities at once, such as eating lunch, working online, or returning emails.

____ 7. I overcommit myself by biting off more than I can chew.

____ 8. I feel guilty when I'm not working on a project.

____ 9. It's important that I see the concrete results of my work.

____ 10. I'm more interested in the outcome of my work than in the process.

____ 11. Things don't move fast enough or get done fast enough at work to suit me.

____ 12. I lose my temper when things don't go my way or work out to suit me.

____ 13. I ask the same question over again without realizing it after I've already been given the answer.

____ 14. I work in my head thinking about future projects while tuning out the here and now.

____ 15. I continue working after my coworkers have called it quits.

____ 16. I get angry when people don't meet my standards of perfection on the job.

____ 17. I get upset when I'm not in control at work.

____ 18. I tend to put myself under pressure from self-imposed work deadlines.

____ 19. It's hard for me to relax when I'm not working.

____ 20. I spend more time working than socializing with friends or enjoying hobbies or leisure activities.

____ 21. I dive into projects to get a head start before plans are finalized.

____ 22. I get upset with myself for making even the smallest mistake on the job.

____ 23. I put more thought, time, and energy into work than into relationships with loved ones and friends.

____ 24. I forget, ignore, or minimize celebrations such as birthdays, reunions, anniversaries, or holidays.

____ 25. I make important job decisions before getting all the facts and thinking them through.

ESTABLISHING ABSTINENCE

An alcoholic who decides to get sober and joins Alcoholics Anonymous is expected to follow simple, black-and-white rules. He or she may be told, "Just don't drink, no matter what" and "Go to ninety meetings in ninety days." But workaholics can't quit working any more than compulsive eaters can quit eating. Transformation involves becoming attuned to shades of gray and making gradual, gentle changes. The goal is not to eliminate work and its joys but to make it part of a balanced life, rather than the eight-hundred-pound gorilla that sits wherever it wants. First, of course, workaholics have to recognize that there's a problem and be reassured that you, the therapist, do not plan to force them to quit work or even necessarily to reduce their work hours.

Just like in my own recovery, in the clinical work I now do with workaholic clients, therapy usually involves an ordinary, commonsense blend of emotional and interpersonal work, cognitive techniques, family-of-origin work, self-nurturing exercises, pencil-and-paper exercises, and behavioral tactics to help people reorganize time and space so that they're not working or thinking about work 24/7. The only thing unique about therapy with workaholics is focusing the microscope so that overwork comes into view as a problem to begin with.

I often tell workaholic clients that the goal is not to cut back on work hours, which they find immensely relieving. The goal, rather, is to create watertight compartments between work and other areas of life and prepare for easy transitions between them. Some solutions are simple, modest, and practical. Mildred, an overweight, forty-three-year-old psychotherapist had no sense of containment for either her work or her diet. She scheduled clients six days a week, any time between 8:00 a.m. and 8:00 p.m. She literally didn't know when her plate was full because, rather than using a plate, she would open the refrigerator and drink or eat directly from a milk container or take-out carton. At my suggestion, she discarded a day planner that listed the hours from 7:00 a.m. to 11:00 p.m. and replaced it with one that stopped at 5:00 p.m. I also suggested that when she ate, she pour the milk into a glass and dish a serving of food onto a plate.

Before she made these changes, Mildred had felt as though she had to be available to all people all the time. But keeping a more limited day planner and serving herself food on a plate reminded her, physically and practically, that she had choices, could set limits, and could decide for herself when she would see a client or have a glass of milk. This empowerment and self-care helped her slowly revise boundaries that had been blurred since childhood, when she had acted as her depressed mother's emotional caretaker. Over time, she was able to question old beliefs that had confused legitimate self-care with selfishness.

PUTTING "TIME CUSHIONS" INTO WORK SCHEDULES

As a clinician, you can help workaholic clients make transitions between work and other activities and learn not to schedule themselves so tightly that there's no time for bathroom breaks or travel between appointments. By showing them how to schedule "time cushions" around appointments, you can help them drastically reduce tension. One man invariably fought with his fiancée when he returned home because she would be eager to talk intimately while he was still tense and preoccupied with work. Once he started to schedule "time cushions," his days became less harried. He also started using his drive home not to chew over the events of the day but to decompress, play enjoyable music, and practice relaxing exercises as he mentally thought ahead to seeing his fiancée. By the time she met him at the door, he was glad to see her and capable of making the transition from hectic schedule to relaxed, intimate conversations.

SEEING THE WATER YOU'RE SWIMMING IN

As a practitioner, I know I'm not alone. Many of you face similar challenges in your own lives. It's one of the hazards of work that is not merely a job but a calling. It's easy for callings to overwhelm other areas of our lives, to become not only our livelihoods but our sole source of spiritual meaning and an oddly safe arena for intense emotional connection without too much personal risk.

Chances are, you, too, are particularly vulnerable to the blurred boundaries that can promote workaholism. We have the dangerous freedom to set our own hours; to juggle training, supervision, workshops, and clinical work; to labor on research projects in our home offices until midnight; to leave our cellphones and laptops on—and we have trouble saying no to clients who insist on evening or weekend appointments.

When we live this way ourselves, swimming in the soup of a work-obsessed culture, it's hardly surprising that we miss the clues our clients and their partners give us about the misshaping power of overwork on their families' lives. By way of analogy, before the 1980s, many therapists who were not aware of the ramifications of alcoholism worked earnestly with couples without directly addressing substance-abuse issues and wondered why they seemed to be treading water.

As mental health professionals, we have also failed to notice that workaholism is the unacknowledged common element in many of our treatment failures. We hear that a man isn't devoting time to his relationship with his wife, and we may be unaware that his compelling and unacknowledged relationship to work may be at the bottom of the couple's distress.

This is a larger issue than it may seem at first. In the case of alcoholism, therapists eventually got more sophisticated and began to see it for what it was, to refer clients to Alcoholics Anonymous or rehab as a condition for continuing therapy, and to understand that until the centrality of the relationship to the substance was addressed, little else was likely to change. It's time we got more sophisticated about overwork as well. We need to see it as yet another way that vulnerable human beings seek, for understandable reasons, a sanctuary from the uncertainties and vulnerabilities of really living their present lives, with all their textures and disappointments. When we as clinicians restore balance to our own lives, we will be far more likely to recognize, and effectively treat, this century's problem without a name when it bedevils the clients and families who come into our therapy offices for help.

Bibliotherapy

✧ Bryan Robinson, *#Chill: Turn Off Your Job and Turn On Your Life* (New York: William Morrow, 2019) provides a wider context for workaholics to use the Twelve Steps to work on moderation one step at a time.

3

How to Spot Work Addiction

*I didn't need to use drugs because my
bloodstream was manufacturing my
own crystal meth.*
—Workaholics Anonymous Member

Roger Loses His Medical License to Work Addiction

As a sixty-five-year-old physician, I was forced into retirement by multiple health and legal issues, and I surrendered my medical license. When I look back, it's clear that the seeds of my work addiction sprouted in childhood. I mowed lawns in junior high, became a construction laborer as soon as I could drive, waited tables in college, and worked two jobs, seven days a week, every summer. I had little if any free time.

In medical school, I worked day and night three days straight in the hospital by choice. As an intern at the San Diego Naval Hospital, I was selected as the "Hot Dog of the Year." As a resident and fellow, I developed numerous clinical and teaching programs that were not required of me, but they earned me attention, distinction, and honors.

I was always busy and loved it that way. I considered work my hobby, not a job. After the internship, I worked eighty-hour workweeks, giving most of myself to my career, and having little left over for my wife and children. I purchased a home with eight acres and a barn where I had plenty to do. Like my father did when I was a child, I took my family on beach vacations but was always ready to get back to work. I rationalized that I didn't want to return to work with a pile on my desk. But truth be told, working gave me a high, making me feel important in ways that nothing else could. Work transcended everything.

While working a full anesthesia practice, I developed a pain clinic that consumed a great amount of my time and soul, plus thousands of hours of work and great effort. I reasoned that the time and effort drain was acceptable because I provided a nice home with a place for my wife's horses and all our children went to the best private schools. I worked my ass off and loved it! Work had become a compulsion. I received awards from the medical society for what I contributed to the medical community and to patients. It was great, and I was having fun. Or so I thought.

As the workload continued to escalate, I couldn't keep up. Then I discovered hydrocodone. The painkiller helped me focus, work longer hours, and churn out a greater quantity and higher quality of work. When back pain started interfering with my productivity, the painkiller became a necessity to keep up with the workload. It was easy to get, often sent to the office as samples.

Altogether, I had five back surgeries, two neck spine fusions, one knee and both hip replacements, two shoulder surgeries, and hand surgery. I was proud that it never took me more than a week to return to work, that my staff was amazed, and that no one tried to stop me. Then one day a representative from the state's impaired physician group visited me, inquiring about a complaint he had received. I assured him I didn't have a problem. Afterward I sought help from an addictionologist on my own. He said I should stop using hydrocodone. But I was blind to my out-of-control work compulsions and didn't know how to change.

I continued working until 2:00 or 3:00 a.m. and got up at 5:00 or 6:00 a.m. to return to the office. I became so tired that I developed fatigue-induced paranoia. I would fall asleep for a few seconds while driving, almost totaling the car more than once. At home, before reaching the bed one time, I damaged our house by a water spill when I fell asleep in the shower.

I continued to perform over seventy injections and other surgical procedures each week and to see patients in the office. I couldn't get ahead of the work, yet I couldn't say no to taking on more. I used eight different medications to keep me going, each on a schedule. And I went to great lengths, making sure I had enough in reserve, so I'd have the energy they provided for me to work. My rut became deeper, but I saw no way out. I couldn't ask for help for fear of being ruined financially and having my personal life destroyed. Constantly anxious, my blood pressure spiked to a dangerous level of 170/110, and I had constant headaches.

Eventually, I was reported to the state board of medicine and was sent to a drug addiction program for evaluation. I told them about my inability to stop working compulsively, yet I was diagnosed as a drug addict. With a wrong diagnosis, I was prescribed the wrong treatment. I had taken charts and a Dictaphone with me so I could continue working in rehab. When they found out, they were upset but still didn't see my problem.

Upon returning home, I tried working without painkillers but couldn't. With my old pill source still in place, I returned to work while going to mandatory AA meetings, ultimately passing ninety-one random urine drug screens over a five-year period. The rut and downward spiral continued for another five years, as did my drug use to support my work addiction.

Hooked on work, I pulled further away from my family and was dying inside. Then came the dreaded call that told me to shut down my practice. I was relieved to receive the call. I enrolled in a high-powered drug rehab program for professionals for three months where I explained that my real problem was work addiction. Again, I was ignored and told "the treatment is all the same."

Once home, I finally found a therapist who listened and made the diagnosis of work addiction with or without drug addiction. I felt like jumping for joy! It had taken only seven years for an accurate diagnosis. Treatment from several other experts on workaholism and many tests all supported the diagnosis of work addiction without chemical addiction.

I can trace my struggles with work addiction to my childhood, when my father worked all the time. He had been a breadwinner for his family since the ninth grade, when his father died. I saw little of him, except when I was in trouble. Although I'd said I'd never do what my father had done, I'd become just like him. I missed my children's youth and sacrificed my marriage for work. I'm sure some of my health problems were caused by my work addiction and the total lack of the ability to treat myself. I'm living out my father's life, and even though I recognize the need to change somehow, I'm still resistant.

My hopes are to avoid dying, feeling totally useless, being a burden to my family and society, and suffering from pain. I'm still in good physical health and have the will and drive to regain my medical license and rebuild my family. Fortunately, my wife and children continue to be understanding and supportive. But the price I've paid for work addiction has been as great as that of any person with a chemical addiction. I'm living proof of that.

The Tell-Tale Signs of Work Addiction

If you're like Roger—addicted to work but unable to see the water you're swimming in—this chapter describes the warning signals so you can recognize when work addiction is staring you in the face.

My research team at the University of North Carolina at Charlotte pinpointed some of the signs of work addiction. We compared a sample of 109 workaholics with nonworkaholics. Across the board, workaholics had statistically higher burnout rates, were more disconnected from their inner selves, and had less self-insight than nonworkaholics. Workaholics were more controlling and more impaired in their communication. In contrast, nonworkaholics showed more clarity, compassion, calmness, and confidence. Research also found that workaholics put in more work hours than companies expect. As a result, they suffer poor work-related mental and physical health such as chronic fatigue, anxiety, depression, insomnia, social dysfunction, and higher somatic symptoms and systolic blood pressure than their cohorts.[1] And it's no wonder. Workaholics tend to focus on the tsunami of work they take on instead of on their mental and physical well-being. Let's look at more of the signs.

The Ten Red Flags

Over the years, I have collected hundreds of case studies from self-described workaholics in my clinical practice. The following ten warning signs were synthesized from these case studies.[2] All ten signs are not present in every case, and they may appear in various configurations in different individuals. But they are useful guidelines to help you recognize workaholism.

1. *Hurry.* "As I'm walking out the door, I glance at my watch and realize I have ten more minutes before my next appointment. I just have to cram in one more thing. So, I rush back to my desk, put in a call . . . and before I know it, fifteen minutes have passed. Of course, I'm late to the appointment."

Nothing moves fast enough for Jim. The more items he can cross off his list, the better. When a job is left hanging, Jim feels anxious and afraid. To curb anxiety, he has two or three activities going at once. When Jim has the cell phone in one hand, he's pounding away on his computer with the other and mentally planning a third project. If you're like Jim, you feel compelled to multitask. Having many things happening at once and engaging in two or three tasks simultaneously gives you the sense that you're accomplishing more, plus it gives you an adrenaline rush. Performing only one activity at a time feels unproductive and boring. Typically, you schedule back-to-back appointments and don't give yourself time to get from one to the next, usually running late. Perhaps you even unwittingly create mini crises such as when you flip out over a shortage of paper clips or a balky computer system.

2. *Control.* "I must write, produce, and star in my life. I really don't have time to develop this new account, but I know if I hand it over to someone else, it won't be handled right. I'll have to work nights to write and design this new ad

campaign, but it's worth it. In the long run, we'll keep the client. I'd rather do it myself than waste time with a bunch of bad ideas from losers."

Sally's successful advertising agency is built on her own strength. As a work-addicted employer, she has trouble delegating authority. Her need to control her life is prompted by insecurity; she's uncomfortable in unpredictable situations. Solo working gives her security. Projects come with a beginning, middle, and end. When she's in control of all three stages, she feels like her entire life is in control.

When you're chained to the desk, you, like Sally, fear that delegating tasks or asking for help will be perceived as signs of weakness or incompetence. And once something is out of your hands, you feel a loss of control. So, you can't and won't ask for help. You tend to overplan, overorganize, and hoard work so your environment feels predictable, consistent, and controllable—all of which inhibit spontaneity and flexibility. Tasks become either your way or the highway.

3. *Perfectionism.* "I think I'm superhuman. I can't be content to accomplish something without laying the groundwork for something else. Fearing that I'll somehow fall behind or get out of control, I constantly must be striving to accomplish a goal or some block of work."

Lyn judges herself and others by inhuman standards. In her view, there's no room for mistakes. Anyone falling short of her idea of perfection is lazy. Doing everything perfectly is the hallmark of work addiction. It's tough to accomplish one goal without laying the groundwork for another project. You're difficult to work for and with. You narrow your life to only those things at which you can excel, judging yourself and others unmercifully. Your common refrain is, "If you want something done right, do it yourself" or "If I do it, I know it's been done the way it should be done." Along with these superhuman standards, failure, and anger for missing the mark are constant companions.

4. *Relationship Difficulty.* "At rehearsals, I would imagine my smiling dad in the front row. He looked so proud of me. His imagined presence really motivated me to learn my part. But when it came time for the actual performance, he had an out-of-town business meeting. He promised to dash back from the airport to catch my second act. All through the first act, I was distracted by opening doors and shuffling feet. I'd investigate the audience, searching for his face. But as always, his meeting ran over, and he missed my school play."

True workaholics are no-shows at a child's recital or soccer game because work calls. If you're anything like Sandy's father, this wouldn't be the first play you missed. You would have a pattern of forgetting, ignoring, or minimizing the importance of family rituals and celebrations. A family member might have to remind you about birthdays, reunions, holidays, and anniversaries. And even if you make it to an event, your cell phone ushers you into the event, and you have trouble concentrating because your mind is back at the office.

Wedded to work, you have little time left over for your spouse, partner, or children. This is called *work infidelity*.

5. *Work binges.* "I self-impose deadlines all the time. The price I must pay for procrastinating just isn't worth it. I go nuts. I panic. I can't sleep. I have such anxiety until a project is completed. Finally, I just buckle down and do it. I get in this altered state where I chain-smoke, don't eat, screen all my phone calls, and avoid sleep. When I'm done, it's like crawling out of a work cave. I look and feel disgusting. But with that finished project in my hand, nothing else seems to matter."

Chances are you've occasionally worked overtime to meet a deadline. But workaholics strangle themselves with unrealistic deadlines and work binges to complete projects. You go into what many describe as an altered state, avoiding sleep, missing meals, working around the clock to finish a project. You would rather work nonstop for days than spread tasks out over a reasonable time period. In extreme cases, you might mimic the alcoholic who stashes booze wherever he or she goes. Instead of hiding your booze, you shove a laptop into suitcases or under car seats. Many workaholics sneak their work, much like an alcoholic sneaking a drink, when their concerned complainers are out of earshot. Even at leisure events, after promising not to work, you slip out your iPhone or shuffle papers inside pant or skirt pockets. It's as if you need a work "fix" everywhere you go.

6. *Restlessness.* "I always have this annoying voice in my head. It tells me I don't have the right to relax or unwind. This voice says, 'Look, fun is a waste of time. What do you have to show for it? Go do something productive, you jerk.'"

This symptom can show up when you feel guilty and useless whenever you are doing something that doesn't produce results. If you're exercising, cleaning, or doing a job-related activity, you feel okay. But if you're hanging out with friends, you might feel restless and irritable because of *work withdrawal*. Leisure activities are viewed as a frivolous waste of time because you have nothing to show for them. And you look down your nose at colleagues who take vacations or leave early, becoming so restless that you turn hobbies and recreation into productivity or money-making ventures.

7. *Brownouts.* Work trances or brownouts are comparable to the alcoholic's blackouts. During a work trance, you have memory lapses during long conversations because you're preoccupied with work. You don't remember commitments or agreements because your mind is in the future or past tuning out the present moment, so you have no recollection of it. Driving while working mentally (DWW) can cause you to drive through stop signs or past designated points on your route. Busily focusing on tomorrow's presentation, you might have trouble paying attention to the road. Chances are if you work and drive, you have a faulty driving record. Melanie described one work trance this way:

It was my boyfriend's birthday, and I'd spent most of the day with him. We were supposed to have dinner together. He was even going to cook. But just before dinnertime, I became so anxious I had to get out of his apartment. I hadn't done one work-related thing all day. I told him I needed to run home to change clothes. But once in my car, I found myself driving toward my office. I told myself I would merely type a few paragraphs and go over tomorrow's appointments. I don't remember the three hours that passed. It was 9:00 p.m. when I rushed to my car and floored it back toward his apartment. I was stopped by a police officer for speeding. I tried to explain my situation to him, but to no avail. When I finally made it back, my boyfriend had already eaten his birthday dinner alone. I felt so terrible. Yet even worse, I didn't know why I did it.

8. *Impatience and irritability.* Since time is your most prized commodity, you hate to wait. You white-knuckle it and drum your fingers during wait times and try almost anything to get to the front of the line at the grocery store, restaurant, or movie. You're easy to spot at the doctor's waiting room—the one hypnotically gazing into a cell phone or open laptop, pad of paper, and a fast-scribbling pen.

You're easily annoyed when interrupted, and in the long run, your impatience results in impulsivity and premature decision-making. You might start projects before gathering all the facts. And sometimes you make avoidable mistakes because your hurried-and-harried actions lead you to bypass research and exploration.

9. *Self-inadequacy.* "Work was my security, promising to fill the hours and give me purpose, meaning, and self-esteem. But as soon as a project was done, the emptiness, unrest, and depression returned. The only time I felt worthy was when I was producing 'things' so that I could constantly prove that I was okay."

Natalie gets a temporary high when she completes a project. In between achievements, she feels empty and lost. This feeling of inadequacy bothers her until she is immersed in her next project. Work is the one thing that used to bring her love and attention from her parents when she was younger. She still believes she has to prove herself in order to be accepted by others.

Overworking promises to fill the hours and provide purpose and meaning, but fear of failure is your constant companion. And you tend to aggravate the inadequacy when you forget, miss the mark, or make a mistake with negative self-talk, name calling, and put-downs. You seek self-worth through performance and achievement. And your self-inadequacy causes you to emphasize production with concrete results that give you a temporary high and feeling of value.

10. *Self-neglect.* Gobble, gulp, and go are at the top of your priority list, and self-care is at the bottom. Your job trumps taking care of yourself. You pay little attention to your mental and physical conditions, which are on a downhill slide.

TABLE 3.1

Warning Signs of Work Addiction

Physical signs	Behavioral signs
Headaches	Temper outbursts
Fatigue	Restlessness
Allergies	Insomnia
Indigestion	Difficulty relaxing
Stomachaches	Hyperactivity
Ulcers	Irritability and impatience
Chest pain	Forgetfulness
Shortness of breath	Difficulty concentrating
Nervous tics	Boredom
Dizziness	Mood swings

Nutrition, rest, and exercise are no-shows in your life, along with the inability to say no to a work task. When coping mechanisms such as chain-smoking, Red Bulls, and junk food are added to the picture, your health deteriorates further. Even when real symptoms such as headaches, ulcers, or high blood pressure crop up, you say you don't have time to go to the doctor. Although you know there's a problem, you convince yourself to ignore it. Table 3.1 presents the physical and behavioral warning signs that accompany work addiction.

The Many Faces of Work Addiction

All workaholics work too much, but not all workaholics act alike. Some are too careless, others too ploddingly scrupulous; some can't get started, others plunge in on a dozen projects and finish little. The result of these differing work styles may look the same from the point of view of a therapist or an unhappy spouse—an unbalanced life dominated by long hours at the office—but each style expresses a different set of emotional and cognitive vulnerabilities, and each requires different therapeutic treatment.

As you consider the signs and traits, keep in mind that not all workaholics fit the general pattern and that work addiction has many faces:

❖ The CEO who sneaks a cellphone and laptop into the hospital where she has just undergone major surgery

❖ The minister zipping down the highway at seventy miles an hour, scribbling notes for his sermon, swearing and promising to remember his cell phone next time so he won't have to slow down

❖ The psychotherapist who cannot say no to the patients who need her and ends up overscheduling herself, burning out in the process

❖ The architect who confides that she mentally worked on a client's house during sexual intercourse with her husband

❖ The supermom who has a career, manages the house, is a driver for the kids' carpool, gets dinner on the table, and perhaps even takes a class at night

Workaholics are not always the Elon Musk's of the corporate world. Sometimes they look more like Martha Stewart. In fact, the number of women workaholics is climbing as women enter more traditionally male-dominated fields. Workaholics are not always in corporate or office jobs, nor are they always in high-paying positions. Plumbers, electricians, waitresses, and maintenance workers are included in the ranks of workaholics.

The broad umbrella term *workaholism* is only a starting point. There are four major categories of workaholism: the *relentless*, the *bulimic*, the *attention-deficit*, and the *savoring* workaholic. Maybe you can see yourself, a loved one, or a colleague in one of the following categories of workaholism.

Typology of Workaholics

	Work Completion (Low ↔ High)	
Bulimic Workaholics (low work initiation / high work completion)		**Relentless Workaholics** (high work initiation / high work completion)
Savoring Workaholics (low work initiation / low work completion)		**Attention-Deficit Workaholics** (high work initiation / low work completion)

Work Initiation

Low ——————————————————————→ High

THE RELENTLESS WORKAHOLIC

The stereotypical workaholics are what I call *relentless workaholics*—those who work compulsively and constantly day and night, holidays, and weekends. How do you know if you're a relentless workaholic? There's no letup and few periods of down time in your life, and leisure and recreation are rare. Gary describes what happens:

> When I'm fatigued and have had only three hours of sleep after staying up all night at the computer, something in my body and my mechanism keeps me moving, even when there's no energy left. It isn't easy for me to give up, no matter what the clock says. I take a break to eat and try to work out once in a while. But I usually don't stop until eleven or twelve o'clock at night, and many times not until two in the morning. Because I want to bear down on myself, I tend to put too much on my list, stay up past the time I should have, and do projects that really could be done the next day. I want to make sure I put forth some blood, sweat, and tears so that I'll remember I've done the work and I didn't come by it in an easy way. I have headaches almost every afternoon to the point that I'm keeping the makers of extra strength Tylenol in business. I'm tired all the time, but I don't allow myself to get the kind of rest I need. I haven't made time for it because there's too much work to be done.

You know you're a relentless workaholic if, instead of dragging your feet on deadlines, you complete work tasks weeks ahead of schedule. When you approach a project with a six-month deadline as if it were due tomorrow, it gives you an adrenaline charge. You let nothing and no one stand in your way of getting the job done. Having the project finished early leaves you time to focus on other work items. Work is more important to you than relationships, and you disregard other people's feelings because you're focused on task completion. Maggie was so praised for her tireless dedication by her hospital bosses that it stimulated her to do more, despite her husband's objections. Her work addiction got so bad she stepped over dog excrement for days on her way out the door because she didn't have time to pick it up. After her marriage ended, Maggie lamented her belated revelation:

> Only after I was separated from my husband did I realize I wasn't supposed to do all of this as part of my job. I'm aware that I've been addicted to my own adrenaline for a long, long time. My mind never stopped at night because I was running on adrenaline. When I couldn't sleep, I'd put a yellow pad by my bed. Every time I had a thought, I'd turn on the light and write the thought down,

thinking it would help me sleep. My husband wanted to know why I couldn't turn it off. But the adrenaline made me feel like I didn't need sleep, except for two or three hours a night. But I wasn't tired. I was having a ball and on a roll!

Once a task is completed, if you're a relentless workaholic, you move to the next item on the agenda and have many activities going at once. You are a hard-driving perfectionist; your work is thorough, and your standards practically unreachable. You are a dyed-in-the-wool workaholic—you take work seriously, performing to nothing short of the highest standards.[3] Overcommitted, you abhor incompetence in others and tend to be productive and highly regarded by others.

THE BULIMIC WORKAHOLIC

The second category is the *bulimic workaholic*, who has out-of-control work patterns that alternate between binges and purges. How do you know if you're a bulimic workaholic? Faced with a time crunch, you create adrenaline as you engage in frantic productivity that is followed by inertia. You overcommit, wait until the last possible minute, then throw yourself into a panic and work frantically to complete the task. Jenny worked for two or three days straight and slept off her work high for two days. She collapsed, sleeping in her clothes, just like an alcoholic sleeping off a drinking binge:

> When I used to binge, I would take on a project and stay up until three or four in the morning to get it finished, just compulsively thinking that morning's not going to come and that if something happened to me, I have to have it done today. That binge would go into fourteen and sixteen hours, and then I'd have two or three hours of sleep and then go on a roll and do this for two more days. Then I would be exhausted and sleep it off. It's almost like I've heard alcoholics talk about sleeping off a drunk. I would sleep off that binge of work. Sometimes I would sleep in my clothes, and I hated it! I just hated it!

In contrast to relentless workaholics, whose productivity is clearly visible, you know you're a bulimic workaholic if you go through long periods where you don't work. In fact, no one would know you're a workaholic if they caught you in one of your down times. When it comes to deadlines, you procrastinate and then put yourself under the gun to finish. Procrastination and frantic working are two different sides of the same coin of work bulimia. Fear that you won't do the task perfectly underlies your procrastination. You might become so preoccupied with perfection that you cannot start a project. Yet while you engage in behaviors that distract you from the task, you obsess over getting the job accomplished. Outwardly, your work bulimia makes it appear that you're avoiding work, but in your mind, you're working obsessively hard.

Although physically present during family gatherings or Workaholics Anonymous meetings, others see you as preoccupied, working in your head. During your procrastination phase, when you feel paralyzed and unable to work steadily and within healthy boundaries, you are what is referred to as a *work anorexic*—someone for whom avoidance of work is as much a compulsion of work addiction as overworking is because of your obsession with it.[4]

THE ATTENTION-DEFICIT WORKAHOLIC

Lee represents the third type of workaholic, the *attention-deficit workaholic*. How do you know if you're engaged in this workaholic style? You are adrenaline-seeking, easily bored and distracted, constantly seeking stimulation. Lee leaves the house most mornings in a huff because either his wife or kids did something to upset him. On the way to work he weaves in and out of traffic, shaking his fist and cursing at other commuters.

By the time he gets to the office, Lee has settled down and is ready to work. You know you're an attention-deficit workaholic when your appetite for excitement, crisis, and intense stimulation is a strategy that you unwittingly use to focus. You're often the revved-up workaholic who clicks her nails on tabletops, twiddles his thumbs, or fidgets, pacing about erratically. You like risky jobs, recreation, and living on the edge at work and in play.

Living on the brink of chaos gives you a constant adrenaline charge. Lee seeks diversion from boredom through stimulation in a relatively safe fashion, such as creating tight deadlines, keeping many projects going at one time, taking on big challenges at work, and being chronically unable to relax without intense stimulation. The adrenaline charge could also cause you to live on the edge and engage in high-risk jobs or activities such as playing the stock market, parachute jumping, or working triage in a hospital emergency room.

You have difficulty staying focused on tasks. You get bored with the details of your work and jump ahead to the next item on the agenda to get another charge. You might even create crises over the smallest things to get the adrenaline rush, possibly throwing a fit because there is no paper in the fax machine. Research shows that it's not uncommon for workaholics to generate the crisis and then get attention and praise for resolving it.[5]

Some but not all attention-deficit workaholics are struggling with undiagnosed attention-deficit disorder (ADD). Adrenaline acts as self-medication that functions as an antidote for the ADD and provides the needed focus that allows you to buckle down to work. Unlike bulimic workaholics, who are paralyzed by perfectionism when they should be starting a project, you start many projects but can't complete them. Unlike relentless workaholics who compulsively follow through, you leave projects unfinished and half-baked to move on to the next excitement. Easily bored with the details of the follow-through stage, you get high from creating ideas and brainstorming the big picture, then launching projects without finishing them.

One expert described this type of workaholic as *the innovators*: "They cannot keep their attention focused long enough to finish what they have created. Moreover, they report boredom with follow-through. Upon deeper investigation, I discovered that these workers were hooked on the adrenaline rush of the new idea and felt let down by the painstaking development work. They jumped to the new projects to get their high. Of course, with inadequate product development, these great innovations were just sitting on the shelves and not making profit for the company."[6]

The compulsion to jump impulsively into work projects before plans have been thought through or solidified makes it hard for you to complete projects in a timely manner. Instead of giving serious consideration to alternate behaviors or possible consequences or waiting and planning, your need for immediacy often locks you into a course of action. You proceed with projects without paying thorough attention to details or receiving valuable input from others. The results can be disastrous if your addiction outruns careful thought and reflection. Nowhere is the adage "haste makes waste" more appropriate. When your lack of forethought causes you to make impulsive decisions without all the facts, you might wonder why you're constantly backtracking to clean up your own messes.

THE SAVORING WORKAHOLIC

The fourth type, the *savoring workaholic*, is a contrast to attention-deficit workaholics because he or she is slow, deliberate, and methodical. How do you know if you're a savoring workaholic? You are a consummate perfectionist, terrified deep down that the finished project is never good enough. It's difficult for you to tell when something is incomplete or when it's finished. You savor your work just as alcoholics savor a shot of bourbon.

When Norm balances his accounts, he'll take eight hours to do some tabulating that most people could do in one hour. According to his wife, Norm has the same sort of intoxication with work that people who eat too much do with food. "He's always working but never seems to accomplish much," Norm's wife said, "Sometimes I look at what he's done, and it doesn't look like he's produced anything. For all I know, he's adding up the same column of numbers day after day."

You know you're a savoring workaholic if you inadvertently prolong and create additional work when you're almost finished with a task. You are notorious for creating to-do lists that often take longer to generate than completing the task would. Norm says he takes great pride and pleasure in producing to-do lists and marking off each item as it is completed: "Creating lists dictated my work life. I always found a way to fill in any extra spaces or lines on my yellow pad with obscure chores, so I'd always be busy." He says each line that's marked off is a great sense of satisfaction for him: "It's a visible trophy to my sense of accomplishment."

When savoring workaholism runs your life, your detailed, self-absorbed work style makes it hard to function on a team. Norm drives colleagues and loved ones crazy with his nitpicking and inability to let things go because tasks rarely seem finished to him. Colleagues complain that you drag your feet because you must dot every *i* and cross every *t*. When others are ready to move on, you hold them back by overanalyzing, taking ideas apart, thinking them through from every angle, getting bogged down in detail, and sending things back to committee fifteen different times. Because projects seem incomplete to you, even when others deem them finalized, you have difficulty with both the closure of old tasks and the initiation of new ones in your work.

Developing a Work Moderation Plan

Abstinence for those who are chemically dependent means total sobriety. But if you have to work, you can find work moderation by abstaining from compulsive overworking and freedom from negative thinking. For some workaholics, an effective work-moderation plan includes specific activities and time commitments. For others, it's a broad framework that provides maximum flexibility and balance in the four areas of life: work, play, relationships, and self. Giving time and thought to your work in proportion to other activities in your life becomes the primary goal. There's a consensus that the best predictor of a positive approach to work is a full life outside work. A full personal life that acts as a psychological buffer can dissipate your work's negative effects and augment the positive ones.

As a beginning to a work moderation—or self-care—plan, imagine your life as four spokes in a wheel: self, relationships, play, and work.

1. *Self*: attending to the personal needs of rest and physical exercise, relaxation, self-esteem, spiritual practices, nutrition, and stress-reduction exercises such as deep breathing or meditation (I include a detailed discussion of the benefits of meditation in chapter 13).

2. *Relationships*: spending time and nurturing relationships with significant loved ones and friends whom you consider your family. Your family can be a spouse; it can include both a spouse and children; it can include unmarried same-sex or opposite-sex partners with or without children; or it can comprise

Computing Your Self-Care Quotient

1. Start by computing your NOW percentage:
   How are you living your life? Indicate the percentage of time you NOW devote to each of the four areas below. (The percentages must add up to 100.)

SELF	_____
RELATIONSHIPS	_____
PLAY	_____
WORK	_____
TOTAL	100%

2. Next compute your GOAL percentage:
   What would be your goal for a more balanced life? Indicate the percentage of time you would devote to each of the four areas below if your life were more balanced. (The percentages must add up to 100.)

SELF	_____
RELATIONSHIPS	_____
PLAY	_____
WORK	_____
TOTAL	100%

3. Then compute your self-care quotient:
   Enter the four NOW and GOAL percentages in the spaces below. Then subtract the NOW from the GOAL percentages to get your self-care quotient. A positive score means the area needs more time. A negative score means the area needs less time.

	SELF	RELATIONSHIPS	PLAY	WORK
GOAL	_____	_____	_____	_____
NOW	_____	_____	_____	_____
BALANCE	_____	_____	_____	_____

4. Your Work Moderation Plan
   After reviewing your four balances, name three or four actions you can take in each area to bring more balance to your life. Putting the actions into practice becomes the basis of your self-care plan. After you try your plan for a week, revise it by deciding what you want to keep, add, or delete.

   Self:

   Relationships:

   Play:

   Work:

other adults such as your parents or siblings. Your family, whether related or unrelated to you, and your friends comprise your major support system.

3. *Play*: spending time in fun activities and social pastimes such as hobbies, recreation, and leisure.

4. *Work*: being effective and productive on the job, enjoying what you do for a living, working harmoniously with coworkers, and working moderately while giving equal time to other areas of your life.

Tips for Clinicians

The symptoms of work addiction are often overlooked. If you're like most clinicians, you'll want to know the symptoms and be able to recognize them. Once you identify the pattern, you can take the first step in treating work addiction by helping clients develop a self-care plan. Together with your client, you can identify his or her type of workaholism, along with accompanying problems, and match counseling goals with the specific type of work addiction. It's important for you to evaluate your own work addiction tendencies and think about a self-care plan of your own if applicable.

USING THE WART

I developed the Work Addiction Risk Test (WART) as a tool to screen for the symptoms of work addiction. The WART has been tested for its clinical preciseness. Statistical studies show that it has high reliability and validity. Scores on the instrument tend to be consistent over time, and it measures what it is supposed to measure.[7]

You can use the WART to identify problem areas and set goals. Together with clients, I encourage you to use the WART to pinpoint areas of concern that need modifying. Then you can apply some or all the tips presented throughout this book. Rereading the test and identifying statements that clients rated 3 or 4 will tell you a lot about how they're living their lives. Then they can think of ways to reduce the risk involved in each situation. In other words, how can they change their lives so that they can honestly rate the statements 1 or 2? You can help clients set goals for each situation that they'd like to change, moving them in the direction of reversing their compulsive work patterns.

Psychologists have modified the WART for those they call *high-powered couples* and discovered that it provides a vehicle for stimulating helpful conversation among couples.[8] Consider encouraging couples to read the WART together and decide how much each item pertains to them. After tallying their two scores—a "mine" and a "yours" score—they can note how they define their own and each other's "work." They can note where they agree and disagree in how they rated themselves and each other. They can note changes in perceptions of each other and answer such questions as "Have you changed in ways that your partner is not recognizing?" or "What small changes in your own and in your partner's work style or work orientation might make a difference in the quality of your day-to-day life together?"

MATCHING COUNSELING GOALS TO WORKAHOLIC TYPE

Some work addicts consistently fit in only one category of workaholic; others mix and match, blending categories or alternating among them. For example, a perfectionist may sometimes procrastinate on a major project like a bulimic workaholic and at other times be unwilling to let go of finished work like a savoring workaholic. And an attention-deficit workaholic may sometimes procrastinate and at other times impulsively start projects, only to lose interest and abandon them. Whatever the type of overwork, a careful assessment can help you unravel the assumptions and fears that lie beneath it and point the way to an effective therapeutic approach.

Workaholics in different categories experience different kinds of job and family problems. I recommend collaborating with your workaholic clients to set therapeutic goals that match your client's type of work addiction. Relentless workaholics need help with impulse control, forethought, and attention to detail. They need to slow down the pulse and rhythm of their daily lives—to deliberately eat more slowly, talk more slowly, walk more slowly, and drive more slowly. Developing a work pace commensurate with that of their colleagues and learning to delegate tasks can give them the breathing room they need to stay in the present.

Goals for work bulimics might include devising a more consistent, steady work style and setting boundaries around the times they work. If workaholics in this category learn to accept imperfection, they can move from a stance of "I either do it perfectly or not at all" to "It's okay if my rough draft contains misspelled words, bad grammar, and incomplete and imperfect ideas." Then bulimic workaholics can get started earlier and spread their work out over more realistic time spans. Some workaholics need more help with procrastination and lethargy, along with concurrent mental obsessions and working. Others need a self-care plan that helps them change their frantic, nonstop approach to work, a plan that might include time out.

In my private practice I have noticed that many adrenaline-seeking workaholics also have a dual diagnosis of attention-deficit disorder (ADD). In your clinical work, make sure you're aware of that possibility and of your client's need for medication when the dual diagnosis exists. Attention-deficit worka-holics perform best in positions where they can initiate ideas and delegate the implementation of them to others. Instead of multitasking, they benefit from making a list of daily (or weekly) goals and sticking with one task on the list until it's completed before starting another one.

The physicians Edward Hallowell and John Ratey, authors of *Driven to Distraction*, describe what they call the high stimulation ADD individual who abhors boredom. Similar to attention-deficit workaholics, the client with high-stim ADD seeks diversion from boredom and is unable to relax with-out intense stimulation. This appetite for excitement and crisis is a strategy that these clients unwittingly use to self-medicate themselves with adrenaline, which helps them focus on their work. Hallowell and Ratey write:

> It may be that the thrill of danger helps focus the individual in a way similar to that of stimulant medication, inducing changes at the neurotransmitter level. Stimulant medications, the standard for ADD, enhance the release of epinephrine (adrenaline) in the brain. High-risk behavior does the same thing. Hence such behavior may constitute a form of self-medication. With addiction, a high-risk situation may supply the extra motivation that we know can help with focusing. When one is highly motivated, once again there is a change at the neurotransmitter level that enhances focusing.[9]

Sometimes it's difficult to treat attention-deficit workaholic clients with-out proper medication, thereby reducing their appetite for crises and high stimulation so that therapy can have the maximum benefit. Once it's clear that medication is not necessary, you can employ other traditional therapeutic tech-niques to reduce stress. You can inform clients that it's acceptable to indulge themselves occasionally by setting aside a block of time to soak in a long, warm bath; relax by a fire or on a cool screened porch; or listen to soft music by candlelight.

Encourage them to block out all work-related thoughts that try to enter their mind. Teach them thought-stopping techniques to make this easier. Advise them that they may feel bored or restless the first time they try it and urge them not to become discouraged. The only way to get over adrenaline withdrawal is to go through it. When restlessness occurs, encourage clients to exercise vigorously, use deep-breathing techniques, or mindfulness medita-tion. In any case, it's important to keep a low-key mood at all costs until the anxiety abates.

Those who practice savoring workaholism can benefit from widening their work lens, functioning as team members, and trusting their work group's assessment of when it's time to move on. They often find themselves becoming productive when they learn to let go, distinguish between perfectionism and high standards, and work more efficiently without getting bogged down with minutiae and losing sight of their goals.

HELPING CLIENTS WITH WORK MODERATION

You can use the form in the "Recharging Your Batteries: Computing Your Self-Care Quotient" section to help clients develop a self-care plan of abstinence that is tailored to their personal needs, lifestyles, and preferences. The plan includes ways to incorporate more time for social and leisure activities, hobbies, and family, as well as personal and spiritual time. A work-moderation component includes setting regular work hours devoid of binges and purges, planning for deadlines, and spreading projects out over a realistic time span. Putting the plan on paper for one week helps clients see how they are spending time and which parts of their lives get overlooked. Such a plan helps them lower their perfectionistic standards and set more reachable goals, delegate, and outsource work in the office and at home.[10]

Bibliotherapy

Bibliotherapy can augment the self-care plan.

✧ Edward Hallowell and John Ratey's *Driven to Distraction* (New York: Anchor Books, 2011) provides more information on recognizing and coping with attention-deficit disorder.

4

Inside the Workaholic Mind

*The longest journey one must take is
the eighteen inches from the head to
the heart.*

—Ramprasad Padhi

Kathy Gets Caught in Quicksand

When I'm honest, I realize there have been workaholic patterns in my life as long as I can remember. On the positive side, I had worked my way to a top senior management position in an international role by my mid-thirties. I was one of the few working females in a male-dominated industry. I had gotten there by sacrificing everything else. I worked Saturdays (if not Sundays, too). Although I enjoyed it, I made it a habit of only socializing with work colleagues.

I did my MBA part-time, which focused on a work project. I was fully consumed by work. I would get to the office by 7:00 a.m. and not leave before 10:00 or 11:00 p.m. for many years. I rarely dated, and if I did, it didn't last long as I was consumed by work. I was easily bored and annoyed. What few friends I had were all long distance, and I liked it that way. They didn't get in the way of work.

At one point, I prided myself on having an operation on a Friday and being back at work on Monday, despite the doctor's recommendation of two weeks' rest. I thought that was dedication. On some level, I loved it, but on another level, it was isolating and painful. Hard to admit, but I felt more comfortable talking about work than anything else. Work was my escape. But from what? I couldn't really answer that until I realized I'd gone too far.

If I could describe it, I was caught in quicksand at work, and the harder I tried, the deeper I sank and failed at my job. I was trapped. It took me a long time to even realize that I was failing. I was caught in a company with some significant growing pains but with my optimism, single-mindedness, and work ethic, I was determined to fix it single-handedly, in spite of the odds. I was working in a foreign land with no way out physically, emotionally, or financially. I felt the daily deck stacked against me—the bullying, lying, unrealistic demands, and plans changing daily. I put my head down, digging deeper into my resolve to keep going.

For the first year, I was considered a star performer. I was the "hero," but little did I realize I was soon to be a "zero." I simply didn't see the signs (or truth be told, I did but chose to ignore them). Over many months, my role was being undermined by subtle unpleasant experiences:

Headcount and budgets were cut. When asked to deliver the same results, I complied.

My boss would set priorities, then add to them or change them, still expecting all of them to be delivered. I kicked myself but also would bend to pressure to say yes. And I said yes.

My boss demanded within one day's notice that I travel five hours to meet him. But on the flip side, he would also cancel meetings at a moment's notice—to all of which I would agree.

Executive meetings were directed to conversations from my peers that I needed to get along with my boss. As humiliating as it was, I would take feedback with a yes attitude.

Over the years, I'd built a reputation of being pragmatic and in some ways bending over backward for both my superiors and subordinates. I would make up for it by working extra effort or time. But this time it had gone too far. One too many yeses. Often, I would kick myself for complying when I really meant to say no.

Having a strong sense of intuition, I had a gut feeling and put the puzzle pieces together of what was coming next. But I could not process it, nor did I know what to do. With all the emotional pressures, I was miserable, exhausted, and trapped in a foreign country. One day, I was summoned to the human resources office and told I would be exiting. I was bitterly disappointed, having been so agreeable and worked so hard. I had never "failed." I had gone from "hero" to "zero" within twenty-four months. I was angry, and mentally and physically exhausted.

The emotional roller coaster of the past two years had taken its toll. I was in pain with heartache, struggling to think clearly, complete tasks, or even get out of bed. I had lost patience with just about everyone and felt isolated. I had never tried so hard and gotten so little in return. I had taken this job in a remote small town with no friends, no social life, and, for that matter, no contact with anyone outside of work. Far from family, I was out of touch.

I secretly thought that being dead wouldn't be so bad. At least I could get some rest.

While it's easy to look at this company as an isolated case, I was in my mid-forties, thinking I had invested two painful years of my life with no benefits. I simply didn't have the wherewithal to endure that punishment again. I could've easily deflected it as a company in turbulent times and moved on. But now I had to examine the cause from my perspective and what I would do differently the next time. I happened to stumble upon an early edition of *Chained to the Desk*. As I was reading the first chapter, I began to cry. So much in the story was like my story and what I was suffering.

In the past, I remember an employee telling me I was a workaholic, but I only looked at it as a good thing. I didn't see the cause or cure of it. Now I was ready to explore the cause. And I mused, "Could there be a cure?"

An Idle Mind Is the Devil's Workshop

Now that you're familiar with the signs of work addiction, let's look beneath the surface at the workaholic mind. This chapter explores in more detail the psychological workings of workaholics that manifest themselves in compulsive behaviors of accomplishing and achieving. In the psychological realm, "an idle mind is the devil's workshop" is the reasoning of many workaholics like Kathy, who feel nonexistent unless they are working.

When you're a workaholic, work defines your identity, gives your life meaning, and helps you gain approval and acceptance, just as Kathy described. It becomes the only way you know to prove your value and numb the hurt and pain that stem from unfulfilled needs. You believe you must earn the right to be, something that nonworkaholics believe is their birthright. Shame is often at the bottom of work addiction—a kind of self-loathing that has earned you the name of human *doer* instead of human *being*, a caricature that reflects your need to justify your existence. Chances are, like Kathy, you believe you must overcompensate and do more than the average person to be legitimate: "For some reason I can't just be average. I have to do more or be more than the ordinary person. I've always felt that way—that I must go over, beyond, and above what other people do. It makes me feel like I'm okay," she said.

Even when friends and family think you're present and accounted for, in your mind you're working constantly—while driving a car, eating dinner, spending time with loved ones, and even while having sex and, sometimes, during Workaholics Anonymous meetings. You believe you can earn respect along with your place among others if you just work hard enough. The constant hurrying, the need to control, and the perfectionism mask your deep feelings of not being good enough. Work addiction has been dubbed the "addiction of choice of the unworthy."[1]

Motivated by low self-worth; you define yourself by what you can accomplish. You gauge your value by what you can produce. And the more you do, the better you feel. As Kyle described: "I associate whether I have worth and value with what I achieve, and if I'm not achieving, I have no worth or value. It's like who I am depends on whether I'm able to achieve, not that I'm a good person, not that I have a lot of good qualities and characteristics. But if I achieve, I have worth and value. That's real distorted, but that's where I'm at."

The Negativity Bias Skews Your Perspective

Kyle is correct. The workaholic mind is skewed, much like an anorexic who looks in the mirror and sees herself as still not thin enough, although she weighs just eighty pounds. The skewed perspective is partly due to what neuroscientists call the *negativity bias*—the brain's built-in alarm system to perceive negativity even when a situation is positive or neutral. As neuropsychologist Rick Hanson puts it, Mother Nature designed the brain "like Velcro for negative experiences but Teflon for positive ones."[2] Just as your rib cage protects your vital organs or a scab covers tender flesh, workaholism protects your psychological vulnerabilities, especially from similar incidents that harmed you in the past.

Here's another example of how the workaholic mind packs heat and is locked and loaded for immediate action. After speaking on a panel with another colleague, I was impressed with her leadership in organizing the speakers. I sent her an email that said, "You were total dope with the way you facilitated our panel today." She wrote back, "At first when I read your email, I thought it said, I was a total dope with the way I facilitated our panel today." She read the email again and told me it was her first time with that kind of national responsibility and was feeling uncertain about it. In other words, her negativity hijacked her executive functioning and distorted my message to fit with the insecurities she felt at the time.

Think of all the times you, too, brooded for countless hours over one negative aspect of a situation when, in retrospect, there was nothing to worry about. Perhaps your negative emotional brain overlooked many positive elements. Your colleagues gave you rave reviews on your presentation, but you couldn't get that one frowning face in the front row off your mind. The majority of your friends attended your dinner party, but that one no-show couple continued to flash in your brain like a neon *failure* sign.

Like a first responder on the front lines of an emergency, your diligent nega-tive brain never shuts down. It works overtime even when you're asleep, on 24/7 alert to protect you from physical danger and less imminent threats such as financial pressures, tight deadlines, health worries, performance anxiety, fear your main squeeze might abandon you . . . the list goes on. Your negative brain plays an important role in your survival, warning and pushing you into action even when positive experiences outnumber negative ones, making your life seem full of mostly negative events that put you on edge or make you angry or explosive.

Once the emotional brain perceives a threat (either real or imagined), it *overestimates* impending doom and *underestimates* our ability to manage it. If you plan to stretch outside your comfort zone, for example, the hardwired negativity bias predicts a negative outcome. Known as *forecasting*, it jumps to catastrophic conclusions about the future without evidence, based on sheer emotion. It collects evidence to support the negativity and waits for the ax to fall, stampeding the prefrontal cortex and throwing it offline, even when there's no rational reason for it.

Suppose your boss walks by your desk. You make eye contact with her, smile, and nod. She looks straight at you but doesn't acknowledge your pres-ence. She might as well be staring at the wall, and your *forecaster* is on red alert. "Holy shit," you hear it say. "I must be in hot water." You shrink inside, rumi-nating over what you might have done to deserve this. Your heart races, and you feel shaky. It's just a few days before your performance evaluation. Sleep-less nights stalk you. You toss and turn as your mind spins with worry over job security. This is the negativity bias in action, making up a story without evidence.

The day of your evaluation, your boss calls you into her office, and your stomach flip-flops. You tremble the way you did in sixth grade when you were summoned into the principal's office. But, to your shock, your boss greets you with a smile and gives you a glowing evaluation. Not only are you not in hot water, but she also calls you a highly valued team member, a laudable success— the exact opposite of what your negativity bias predicted and a feather in your cap.

All that worry and rumination for nothing. But it has already taken a toll on your body. Studies show that 90 percent of the worries that your forecaster scares you with are false alarms that never manifest. Still, your negativity bias prioritizes and remembers the negative experiences to prevent life's unexpected curve balls from ambushing you. If you're like most people, you believe the negative voice and stay in the safety of its cocoon. And in the final analysis, you end up feeling lost and questioning who you are, alienated from others, life in general, and isolated from your "self."

Had you *thought about it*, you might have realized there are several benign reasons your boss didn't acknowledge you when she walked by your desk. Perhaps she was distracted by her own worries, deep in thought over an upcoming meeting, or simply just didn't see you. But your negativity bias jumped into action, focused only on the disastrous possibilities. It blew your thoughts out of proportion, sending you into spirals of rumination. And you fell for it hook, line, and sinker.

To offset the negativity bias, the workaholic mind feeds on tangible success, quantifying observable outcomes. Outward manifestations of your importance include how much money you make, how many sales accounts you land, how many pieces of real estate you sell, how many projects you can complete around the house, and how quickly you can get superb food on the table. Typical of most workaholics, you're a list maker who takes great delight in marking off each completed task. And "enough is never enough."

This type of rigid thinking is typical of workaholics who hold tightly to their unrealistic expectations of themselves and others. Although you exceed most people's expectations, you can't seem to meet your own because your standards (not unlike the anorexic's) are unrealistic and, therefore, doomed to fail. On the inside you might feel like the small child who never does anything right, judging yourself harshly for the most minute flaws. When you eventually do make a mistake, you kick yourself for your shortcomings.

Some experts say that the workaholic's to-do lists become a tight girdle instead of a flexible guide: "One woman allots a certain amount of time each day to spend with her children. If the children are not willing or available between three o'clock and five o'clock, they get no time with their mother. The list is a link to our stash. It tells us what we have accomplished and what is left to be done. The problem, for the work addict, is that the list is never done. There is always another list."[3]

Instead of thinking, "What can I realistically accomplish?" your workaholic mindset says, "What would be so great an accomplishment that everyone (myself included) would see how valuable I am?"[4] The attorney tells herself that winning one more case will put her on top. The writer believes she will be revered after just one more book. The construction worker will have all the money he needs after building just one more house. When part of a compulsive pattern, all these acts convey similar messages: "Look at me: I am worthy; I have value." But after all is said and done, the workaholic is on to the next fix.

The Impostor Syndrome

It was January, and snow covered the ground. Inside my office, Lois was having an anxiety attack because she feared she would not be able to succeed in the highly competitive real estate field in which she had worked day and night for several years. She believed it was only a matter of time before her incompetence was revealed and she would lose her job. The paradox was that she had just received an award and a bonus for top million-dollar salesperson in her company the previous year. I was puzzled at the contradiction. I saw her as bright, friendly, and obviously capable and accomplished. She said to me: "At first, I felt good about it, but that only lasted for about twenty minutes. Then I realized it was a fluke, and I'll never be able to pull it off again. I feel like I'm going down the tubes this year."

Although puzzled, I also understood that her nagging workaholic voice clouded her vision from internalizing success, afraid she would slack off and ultimately flop, throwing her into *impostor syndrome*—the chronic fear of being exposed as a fraud, that her accomplishments were not genuine. Instead of embracing success, workaholics are more likely to minimize it and maximize inadequacy.

Distorted workaholic thoughts can make you feel like an impostor. You've been able to fool people that you're competent, even though you're not convinced yourself. You think if they really knew you, you'd be discovered for the fake you are. Your rigid beliefs tell you that you have to work even harder to keep up the charade. One financial consultant said: "I want to achieve everything there is to achieve in my profession. I am humble in the spotlight, but I am afraid of not being in the spotlight."[5]

Work addiction drives you to produce more and more and take on mountains of work even when your professional and personal life are already overloaded. You set yourself up for failure because your standards are so high that no one could ever meet them. Lois described the sabotage of her workaholic mind: "I feel like people judge me on what I do—on what I accomplish, achieve, and on what products I produce and what effect I have on the world. And if I'm not doing the best job I know how, I feel like a failure. And because I can't possibly be doing the best job at everything, I feel like a failure most of the time. Any time I set a goal for myself that I can achieve, I think, 'That wasn't worth it; that was nothing.' So, I create a higher goal that I can't possibly reach."

If you suffer from *impostor syndrome*, you're not alone. Some of the most accomplished personalities on the planet have struggled with self-doubt. Journalist Jeff Jarvis said "like most other creatives, I struggle with self-sabotage, self-doubt, and feeling like an impostor more often than not." When Jane

Fonda won her second Oscar, she told a talk show host that she felt like a phony and feared the Academy would find out how talentless she was and take the award back. Even American author and poet Maya Angelou lamented, "I've run a game on everybody, and they're going to find me out." Other well-known people such as actor Tom Hanks and former First Lady Michelle Obama have also spoken publicly about feeling like an impostor.

Rutgers organizational management expert Gayle Porter suggests that workaholics struggle with low self-esteem to such an extent that they have distorted patterns of working with others, because they focus on how interactions enhance their self-esteem, not on how they can enhance the quality of the task itself:

> The good of the organization, the department, or the work team is secondary to choosing the task or method that will protect the workaholics' self-concept and possibly highlight their efforts. . . . When choices are available, workaholics may redirect effort in a way that does not risk damage to self-esteem. The job outcome is secondary to ego protection. The most common response to any problems will be to work more hours. It would also be important that the ego be protected from any possible connection to lack of results to accompany those added hours. This requires finding a way to assign external blame when the work does not go well rather than focusing on genuine efforts of problem resolution.[6]

Your workaholic mind tells you that you're the only one who can solve a certain problem at work, when the truth is that the work could be delegated. The belief that only you can do it in the specific right way or at the speed necessary gives you a sense of superiority and bolsters your self-worth. Being able to handle heavier loads more swiftly than your coworkers makes you think you measure up to the performance of others. But, of course, when you have to denigrate others to prove your own adequacy, it only calls more attention to your insecurities.

When you stay at the office past five o'clock, after everybody else goes home, you often quietly fume or smugly demand that coworkers and subordinates put in equal time. The thing people applaud you for most, your work ethic, is also the thing people close to you dislike the most. Despite your superior attitude, you're often surprised to learn from office surveys that business associates don't admire you for your abusive work habits. You're shocked to discover that you're viewed as narrow-minded, difficult to work with, and lacking in vision.

The World through Workaholic Eyes

Your workaholic mindset keeps you stuck in an addictive cycle. We unwittingly enter situations with a mindset that doesn't necessarily fit with the actual situation. After a three-week trip to Asia, for instance, I returned to my job at the university. I remember walking into another faculty member's office and noticing a partially covered book on her sofa, only half of which I could see. I read the title as *Tea Ching* and thought she, too, must have an avid interest in Asia.

As I came further into the room and examined the entire book cover more closely, I chuckled to myself when I saw the actual title was *Teaching in the Elementary Schools*. My Asian frame of reference caused me to view that situation differently than I ordinarily would have. We're often unaware of how we bring our own mindset to a new situation, and we expect things to be a certain way. So, we think and behave in ways that make our thoughts come true, a phenomenon known as the *self-fulfilling prophecy*.

The human mind works in such a way that you believe what you learn about yourself as a child. Then, in your adult life, you collect evidence to support this belief. Jason's father used to tell him that he'd never amount to anything. That critical voice, echoing in his head, reminded him that nothing he ever did was enough, driving him deeper into work addiction. Today, he knows that his father's criticisms, although directed at him, reflected his dad's own inner frustration, low self-worth, and deep unhappiness.

Perceptual studies conducted with animals have implications for the workaholic mind. In a laboratory experiment at England's Cambridge University, the visual field of baby kittens was restricted to horizontal lines (——) from birth.[7] They were never exposed to vertical lines (|) while growing up. As adult cats, they could recognize horizontal lines but not vertical ones. They could jump up on horizontal tabletops, but they consistently bumped into vertical table legs. Vertical lines were not part of the adult cats' perceptual reality because they had never experienced such lines as kittens. Another way of putting it is that because of their restricted past, the cats had developed a restricted view of the world.

If you're a workaholic, chances are you were held to high standards that you couldn't reach. These repeated failures restrict your beliefs about your capabilities, so what you see as an adult is set in a certain direction, like the cats' difficulty with vertical lines. If you believe you don't measure up, you develop a mindset that tells you you're inadequate, defective, inferior, undeserving, unworthy, and unlovable. In adulthood you're driven by the belief that you're not good enough, and you unwittingly collect evidence to fit with this belief. You're looking for the horizontal line because that's the template that shaped you. You devote your thoughts and actions to disproving your inadequacy and proving your worth by overcompensating, overdoing, over-caring, overachieving, and generally going overboard with work. But the consequence is the opposite—you prove to yourself that you're inadequate because you continue to believe the template.

Give this exercise a shot. Ask a friend to spend one minute looking around your office or whatever room you're in right now. Ask the friend to list mentally as many items as he or she can that are blue—perhaps the carpet, wallpaper, bindings on books on shelves, curtains, the sofa. After a minute have the person close his or her eyes and name out loud all the items he or she can remember that are yellow. Most people go blank and cannot remember any yellow items. Your friend might have rolled eyes and look at you sideways, wondering what kind of prank you're pulling, and say something like, "I didn't see any yellow, because you told me to look for blue." However, if you had instructed the friend to see yellow, he or she would have seen yellow items. Even if there were only a few of them, the friend would have blocked out everything else to focus on whatever yellow objects were in the room.

The point of this exercise is to demonstrate that the mind sees what it expects to see. Essentially, your workaholic outlook makes present experiences coincide with your mindset. Your perfectionism verifies your unworthiness by unconsciously proving how inadequate you are. You get a 98 on an exam and condemn yourself for not making 100. You receive a promotion, but it's still not high enough up the corporate ladder. You're named salesperson of the month but still didn't break the all-time sales record. You get the bronze medal, but you should have won the gold.

When feedback from people conflicts with your perception of yourself, you change it to fit with your belief system. In other words, you turn positive situations into negative ones. If you think you're inadequate (let's call that the blue), you frame each experience through that belief system and collect evidence to fit with it. Any situation that contradicts the belief that you're inadequate (call that the yellow) is ignored, discounted, minimized, or is not taken in as part of your personal experience. In these ways, you continue to look for blue, even though you're confronted with a veritable rainbow every day. Compliments sail over your head. You tell yourself that your triumphs are accidents, and your failures are proof of who you are.

You're constantly looking for the blue, and you find it because you see what you expect to see. Your rigid beliefs tell you that you must earn the right to be. And when you believe you never achieve enough (the blue), perfect is never enough. So, you're usually feeling bad about yourself; striving to disprove your negative ideas about yourself; pushing yourself to try harder; working longer hours; neglecting yourself and loved ones, and going deeper into performing, achieving, being out of control, attempting to feel better, and hoping to be the best. Elaine said, "If I wasn't accepted, I had to excel, I had to keep pushing to keep working, to prove myself to somebody out there so they would recognize me and think I had something on the ball."

Ten Workaholic Mind Traps

You can see how easy it is to get swept away by your negativity bias into a whirlpool of addictive thinking patterns. Under workaholic stress, negative self-talk pops up with such lightning speed that you might not even notice. Work addiction is kept alive by the exaggerated conclusions we draw, most of which are distorted. And you continue to draw wrong conclusions because you keep falling into *mind traps*—rigid and irrational thought patterns that blind you to the objective facts and cause you to make errors in judgment. These illusions or visual distortions—although meant to keep you safe—cage you with limited possibilities, undermining your ability to cope with inevitable job challenges.

1. All-or-nothing thinking: "I can be either a good mom or a good employee, but I can't do it all." You categorize life into the extremes of black and white and blind yourself to the shades of gray, where truth lies. *Takeaway:* Listen for yourself using words like *always, all, everybody, either-or, nobody, never,* or *none*. Let that be a cue that you're immersed in exaggerated thinking.

2. Mindreading: "She didn't call me back. Obviously, I made a bad impression." You convince yourself you know what others are thinking and feeling. You connect the dots about a situation based on your workaholic thoughts, not facts. When you automatically accept your thoughts as truth, instead of questioning or checking them out, you've sold yourself a bill of goods. *Takeaway:* Remind yourself that your assumptions are not the truth. You can check out the facts before making conclusions to save yourself a lot of unnecessary worry and stress.

3. Catastrophic forecasting: "I'm gonna fall flat on my face in the interview." You forecast the worst possible outcome of a situation without evidence. Even when facts contradict your negativity bias, you continue to predict things will turn out badly. *Takeaway:* When you catch yourself worrying over something that hasn't happened, identify your negative prediction. Then ask yourself, "Where's the evidence for this conclusion?"

4. "Shouldy" thinking and "musterbation": "I *should* have gone to church on Sunday." The words you use can make you feel in charge of your career or at the mercy of it. Oppressive words like *should, ought, must,* and *have to*

can cause you to feel you're a slave instead of a master of your emotions. Notice the difference in tone when you replace just one word: "I *could* have gone to church on Sunday." *Takeaway*: Ask yourself if your self-talk opposes or supports you and if it traps or frees you. Replacing negativity with uplifting words turns burdens into opportunities and empowers you. Now, notice the difference when you change just one word from "have to" to "get to": "I have to work on that project" becomes "I get to work on that project."

5. Overgeneralization: "I really screwed up on that sale. I'm such a loser." You make a sweeping conclusion about your capabilities based on one negative event. You believe if something's true in one case, it's true in all the others. *Takeaway*: When you catch yourself viewing a negative event as a never-ending pattern of defeat, look at the proof. You'll likely not find evidence for the exaggeration.

6. Filtering and discounting the positives: "I won top broker of the year, but that was a fluke." You downplay your accomplishments or positive qualities and dwell on the negatives. This mind trap can keep you stuck in depression and anxiety and create an outlook of hopelessness. *Takeaway*: There's usually a "but" in this mind trap that can help you catch yourself when you insist that your positive aspects don't count. Pay attention when negatives outweigh positives and give the positives equal weight.

7. Magnification or minimization: "I have to get this job promotion, or my career goes down the tubes." You blow the negative aspects of a stressful situation out of proportion while shrinking your ability to overcome it. Or, on the flip side, you downplay your ability to surmount a stressful situation, "Oh sure, I got the last promotion, but that was because the boss liked me. I don't know the new boss." *Takeaway*: Try to be aware when your outlook about a stressful situation is at one extreme or the other. Take the point of view of an outside observer and put it in perspective.

8. Blame: "It's my fault the new employee didn't work out; I shouldn't have hired him." You're overly responsible and blame yourself for conditions beyond your control. Or, on the flip side, you blame others, overlooking your part in an outcome, "I took your advice, and hired the new applicant; it's all your fault it didn't work out." *Takeaway*: Ask yourself if you're blaming someone for conditions beyond their control. Then think about how much of the situation you're truly responsible for. Be willing to take ownership for your part but avoid becoming overly responsible for situations outside your control.

9. Emotional reasoning: "I feel hopeless about my job, so it must be over." You make judgments about people and situations from how you feel. And how you feel about something makes it true in your head, even if there's proof to the contrary. *Takeaway*: Acknowledge your feelings first. Then see when you can separate them from the facts to determine if your conclusion is indeed true, "Yes, I'm feeling hopeless about my job, but that doesn't mean it's hopeless. There are steps we can take to make it better."

10. Labeling: "I blew it with my boss; I'm such a jerk!" Instead of telling yourself that you made a mistake, you tell yourself *you* are the mistake. You put a negative label on people and situations because of one incident instead of looking at the entire picture, "I didn't like that movie; that theater sucks; I won't go there again." *Takeaway*: Save labels for cans and jars and be willing to look at the big picture, "I stumbled in the performance review, but my boss knows and appreciates the quality of my work."

Much of what the workaholic voice whispers isn't true, but you believe it because you hear it in your mind's echo chamber. Raising your awareness and learning to identify the origin of your fears, enables you to avoid taking the whispers seriously and believing them as facts.

Tips for Clinicians

Recovery from work addiction is not something clients can dash through like a commuter rushing to catch the five o'clock train. Most of us have spent a lifetime developing our work thoughts and habits. Changing them requires a reversal of our mindset. As a clinician, you can help clients get in touch with the beliefs that drive their workaholism, make appropriate changes, and begin to set realistic expectations. After you help them understand that their self-worth is not tied to what they do, they can begin to adopt an internal instead of an external focus.

WRITTEN EXERCISES AND BEHAVIORAL TECHNIQUES

A pencil and paper exercise may bring to the surface the catastrophic, all-or-nothing thinking that lies behind some workaholic patterns. One man said to me, "I can spend time with my family or provide for my family financially, but not both." Another client, a successful, thirty-eight-year-old heart surgeon, had not gone on a vacation in ten years because he was convinced that if he took even a week off, his multimillion-dollar business would crumble. I asked him to draw a line across a sheet of paper and write his two extreme beliefs on each

From "Tor-mentor" to Mentor

Elizabeth, once a dispirited wage earner, was able to stop blaming the workplace and accept responsibility for her job choices: "I have picked high-pressure jobs for my last three positions. I wasn't aware of it going into them, but now I see I'm doing that. Nobody's doing that to me."

When the workaholic voice snares us in circling thoughts, it's trying to help us out of a threatening situation, but its made-up story often distorts our perspective, causing us unnecessary worry or anxiety. It helps to reframe your workaholic voice not as your *tormentor*, but as your *mentor*. It takes practice, but you can learn to test the truth about the workaholic's made-up stories in the very moment they rear their heads. Over time, you can become mindful of how you assign meaning to events that often turn out to be untrue.

If you're a workaholic, you can outsmart your mind traps by making an intentional effort to be mindful of them and naming the addictive thoughts that have become part of your inner dialogue. Once you've changed your perspective, you can commit to changing your work habits, instead of blaming your family, the media, society, the job, the economy, or the dog. The way to change is to change your perspective. Here's an exercise to help you notice your mind traps:

Think about what you say to yourself right before, during, and after a workday. Then answer the following questions:

1. Which of the mind traps do you fall into the most?
2. What conclusions do you draw about your work and yourself?
3. Are your conclusions accurate, compassionate, and helpful?
4. If you were on the outside looking in, how would you evaluate the conclusions you make?
5. What would you say to a loved one who thinks this way about his or her work?

end. He put "I must work nonstop to build my business" on one end and wrote "If I take a vacation, my business will crumble" on the opposite end.

This helped him externalize and dispassionately examine the unspoken assumptions that had driven his financially successful but lonely and harried life. I asked him to consider an option and write down a new phrase at the line's midpoint: "It is possible for me to take a week's vacation and for my business to continue to grow." I call this simple process "accessing the 'graydar,'" because it helps clients get in touch with their internal radar, attuning themselves to shades of gray rather than extremes.

Sometimes I teach simple behavioral techniques to stop intrusive work thoughts from elbowing their way into every waking moment. Once, for example, I taught a financial planner who worried obsessively about his job to compartmentalize his intrusive thoughts by mentally placing each one in a box, putting a lid on the box, and setting it on a storage shelf in a basement or attic. He was to take the thoughts off the shelf and out of the box only when he planned to give them his full attention. This simple strategy helped him sleep better, be more present with his wife and young son, and tackle work problems with greater clarity and energy.

COGNITIVE PSYCHOTHERAPIES

Cognitive psychotherapies are excellent approaches to treat work addiction because they capitalize on the workaholic's reliance on thinking and cognition rather than on feelings and intimacy.[8] As these beliefs begin to change, the motivation to overwork subsides. By helping workaholics change their rigid belief systems, you also help them develop a more flexible, balanced perspective on themselves that automatically translates into a healthier, more balanced, and more flexible lifestyle.

In your clinical work, you can help clients make a mental shift to get them out of the workaholic cycle by following these four steps:

❖ *Step 1*: The first step in modifying incorrect beliefs is for clients to become more aware of them. Start helping clients identify their negative thoughts by suggesting that they pay attention to and keep track of their self-referencing, negative thoughts for a one-week period. Tell them to notice each time they have critical dialogues with themselves and write down the negative thoughts, without censorship, in a daily log.

❖ *Step 2*: Once the log has been generated, ask the clients to look at it and star the criticisms that occur more than once. They may be surprised at how often they call themselves names such as "stupid" or "unworthy," use shame-based words such as "should" or "must," and otherwise downgrade themselves. Next, have clients write beside the thought whether the belief is true (these thoughts are almost always untrue). For example, are they really losers? Is it true that no one loves them, or that everything they do is wrong?

❖ *Step 3*: Have them get a sheet of paper and draw two lines down the page, making three columns. In the left column have them list each negative thought. In the middle column, have them identify the mind trap in each statement, or explain why that addictive thought is not true.

❖ *Step 4*: In the right column, have clients rewrite each addictive (or exaggerated) thought by substituting a truer statement, more rational thought, or positive affirmation about themselves. For example, if they had thought, "I'm a loser," a more honest replacement might be "I'm competent and capable" or "I'm a worthy person." Positive statements usually represent a more accurate view of the workaholic and the perspectives of others.

The positive statements, more than the negative ones, tend to be accurate portrayals of how clients are viewed by others. The positive statements can become affirmations that clients repeat silently to themselves from week to week. The more they use these positive statements, the more they come to believe that they are true. The use of positive affirmations, repeated silently during the day, before the morning mirror, or written in a journal, helps strengthen the nurturing voice so it can trump the self-critical voice. Research shows that self-affirmations serve as "cognitive expanders," providing a bird's-eye view that helps diffuse the workaholic voice's tunnel vision of self-threats.[9] Positive affirmations can be put on mirrors, refrigerators, desks, or even telephone answering machines. You can suggest that clients keep a bulletin board with all the affirming letters, notes, gifts, and sayings that loved ones, friends, and business associates send them and look at them often as reminders of their inherent value.

THE ABCS OF STRESS MANAGEMENT

The ABCs of stress is a way of bringing the rational brain or prefrontal cortex on board to stay calm and productive when workaholic clients feel like pulling their hair out. You can use the following example of how external events create internal stress when clients don't realize it.

Suppose you're stuck in traffic, late for a meeting. You bang on the steering wheel and explode, "Damn traffic! Now, I'll probably get fired!" The workaholic thoughts just bypassed the rational brain, blamed the traffic, and added a catastrophe (getting fired) for which there's no evidence. Heavy traffic is just heavy traffic. It didn't happen to make life miserable. The negative thoughts about the traffic caused the distress, not the traffic.

In this scenario, A + B = C. A stands for the external event (traffic jam); B stands for your automatic workaholic thoughts about the event (I'll probably get fired); C stands for your reaction to the event because of B (getting upset and banging the steering wheel). You jumped from A (traffic jam) to C (banging the steering wheel and blaming the traffic) and bypassed B where your "thinking brain" plays a starring role. Now let's go back and consider B (your automatic thought), which is what creates most of C. The key is to bring your "thinking brain" back online to the irrational thoughts.

The conclusions you draw in threatening situations raise your stress level because you believe the thoughts—even when they're exaggerated—simply because you think them. Once you practice paying attention to B and your "thinking mind" registers how irrational the thoughts are, you feel calmer. And over time this shift reduces your reactivity. Why? After your reactive emotional brain calms down, your prefrontal cortex comes back online.

Think about one of the curve balls life threw at you and how you handled it. You probably remember the upsetting event (A) and your reaction (C). But you might have overlooked your irrational thoughts at the time (B). Now go back and think about the automatic thought that upset or caused you stress. Once you're aware of the trigger, you can change your perspective by bringing your rational thoughts to bear on the situation. Then write down a more rational thought that might mitigate your knee-jerk reaction. Here's an example:

A= Triggering event: my computer crashed.
B= Automatic workaholic thought: *I'll never get this project finished on time.*
C= Your emotional reaction: You blow your top.

Intervention:

B= Now go back and insert a rational perspective to mitigate the workaholic reaction: *Computers sometimes crash. It sucks, but I'll find another way to finish the project.*
C= Response: You notice a rise in calm, clarity, confidence, and other "C" words.

When unexpected events zing you (A), and workaholic thoughts impale you with frustration or anger (C), it adds insult to injury, making the misery worse. The obstacle (A) (stuck in a traffic jam or computer crashing) is unpleasant for sure, but sometimes the real distress comes from (B) your emotional reaction (the irrational belief freaking you out).

Bibliotherapy

The following readings are excellent resources to help clients learn that their power comes from inside out instead of outside in:

❖ Judith Beck, *Cognitive Behavior Therapy: Basics and Beyond*, 3rd. ed. (New York: Guilford, 2021).

❖ David Burns, *Feeling Good: The New Mood Therapy* (New York: Harper-Collins, 2017).

❖ Albert Ellis and Windy Dryden, *The Practice of Rational Emotive Behavior Therapy*, 3rd ed. (New York: Routledge, 2021).

❖ Rick Hanson and Richard Mendius, *Buddha's Brain: The Practical Neuroscience of Happiness, Love, and Wisdom* (Oakland, CA: New Harbinger Publications, 2009).

5

The "Off Duty" Workaholic Brain

When we pause, allow a gap and breathe deeply, we can experience instant refreshment. Suddenly, we slow down, look out, and there's the world. It can feel like briefly standing in the eye of the tornado or the still point of a turn wheel.

—Pema Chödrön

George Is Strung Out on "Work-ahol"

Like many workaholics, my battle began in childhood. I was born in the rural South, the youngest of four children. My father, who was twenty years older than my mother, became severely handicapped from a stroke when I was five years old. My strong-willed mother had to take care of my father, her three teenage children, and me, insisting that we rise above our rural environment and become successful in a more sophisticated world.

My siblings were victims of my mother's tenacity, insistence on perfectionism, and relentless criticism when the highest results were not achieved. But I was more defiant and strong-willed like my mother. As I grew into adolescence, Mother and I constantly fought, but she instilled in me a strong sense of survival, achievement, perfectionism, and ego. Her psychological demands of perfection and accomplishment, along with my need to demonstrate to the world that I was worthy, ultimately spawned my workaholism.

My drive for achievement, success, and hard work became evident in high school. I was student body president, voted most popular, inducted into the national honor society, selected as "king teen," and accomplished records in track. In college, the pattern continued when I was elected president of my class each year, achieved the dean's list, made captain of the track team, and managed several money-making endeavors.

After college, I attended officer candidate school, where I graduated as a distinguished military graduate. In my three-year tour of duty in Germany, I met and married a wonderful German woman who was graduating from the university. After my tour of duty, we moved back to the United States. Perhaps I had an instinctive sense of what I needed to maintain my work addiction because my wife was kind, bright, nurturing, and supportive—all traits that fed my workaholic control and drive for perfection.

After returning stateside, I enrolled in a prestigious MBA program, where I was informed that the student with the highest-grade point average in the first year would be granted a full scholarship in the second year. This challenge was just the spark to ignite my workaholism, my need to demonstrate that I was worthy. My incessant studying—ten-to-twelve-hour days, seven days a week—landed me the scholarship while simultaneously enabling my workaholic behaviors.

Despite the fact that we were newlyweds and my wife was adjusting to a new country, I increased my workload. I became an officer in the National Guard and a student consultant with a local real estate firm. After completing my MBA, I saw that with a "little extra effort" (three weeks of studying nonstop for sixteen to eighteen hours a day), I could get my CPA as a "tag on" to my MBA, before starting my employment with a national accounting firm shortly after graduation. As the world applauded, little did I see the toll it was taking on my marriage and my own mental well-being.

Once I started my career, my workaholism flourished. I was promoted to manager in three years, which normally took five; in three additional years to senior manager, which usually took five; and then to partner in three more years, which took five for most people. I had to prove to the world and to the insecurity inside me that I was worthy and measured up. It was essential to be the best. I didn't understand that "even in the fast lane there is a speed limit."

Early in my career we had two children, a daughter, then a son two years later. My wife didn't work outside the house and basically raised the children. One could argue that parenthood is a partnership with each partner assuming an appropriate role. In our case, the scales tipped too far in the direction of me doing too much of the wage earning and too little parenting. I rationalized that I was providing my family with material riches that would make them happy. What they wanted, however, was more of a father and husband.

My wife complained that every Friday the fathers in the neighborhood were home in the early afternoons, while I worked until seven and eight o'clock at night and returned to work on Saturday. My children wondered why Dad would take work with him on vacation and silently slip off to work while Mom did fun vacation things with them. Later in life, my daughter vowed to never be like her father; to her credit, she learned the importance of balancing work and family early on.

Although there was constant stress among the four of us, my wife struggled to keep the peace among the kids so I could work more, unwittingly enabling my addiction. Often, I would displace my stress on her, becoming verbally abusive, condescending, and manipulative. With my children, I was controlling and didn't give them the strong emotional guidance they needed from a father. Even though my career soared as top producer, it didn't satisfy me or make me truly happy. I continued to raise the bar without stopping to "smell the roses."

At its peak, my workaholism manifested itself in many ways. I worked incessantly at the office and at home, ignoring the emotional needs of my family. I was competitive and measured in everything I did. When I exercised, I had to exhaust myself; when reading "for pleasure," I timed myself to see how many pages per hour I could read; when I played games with others, I had to win. I was impatient in grocery lines, in traffic, or jockeying for a position getting into sports events. I attempted to control and manipulate everything in my work and social environment. I was a ticking time bomb headed toward a classic workaholic disaster. Only my strong constitution kept me from being totally burned out. Still, the workplace and society applauded, adding fuel to my workaholism.

Recovery sometimes comes in strange ways. At sixteen, my son started on a journey that ended up with him becoming a heroin addict. Little did I know that his addiction would become my salvation. My wife and I tried to "fix" his addiction, and the more we tried to help, the more we enabled him, and the more our lives spun out of control. We put him in numerous treatments, but nothing worked. As he continued his drug addiction, dismissed by society as a "loser," I continued my work addiction, applauded by the world as a "winner."

To deal with our son's problem, my wife and I found Al-Anon, where people search for serenity after dealing unsuccessfully with addicts in their lives. Al-Anon saved my marriage, my sanity, and my career. I quickly learned that recovery must be focused on me, not on controlling things outside my control, including my son. Al-Anon's serenity prayer taught me to ask God to "grant me the serenity to accept the things I cannot change, the courage to change the things I can, and the wisdom to know the difference."

Even though I attended church regularly, the Twelve-Step program brought me more in touch with my Higher Power. I admitted that my life was out of control, that my work was consuming me, and that I had to turn my life over to a power greater than me. I examined my character defects as well as my asset traits that hindered or facilitated serenity. I came face to face with such shortcomings as impatience, control, rage, ego, enabling, fear, and out-of-control drive for more and more achievements. The epiphany came when I realized that most of these character defects fueled my work addiction, and that to achieve serenity, I had to become aware of these defects and then take action to address them.

With movement toward serenity, gratitude has flowed. No longer do I dwell in the past or become obsessed with the future. I attempt to live in the present and am happy to report that I have more balance in my life. As an active workaholic, my "asset allocation" was 90 percent work and 10 percent life. Through my recovery program, I am balancing work, play, family, and self. I am better at setting boundaries of what I'm willing and not willing to do. If I relapse into old behavior, I'm able to recognize what's happening and employ remedial action.

I'm quick to point out that I'm a work in progress. I know I'll relapse in the future. But when I do, I'll forgive myself and continue to work through progress, not perfection. I understand that once a workaholic, always a workaholic, and I need to go periodically to my Higher Power as I seek self-help. Plus, I've come to understand that achieving balance and serenity is not a destination; it's a journey that needs ongoing maintenance. The good news is I can now sit in a chair and read a great book, spend an afternoon in the park with my grandkids, or have a nice dinner with my wife without keeping my ear on the phone or my eye on my email!

Knowing Your Gray Matters

As you can see from his story, George was able to recover from workaholism because he shifted his mental outlook. As he commented, he realized that even the fast lane has a speed limit and took a different course of action. From a neuroscience perspective, because he took charge of his workaholism and changed old unhealthy work habits, George actually changed the neural pathways in his brain. I realize this sounds far-fetched, and I'll get to how you can change your brain in a minute. But first let's get to know your brain. If you're like most people, you might not even know about your own brain, yet your brain is who you are. It's the boss of your mind and body. So, it's important for you to know what it's up to, especially when work addiction has you in its clutches.

Your brain is about the size of your fist and weighs about as much as a cantaloupe—approximately three pounds. Although it's made up mostly of water, the human brain contains as many as 100 billion neurons. These neurons connect through long, spidery arms and communicate with each other through electrochemical signals. Your brain never shuts down; it's active even when you're asleep.

With modern imaging techniques, science has advanced our understanding of this amazing organ and of the aftermath of prolonged work stress. Brain scans of compulsive gamblers, for example, are associated with blunted mesolimbic-prefrontal cortex activation.[1] That means problem gamblers have an underactive brain reward system similar to drug users so that they're drawn to ways of stimulating their reward pathways, including the highs of gambling and drug use. Although brain imaging studies haven't been performed with workaholics, I'm convinced that in many cases significant brain differences exist between workaholics and nonworkaholics in which workaholics are seeking the psychophysiological payoff of overworking.

Working from Your Lizard Brain

If you're a workaholic, you probably work from your survival brain. When you're besieged by work stress, studies in neuroscience explain what happens on a cellular level to spark your inner workaholic firestorm. As you have seen, the brain is prewired to kick into red alert to keep you safe. It constantly scans your inner and outer worlds for danger, reacting automatically to perceived threats, even though you're not fully aware of it.

At one time in our species' history, the primitive fight-or-flight response (also known as the stress response), would have switched on at breakneck speed to help you survive attacks from other tribes and wild animals. Our laid-back ancestors who didn't worry about danger were killed off by unsuspected attackers, but our vigilant ancestors survived. As a result, our DNA carries an evolutional heritage that leaves us with ruminations and worries about what could have been in the past and about what is yet to come.[2]

Even though you don't have to worry about attacks from lions or tigers (unless you work in a zoo), your brain and body carry the heritage of these old fears. Emotional reactions come from the limbic system, sometimes called the lizard or reptilian brain or "emotional brain"—the part of the human brain that corresponds to the brain of vertebrates before the evolution of mammals and is mainly concerned with survival. When this part of your brain registers situations as threatening, your stress response fires up. The limbic system is a complex set of brain structures (including the amygdala, hypothalamus, and hippocampus) buried beneath the prefrontal cortex on top of the brain stem. It's responsible for the formation of memories and emotions related to survival, such as anxiety, fear, and anger.

When you're in workaholic mode, threatening situations like tight deadlines, having to make a complicated presentation at work, relentless pressure from a difficult boss, racing against the clock, threat of job loss or unemployment, and intrusive electronic devices all activate your fight-or-flight response. Your hypothalamus acts as a thermostat for your limbic system, controlling balance in bodily functions such as hunger, thirst, sex, and response to pain.

This primitive mechanism sends emergency instructions to the rest of your body through one arm of your autonomic nervous system—the sympathetic nervous system (SNS)—squirting out a neurophysiological cocktail of adrenaline and cortisol. These messages amp up your SNS to increase sweating, heart rate, blood pressure, and breathing; it tenses muscles and slows digestion, priming your body for action against the threat. Under the workaholic gun for prolonged periods of time, your inner alarm system stays on red alert mode, raising your risk of heart disease, type 2 diabetes, chronic pain, and a compromised immune system. Even if you're not a workaholic, you might be working like one. Studies show that 40 percent of all workers today feel overworked, pressured, and squeezed to the point of anxiety, depression, and disease.[3]

THE AMYGDALA: GETTING IN TOUCH WITH YOUR INNER REPTILE

Whether you're a workaholic or not, work stress can cause you to rant and rave, freeze in fear, or try to escape. Your brain's reaction in the present is often driven by past events that are no longer deadly or unsafe. In other words, your workaholic brain and body overreact to small things that create unnecessary and unpleasant stress in the present moment—all to keep you safe.

Here's how that works. Imagine peeking inside your own brain from a side view (see figure 5.1). The limbic system, or "reptilian brain," houses old hurts from the past. Current events that echo ancient hurts can trigger reactions from the past, activating memories of earlier situations buried deep within your reptilian brain that angered, hurt, or scared you.

A tiny, almond-shaped gland called the amygdala resides in the center of your limbic system. This gland contains a library of old feelings linked with past events that protect you from harm. Your amygdala senses present threats like those already recorded by the reptilian brain, and it kicks into survival mode to defend you. When your buttons get pushed, you can feel the moment your amygdala dumps a tonic of enzymes into your bloodstream making your heart pound. Like a tidal wave, the surge of adrenaline and cortisol hijacks your thoughts and leaves your emotions in control.

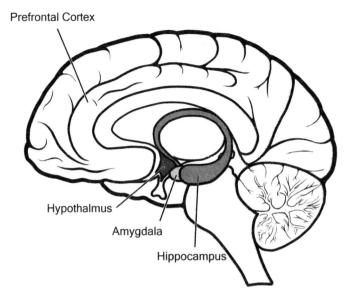

Prefrontal Cortex

Hypothalmus

Amygdala

Hippocampus

Figure 5.1. Side view of the human brain.

Dousing Your Inner Firestorm

See if you can recall an unpleasant or traumatic situation that you experienced early in life. Then make two columns labeled "present" and "past." In the "present" column, jot down what situations make you sizzle today because of your past. Then jot down the past experience in the second column. What does your blueprint from the past tell you about what is written in the library housed in your amygdala? And what role, if any, do you think your amygdala might have played in these episodes? George's amygdala blueprint said he wasn't good enough, that he had to exceed the standards of others. So, he constantly tried to prove himself in the present at school, at work, and even at play, outpacing others in grocery lines or jockeying for seats at sporting events—while simultaneously sacrificing his mental well-being and relationships with loved ones.

The Big Chill: Rewiring Your Brain to Stay Cool under Pressure

Over time, your brain's perceptions of threats in your self-imposed workaholic demands and deadlines can result in chronic mental and physical problems.

Whether you're a harried parent, a driven businessperson, or a worried retiree coping with an uncertain future, eventually these stressors catch up with you. They force your brain to adapt negatively to them as only it can. But there's good news. When you're off duty, the same process of negative adaption can be used to heal as well as harm. Did you know that you can reengineer your brain to calm your knee-jerk reactions? Sound like frontier science fiction? Hold on. I can see you rolling your eyes. But your brain is prewired to be pliable, just like a cut on your hand prompts your body to produce new, healthy skin.

Neuroplasticity

An innate ability called *neuroplasticity* allows you to use your mind to rewire the structure and functioning of your brain, no matter how old you are. Your brain can change its own structure because of your taking different actions in response to changing circumstances, as you saw with George at the beginning of this chapter.

Scientists at the National Institutes of Mental Health report that your brain can change its wiring and grow new neural connections through regular practice and repetition of tasks.[4] In other words, you can create a healthier brain by bringing balance to old workaholic habits. The new practices reshape nerve cells and change the way your brain works.[5] For workaholics, a rewiring could happen by intentionally activating your parasympathetic nervous system (PNS)—the second branch of your autonomic nervous system—with relaxing and calming activities. Examples are meditation, yoga, relaxation responses, tai chi, qigong, deep breathing, and various mindfulness techniques. Some experts go so far as to say it would take less than two months for you to alter your neural functioning.[6] Other examples of rewiring your workaholic brain include intentionally slowing down your work pace, rearranging your life's priorities, paying more attention to loved ones whom you've ignored, or spending time doing fun things you've never done before.

Remember that old saying, "whatever fires together, wires together?" By making micro-adjustments to your old workaholic patterns (such as getting home for dinner at six o'clock as promised, instead of working until nine), you can wire more positive work habits with healthier actions and get calmer as a result. With some dedication to intentionally changing your old habits, you can change the way your brain is firing in the moment. So, when you do something different, the firing of neural pathways wires the different approach and its outcome. After practicing them regularly, you'll find that relaxation, spontaneity, and balance start to feel as comfortable as an old pair of faded jeans.

Activating Your Parasympathetic Nervous System

Your autonomic nervous system (ANS) plays a starring role in your mental work life when it is engaged by your hypothalamus (see figure 5.1). Usually, you're not aware of your ANS except when your workaholic mode stresses you out and your ANS revs up your body functions. As I mentioned in chapter 1, your ANS is composed of two parts (see figure 5.2): (1) The *sympathetic nervous system* (SNS) is the *gas*—that part of your autonomic nervous system that functions in opposition to the parasympathetic nervous system by mobilizing your body's defense systems to induce your stress response for survival. (2) The *parasympathetic nervous system* (PNS) is the *brakes*—that part of your autonomic nervous system that functions in opposition to the sympathetic nervous system by calming your body's defense systems to induce your "rest and digest" response.

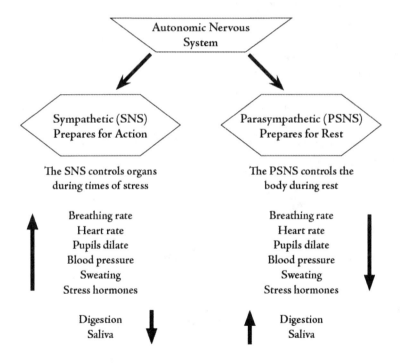

Figure 5.2. Two branches of your autonomic nervous system. Reprinted from Elaine Miller-Karas, *Building Resilience to Trauma* (New York: Routledge, 2023). Used with the author's permission.

Your Decision-Fatigued Brain

When you make decisions after working days on end, chances are they'll be different from the ones you'd make after your brain has had a rest period. Why? Scientists have discovered a phenomenon known as decision fatigue—which is what happens when your brain is worn out and depleted of mental energy.[7] Decision fatigue is why many workaholics have no mental energy left over for activities outside of work.

After hours of nonstop working, your brain gets fatigued. The longer you work and the more choices you make in those extended work hours, the more difficult it is for your strained mind to make decisions. It becomes hard to make even ordinary decisions, such as what to wear, where to eat, how much to spend, or how to prioritize work projects. So, you start to take short cuts, permitting your newly licensed teenager to drive the car on an icy night or opting out of responsibilities and decision-making at home. You're short with coworkers and loved ones; you eat junk food instead of healthy meals; you tell your spouse to pick what restaurant to go to.

The solution is to activate your rest and digest response. Your brain needs restorative rest just like your body does when you're tired. Ask yourself how much time you devote to your PNS to keep your mind and body in harmony. If you're like most workaholics, your answer would be "not enough." You can switch on your PNS instead of your SNS by engaging in certain activities such as brisk exercise, yawning, relaxing in nature, and power napping, and in practices such as deep breathing, progressive muscle relaxation, prayer, meditation, laughing, yoga, massage, and tai chi.[8]

When you're under siege by hard-driving workaholic impulses, the SNS activates your body functions to help you deal with your "urgent tasks." Your parasympathetic nervous system (PNS) dampens down your body functions in non-emergencies, allowing you to relax. As noted earlier, your SNS and PNS work in opposition to each other. Your SNS acts as the *gas* to help you meet deadlines, stand before your coworkers, and make a challenging presentation, or compete with your peers for higher positions. To help you become productive and successful when facing stressful conditions, your SNS dilates your pupils, increases your heart rate, opens bronchial tubes in your lungs, and inhibits secretions in your digestive system. Your PNS acts as the *brakes* so you can slow down, relax, and give your inner alarm system a break. It constricts your pupils, decreases your heart rate, constricts your bronchial tubes, and stimulates activity in your stomach and intestines.

SELF-REGULATION AND RECOVERY FROM WORK ADDICTION

Both systems are vital for life and bringing a balance between the two is the holy grail of workaholic recovery. When workaholic behaviors cause your SNS to dwarf your PNS to the point where your mental and physical health are at stake, you can activate your "rest and digest" response. "Off duty" workaholics learn balance and self-regulation, are more attuned to themselves, and see work as simply a necessary and sometimes fulfilling obligation. Self-attunement activates your PNS, creating a soothing, calmer approach to work tasks and giving you greater satisfaction and joy on the job.

Brain scans demonstrate that contemplation of nature, meditating, and praying activate your brain's frontal lobes (behind your forehead) and reduce activity in the parietal lobes (at the top rear of your head). These changes heighten your body's production of dopamine (a neurotransmitter released in the brain that creates euphoria and a sense of well-being) and dampen the production of epinephrine (a hormone associated with stress). Neuroscientists say these neurological changes create a feeling of calm, unity, and transcendence—a feeling of unification with God or heightened consciousness.[9] The appendix showcases a sampling of quick Microchillers, designed to activate your PNS and regulate your nervous system.

Beefing Up Your Prefrontal Cortex

Your prefrontal cortex is the part of the brain located behind your forehead in the frontal lobes. It is responsible for executive functions that allow you to reason logically, predict outcomes, judge right from wrong, and think rationally and abstractly.

Neuroimaging techniques show that stress diminishes activity in your prefrontal cortex and that long-term work stress can damage neurons, shrink areas of your brain, and impair thinking.[10] But if you want to be more alert, kinder, and more productive at work, you're in luck. Brain scans from Harvard University and the University of California show that through the regular practice of meditation, you can minimize brain shrinkage and cognitive decline and build thicker neural tissues in the prefrontal cortex.[11] Once beefed up, your gray matter sharpens your attention, amps up your immune system, neutralizes the amygdala's hot-headed reactions, heightens your awareness, and shifts you into a calmer, clearer, and more compassionate state of mind that I call the *C-Spot* (See "Finding Your C-Spot" in chapter 12).

REWIND THE MINI-MOVIES PLAYING IN YOUR HEAD

The authors of the book *Buddha's Brain*, describe what they call "mini-movies" that play in your head.[12] Think of your brain as a simulator that is constantly running mini-movies—brief clips that are the building blocks of conscious mental activity. These mini movies of past or future events at one time wired you for survival because through repeated neural firing patterns your brain strengthened your learning of successful behaviors.

Today, because of your genetic heritage, your brain continues to produce short movie clips that have nothing to do with survival or with what's happening in the present. But even if you know that, it's easy to get caught up in the movie's story line and stress yourself out in the heat of the moment. During work, the movie clips can pull you out of the present and create stressful thoughts and feelings. The movie might take you a thousand miles away, where you fret about a lost account, agonize about an unreachable work goal, or rehearse for a challenging presentation at work. Your mini-movies can become bars on an invisible cage that trap you in a life smaller than the one you could have—much like a tiger released into a large zoo park that continues to crouch as if it's still confined in its old pen. You have the power to create a horror movie or a musical comedy in your head. Keep reading, and you will learn that the choice is yours!

Overriding Your Lizard Brain's Threats

When you're frazzled from overworking, you can avoid urgent, impatient action and cool down your amygdala by using your executive function to challenge perceived threats. Here are some examples of how to do that:

❖ Try to see the upside of downside situations—to see the roses instead of the thorns: "I have to pay more taxes this year than ever before" becomes "I made more money this year than I've ever made."

❖ Be adventurous and take small risks in new situations instead of predicting negative outcomes without sticking your neck out: "I won't go to the office party, because I'm afraid I won't know anyone" becomes "If I go to the office party, I might have a chance to meet new coworkers."

❖ Make an effort to focus on the good news wrapped around bad news: "COVID-19 made me miss the chance to shine in the presentation at work" becomes "I missed the presentation, but I've recovered now, and the colleague to whom I delegated the task landed the account for the firm."

❖ Avoid blowing things out of proportion and letting one negative experience rule your whole life pattern: "I didn't get the promotion, so now I'll never reach my career goals" becomes "I didn't get the promotion, but there are many more steps I can take to reach my career goals."

TAKING A BIRD'S-EYE VIEW

Another way to change your brain's wiring is to get in the habit of engaging your prefrontal cortex when workaholism blindsides you. Your prefrontal cortex gives you the capacity to take a breath, step back, and regain the perspective of an outsider during threats.

Next time you're pressed, go inside yourself and focus on your inner experience. Acknowledge and listen to your feelings. Then ask, "What am I feeling in my body right now? What are the feelings telling me? If my heart wasn't slamming against my chest, what would I do right now?" When in response to pressure you engage the executive function of your prefrontal cortex, it's easier to separate from automatic limbic reactions, stay cool, and make smart decisions.

When I realize that my limbic system is activated, I check in with myself and ask if I'm angry, upset, or worried. I acknowledge those feelings as parts of myself. Then I have a dialogue with those feelings: "I know you're upset. How can I help?" This gives me immediate separation from the reactive parts, throws the switch in the executive function of my brain, and enables me to act instead of react (See chapter 14 for more on how to separate from your workaholic part).

Tips for Clinicians

By now you might be dehydrated because the brain can be a dry subject. But there are many clinical approaches you can take to help workaholics understand the neuroscientific risks of what's happening to their nervous systems and what they can do to reduce those risks.

SELF-REGULATION ACTIVITIES

You can share short Microchiller activities with workaholic clients that activate the parasympathetic nervous system, many of which I describe in the appendix. Over time, these practices have an automatic effect of regulating the stress response. You can remind clients of the importance of calming the mind and body to put the brakes on the sympathetic nervous system. You can also cite the latest findings in neuroscience and how they demonstrate that the basics (exercise, sleep, and good nutrition) never go out of style. Research shows that under prolonged stress such as a workaholic lifestyle, the brain loses its self-regulating capacity. Overloaded with work stress, the human brain becomes dysregulated, and brain cells shrivel up and die. But because of the brain's plasticity, exercise can switch on certain genes that pump up the brain's level of *galanin*—a peptide neurotransmitter that tones down the body's stress response by regulating the brain chemical norepinephrine (or adrenaline). In other words, exercise, in effect, protects brain cells from being destroyed by stressful overwork.[13]

ENCOURAGE CLIENTS TO "WATCH" THEIR INNER WORKINGS

Most workaholics approach work as if they're under threat, as if something bad might happen when they're not chained to the desk, even when there's no reason to be. Remind clients that the limbic system is designed to exaggerate their fears and worries for their protection. Encourage them to get curious and see if they can gain more clarity about why they're on red alert for no good reason. To help them get underneath the red alert, suggest that they ask themselves questions like, "What am I afraid of?" (They probably fear not being good enough or being ineffective), "What are the chances of that really happening?" and "What is the worst thing that could happen?"

Then have them call on their brain's curiosity, instead of self-judgment, as the gateway to clarity and calm. This approach keeps them from attacking themselves, cultivates compassion, and makes it easier for them to see what's really going on. In addition, it kicks in the executive function, creating an impartial and bird's-eye view of their out-of-control work patterns and self-created, stressful work situations.

Bibliotherapy and Psychoeducation

I recommend encouraging workaholic clients to read about neuroplastic transformation and how they can re-regulate their own nervous systems. You can help them understand the consequences when their limbic system reacts to workaholic stress as if they are in physical danger. After a while, the sympathetic nervous system stays on for an inordinate amount of time and the body becomes unable to tolerate down times. So, it's very difficult for workaholics to relax and have a normal life. Consequently, they are drenched in the adrenaline and cortisol cocktail that I discussed earlier, which causes multiple health problems and truncates the trajectory of their work careers.

Bibliotherapy helps workaholics gain an understanding of what happens when they overload themselves with work projects, multitask, shackle themselves to electronic devices, or bite off more work tasks than they can complete:

- Daniel Amen, *Change Your Brain, Change Your Body* (New York: Three Rivers, 2010).
- Norman Doidge, *The Brain That Changes Itself* (New York: Penguin, 2007).
- Norman Doidge, *The Brain's Way of Healing* (New York: Penguin, 2015).
- Lisa Miller, *The Awakened Brain: The New Science of Spirituality and Our Quest for an Inspired Life* (New York: 2021).
- Richard Davidson and Sharon Begley, *The Emotional Life of Your Brain* (New York: Penguin, 2012).
- Martin Rossman, *The Worry Solution: Using Breakthrough Brain Science to Turn Stress and Anxiety into Confidence and Happiness* (New York: Crown, 2010).
- Ronald Siegel, *The Mindful Solution: Everyday Practices for Everyday Problems* (New York: The Guilford Press, 2010).

When Work Addiction Hits Home

Wedded to Work Is a Family Affair

Machines have less problems. I'd like
to be one. Wouldn't you?
                                        —Andy Warhol

Jena's Life Revolves around a Workaholic

For years I lived with loneliness, disappointments, broken promises, anger, and chaos, created by my husband's addiction to work. Nobody can ever understand my pain when they see the million-dollar house I live in or my beach house, the cars, boat, clothes, travel. I have luxury that some people don't even dare to dream about, and most importantly I have my dedicated husband who works so hard for the family.

I've been living like a single mother for my three sons, watching my husband's work addiction run out of control. Hudson is competitive, seeking perfection in everything he does, killing himself working weekends until 3:00 or 4:00 in the morning, taking no lunch breaks, conducting business while wolfing down meals, even while in the bathroom. He works while driving and has had several accidents as a result. When Hudson is not working, his mind is constantly on work. On the beach in Europe, Hawaii, or Florida, he's thinking about work, oblivious to what's going on around him. We go to dinner with friends, and he misses lengthy conversations that took place during the evening. He cannot relax and feels he's wasting time if he's not engaged with work.

Our life revolves around his impossible work schedule. I'm pursuing him, and he's constantly distancing himself. I enabled him without realizing it, at the time thinking I was being supportive, but then things got out of control when he couldn't draw the line.

He told me his job needed him more than I did. He ignored my birthdays and holidays because he didn't have time and we could always "have them later." Of course, "later" never came. Meanwhile, family and friends concluded that something had to be wrong with me, something he was trying to avoid, something driving him to work so much. It seemed an unlikely explanation for the behavior of a man who often worked at his computer seventy-two hours straight without food or sleep. But I accepted it and believed that there was something I needed to do differently.

After twenty-five years of marriage, it grew more difficult to hold out hope that our life would ever change, that Hudson's walls of denial would break down, that he'd ever begin any kind of recovery process. Then I began to struggle with severe bouts of depression. As I became more miserable and lonelier, I sought counseling. Hudson wasn't part of our daily lives, and I became weary of filling him in on our details and schedules. Tired of being a single parent, I spent many hours drumming into him the importance of his role as husband and father. He was an outsider, a stranger to the kids and me, as if he didn't know his own family. Plus, it was hard to watch the kids deal with the fact that they couldn't change their dad, a tremendous heartbreak for them. Still, I was obsessed with trying to figure out how to get him to cut back his time at work, be part of the family.

Counseling helped me see that I had to let go of my obsession, release my focus on Hudson's workaholism. I began to look at my own behavior. It was difficult to admit that I couldn't fix my husband, more difficult to admit that much in me needed fixing. And that's what I focused on. If I obsessed about him, nothing was going to change. It was a frightening time because it meant letting go of all the habits and ways of dealing with what was familiar to me. It meant stepping into the unknown, but that's when I started to see genuine progress in my own recovery from workaholism.

As Hudson's work addiction progressed, my loneliness increased, not just from Hudson's absence but from the pain inflicted by a lack of understanding from friends and professionals. No more wry smiles and patronizing pats on the back for me when work addiction is mentioned. It's a devastating addiction and it hurts.

Out of the Shadows

Now that you know the signs of work addiction and how to recognize it, let's look more closely at how it affects other family members, giving them a whole set of mental health problems of their own. My research suggests that workaholism has devastating systemic effects on other family members that can be as severe as—or even more severe than—the familial effects of alcoholism.[1] But there is one major difference between the spouses and children of alcoholics and those who live with workaholics: Clinicians give the partners and children of alcoholics understanding, professional help, and referrals to self-help programs like Al-Anon. When the partners and children of workaholics complain, they get blank looks. As you have seen, therapists—some of whom are workaholics themselves—often suggest that the partner simply accept and adapt to the workaholic's schedule or tell the spouse not to be a "pop psychologist."

Asked what a spouse can do to change a workaholic, one management consultant gave some less than helpful advice in a 1980 *Psychology Today* interview: "Family members should make every effort to be exposed to the workaholic's work world. They should meet for lunch if possible. Even a small child can be taken to the office, shop, or lab on a weekend. To make time together enjoyable, they must simplify household chores—pay bills and shop by phone, for example, and buy a microwave oven. Most important, they should anticipate spending a lot of time on their own. As one stockbroker told me, 'I may be a lousy father, but when Merrill Lynch needs me, I'm here.'"[2]

Back in the day the message was to center your life around the workaholic and his or her work schedule, join in the addiction whenever possible, and settle for being alone a lot. In other words, bite the bullet and enable the problem to continue.

Although our culture still often admires this sort of "dedication" to work, it's not surprising that wives and husbands often bring their workaholic partners into my office, insisting that the partners invest in the marriage. As you saw in Jena's case, spouses of workaholics say they feel like widowed partners and solo parents. With little support from the workplace, the mental health system, or their families, many in today's world are still self-doubting and depressed.

"There are times when I feel I would actually be relieved if my husband were dead," said Dora, married to a driven attorney. "He doesn't hit me, he doesn't drink, and he doesn't use drugs. There are a lot of things he *doesn't do*—the most important being that he doesn't do anything with me or our three kids." When Dora asked him to spend more time with the family, he called her an ingrate and said he was only working day and night for her, the kids, and their future.

Treating Workaholism as a Family Disease

In exposing work addiction's nature as a disease, I employ a family systems addictions model. The principal view from this perspective is that addictions are transmitted through the breakdown of the family system, rendering it dysfunctional. If you're a workaholic, this breakdown is shown in the behavior from your family of origin and in your intimate relationships as an adult, including those with your children. Addictive behaviors are intergenerational, passed on to future generations through family dynamics, which often change from one generation to the next. Through the way the family operates—its rules, beliefs, and behavior patterns—addictive behaviors such as alcoholism, work addiction, and codependent relationships can become an intergenerational cycle. Work addiction is viewed as a learned addictive response to a dysfunctional family of origin. It requires a nonmedical model of treatment such as family-of-origin work and marriage and family therapy.

Work addiction is a family disease, one that affects you and other members of your family in a devastating way. Thinking of the family unit as a system can help you understand the disease concept. Suppose I wanted to know how the cardiovascular system works. I might go to a medical lab, locate a heart and the attached blood vessels, and then carefully dissect and study them. I would learn something about the basic structure of the cardiovascular system, such as that the heart has four chambers and several valves. But I would still not know how these chambers and valves work, because the heart would not be functioning. Only by studying the cardiovascular system while it is functioning in a living person could I see how the chambers and valves pump blood through the body. And I cannot know what happens to the heart when a person is running, for example, without seeing the cardiovascular system in relationship to the whole-body system. This holistic approach teaches me that while the person is running, the muscles of the body require more oxygen than they do at rest and the heart beats faster to supply that oxygen. In other words, the total body system is affected by the running and must change to adjust to it.

The same is true of the workaholic family. It's difficult to fully understand what happens to you as a family member without understanding the innerworkings of your total family system. When you look at your family, you'll see that each member is part of a functioning system, with each person interdependent on the others. As your family works together to run smoothly, change in one part of the family system results in changes in the other parts. Your family system will always try to keep itself balanced, organizing around problems, and thus often causing them to continue. Your workaholic family automatically alters how it functions to accommodate the workaholic's extreme work patterns. Out-of-control working throws your whole family off kilter, causing the other members to shift the way they function to keep themselves in stasis and maintain a closed system.

You and your family members are negatively affected by work addiction and often develop mental health problems as a result. The workaholic's career dictates your family's rules, which get enforced despite their negative effect on the emotional well-being of individual members. There's often a tacit family contract that allows workaholics to work, while their partners align with the children against them, and the workaholic forfeits a hierarchical family position in order to pursue a career.[3] To better understand the workaholic family structure, let's look at the Smith family.

Family Ties: The Smith Household

Because of failing health, Jack Smith, a forty-three-year-old workaholic, saw his physician, who said that the best antidote for Jack's addiction was taking long weekends and vacations. Jack complied with the doctor's orders, but he lugged his legal files across Europe and halfway around the world. His wife, Dorothy, said that both Jack and she knew those files would never be opened, because she would not allow it. For years she had complained to Jack's doctor about his constant working and how lonely she was on trips, visiting museums alone while Jack holed up in the hotel working. Even when they took long weekends to their Adirondack Mountain retreat, Jack carried a phone in his fishing boat. According to Dorothy, Jack maintained direct and constant contact with the other attorneys in his law firm in New York City. A constant source of conflict in their marriage, Jack's workaholism had driven a wedge between the couple and between him and his now-grown children.

When the three children were small and came along on picnics, Dorothy carried the blanket and picnic basket while Jack carried his briefcase. Jack's preoccupation with work angered Dorothy, who felt like a single mother rearing the children on her own. And the children are angry at their father because he kept them at arm's length. Although the children have become successful adults, they admitted to Dorothy that they never believed they could do anything good enough to please their father.

Dorothy regretted that Jack was "missing in action" during most of their marriage, while she was "left holding the bag." When it came to child rearing, managing the house, or attending social gatherings, Jack would often break promises to meet her at various places. The family's tone and activities revolved around Jack's moods and whims. Family members postponed their plans, hoping by chance to be able to grab some time with Jack.

The children learned they could have these special times with their dad by photocopying legal papers for him or going to his law office on Saturdays and playing in an adjacent room while Jack worked on important cases. Even when they went fishing, the children resented their father's brownouts when his mind was back at the office. Dorothy even went to school to become a paralegal and took a job in Jack's office, working alongside her husband "just to nab some time with him." On those rare occasions when Jack tried to take an active role in his family life, he said he felt rebuffed by his wife, who felt he was intruding on her turf.

During marriage therapy, the wise therapist introduced the concept of workaholism to Dorothy, which helped her see her husband in a different light: "Workaholic, huh? That sounds as if my husband's a sick man. That gives me a whole new way of looking at him—with more compassion and understanding."

Underlying Patterns of the Workaholic Family

The structural patterns of the Smith family are such that Dorothy and the children become extensions of Jack's ego, inevitably leading to family conflict.[4] Tending toward self-centeredness and self-absorption, workaholics typically need an overabundance of attention and want family members to cater to their work habits.[5] With the timing and synchronization of a Julianne and Derek Hough dance routine, each family member gets drawn into the act by waltzing around the workaholic's schedule, moods, and actions, which determine the family's schedule, moods, and actions.

CIRCULARITY

If you're a family member of a workaholic, you may have noticed that, over the course of time, you unwittingly developed certain habits in response to the work addiction. As workaholics work longer and harder, chances are that as a spouse, not unlike the spouses of alcoholics, you react by trying to get your workaholic to curb the compulsive behaviors and spend more time in the relationship. And chances are that your workaholic mate hears your reactions as demands, criticisms, or nagging and reacts by digging his or her heels in deeper, thus retreating further from the family. Feeling lonely, unloved, isolated, and emotionally and physically abandoned, you might align with others against the workaholic and retaliate with verbal resentment and emotional distance. Eventually, your workaholic mate is left outside your family unit because of his or her self-distancing and your retaliations and coalitions.

As a family member, it's natural for you to complain or become cynical about living with abusive work habits. A common refrain is that even when workaholics are physically present, they are emotionally unavailable and disconnected from the family. As with Jena and Dorothy, spouses often single-handedly raise the children, complaining about having had the major portion of parenting responsibilities dumped on them. As a result of this one-sided arrangement, if you're like most workaholic spouses, you react with anger and resentment. Your workaholic partner, in turn, cites your verbal complaints to justify his or her physical and emotional aloofness. Thus, circularity often results: the workaholic claims that "I wouldn't work so much if you didn't nag all the time," whereupon the partner retorts, "I wouldn't bug you so much if you didn't work all the time."

Dorothy's presenting problem in therapy was Jack's remoteness and his exits from the relationship through work; Jack's presenting problem was Dorothy's constant criticism and his resulting feeling that he couldn't please her. He felt that even his successful career was not enough to satisfy her. He rationalized his intentional exits from the marriage by demanding, "Why would I want to spend time with someone who's on my back about something all the time?" Dorothy had started to withdraw because she felt she was getting nothing from Jack emotionally. Jack defended himself with denial, claiming his hard work was for Dorothy and the kids, and he couldn't understand how she could criticize him on one hand and reap the benefits of his efforts on the other hand, much like Jena's husband did. As two experts observed, "for the suffering family, the final blow usually comes when the workaholic passes the blame by saying, 'I'm doing all this for you!'"[6]

POWER STRUGGLES AND ENABLING

Could your family's behavior patterns enable the very work addiction that you protest? If you're like Jena and most partners of workaholics, you might be playing the role of resentful enabler, trying to limit your partner's overwork while unwittingly supporting it. Just as many wives and husbands of alcoholics cover bounced checks or serve a hot dinner whenever the drinker returns from the bar, many partners of workaholics cover the workaholic's home chores, give alibis to children and party hosts, build family activities around the workaholic's impossible work schedule, and put dinner on the table at midnight for the umpteenth time after the workaholic promised to be home by 7:00. Barbara, the wife of the founder of Workaholics Anonymous, said, "Our lives revolve around the workaholics we married—around making excuses to friends why our spouses aren't at parties, making excuses to our children why daddy can't make birthday parties and baseball games."[7]

Partners of workaholics often plead, threaten to leave, insist on weekends together, and otherwise try to control the addictive behavior. Much as the partner of an alcoholic searches for hidden gin bottles—the way Jamey had once searched my luggage for work—these unhappy spouses live with loneliness, try to control the uncontrollable, and build up enormous amounts of resentment, experiencing the workaholic's emotional unavailability and unreliability as a personal rejection and failure.

I realize this sounds counterintuitive. But by assuming child-rearing duties, household responsibilities, and social commitments, you the family member provide the workaholic with the necessary freedom to work endlessly. Shielding workaholics from domestic worries and working alongside them, as members of the Smith family did, have the effect of enabling the compulsive working.

Even if you're a frustrated family member, demanding that your workaholic partner moderate his or her busy pursuits, you could unwittingly be enabling the work addiction. It's possible that you become just as obsessed with trying to get your workaholic to cut back on work hours as he or she is obsessed with working. The more you press her or him to take a break, a day off, or a vacation; to slow down; or come home early, the more threatened your partner feels and the more tenaciously she or he resists and retreats into work.

Typically, workaholics interpret these pressures as an effort to undermine their control. Cheryl said: "The more my husband complained about my working too much, the harder I worked." If you're a husband who dictates how his workaholic wife should set boundaries or reprimands her when she relapses, the more shamed and out of control she feels. From her point of view, the only solution is to escape further into a satisfying activity—her job—to gain control and relief. Challenges to the compulsive working often result in defensive reactions. As you saw with Jack, he rationalized his long work hours as providing a better life and future for the family.

VILIFICATION OF FAMILY MEMBERS

If you're the family member of a workaholic, chances are that your hands are tied in many ways, giving you few options for dealing with the problem. Workaholism's looking-good camouflage, supported by our society, enables work addiction. As you saw with Jena, spouses often are branded as ingrates and blamed for wanting more even though their workaholic partners have given them abundant material comforts. With little or no support, Jena ended up in counseling for depression.

In another workaholic marriage, Madge ended up at the Duke University Medical Center to be treated for allergies, headaches, stomachaches, and other stress-related symptoms that workaholics have. The paradox was that Madge was the *spouse* of a workaholic: "I had to remove myself from my husband, or I was going to die. I had taken on his work addiction, and it was killing me. His multimillion-dollar business is everything to him. He's always working, always on a 'high.' People ask me why I complain. We have two beautiful kids, he has a great job, he makes lots of money, and I don't have to work. I have the dream life; why am I never smiling?"

If you're a family member, your fear of appearing unappreciative can have the effect of censoring you, preventing you from speaking out or seeking help, which further cements your family's denial. This denial can also cause you and other family members to wonder if you *are* the problem. If your friends and colleagues heap praise and financial rewards on your workaholic spouse, you might think that something is wrong with you, that you're terminally flawed or don't measure up in some way. And when you relax, you might feel unproductive and inferior.

PARENTIFICATION

When the generation lines that insulate children from the parental adult world get violated or blurred, children can become what family therapists call parentified.[8] As you saw in chapter 1, parentification refers to the process through which children of workaholics are assigned the tacit role of an adult in the family system, taking on both emotional and functional responsibilities that typically are performed by parents. Overwhelmed by family caregiving roles and responsibilities, parentified children in a workaholic family system have trouble with developmental tasks.

If you were a *parentified child*, you became a parent to your own parent who has forfeited their role. You unwittingly set aside your own emotional needs for attention, comfort, and guidance to accommodate and care for the emotional needs and pursuits of a parent or another family member. Workaholics who were parentified as kids often pass their own parentification to their offspring, who are sometimes chosen to be emotional surrogates for the missing workaholic parent.

A typical example is the child who is elevated into an adult position within the family system to accommodate a parent's emotional need for intimacy by becoming the adult of the house during the workaholic's physical or emotional absence. Or the nonworkaholic spouse may be consumed by the single-parent role during the workaholic's absence, with the children (usually the oldest) becoming parentified—required to become overly responsible at a young age before they have reached emotional maturity themselves. They may assume household chores or caretaking responsibilities for young siblings to bring homeostasis to the family system. The void left when you must sacrifice your childhood shows up years later as an oft-described "empty hole inside."

Twelve-year-old Katie became her mother's little helper when her father died. Her mother had to take two jobs to support Katie and her younger brother, and she was gone from early morning until late at night. Katie was only twelve, yet her little brother became what she called "her baby":

> I got him up every morning, made sure that he got his breakfast, had his lunch, and learned to read when he came home from the first grade every afternoon. I helped him with his *ABCs*, made the beds, and cooked meals. Mother would come in at supper time, tell me I had made a good meal, and go to her second job. My world was falling apart around me, and by grasping onto those duties, I was able to gain control over my life. I could take care of my brother, clean the house, make cakes, and do a multitude of chores that would make my world stable. And I have been doing this all my life.

The tacit family contract here was that mom would fill the father's role as breadwinner, while Katie moved into the mother's role as partner to Mom and mother to the "baby." Katie's hectic childhood contributed to a stressful bout with work addiction and a broken marriage by the time she was fifty, at which point she was working day and night as a nurse administrator.

TRIANGULATION

Triangles across generations can occur when spouses become competitive with each other or the parental bond becomes more valued than the marital bond, as when a mother aligns with her daughter by sharing her despair over the workaholic father's emotional absence. The father is excluded, and the mother-child bond is strengthened at the expense of the marital bond.

This boundary violation can exacerbate the child's resentment of the absent workaholic father and increase tension between them. As emotions surface between father and offspring, the mother may intercede on the child's behalf, further eroding the marital and paternal bonds while solidifying the maternal bond. As alliances form, workaholics feel like bystanders in their own homes. They complain about feeling insecure and not fitting in with their families. Hudson believed that Jena and their three sons were conspiring against him. He blamed them for his unhappiness outside the office. In fact, he had helped create the barriers by extricating himself from their conversations and activities, because his mind was on work. He felt like an outsider, but he couldn't see how his own actions had contributed to the situation.

The Japanese would call Hudson a "seven-eleven husband," their term for marginal fathers who work from dawn to dusk and live on the fringes of their families: "For overworked and exhausted husbands, the home becomes just a place where familiar sleeping facilities are provided without much emotional nourishment. Such husbands tend to feel like fringe dwellers whose main responsibility is to bring money home, but not to be directly and significantly involved in family activities and raising their children. The seven-eleven husband is often so tired even on the weekends that family outings and chores around the house sometimes become additional sources of stress and fatigue. He tends to have a rather marginal family membership and receives only limited substantive validation for his familial self from the family. When the family forms an internal alliance excluding the marginal father, he is likely to feel displaced and unwanted at home, which in turn reinforces his wish to be back in a familiar working environment."[9]

After alliances are solidified, spouses often resent having their turfs violated when workaholics try to become more actively involved in their families. Older children often rebuff the workaholic's attempts to reestablish close contact because they feel the reentry is too little, too late.

The Workaholic Family under the Microscope

My research team at the University of North Carolina at Charlotte and I tested anecdotal reports by conducting two empirical studies that showed family members are harmed by work addiction.

We launched the first study because we wanted to know if there was a relationship between work addiction and family-of-origin or current-family functioning.[10] After all, family systems and psychodynamic theories suggest that adult behaviors have their roots in the family of origin. A body of research had already linked a healthy family of origin to healthy functioning in adulthood, positive marital experiences, and overall family relationships. We conducted the study below:

We administered a battery of tests to 107 members of Workaholics Anonymous from Canada and five regions of the United States. Of our sample, 14 percent came from the Northeast, 24 percent from the Southeast, 4 percent from the Northwest, 39 percent from the Midwest, 18 percent from the

Your Unspoken Workaholic Family Contract

Look over the section titled "Underlying Patterns of the Workaholic Family." Then ask yourself the following questions to get a picture of your family's unspoken contract with the workaholic:

1. Is CIRCULARITY present because of workaholism in your family?
2. Has anyone in your family ENABLED the workaholic?
3. Has a family member ever been VILIFIED when he or she complained about work addiction?
4. Does PARENTIFICATION exist among children in your family?
5. Is TRIANGULATION present because of workaholism in your family?

If you answered yes to any of these questions, write a description below of the patterns you detect. Then describe what can be done to correct the patterns:

Southwest, and 1 percent from Canada. The average age of the participants was forty-four, and 65 percent were women.

Respondents were classified into two groups based on their responses to the following question: "Have you ever joined group therapy or talked with a professional counselor about your work habits?" Seventy people answered yes and were defined as the clinical group of workaholics; thirty-six said no and were defined as the nonclinical workaholic group.

Despite the clinical observation that workaholic adults come from dysfunctional families, we found no relationship between work addiction (based on WART scores) and family-of-origin dysfunction in the overall sample. But when the sample was divided into clinical and nonclinical groups, the findings changed. Clinical workaholics who had sought help for their condition, compared to those who had not sought help, were more likely to rate their families of origin as dysfunctional and lower in intimacy.

Our findings also positively linked work addiction to the family's current functioning, showing that workaholism wreaks havoc on the family. The more serious the work addiction, the worse the family was at communicating, solving problems, expressing feelings, valuing others' concerns, and functioning as a unit.

Using scores on the WART, we divided the sample into three groups: those at low, medium, or high risk for work addiction. The high-risk group rated their families as having greater problems in communication and in the exchange of information than the other groups did. In addition, those at high risk were more likely to rate their family members as having unclear roles and less established behavior patterns for handling family functions, compared to respondents in the low- and medium-risk groups. High-risk respondents also said their families were less likely to appropriately express feelings about various events occurring in the family. High-risk adults said their family members were less likely to be interested in and value each other's activities and concerns. And they perceived their families as unhealthy and more likely to have problems functioning in general, compared to respondents at low or medium risk.

Maintaining social and intimate relationships was also a problem for workaholics in the sample because of their work. The social relationships of men were affected to a significantly greater extent by their work than were those of women. Intimacy was a problem for the clinical workaholics, both in their families of upbringing and in the families that they established as adults. Perhaps workaholics in the clinical group (with more intimacy problems from their families of origin compared to those in the nonclinical group) had more problems with intimate relationships in adulthood, which may explain their motivation to seek help.

The second investigation conducted by my research team examined the influence of work addiction on adults who grew up in workaholic homes—the first study ever conducted on adult children of workaholics.[11] That study, as well as the earlier one, strongly supported clinical evidence suggesting that work addiction is associated with ineffective communication and that it contributes to brittle family relationships, marital conflict, and overall dysfunction within the family system.[12] More recent research corroborated the link between work addiction and the family system. Parental workaholism was tied to a rise in parental unhappiness and family conflict and a reduction in family happiness, along with an increase in the children's emotional and behavioral problems. Work engagement, on the other hand, was tied to a rise in family harmony and family happiness and a decrease in children's emotional and behavioral problems.[13]

Tips for Clinicians

You can take a variety of clinical approaches when workaholic clients and their loved ones are entrenched in denial. You have seen that family members often are reluctant to come forward for fear of being vilified as ungrateful for the material rewards generated by the workaholic lifestyle. Typical workaholic families dance around this "elephant in the room" without acknowledging its presence, which builds tension and resentment. When you help couples identify and express their feelings about the problem, you can reduce tension and reactivity and set the stage for further work.

INITIAL SCREENING AND FAMILY CONTRACTS

As part of the initial screening, I recommend that you identify the structure of the workaholic family. Is there a tacit family contract, for example, that permits compulsive overworking? Are there unspoken expectations of children that place them in parentified roles that could cause long-term emotional problems? If you can bring these hidden factors into the light, you'll have more success in helping families restructure their behaviors.

Together with family members, you can diagram the structure of the family system to help clients see clearly where alliances, triangles, enabling, or exclusions exist. You will see cases where the marital bond has weakened (perhaps replaced by parent-child alliances or the elevation of children above the generational boundary into adult surrogate roles). Then you can work with couples to strengthen their relationships, consciously work at reinforcing the generational boundary, and perhaps even prevent further parentification of the children. After revealing the tacit family contract, you can assist families in rewriting a more deliberate and functional family contract that clearly defines family roles for each member and provides methods for encouraging open communication, valuing each other's concerns, and openly expressing feelings.

INTRODUCING THE CONCEPT OF WORK ADDICTION AS A FAMILY DISEASE

When you present the disease concept of work addiction to families, it usually brings them great relief, and in many cases arouses compassion, as in the case of Dorothy. It can also help families reframe the problem, to go from seeing it as personal rejection to seeing it as a more complex condition that workaholics bring to the marriage. The disease concept also helps family members understand how they are affected in subtle ways that they're not aware of. With the disease concept, you can introduce a Twelve-Step approach and many of the principles of Alcoholics Anonymous and Al-Anon that have been extrapolated to work addiction. Some family members, like Jena, benefit from help in learning to detach from the addictive process and to focus on themselves and their children when offspring are involved.

As you have seen, work addiction is a "pretty addiction" that also looks good on the workaholic's offspring. It's important in your clinical work to educate yourself about the insidious damage that work addiction inflicts on workaholics' children and to tailor your approach to examine unrealistic expectations the family might have of children. Once you ascertain the family structure, you can look beneath the surface of this pretty addiction and discern potential anxiety and depression among children. Breaking the cycle of work addiction also is important. Protecting children from out-of-reach aspirations, unreasonable expectations, and parental perfectionism can prevent the development of Type A behaviors and the intergenerational transmission of work addiction.

CONFRONTING THE ENABLING

In your sessions, I suggest that you raise the awareness of spouses and children about ways they are repeatedly pulled into the addictive work cycle. Then you can explain how to avoid enabling the addiction when loved ones are desperate to spend time with the workaholic family member. You can help families explore whether they have put their own lives on hold for their workaholic family member. You can help them understand that, as with any addiction, building their lives around the addict's behaviors only sets them up for further hurt and disappointment. Then help them explore ways they can include workaholics in family plans but without stopping the family's life. I discuss this issue in more detail in the section called "Recharging Your Batteries: The New Normal," in chapter 7.

TWELVE STEPS AND REFERRAL TO SUPPORT GROUPS

In conjunction with individual therapy, you can refer families to support groups composed of other people struggling with various addictive behaviors. In group therapy, members help one another see past denials and distractions that have prevented them from taking responsibility for their actions and putting balance in their lives.

Most large cities have support groups such as Workaholics Anonymous (WA) that provide literature and weekly meetings for workaholics. You can inform clients of Twelve-Step programs such as Workaholics Anonymous or Al-Anon to complement their individual therapy plans (see the appendix for more information on WA).

The Twelve Steps have worked for millions of people with a variety of addictions, including to alcohol and other drugs, food, gambling, and shopping. Continuing in the Twelve-Step tradition, Workaholics Anonymous provides a setting that is accepting, anonymous, and safe where workaholics share their strength, courage, and hope. Following the Twelve Steps, they work with other recovering workaholics and sponsors with solid records of personal growth who mentor newcomers. Under the guidance of their sponsors, members are encouraged to develop their own self-care plan for work moderation. Abstinence from compulsive working on a physical level is encouraged, as is developing a positive attitude that comes from surrender to a Higher Power.

The work plan is a guide to daily work that provides healthy limits and moves Workaholics Anonymous members toward a more balanced way of life. Elizabeth described how she benefited from Workaholics Anonymous:

> Workaholics Anonymous gives me the opportunity to go and sit down with other people like me with anonymity. I don't have to worry if I don't want the world to know about me, that what I say will go out of that room. It gives me an opportunity to share with others and to hear myself for an hour. It gives me a chance to calm down. It's very soothing to be with other people just like you who understand and know what you feel. At the same time, listening to them and what they've done to change their behavior helps you realize what you can do, because they share their experience, strength, and hope. They don't give advice.

SUPPORT FOR FAMILY MEMBERS

Family members often need help expressing their feelings of emotional abandonment, guilt, inadequacy, anger, resentment, and hurt to their overworked loved ones. Partners especially need help in developing constructive outlets for their feelings, such as keeping a journal, joining a support group, or getting individual therapy. They often benefit from understanding that they didn't cause and can't cure or control their partner's work addiction, and that their partner's problem is a cover for low self-esteem, past hurt and fears, and intimacy problems that remain unresolved.

An organization called WorkAnon was founded in suburban New York at the same time that Workaholics Anonymous started. WorkAnon serves spouses, other family members, and friends of workaholics in the same way Al-Anon serves as a family adjunct to Alcoholics Anonymous. Barbara, the founder of WorkAnon and wife of one of the WA founders, got a call one night from a distraught woman who had planned a special dinner for her twenty-fifth wedding anniversary, for which her husband never showed. The woman put his gift on the dining-room table and went to Barbara's house, and the two of them started WorkAnon. Some people come to WorkAnon with the idea that it will help them cure their spouse, relative, or friend of work addiction. But, like Al-Anon, WorkAnon is there to help nonworkaholics deal with their personal feelings about work addiction, not to cure their work addicted partners or friends. Workaholics have to decide for themselves that they need help and take responsibility for getting it.

In your work with workaholic families, consider establishing structured support groups for partners of workaholics like Al-Anon or WorkAnon. These special groups can help spouses cope with their own bruised self-esteem and feelings of guilt, stress, and isolation. It can be a haven for many families who feel alone and hopeless and who fear that going public will lead to accusations and insults aimed at their lack of gratitude. Groups of this nature can provide support to help spouses feel connected to others who understand and achieve greater clarity about constructive actions they can take to change their lives.

Bibliotherapy

Several good resources for clinicians to consider work addiction as a dynamic in the family system are:

❖ Lindsay Gibson, *Adult Children of Emotionally Immature Parents: How to Heal from Distant, Rejecting, or Self-Involved Parents* (Oakland, CA: New Harbinger Press, 2015).

❖ Sue Johnson, *Attachment Theory in Practice: Emotionally Focused Therapy (EFT) with Individuals, Couples, and Families* (New York: The Guilford Press, 2019).

❖ Harville Hendrix and Helen Hunt, *Getting the Love You Want: A Guide for Couples* 3rd ed. (New York: St. Martin's Griffin, 2019).

❖ Toni Herbine-Blank and Martha Sweezy, *Internal Family Systems Couple Therapy Skills Training Manual: Healing Relationships with Intimacy from the Inside Out* (Eau Claire, WI: PESI Publishing, 2021).

7

Spouses and Partners of Workaholics

*Leisure is only possible when we are
at one with ourselves. We tend to
overwork as a means of self-escape,
as a way of trying to justify our
existence.*

—Josef Pieper

Loretta Calls Herself an Unkept Statistic

The simple fact is that my husband's work addiction was stronger than anything else in the family. And we're now an unkept statistic. My children and I carry the oh-so-common legacy of pain that lies in the wake of every soul-destroying obsession. For Ron, a normal workday lasted eighteen hours, six days a week. Sunday was only a twelve-hour day. In the busy season, there were twenty-to twenty-four-hour days for weeks on end. Ron's need for sleep has been his lifelong enemy. It's amazing he hasn't had a heart attack yet or an accident.

My eyes were opened late one night when I was alone with the baby in our isolated farmhouse and two drunk men began pummeling on the doors, running around to each of the windows, trying to break in. When I called my husband, who was half a mile away, he was too busy with paperwork to come home. Instead, he called the police. I spent forty terrifying minutes crouched with a knife in front of my son's bedroom door until the police came. Ron's response to my upset? "What's your problem? The doors were locked. You weren't in any danger."

When my son was one year old, I became ill but even that wasn't enough for Ron to find time to come home from his work. I locked the baby in a bedroom with me so that if I passed out, he wouldn't get hurt. I could make it into the bathroom if I crawled. It worked, but I managed to piss Ron off because there was no food prepared for him when he flew in for one of his stopovers.

During his ten-day business trips, I never knew which state or city he was in. To contact him, I'd have to call one of his business partners to find out where he was. Although we never knew when he'd be home, we were lucky to have him there for a meal once a week. Even then we were lucky if we got twenty minutes of him before the phone rang, and he never once told anyone to call back after supper. The house and yard were wired so that he could hear all three phone lines no matter where he was. A two-way radio was perched in the kitchen, volume on high, so that he would hear and contribute to conversations between all employees and his business partners. I was forbidden to lower the volume even when he wasn't in the house, and he expected me to keep up with who said what to whom and when.

At one point, I was hospitalized for three days with a serious infection. He dropped me at the emergency room door, and I didn't see or hear from him again until the medical staff called him to come get me. Foolishly, I believed him when he said his commitment to work was the only thing keeping us from starving. And I always felt guilty putting an extra burden on him when I was sick. I watched other husbands in amazement when they'd ask their wives and children, "How are you doing?" or "What can I do to help?" Then I told myself that if I worked harder, was more patient, more supportive of him, that one day I would also enjoy a relationship like that.

I envied single mothers who shared parenting by dropping the kids off at their dads' for the odd weekend. I was the one to teach both children to ride a bike, swim, play ball, paint a room, and hammer a nail. He was too busy. He never put a single present under the Christmas tree for me. But if I complained, he would chastise me for being selfish. One Christmas, my nine-year-old daughter looked up at me from her pile of gifts and said, "Gosh, Mom, it would be awful to be you." She was right. It was.

Ron spent holidays with laptop, cell phone, faxes, and day trips to research more of his projects. He saw it as an opportunity for his family to prove our love for him by joining him full time in the delight of his work. In public, he would work the room, the plane, the subway, the traffic jam. During one trip to the Caribbean that we were supposed to have to ourselves, he hammered away at his laptop. He never spoke to me the entire day, leaving the computer only to go to the bathroom. He didn't need me because he had his fix.

After I began reading about work addiction, I asked him what the best thing in life was. His eyes lit up and his immediate reply was, "Doing a deal. There's nothing like it!" That's when I knew no matter how hard I tried, I couldn't compete with the rush a deal could give him. Because drugs and alcohol had always kept a stronghold on the men in my life, I had looked for a sober, drug-free man to father my children. When I met Ron, I had congratulated myself on having eliminated addiction from my life. But the insidious monster in my house had a life of its own. It grew an arm here or a leg there based on how I was situating myself in the relationship.

In the aftermath of my family's disintegration, I drove away from the community where I had spent my marriage and raised our children for the last time. I stopped and looked at the memories I was leaving behind. There was the hospital where the kids were born, the schools they attended, the swimming pool, the community center where I alone watched them play soccer. But not one building or place housed a memory I had with my now ex-husband. No restaurant or bar where we socialized, no mutual friends where we'd been entertained, no dance hall. Nothing. Ron was too busy for a social life unless it was work-related, in which case he would buy me a drink and disappear for the evening.

The night we separated, Ron carefully entered me into his address book, last name first, followed by a comma and my full first name. I watched him do it, frozen in disbelief. The main thing that stuck with me was that at least he got the spelling right.

Married to the Job

You have seen how the childhoods of workaholics predispose them to being more object-focused than people-focused. You also have seen how the workaholic mindset is outer directed, geared almost exclusively toward task completion, to the point where workaholics neglect the emotional needs of themselves and their loved ones. This chapter illustrates how workaholic neglect can negatively affect committed relationships with spouses and partners.

WHAT'S OUT OF WHACK?

Loretta's painful story of living with a work-addicted husband follows a pattern common among partners of workaholics who feel alone and isolated. Loretta may have felt alone, but she isn't. My research team studied a random sample of 326 women, asking them to fill out questionnaires on their husband's work habits and the state of their marriage.[1] The 22 percent who said they were in workaholic marriages also reported far more marital estrangement, emotional withdrawal, and thoughts of separation and divorce than those whose partners were not workaholics. The workaholic husbands worked an average of nine and a half hours more a week than the nonworkaholic husbands. And only 45 percent of the women married to workaholics were still married, compared to 84 percent of the women married to nonworkaholics. The spouses of workaholics also felt more helpless: they were more likely than partners of nonworkaholics to say that external events controlled their lives.

We repeated this study with a random sample of 272 men, asking each to rate his wife's work habits and the state of their marriage. The more the husbands perceived their wives as workaholics, the more likely they were to say the women worked longer hours and that greater marital estrangement and negative feelings characterized their marriages. A later study found that workaholism among women was tied to low marital satisfaction and work-family conflict. Together, these three studies suggest that the strength and cohesion of a marriage is associated with the presence or absence of a spouse's workaholism.[2]

ISOLATION AND VILIFICATION

"Earl D. Rhode, 28, a bright executive climbing the ladder of success, fell victim to a national aberration—workaholism. He returned to his suburban home in Washington, D.C., one evening after a long day at the office, with a briefcase bulging with work. The executive secretary of the Nixon administration's Cost of Living Council rested on the living room couch as his wife approached and then calmly put a bullet in his head. Then she killed herself. A newspaper story quoted neighbors as saying she had been complaining about her husband's seven-day workweek."[3]

Although most workaholics die from stress-induced illnesses, this rare case exemplifies the frustration many partners feel. Spouses of workaholics describe the intimate, isolating times within the confines of the house and family as maddening. Some, perhaps even you, say life with their mates is a nightmare, because they have little support from the mental health system, relatives outside their nuclear family, friends, and, least of all, the workplace. Has your partner failed to appear at family gatherings too many times because of work? Has she promised to spend more time with you and not delivered because work comes first? Has he said, "I'll quit tomorrow," but tomorrow never comes? Or has she stood you up or kept you waiting because of work? If you answered yes to these questions, your partner may be suffering from work addiction.

Trudy complained that her husband had been away from the family for so long he'd grown a beard and mustache. When he showed up after six months, his two children didn't even know who he was. Melinda was so chained to her bank job that on school holidays, she took her three children to work with her, leaving them in her car in a parking deck. She justified her actions by insisting that she had to finish a report and said that she went down to check on her kids every hour. After Seth arrived home from a hard day's work, his wife asked where he had left their son, whom he had taken to work for the day. Searching the car, Seth freaked out, exclaiming, "Oh, my God! I forgot and left him at work!" The common theme in all these real-life examples is the workaholic's emotional and/or physical absence from intimate relationships.

If you're the mate of a workaholic like Loretta, you probably feel alone as a partner and parent, as if you've been left with the responsibility of holding the family together. You feel unimportant and minimized, even innately defective, because you get so little attention from your workaholic partner. You might even harbor feelings of anger, resentment, sadness, and guilt. Or you may live under a distinct set of unwritten and unspoken rules, dictated by your partner's work habits: Handle everything at home. Don't expect anything from me because I have enough on my plate at work. Put me at the center of your life and plan the household and family and social life around my work schedule. I'm depending on you to do your best, be perfect, and not let me down.

If you have a workaholic partner, chances are he is extolled by friends and society as a super achiever, dedicated worker, and good provider. So, what do you possibly have to complain about? You must watch your step in how you express your concerns. Along with the general acclaim for the workaholic and the shaming from friends and clinicians in response to any complaints, spouses often blame themselves for their gut sense that something is wrong. Karen, the wife of a New York lawyer, said: "I know how pathological it sounds, but my feelings of rage, confusion, and abandonment are such that I often wish my husband would bruise my face or break my arm. That would enable me to say to myself and everyone else, 'See, he really is hurting me. He's doing something terrible to this marriage, and it's not my fault.'"

Karen's relatives looked at her expensive townhouse and European vacations and couldn't understand what she was complaining about; she had tried couples counseling, only to be told by the therapist in the first session that she was overreacting. Without support from her family or friends, she tucked her feelings neatly away inside and tried to fix some faulty aspect of herself that she couldn't put her finger on.

Stella also reported that she gets vilified: "To everyone else, my husband is perfect. I feel like I'm one of his employees, even at home. He denies there's anything wrong and gets hostile if I confront him about his workaholism. Our friends always want to know why I'm always complaining. I have become the bitchy wife in the eyes of our friends, but they don't understand what it's like being alone."

Till Death Do Us Part

My research has shown that couples in which one spouse is a workaholic are more likely to divorce than couples in which neither party is a workaholic. In addition, a survey by the American Academy of Matrimonial Lawyers cited preoccupation with work as one of the top four causes of divorce. It makes sense that workaholic families would experience problems similar to those of alcoholic families, because of the similarity between the two addictions.

The lawyers' group surveyed four hundred physicians about their observations of workaholics as marital spouses. What follows is a summary of how the physicians would describe your partner, had he or she been a workaholic patient:[4]

1. Devotes an inordinate amount of time and effort to work for the following reasons, in descending order of frequency: inferiority feelings and fear of failure, compulsive defense against strong anxiety, need for approval, fear of personal intimacy, and sexual inadequacy

2. Tends to choose spouses with more dissimilar than similar personalities

3. Has higher than normal expectations for marital satisfaction

4. Is much more demanding of achievement in the children

5. Fills leisure time with work activities

6. Avoids confrontation and marital fights with passive-aggressive maneuvers such as silence and sulking

7. Engages in extramarital affairs more than his partner

8. Engages in marital sexual relations less frequently than other couples

9. Is more prone to alcohol abuse than nonworkaholic peers

10. Frequently has the following sexual problems, in descending order of frequency: emotional detachment, lack of sexual desire, routine and unvarying practices, inhibition of arousal, and inhibition of orgasm

An Office Affair

Sometimes partners feel jealous, even suspicious that their workaholic mate is having an affair because of the long and late hours he or she spends away from home. *Exec* magazine surveyed the work habits of three thousand men and found that spending excessive time at the office wreaks havoc on family life.[5] One-third of the men said they'd been accused of having an affair due to long hours on the job. And 86 percent said their personal relationships were marred by work-related stress. In a survey by *McCall's* magazine, 80 percent of the readers said their husbands worked too much.[6] The phrase "wedded to work" illustrates this condition, and it knows no gender boundaries. When women are addicted to work, men become the suffering partners, as Elizabeth confessed: "I remember my ex-husband saying to me, 'I feel so lonely. You're here in this house and I feel so lonely.' At the same time, he was saying that I felt lonely, too. And we couldn't come together. Work was what was filling us up. He wanted me to fill him up, and I couldn't."

Another feeling frequently expressed by partners of workaholics is reflected in Eric's comment: "I feel like one of her employees, that the only way to be close to her is to join her in her work." And that is exactly what many do. Tears in her eyes, Valerie expressed her struggle between intimacy and work addiction:

Profile of Partners and Spouses of Workaholics

If you're a spouse or partner of a workaholic, chances are you . . .

❖ Feel ignored, neglected, shut out, unloved, and unappreciated because of your spouse's physical and emotional remoteness

❖ Believe you're carrying the emotional burden of the marriage and parenting, which makes you feel lonely and alone in your relationship

❖ Think of yourself as second to work, because family time is a low priority, dictated by work schedules and demands

❖ Perceive yourself as an extension of your workaholic mate, whose addiction demands to be center stage

❖ View yourself as controlled, manipulated, and sometimes rushed by your partner, who calls the shots

❖ Use attention-seeking measures to get your partner to see you or agree to conversations and activities related to work in order to connect with the workaholic

❖ View your relationship as serious and intense, with a minimum of carefree time or fun

❖ Harbor guilt for wanting more out of the relationship, while your partner is applauded by colleagues and society for accomplishments

❖ Have low self-esteem and feel defective, in some way unable to measure up to your spouse, who is often put on a pedestal

❖ Question your own gratitude and perspective when faced with the accolades bestowed on your workaholic partner

People think the workaholic doesn't love them, and that's not true. It hurts me more than anything that my friends and family would think they're not important to me. Work addiction is like alcoholism, and workaholics have unfulfilled needs that they're trying to fill. It's sometimes uncontrollable. It just takes me over and carries me away. So, family and friends need to be patient and need to educate themselves. That will help them understand the person they're with and care about. Work addiction is self-destructive, but it's also destructive to the people around you, if you're not careful.

Romancing the Grindstone

There's a common misperception that workaholics must enjoy their jobs to be addicted to work because they spend so much time with nose to the grindstone. Truth be told, workaholics work for the sake of working. Regardless of work conditions or salary scales, they're willing to do whatever it takes and go the extra mile to get the job done—even when the company doesn't financially reciprocate.

The reason they are accused of "romancing the grindstone" is not necessarily that they love their work. What they love is the escape from intimacy that the work gives them, along with the boosts of self-esteem. Immersion in work feels safe and secure for workaholics, whether the work itself is satisfying.

THE GREAT ESCAPE

Workaholics tend to be what family therapists call minimizers in their couple relationships.[7] Emotionally detached and withdrawn, they withhold and ignore their feelings because intimacy is difficult for them. In marital arguments, minimizers are tight-lipped, cold, uncommunicative, and unfeeling. Constant work keeps feelings buried in the deep freeze, emotionally disconnected, and numb from hurt.

Workaholics handle intimacy issues by wishing them away, putting them off, or ignoring them altogether. They preserve their own space by keeping their thoughts and feelings to themselves, making it difficult for their partners to know what they think or feel.[8] When workaholics share anything with their partners, it's more often about their work or logical and rational thoughts. A request for closeness feels like a demand to a workaholic, a distraction from his or her goal-directed job. Workaholics feel hounded by concerned family and friends who say, "Why don't you just cut back?" Their well-meaning loved ones don't understand that cutting back isn't as easy as it sounds.

MARS AND VENUS

If your partner is a workaholic, chances are you are coming from two totally different emotional worlds, caught in the pursuer-distancer interaction style—a dynamic in which the workaholic wants distance, and you want closeness. So, you pursue your workaholic mate for emotional closeness and affection. Feeling threatened, the workaholic retreats further into work and becomes even more emotionally unavailable. The more you pursue, the more your workaholic partner flees. This interaction, which becomes circular, was shown in the Smith family by the stereotypical—but true—nature of Dorothy's nagging and Jack's withdrawing (see chapter 6).

As the mate of a workaholic, you more than anyone else feel the shield your loved one uses as protection from intimacy. The barriers are hard to penetrate, and workaholics have few or no friends. Their tools of trade are their best friends, because they don't have to worry about disappointing their computer screen, falling short of the iPad's standards, or hurting the feelings of their cell phone. Immersing themselves in predictable and controllable jobs is safer than slippery intimate relationships.

Workaholics who excel at work but not at home engage in areas where they feel more competent—their work—which reinforces their disconnection. Perhaps the workaholic in your life treats your relationship like he treats his job, because that's what he's best at doing. Chances are, he uses the same control and hard-driving perfection to relate to you and other family members that he uses with coworkers. Dictating and organizing, workaholics run their households like a work camp. Like Loretta, you might feel treated like an employee on work detail. Your teenage son's ballgame with his father must be scheduled, and you might be expected to share intimacy on command.

Your workaholic probably forgets, ignores, or minimizes important family rituals and celebrations such as birthdays, anniversaries, or children's recitals. He might be unable to stop work long enough to participate fully, because such events represent a distraction from his commitment to work—even in emergencies, as a terrified Loretta found. Accomplished in his field, the workaholic might still have few social skills and few interests outside work, often remaining disengaged in social conversations that don't pertain to his work interests.

WET FALLEN LEAVES

Japanese wives use the derogatory term *nure-ochiba* (a wet fallen leaf) to refer to retired workaholic husbands who don't know what to do with themselves when they're not working and who hang around the house expecting their wives to plan their spare time: "They follow their wives around, like unwanted, wet fallen leaves which are stuck to the bottom of one's shoes. Thus, competencies developed at work are not necessarily transferable to a post-retirement lifestyle. The wife has lived all these years without her work-immersed husband's support and has achieved emotional independence and ego-identity. She possesses appropriate skills for social survival and networking. On the other hand, the husband may lack such skills. He is like a fish out of water, becomes dependent upon his wife, while the latter feels annoyed with him who constantly disrupts her routine and demands her attention."[9]

Many Americans report that their workaholic partners experience a sense of lostness or helplessness especially noticeable during down times like vacations, holidays, and retirement. On their trip across Europe, Wendy handled all the details of the plans, keeping Tim's wallet and passport and arranging their daily trips to museums, tours, and sightseeing. Tim dutifully followed her lead from Scandinavia to the Mediterranean, almost as if they had an unspoken bargain: "I'll traipse all over the world with you and indulge your every whim, but I expect you to let me work without interruptions or complaints." In this way a tacit contract gets played out in ways that couples don't realize. Some workaholics bargain to win release from family obligations by telling a spouse, "I'll go with you to the wedding next weekend if you'll keep the kids out of my hair today and tomorrow so that I can finish the sales report." Promises to cut down on work or spend more time with family are more often broken than kept. As the weekend approaches, there's more work to be done, accompanied by an apologetic refrain: "Sorry, honey. Looks like you and the kids will have to go without me."

Work Infidelity

You might've noticed that your workaholic doesn't tolerate obstacles to working. If someone stands in her way, she takes either an aggressive approach of blowing up or a passive-aggressive approach of sneaking to her stash, as I once did to avoid repercussions. This concealment and deceit are known as *work infidelity*.

Work goes everywhere the workaholic goes, regardless of what family or friends say: in briefcases or luggage, under car seats, in glove compartments, in car trunks, beneath spare tires, in dirty laundry bags, stuffed inside pants or a skirt, and, in at least one case, hidden in a secret compartment of another person's suitcase, unbeknown to that person. Once workaholics start bootlegging their work compulsions, you might as well admit it: they're desperate; they must get their fix at all costs, even if it means being deceitful and dishonest, even if it hurts the ones they love the most.

If your partner is like most workaholics, she caves into your demands by concealing work to please you and avoid criticisms, much like an alcoholic who hides beer bottles.[10] Your workaholic might hide memos or files in a suitcase, pretend to rest while you're off at the grocery store, or feign going to the gym and working out at the end of the day to sneak in an extra hour or two of work.

Mildred committed work infidelity to deal with the stress and anxiety caused by her husband's expectation that she be home with him by 5:00 p.m. She told him she'd enrolled in an aerobics class after work. Her husband was thrilled that she was finally taking an interest in activities outside work. But the truth was that Mildred was working two hours overtime, changing in her office from business outfit to aerobic garb, tousling her hair, and dampening her tights with water—all to convince her husband that she was coming around.

In his book *Working*, Studs Terkel describes how the broadcast executive Ward Quaal concealed his working from his family:

I get home around six-thirty, seven at night. After dinner with the family, I spend a minimum of two and a half hours each night going over the mail and dictating. I should have a secretary at home just to handle the mail that comes there. I'm not talking about bills and personal notes; I'm talking about business mail only. Although I don't go to the office on Saturday or Sunday, I do have mail brought out to my home for the weekend. I dictate on Saturday and Sunday. When I do this on holidays, like Christmas, New Year's, and Thanksgiving, I have to sneak a little bit, so the family doesn't know what I'm doing.[11]

Kate's work obsession became her weekend lover. She lied to her family so she could rendezvous with work at the office: "I'd tell my family I was going shopping on a Saturday, and I'd end up in my office working. Or I'd tell them I was going to my girlfriend's house. After calling my girlfriend's and not finding me, they'd call the office and say, 'I thought you were going to Dottie's.' I felt like I'd been caught with my hand in the cookie jar." As I related in the introduction, in the throes of my own work addiction, I, too, committed work infidelity, smuggling projects on vacation, and sneaking a fix when others were out of eyesight and earshot. Concealment serves the purpose of lowering tensions in the couple relationship, as it did for Jamey and me. Once the truth is revealed, though, partners often feel betrayed and mistrustful, and relationships suffer severe, sometimes irreparable, damage because of the deceit. Once workaholics have entered the lying and concealment stage, it indicates their desperation and inability to say no. At this juncture, professional help is often needed for workaholics and their partners.

The New Normal

Have you put your life on hold because of a workaholic mate? If so, you could be enabling the very addiction you wish to erase from your life. Many partners and spouses build their lives around the workaholic because they want to feel connected and supportive. That's natural, right?

But as with any addiction, molding your life around a workaholic spouse only leads to disappointment and enabling. The key to avoid enabling, when you're desperate to spend time with your workaholic partner, is to stop postponing your life. If you plan a trip to the zoo with the kids and the workaholic cancels (for the umpteenth time) because of last-minute demands at the office, go without her. When your workaholic promises to be home in time for dinner and never shows, consider eating on time without him and, instead of putting dinner on the table at midnight, let him fix his own meal.

You can refrain from such activities as bringing your loved one work when he goes to bed sick, making alibis for her absenteeism or lateness at social functions or family gatherings, and let the workaholic take responsibility to explain. You can stop assuming your workaholic's household duties, returning phone calls for him, or covering for her by lying to business associates on the telephone—all because the workaholic is too busy working.

Although it's important for you to include your workaholic in your plans and let him know he was missed and how disappointed you were by his absence, you don't have to continue putting your family's lives on hold. Here's a real-life example: "My husband used to be late for everything—parties, dinners, movies—because he always worked overtime. Then one night, our friends came to pick us up, and as usual, he wasn't home yet. So, I left without him, but I wrote him a note that read, 'You're always late, and it's embarrassing. We're at the restaurant. I hope you get home in time to join us.' He's been much more considerate ever since. He even gets home early enough on Fridays to take me to the movies!"[12]

Your workaholic might comply with pressures to curb work by the "white-knuckling approach"—going through the motions of being at a cocktail party or on a Caribbean vacation, attending a child's ballgame or recital. Although present in body, in her head she's back at the office working. Cynthia described her husband's inability to let go and be present: "It's difficult to pull him away from any of his work activities. He gets anxious when he's not working, and then I feel guilty if I try to get him to do something with me other than work. I wind up feeling as if I have deprived him of something."

Tips for Clinicians

If you're a clinician, you can provide counseling for couples whose marriages have been damaged by work addiction. Change, however, doesn't come easy or fast for workaholic couples, and change is necessary for all family members if the damage is to be repaired.

ADDRESSING THE CHICKEN EGG CYCLE

When family members expect workaholics to change, they also must examine the reaction patterns they've built in response to the workaholism and be prepared to change as well. They may have gotten into the habit of complaining or being cynical about the compulsive working, and workaholics may have withdrawn into "vital exhaustion"—total shutdown and detachment from the relationship.

If you work with couples to restructure the family system, be prepared for resistance on both sides. The parent who has single-handedly raised the kids, for example, may become resentful when suddenly the work-addicted partner decides to take a more active role in parenting. Reversing these types of patterns can evoke anger and hurtful feelings, leading to turf battles and questions like "Where were you ten years ago?" Family members may be sending the workaholic mixed signals by complaining about his or her absence and then, as the workaholic begins to move back into the family system, complaining about his or her attempts at reintegration.

You can also make family members aware of the double bind they create by complaining about the work addict's overworking in one breath and making unreasonable financial demands in the next. In some cases, they must be willing and prepared to sacrifice financial advantages in return for the workaholic's increased presence and participation in the family and less time spent working.

You can take several clinical approaches to help workaholics and their loved ones—who, not unlike alcoholic families, are entrenched in denial. Outwardly, workaholic families appear immune to the effects of the hard-driving, compulsive behaviors of the addict. Workaholics in particular mask their anxiety, depression, or fear of not being in control by demonstrating resiliency, perfectionism, over responsibility, or self-reliance to the point of having difficulty asking for help. Family members often are reluctant to come forward for fear of being branded ungrateful for the material rewards generated by the workaholic lifestyle. Typical workaholic families avoid acknowledging this issue which leads to tension and resentment. By helping couples identify and express their feelings about the problem, you can reduce their tension and prepare them for further work.

IDENTIFYING THE PURSUER-DISTANCER DYNAMIC

During the therapeutic process, try to be aware of the troublesome pursuer-distancer dynamic and take steps to help couples identify and correct it. Keep in mind that when there's an ingrained pursuer-distancer pattern, the behavior of one partner provokes and maintains the behavior of the other.[13] John Gottman's research on thousands of couples, revealed that when partners get stuck in this pattern early in marriage, they have more than an 80 percent chance of divorcing in the first four to five years.[14] When you name the pursuer-distancer interactional style in therapy sessions, you help couples recognize it and give them something concrete to work on in their daily interactions. You can help couples understand the transmission of their respective roles from their families of origin, which can foster their taking responsibility as a couple for their relationship, instead of blaming each other.[15]

Workaholics often "check out" during therapy sessions, and when they do you can gently prompt them to invest more of themselves to effect change. The family therapist Stephen Betchen cautions you, the clinician, to not enlist or enable pursuers to play co-therapist, which often unconsciously happens. If you align with a pursuer, the workaholic spouse will feel ganged up on and withdraw even more. Because pursuers often take responsibility for their part in the relationship plus that of their spouse, Betchen recommends the following approach: "Clearly, the pursuer is the over functioning, over responsible spouse, and I often tell her that she overworks her relationship. I let the under responsible distancer know that when he abdicates responsibility in his relationship, he is more likely to be controlled by his spouse—something I know he is deeply concerned about."[16]

When working with couples affected by work addiction, I have observed that the more one spouse pursues, the more the other retreats. I often use this analogy with clients: "When it's hailing [the pursuer], the turtle pulls its head in its shell [the distancer]. And if it's hailing, the turtle is not going to stick its neck out." To break this cycle, I suggest that pursuing spouses consciously and deliberately pull back or take a vacation from working on their relationships. This strategy gives workaholics the space to take more responsibility for their part by becoming the pursuer. Each party must embrace part of the role of the other. You can recommend that pursuers change by ceasing to offer unsolicited advice, no longer expecting distancers to join them at social events, no longer pushing for physical contact, or ceasing to constantly ask distancers if they love them. You can encourage distancers to express their intimate feelings, create romantic dinners with candlelight and flowers, invite the pursuer to special social events, and initiate conversations by asking their partners about their day.

The effect of having pursuers withdraw is that it gives distancers the psychological space they need to take more initiative in the relationship. As distancers increase their interest in and attention to the relationship, pursuers ultimately get the closeness they have been seeking, and the couple is able to meet at an emotional halfway point. Other clinical evidence documents that distancers move closer to their partners when pursuers reduce their pursuing.[17]

NOURISHING THE OVERWORKED RELATIONSHIP

Typical twenty-first-century couples overwork their relationships. After spending all day at the office, couples spend evenings cooking meals, attending to children, and, in some cases, preparing work for the next day. Busyness and doing infiltrate the relationship to the point that intimate relationships are replaced with business relationships: discussing financial concerns, hassles at work, headaches with the kids, problems with day care or school; juggling family schedules and children's activities; and preparing meals for the next day. Eventually, couples in these overworked relationships start to show the same signs of stress and fragility as the individual workaholic: irritability, tension, exhaustion, and burnout. In problematic relationships, couples may shut down completely and not talk at all, in which case television or late-night work often becomes a replacement for companionship.

Relationships need attention to stay vital. You can assist workaholic families in negotiating boundaries around the amount of time they spend working together, talking about work, or discussing family business or scheduling issues. These boundaries can be tailored to the unique schedules and lifestyles of each couple. One possibility is to eliminate work after a set evening hour and to carve out a set time every evening (without the internet or television) for intimate conversations about matters not related to work. Meals are great times to put these boundaries in place; another possibility is to set aside the time immediately after both parties arrive home.

Couples can learn not to let work dominate their conversations, but still discuss work frustrations and successes as all healthy couples and families do. They can set boundaries, making weekend working the exception rather than the rule and barring work from vacations. Establishing appropriate boundaries around work is essential to protect fragile relationship intimacy in today's intrusive wireless world.

You can guide couples through a couple-care plan to achieve balance in their relationship by using the procedures for the work moderation plan outlined in chapter 3. Using the categories of (1) couple relationship, (2) family, (3) play, and (4) work, couples can separately and together compute their scores for each area and then name three or four activities or goals for each area to bring healthier boundaries and greater balance into their relationship. The content of the couple-care plan can make for lively discussions and invigorate an otherwise neglected or overworked relationship.

HELPING PARTNERS COMMUNICATE

As the family unit shifts its dynamics, you can tackle additional goals such as effective problem solving, better communication, more clearly established family roles, greater affective responses, more affective involvement, and higher family functioning in general—all of which are frequently cited problem areas within the workaholic family system.[18]

Tension builds in families whose members have refused to acknowledge and discuss their problems. Angry outbursts occur over trivial events that have little to do with the real problem. Here's another area where clinicians can help families talk about their problems and feelings by providing a communication structure such as the couple's dialogue—the framework created by Harville Hendrix and Helen Hunt in Imago Relationship Therapy—to ensure that listening, understanding, and empathy are reciprocal.[19]

Imago Relationship Therapy is an effective approach to build communication between couples, developing their relationship vision, and helping them understand how their family-of-origin experiences get recast in unconscious ways, causing problems in their current relationship. The Imago (pronounced eh-MAH-go, Latin for "image") works such that your romantic attraction is based on a composite picture of the caretakers who influenced you most strongly at an early age. You and your intimate partner activate in each other stressors that plunge you back into the central conflicts of your upbringing in order to have it turn out better the second time around. Your workaholic mind, in effect, returns to the scene of the crime without realizing it. You click with a mate who in some way matches your Imago template, duplicating the unmet needs you felt with your childhood caretakers, to right the wrongs of your past.

By facing these problems and getting their feelings out in the open, families can reduce tension and address the real source of conflict. Treatment issues address intimacy problems as they manifest in the present family and social functioning of the workaholic. The most common clinical observation, as I mentioned earlier, is when workaholics hide behind a psychological shield to avoid closeness with their families. You can help workaholics identify when and why they dissociate and learn to stay in the present and communicate with loved ones. In addition, you can facilitate the process for partners of workaholics, helping them express to the workaholic their feelings of isolation, abandonment, anger, resentment, guilt, hurt, and sadness. This allows partners to share their hopes and dreams for, as well as disappointments with, the relationship. They can share their fears of drifting apart, how it feels to be kept waiting or stood up, or what it's like living with a stranger who escapes into work. With the right help, partners of workaholics can develop compassion for the difficulty their companions have in controlling work compulsions without making themselves doormats to the abusive work habits.

INTERVENTIONS

You can assist family members with interventions when work addiction becomes life threatening. Forgetfulness, chronic fatigue, grouchiness, mood swings, and physical ailments related to stress all indicate that the body is burning out. Families can lovingly share their concerns about their workaholic's health and encourage him or her to consult a physician. They can ask the addicted family member to go with them for counseling and, if the addict refuses, get help for themselves through a support group or continued individual therapy.

In severe health cases, a family intervention might be appropriate. Family interventions with workaholics are like those used with alcoholics. The workaholic is lovingly confronted by family, friends, and significant colleagues (for example, employers, supervisors, or employees) under the supervision of an experienced family therapist. Each person tells the workaholic how it feels to watch him or her deteriorate and explain what the intervener plans to do about the relationship (threats are never used) unless the workaholic gets help.

Bibliotherapy

The following readings relate to the content of this chapter:

❖ Terry Gaspard, *The Remarriage Manual: How to Make Everything Work Better the Second Time Around* (Boulder, CO: Sounds True, 2020).

❖ John Gottman and Nan Silver, *The Seven Principles of Making Marriage Work* (New York: Random House, 2015).

❖ Harville Hendrix and Helen Hunt, *Getting the Love You Want: A Guide for Couples* (New York: St. Martin's Griffin, 2019).

❖ Harville Hendrix and Helen Hunt, *Getting the Love You Want: A Couples Workshop Manual* (New York: Institute for Relationship Therapy, 2003).

❖ Sue Johnson, *Hold Me Tight: Your Guide to the Most Successful Approach to Building Loving Relationships* (New York: Little, Brown, 2011).

8

The Legacy of Children of Workaholics

My child arrived just the other day,
came into the world in the usual
way, but there were planes to catch
and bills to pay; he learned to walk
while I was away.
                        —Harry Chapin

Charles Cannot Get His Father's Attention

My father had two loves: work and bourbon. He also, of course, loved his two children but we learned at an early age that being close to our father required entering his world of ambitious interests and endless cycles of working, drinking, and sleeping. Our house ran on our father's energy. When the phone rang, as it frequently did just as we sat down to an already delayed, late-evening family dinner, it was usually a graduate student or colleague calling for my father. "Oh, damn!" he'd say, jumping to his feet, racing from the dining room into his study. Sometimes I'd groan as he made his quick exit, but usually my mother, brother, and I would just sit in silence, staring and continuing to eat until he returned with the latest tale of upheaval in the department or of the almost nervous breakdown his advisee was having over an oral comprehensive exam.

My father's life seemed exciting, passionate, and important. By comparison, everyone else's life seemed less so. Childhood pleasures like the state fair, shooting basketball hoops, picnics, going fishing or to the pool, learning to ride a bike without training wheels, or carving the Halloween pumpkin were all scheduled around Dad's work and often were simply endured by him in a state of irritation or, worse, exhaustion after long hours "at the office." It was clear from the start that family life and "traditional" family activities came second and were rather trivial compared to the adult world of work, politics, ambition, and collegiality. Even vacations to the beach involved taking along favored graduate students. If students couldn't come with us, my father would make contacts with colleagues and former students in a nearby town and ask them to come visit. Over shrimp and beer, they'd give him the latest scoop on the local school system or reminisce with him about his early years as a bachelor high-school chemistry teacher in this same nearby beach town. My father's (and thus also my mother's) friends were his students and former students. I realize now that his mentoring of these young, admiring professionals occupied his time and energy and left me, his older child, competing with handsome, bright male graduate students for his love and attention.

When he brought home his favorite students or colleagues to drink and "talk shop" late into the evening, he was at his best: happy, lively, and eloquent. As a small boy on these nights of discussion and drinking, I would run rambunctiously in and out of the living room where he was holding forth. In childish ways, I'd compete for his audience's attention or for his attention by asking questions, making noises, or hiding and jumping out from behind the sofa to scare everyone. Usually, Dad would just give me a hug and then firmly direct me out of the room to find Mom (who was sequestered in her bedroom) so that she could give me a bath and put me to bed, usually well past the designated hour. These were the fun nights in the house filled with my father's work companions, their laughter, their serious and meaningful conversation. I remember nights like these throughout my entire childhood and adolescence.

As I grew older, I learned to sit quietly, listen, and watch Dad as he talked to his students and colleagues. If I was quiet and didn't interrupt, then I could stay in the room with him, and this was very important to me since it was often the only contact that I would have with him for days at a time, except for when he would sleepily drive me to school (and almost make me late) the following mornings. I learned to enter these conversations about philosophy, politics, child development, educational curriculum, John Dewey, Martin Buber, and other topics of interest to my dad, and thus topics I too attempted to read about and understand. I did my ninth-grade English project on existentialism. I learned to make strong percolated coffee and serve it to him in his study when he would write until two, three, or four in the morning. My bedroom was next door to his study. I loved to try to stay awake reading as late into the night as his light was still on. And I'd get out of bed, go to his study door, and see him sitting at his desk in his black horn-rimmed glasses, focusing intensely. It seemed as if I was constantly interrupting and distracting him from something very important.

My father was always "at work," at the office, hovering over his desk at home, or entertaining his students and "talking shop." When I was very little,

I'd beg him to play with me in the evenings when he would come home from his office without his students. "Daddy's tired," he'd say, as he slumped in a chair. I'd grab his arm and pull him to get up to play cowboys with me, which at times he would agree to do, grudgingly. Then in a less than enthusiastic tone, he would respond to my piercing war cries with a distracted "bang, bang." Even then I remember feeling mad at him for being so tired and uninterested in my childhood fantasies and dramas.

I was always the little warrior in our family. I raged and cried at canceled camping trips, at my father's out-of-town consulting jobs, which took him away for days, and at his sleeping until noon on the weekends when I wanted him to be up with me.

At a young age, I would follow him to his university office on Saturday and Sunday afternoons to play in the science lab with the hamsters and gaze at anatomy books by myself while he labored in a nearby office. It was lonely, but it was a way to be near him, so I always behaved and was trusted to take care of myself and not interrupt him too often. When he'd take a coffee break, we'd walk to the store across the street. I'd get a vanilla ice cream cone and, on our way back to the office, I would ask him to "Watch!" as I balanced myself walking along the ivy-covered stone wall beside the sidewalk. I was happiest when I was with my dad, even if it meant learning the importance and priority of his work over my childish whims and wishes.

When I cried and yelled at him for "always working," my little brother just sucked his fingers and watched quietly. Mom was depressed and often in her bedroom or even hospitalized for extended periods with what later was diagnosed as manic depression. Manic depression, I now think, was an appropriate illness to have in my family. If she was to have a mental illness, manic depression certainly complemented her husband's waxing and waning energies. Dad's work cycles of all-night writing binges, teaching, and long hours with students at home or at the office were always followed by periods of intense exhaustion during which he would sleep for long periods or sluggishly mope around the house, relax with his bourbon, and sleep more.

Dad had his first heart attack at forty-two. In my fifteen-year-old eyes, he seemed so old, even fragile. His doctors told him to quit smoking his four packs per day, drinking caffeine, and eating the New York strip steaks he loved to cook and generously serve to his protégés during those late-night sessions after bourbon rendered them ravenous at ten o'clock, when they'd gone without dinner. His doctors also told him to exercise more, work less, reduce stress, and consume no more than two alcoholic beverages a day. In other words, at forty-two, my father was told to change just about every aspect of his life that had been so much the source of his greatest success and pleasure: hard working, hard drinking, smoking, and late-night talking and dining. Although at the time, in my usual fashion, I was so angry at him and his failed attempts to reform himself, I now realize how sad it was to watch his feeble efforts to smoke less, drink less, and be with his students less.

In the year before he died, I remember he would sometimes spend an entire weekend in bed or in a recliner reading a novel. In my early twenties, when I would return to my parents' home for visits, the students didn't come to the house as much, and I didn't hear about his dreams of starting experimental schools or becoming president of a university any more. He was at home more, less busy, quieter, and sadder. I didn't realize then what was happening. I thought he was just getting older—after all, he was almost fifty. He died of a coronary at fifty-one after a full day at the office. My grandmother, his mother, said my father would have wanted it that way—to have worked every day of his life until he died. I was twenty-four when he died. I'm now forty-two, and fifty-one doesn't seem all that old.

Sometimes, I go to professional baseball games and watch the fathers with their sons and daughters. The kids are so excited, and the fathers buy them things, hold them on their laps, and talk to them about the game, pointing, whispering in their little ears, and the kids jump up, arms waving, with loud joyous cheers. I don't really like ballgames now; they're boring, no fun, and a waste of time. But when I was a child, I wanted so badly for my father to take me to ballgames like other dads. But he was either too busy or too uninterested in sports and the heroes that eight-year-old me adored, like Mickey Mantle and Roger Maris. Who knows? Maybe if he had taken me to some of those games before the age when my stodgy boredom set in, I would know how to enjoy baseball now.

When I watch those children with their dads at ballgames, I get a glimpse of what it means to have lost the moments childhood offers us all, however so briefly, to know pure excitement over something simple and playful. My father worked through most of my childhood. And he hasn't been around for any of my adulthood.

Carrying the Legacy of the Best-Dressed Addiction

In 1983, Janet Woititz wrote a small book called *Adult Children of Alcoholics* that sold millions of copies and started a movement among legions of adults who had been damaged growing up in alcoholic homes. During the 1980s, a lot of research on adult children of alcoholics was published, showing this population to be at risk for a variety of problems.[1] Parental alcoholism was linked to low self-esteem in children and, in adults, to a higher external locus of control (which means they believe that they are controlled by external circumstances instead of by their own internal fortitude), depression, and anxiety. Adult children of alcoholics came to realize that they carried an insidious legacy that affected their current mental health, their intimate relationships, and, in some cases, their careers. The Woititz book, credited with starting the recovery movement of the late 1980s and early 1990s, opened the floodgates for other popular books on codependency, dysfunctional families, and the inner child.

This chapter is about a parallel problem with workaholism and how it damages children—the addiction that looks so good on parents, it's also pretty on their children. Despite the abundance of studies on children of alcoholics, the research on children of workaholics is sparse. Clinical reports suggest that, while attempting to medicate emotional pain by overworking, workaholics suffer some of the same symptoms as alcoholics.[2] My early clinical observations suggested that children in workaholic families were subjected to subtle yet harmful influences, yielding coping problems like those of children of alcoholics.[3]

Children of Workaholics under the Microscope

Near the turn of the twenty-first century, not one scientific study had been conducted on children of workaholics. This sad situation prompted my university research team and I to launch the first study on children of workaholics using similar methods that scientists had used to study children of alcoholics.[4] We gave a battery of tests to 211 young adults (average age twenty-four), asking them to rate their fathers on workaholic tendencies. Based on the WART ratings, fathers were categorized as either workaholics or nonworkaholics. We also asked them to rate themselves on depression, anxiety, and locus of control. Adult children of workaholic fathers had statistically higher levels of depression and anxiety and were more prone to believing that external events controlled their lives compared to adults from homes where fathers carried an average workload.

Our findings showed that children with workaholic fathers carry their psychological scars well into adulthood, as Charles did. These scars manifest as an outer-directed reliance on others for decision making, and a lack of inner confidence that is tied to greater anxiety and depression than in the population at large. These results parallel similar findings on adult children of alcoholics, compared to adult children of nonalcoholics.[5]

Other studies replicated our findings with different populations. Studies conducted at the California Graduate Institute and the University of South Australia found that children of workaholics, compared to children of nonworkaholics, had significantly higher depression and anxiety levels and more incidences of obsessive-compulsive tendencies, rated their families as more dysfunctional, and were at higher risk for workaholism themselves.[6] Later findings also suggest that parental workaholism is related to children's happiness and emotional and behavioral problems. Once grown, children of workaholics are more likely to have lower levels of well-being and self-acceptance, more health complaints, and to become workaholics themselves.[7]

In another study, my research team wanted to see if there was a difference in psychological adjustment between children of workaholics and children of alcoholics. We tested a group of 207 young adults of which average age twenty-five. Those who reported growing up with a workaholic parent had higher depression levels and higher rates of parentification than a control group of adult children from alcoholic homes. Additionally, the children of workaholics said their parents worked significantly more hours than what the children of alcoholics reported.[8]

Picture-Perfect Childhoods? Really?

These statistics match the stories I've received from readers far and wide who describe patterns of failed marriages, anxiety, and depression with no obvious causes, but who came from seemingly picture-perfect childhoods. If your father drank too much, you could point to the bottle; if your mother was strung out on pills, the drugs might explain her unusual mood swings. But if you grow up in a workaholic home, there's no tangible cause for your feelings of confusion, guilt, and inadequacy. The American work ethic prevents us from faulting a parent for hard work and from viewing workaholism as a problem. If you're the offspring of a workaholic, you examine your supposedly picture-perfect life and conclude that "something must be wrong with me." After all, workaholic parents are usually highly successful, responsible, and may even hold leadership positions in the community. Their overachieving is sanctioned by society, the community, and even religious organizations.

So, you silently reprimand yourself for complaining because your workaholic parent is an upstanding contributor to society. When you acknowledge the problem, it can bring up feelings of guilt and disloyalty. After all, your family is perfect, which makes you the ungrateful child. This scenario is why I say it's the best-dressed of all the addictions and why the children of workaholics, such as Dana, carry the pretty addiction into adulthood:

> My dad was such a workaholic that he got his thank-you notes out the day after Christmas. He does it right and holds everybody to those same standards. If he could do something, then everybody else ought, and should,

be able to do it, too. Wasting time was not allowed in my family, and both of my parents were always busy. And there was no obvious dysfunction to point to as a reason for my feelings of discontent, emptiness, and frustration. My parents were avid churchgoers, civic leaders, and good parents who worked hard to send us to summer camp. They wanted to be Ozzie and Harriet, and they tried hard to be. They were so perfect that the logical conclusion was that there must be something wrong with me for wanting to have intimate conversations and relationships and for feeling like I wasn't loved or accepted. If I have children, the biggest thing I would hope to do would be to promote an atmosphere of intimacy, to be the kind of mother who would want to hear how my children's days went and to talk about how my children and I were feeling.

When Relationships Feel Like a Death Sentence

If you're the grown-up child of a workaholic, you're likely to either shun intimacy altogether or become enmeshed to the point of reinventing yourself to accommodate to your partner. On the inside you feel trapped in a lifelong legacy of personal emptiness, disappointment, and depression, much of which materializes in your adulthood. You might have a pattern of getting involved in long-term relationships with people whom you're constantly trying to please, who are emotionally distant, and whom you're always disappointing. In other words, you become intimately involved with someone who reminds you of your workaholic parent.

Helen is example of the many adults I have seen in my practice who suffer from having grown up in a workaholic household. Her first marriage ended during a vacation in Yosemite National Park. Relishing the sunshine on her face, the smell of the clean fresh air, and the breathtaking natural beauty, she turned to share the experience with her husband—who was on his cell phone with someone in Argentina, grunting and kicking the dirt. He'd just lost a huge business deal. The loneliness Helen felt in this marriage paralleled the loneliness she had felt with her father, a physician who was physically and emotionally absent during her early years.

Now, as she and her second husband sat before me, their marriage was on the rocks, partly for the same reasons. Huge tears ran down her cheeks faster than she could dab them away. Her guilty conscience said she should stay in the marriage and make it work (even though she didn't want to) and sacrifice her needs. Another part of her desperately tried to figure out who she was. After all, she'd spent both marriages pleasing her husbands. Since the age of five, she'd been taught that performing, being perfect, and accommodating the needs of others should be her life's work. Never mind what she wanted, needed, or felt. Play the role, produce, achieve. Both husbands had been emotionally vacant, and she felt disconnected and emotionally sterile living with them. The distance felt familiar to her because it echoed the painful loneliness that she had felt growing up with her workaholic father.

This scene is repeated over and over in therapists' offices around the country. There is no label for it. But millions of adult children of workaholics are confused, in pain, and don't understand why. In some cases, they're unaware that their parents were workaholics or that parental work addiction insinuated itself into their lives at an early age, let alone that it continues to play a role in their adult mental health. They are fumbling badly in relationships and are self-critical, anxious, depressed, and willing to accommodate their current partners. Most of what we know about children of workaholics is based on case studies, clinical observations, and a handful of scientific studies. Although embryonic, this information is insightful. The following section is painted from this small body of literature.

Profile of Adult Children of Workaholics

If you're an adult child of a workaholic, you might fit the profile of this group:

- ❖ Outwardly focused conformists
- ❖ Self-critical
- ❖ Self-disparaging people who feel unworthy and incompetent for not being able to meet others' expectations
- ❖ Prone to depression
- ❖ Approval seekers striving to make up for self-inadequacy
- ❖ Performance-driven perfectionists who judge themselves by their accomplishments, rather than by their inherent worth
- ❖ Overly serious people who have difficulty having fun
- ❖ Prone to feelings of disloyalty and guilt for acknowledging a problem in their picture-perfect family, which, on the surface, has provided them with everything
- ❖ Angry and resentful
- ❖ Prone to generalized and performance anxiety
- ❖ Unsuccessful in adult intimate relationships
- ❖ Chameleons with an undeveloped sense of self

"Daddy Gone": Growing Up with a Workaholic Parent

Case studies indicate that workaholics are physically and psychologically unavailable to their kids, generally don't take an active role in their children's development, and, as a consequence, their offspring become resentful of their emotional absence.[9] According to one management consultant, "it is easier for him [the workaholic] to be a mentor than a parent, because there is more distance. I have heard workaholics talk in glowing terms about students and subordinates and yet never speak with such delight about their own offspring."[10]

In interviews, adult children of workaholics have revealed that they had four major concerns regarding their parents' work addiction.[11] *Preoccupation* was the most significant concern. The second was *haste*, because their parents were always rushing around. The third was *irritability*: the parents were so deeply involved in their work that it made them cross and cranky. The fourth concern was that children felt that their work-addicted parents took work too seriously, lacked humor, and showed *depression* about work. All four signs were present in the case of Charles.

Desperate for love and attention, Charles pulled every antic his child's mind could dream up to get his father to notice and spend time with him. These kinds of futile quests, which made him a lonely and angry child and an empty adult, are a common refrain among children of workaholics. Tom said: "The second words I learned to say were, 'Daddy gone.' That indicates to me that I was missing my dad at a very young age, and it shocks me that I am doing the same thing to my kids."

Children like Charles, who are hungry for attention from their psychologically absent parents, complain about their parents' mental absenteeism. But their natural way of handling the disappointment is to defer their emotional needs by joining in the workaholic pattern to get approval. If this were you, you'd work alongside your workaholic parent or accompany him or her to the workplace in hopes of stealing a few moments of attention, the way some children of alcoholics let themselves be propped up on the counter at the corner bar in order to have time with "Daddy."

At thirty-five, Nell smuggled memos and contracts into her dying father's hospital room. "It was the only way I could be with him," she said, fighting back tears. "The only time he'd pay attention to me was around the subject of his work." Desperate to connect with the unavailable workaholic parent, children unwittingly enable the working parent by helping him or her. Nell's father died working, a pen in his hand. Now she lives with the guilt of hastening his death.

The Deck Stacked against You

When workaholics actively parent, it's often to make sure their children are living up to their perfectionist standards. Workaholic parents push achievement and accomplishment over unconditional acceptance of their offspring. Their love and approval are unwittingly doled out on the condition that a standard is reached—one that, from the child's perspective, is often unattainable.

At the age of forty-three, Pat remembered how difficult it was living up to her workaholic mother's expectations: "In some ways growing up with a smart, hard-working mother was hard. I've never felt like I could measure up to her success in either of the domains of running a family or having a career. And while I have never competed directly with her, I know that working extra hard and being successful is the only real way to feel good about my efforts. I worked hard but have never felt like I'm successful because I could've done more."

Chances are, if you're the child of a workaholic, you felt loved only if you performed well. Because of a perpetual fear of failure, you might have performance anxiety about challenges at school, in work, and even in relationships. Haunting perfectionism is your lifelong invisible companion. Being good and doing well become your standards. Marsha's workaholic mother ran the household according to the motto: "Your best is always better yet." She believed no matter how hard you work, you could work harder, earn more, do better. Marsha shudders at the memory of traveling home after her high school graduation—not just because there'd been a late spring snow and it was cold outside, but also because of her mother's chilly attitude. Even though Marsha had been honored for having the second highest grade point average among two thousand students, her mother had been distant and unenthusiastic all day long. As tires crushed the ice on the road beneath them, Marsha's mother broke the ice inside the car. "Why couldn't you have been number one?" she demanded.

Something Must Be Wrong with Me

The takeaway from a workaholic parent is, "You can't measure up" or "You need to be someone other than who you are." With parental expectations out of reach, you internalize failure as your own inadequacy. The anecdotal literature suggests that like many children of workaholics you're apt to carry the same best-dressed legacy of your workaholic parent: you become other-directed and approval seeking, trying to meet adult expectations. Or you go in the opposite direction: you see measuring up as a hopeless task, give up trying, and act out your frustrations, anger, and hostility. You might become an underachiever or develop a behavioral problem, displacing anger and aggression at school.

Science supports the clinical observations. Families in which parents have high achievement expectations or evaluate a child's performance based on others' performances promote the development of Type A behaviors such as competitiveness, aggression, and hostility, as well as decreased self-esteem and perceived control, in children.[12] In addition, an unsupportive family environment and a lack of positive familial affiliation are linked to children's anger and hostility.[13]

Asked if workaholics are demanding of achievement in their children, 88 percent of four hundred physicians responded, "more demanding." The study concluded that because workaholics regard their spouses and children as extensions of their egos, family conflict is inevitable. As children of workaholics learn that parental love is contingent on their perfect performance, they react with resentment and become hostile and rebellious.[14]

These children learn to measure their worth by what they do rather than by who they are. When they ultimately fail, they internalize the experience as a lowering of self-worth. They feel incompetent, as if nothing they do is good enough. They often feel inherently defective for being unable to meet parental expectations, and they describe themselves as failures even when they succeed.

Dana described how she was caught in this no-win cycle:

> There was little open conflict in my family. Everybody was always trying to do everything right and anticipate anything that could create trouble before it happened. We operated from the avoidance of conflict. My dad didn't get angry; he got cold and sarcastic. I learned early that the wrongdoing around my house meant freeze time, an awful, tangible chill! I'd rather have been beaten. It was worse than a slap across the face. I always feared that if I didn't meet my parents' expectations, they would withhold their love and abandon me emotionally. That had a big effect on my self-esteem. The way to have self-esteem was to be good, to be right, to do well, to be perfect. I never had a sense that my parents were people to talk to or to turn to when I was in trouble. I didn't feel loved and accepted, even though I know my parents were well-intentioned. They were always the last people on earth I wanted to know my business, because there was no history of that kind of intimacy. There was a focus on the belief that "you are what you do."

The Making of a Chameleon

When Dana was a child, her dad gave her a dollar every time she read Dale Carnegie's *How to Win Friends and Influence People*, a book that she internalized:

It emphasizes the people-pleasing stuff—tuning in to others and making them feel important. Underneath all that manipulation is the need to control how others feel about you. That's how I can feel okay about myself. As an adult, I still struggle with whether it's okay for me to be different from others. It's been okay for other people to be different from me, but the issue of my being different from them is based on a security within myself that I'm okay even if others don't like me. Being accepted and understood has been one of my own coping devices, being a good girl, a good daughter, doing all the things I'm supposed to do. I often laid myself open too much, too soon and ended up hurt and resentful in my adult relationships with a lot of self-doubt about not being smart enough to figure out who to trust and how much.

If you're a child of a workaholic, you might have learned to conform and become an approval seeker, searching for the acceptance you never had. Chances are, you learned early in childhood that doing "right"—which often means doing what others want—is more important than being who you are. You learned to mold your attitudes, emotions, and behaviors around the wishes of others, usually the dominant workaholic parent.

Whose Drum Do You Dance To?

What about you? Have you disowned your true self and tried to measure up outwardly, becoming whoever and whatever it took to get the approval you craved? If so, somewhere along the way you lost touch with who you are on the inside, becoming a chameleon, yet one who is viewed as accomplished and held in high regard. You developed an outward focus (or an external locus of control), an undeveloped sense of self, and a lack of differentiation. Simply put, this means you became other-centered and perceive yourself as being "at effect" instead of "at cause." People with an external locus of control tend to be more pessimistic and to respond more negatively in general to the vicissitudes of life. They are at risk of being victimized by life rather than empowered by it and having codependent relationships as adults.[15]

Case studies of adult children of workaholics confirm that, in order to gain parental attention, the children learned to gauge their emotions and behaviors according to the expectations of their high-achieving parents.

Everything I did as a kid was based on accomplishment and goals. I tried hard and got awards for everything: outstanding academic scholarship, band, choir, being captain of the football team. But the one award I never won was my dad's love and attention. He was always working. Oh, yeah, he

Making Amends

There's almost always unfinished business between workaholic parents and their children, whether kids are twelve or twenty. As a parent, you might not have the luxury of quitting your job to mend damaged relationships. Nor do you need to. But if you're a workaholic, part of your Twelve-Step recovery is to repair tense and broken relationships (see the appendix for more information on the Twelve Steps). Step 8 says: "We made a list of all persons we had harmed and became willing to make amends to them all." And Step 9 says: "We made direct amends to such people wherever possible, except when to do so would injure them or others."

Sound advice comes from an interview with Bill Smith, who suggests that workaholics use the tools of their trades to revive closeness: "Write a love note to your son or daughter or wife telling them how much they mean to you. Pull out your calendar and make appointments to meet with your children one by one. No one on their deathbed wishes they'd spent less time with their family."[16]

Think of special activities you can initiate with your children, such as long walks and heart-to-heart talks. Take an active interest in their lives by listening to what they have to say, finding out what they've been up to, and paying attention to how you interact with them. Everybody has bad days but try to avoid coming home in foul moods or unloading your anger on family members. Focus on the positive things your children do instead of harping on the negative.

Save newspaper reading or work until young children are asleep. Consider carving out quality time with youngsters, perhaps helping them with homework, playing games, scheduling weekday or weekend family outings, or facilitating family projects. Preparing meals together and having pleasant mealtime conversations (with the television and all other electronic devices turned off) is another way to restore family rituals and celebrations that have disappeared. Practicing daily rituals is the glue that holds your family together. This glue is neutralized when workaholics forgo the bedrock ritual of nightly dinners. Family members become virtual strangers, losing track of who's doing what and how each one is feeling about his or her life. Research backs the idea that rituals keep loved ones stabilized and help them fare better amid the chaotic juggling of each day's diverse activities. So, make it a point to celebrate birthdays, holidays, and anniversaries.

If you're like many adult children of workaholics, no matter how hard your parent tries to mend past mistakes, you feel the divide is too great, that your workaholic parent's overtures are too little, too late. If that's the case, consider discussing your natural resentment with a trusted counselor to see if it's possible for you to work toward reconciliation with your workaholic parent.

would come to my games and criticize what I did wrong. He *always* looked for a better way to do things. His way was the right way. What about all those things I did right? "I'm proud of you" would've been nice. I just wanted him to play catch with me or hit me on the head with a pillow and say, "How ya doing?" To this day it's hard for me to sit in a room without having a project or a product. I guess something in me is still trying to grab my dad's attention.

You must be perfect to receive love, so you try to please, even if it means being someone you're not. And you often don't think for yourself or venture outside a safe comfort zone for fear of ridicule. In attempting to please, you gauge your emotions and actions by those of your workaholic parent. In short, you learn to dance to the beat of your workaholic parent's drum instead of your own.

Tips for Clinicians

As a clinician, you will be called on to work with children of workaholics who have a variety of needs. There's almost always unfinished business in family relationships on the part of parents, their children, or both. You might work indirectly with children through their workaholic parents—children struggling to alter their lives to accommodate their families. Or you might work directly with young children or, retrospectively, with adult children of workaholics.

REPAIRING RELATIONSHIPS WITH CHILDREN

Workaholics' self-care plans usually address how they can put more thought, care, and time into their often-neglected relationships with their children. This is an important area for you to explore with workaholic clients. Understanding the nature of the parent-child relationship and setting goals to repair damaged relationships are essential parts of the workaholic's individual psychotherapy.

Your workaholic clients will benefit from knowing that investing in relationships is a good use of their time. After assessing their view of relationships, you can help them set aside time to rebuild damaged relationships and make time for the people they're with now.

Explore the importance of family time with workaholics. Research shows that families are not as close when they eat on the run or in shifts as when they sit down together for a meal. Households where holidays are observed, and birthdays and anniversaries are recognized and celebrated have stronger relationship bonds than homes where life's markers are ignored. Rituals such as a family dinnertime provide an anchor when loved ones are caught in the whirlwind of today's fast-paced society. Together time heals tensions and teaches kids the importance both of togetherness and of having plans and seeing them through. Rituals provide stability and dependability and make family members feel they have something to count on. When families value and practice rituals, they generally have less anxiety and fewer signs of stress related to burnout. You can explore with clients the rituals they can put back in their lives to restore family cohesion and heal tensions in relationships.

WORKING WITH SUBPERSONALITY PARTS

One of the most effective ways to help workaholics rebuild relationships is working with their subpersonalities or parts.[17] Internal Family Systems Therapy (IFS for short), developed by Dr. Richard Schwartz is one of the best approaches for working with the workaholic subpersonality or part of the individual client (I discuss the IFS approach in detail in chapter 14). A *subpersonality* is an aspect of your personality or a part of you that shows up on a temporary basis to help you cope in different situations. You can be forceful at times, yielding at others. Sometimes you're in the mood for a burger; other times you prefer a salad. Using IFS to isolate and work with the workaholic part helps clients see that they are multidimensional—more than their workaholic label—more than they think of themselves as being.

This approach gives clients a broader perspective to explore their disowned parts, embracing aspects of themselves that their workaholism unwittingly eclipsed. Most workaholics have highly developed manager parts—the part of the character that brings home the bacon, focuses on goals, and exercises the virtues of strength, persistence, decisiveness, self-denial, and determination. Individual counseling shows clients how to develop the other aspects of themselves that form connections to others, love fun, and are calm, centered, confident, and compassionate.

Reese, the forty-six-year-old president of a large computer company, had built a business from the ground up with the determination and perseverance that had taken him from poverty to great wealth. But his workaholic part's singular focus on goals led to communication problems, causing disgruntled employees to leave in droves. His workaholism left his wife fed up and produced teenaged children who, feeling they could never meet their father's impossible standards, used drugs and got into trouble at school. Labeled the tyrant workaholic at work and the Nazi parent at home, he had a genuine desire to change.

I encouraged Reese to continue to value his determination and hard-working parts but also to get in touch with his wise, creative inner elder who helped him slow down, see the magic of process, stay in the present moment, smell the flowers, and enjoy each instant of life as he moved toward his accomplishments. The wise elder helped Reese control less and delegate more, trusting his employees to be creative and find their own ways to get the job done.

I also helped Reese get in touch with his compassionate self, which allowed his caring and love to flow, as well as his passion and commitment. His compassionate self helped Reese be more accepting of all people, especially his employees, wife, and children. It helped him recognize human frailty when his workers made mistakes or revealed weaknesses. He used this part to listen, show genuine appreciation for his employees' hard work, and praise them for good work, which his workaholic part had often failed to do. The compassionate self also pulled out his iPhone, scheduled date nights with his wife, and carved out special moments to be with his children.

Reese also discovered his clown—the fun-loving and playful part of him—to restore the joy and freedom he had forfeited to complete tasks. The clown helped Reese see the lighter side of life at home and work, as well as to enjoy laughing and being with people. He started planning trips with his family and instituted birthday celebrations and employee picnics to boost morale at work. He became less serious about financial security, less perfectionistic, less explosive, and more lighthearted.

YOUNG CHILDREN OF WORKAHOLICS

Professionals who work with children often fail to assist those who come from workaholic homes because, as we have seen, these children appear to be immune to the effects of the parent's hard-driving approach, competitiveness, and perfectionism. As adults, these children are usually well liked and accomplished, and they excel in their careers. Their low self-esteem, anxiety, or depression are often masked by resiliency, over-responsibility, and exaggerated self-reliance. You can look underneath the veneer to see if young and adult children of workaholics are driving themselves for approval, providing the following tips to workaholic parents or directly to children of workaholics:

❖ Be on the lookout for "overly competent" children who appear to be functioning at their maximum. It's important to mention that not all successful or competent children are suffering in the way described in this chapter. When you find children with an *overdeveloped* sense of accomplishment, responsibility, and perfectionism, you can make sure that they get as much attention as other children who may find it easier to show their needs or ask for help.

❖ Insist that children of workaholics do not sacrifice or forgo potential benefits derived from activities, experiences, or interactions because they are too busy putting others' needs before their own.

❖ Avoid being overly critical, comparing the child to others, overencouraging him or her or setting unattainable goals, and overcommitting the child to activities without evidence of a natural interest or consent.

❖ Continue to present children of workaholics with challenges that match their developmental abilities but help them learn not to take on too much. Avoid having unusually high expectations and burdening these children with adultlike responsibilities, even when they are eager to accept and capable of accepting them.

❖ Let children know that it's okay to relax and do nothing. Reassure them that they don't always have to be producing to please someone else, that it's acceptable to please themselves—which can include doing nothing.

❖ Encourage youngsters in their successes and enjoy their accomplishments with them but let them know that it's also acceptable to fail and that they don't have to be perfect in everything they attempt. Encourage significant adults in their lives to let youngsters see them fail and handle failure in a constructive way.

❖ Affirm children and provide them with unconditional support for who they are, regardless of their achievements. Let them know they're valued even when they're not producing, that they're accepted regardless of whether they succeed or fail. Be there for them in case of a big failure or letdown. Help children understand that success is built on failure.

❖ Encourage children to identify their true feelings and to express them often in conversations or through creative outlets.

❖ Provide children with guidance as they make difficult decisions that parents have left up to them, such as how and where to spend their after-school time.

❖ Provide children with opportunities for noncompetitive games so they can enjoy the sheer fun of play and enjoy their childhood with other youngsters their age, rather than spending all their time with adults in adult activities. Welcome laughter, giggling, and even silliness by building in funny stories or experiences during the day and suggest creative here-and-now activities to balance out the focus on products and future-oriented activities.

ADULT CHILDREN OF WORKAHOLICS

Children of workaholics often grow into adults who are envied by everyone: responsible, achievement oriented, able to take charge of any situation. At least that's how they appear to the outside world. Inside, they often feel like little kids who can never do anything right, holding themselves up mercilessly to standards of perfection.

You can screen for work addiction in the families of origin during the intake process with any client, just as you would for alcoholism and other addictions. When you identify work addiction, you can use this information to implement a therapeutic plan for adult clients. In cases where adult clients identify living or having lived with a workaholic parent as the presenting problem, you can help them learn how to avoid enabling parental work addiction. You can inform clients of the potential damage of joining in the compulsive work habits out of their need to spend time with their parents and of bringing them work to do when they go to bed sick. You can help clients refuse to make alibis for their parents' absenteeism or lateness at parties or family get-togethers and let their parents be responsible for explanations. Consider pointing out the importance of not enabling workaholics by refusing to assume their household chores, return phone calls, fulfill family obligations for them, or cover for them at business meetings or social gatherings. It's important for the children to understand that building their lives around the workaholic's busy schedule only sets them up for further hurt and disappointment.

Try helping adult children of workaholics lower their perfectionistic standards to set more reachable goals and delegate tasks in the office or at home. Help them to be less self-critical and to strengthen their inner, nurturing voice, and teach them to affirm themselves for who they are and not just for what they do. Providing unconditional support for themselves as individuals— not just measuring their worth by what they produce or achieve—can be a major step forward for people who have spent their lives measuring their value according to the standards and approval of others.

You can teach stress-relief exercises or refer adult children of workaholics to workshops or special classes where they can learn yoga, mindfulness meditation, and other relaxation techniques to help them live more in the moment. Inform them about how to use "Microcare"—*small* micro-adjustments in your work habits that make a *big* boost in your work health and wellness—to promote their mental health while working (see the discussion in chapter 9).[18] And teach them how to develop flexibility by building in spontaneous, spur-of-the-moment activities and welcoming fun and laughter, perhaps by deciding to go to the beach at the last minute, or by walking barefoot and umbrella-less in a summer rain shower.

Encourage clients to deliberately do something imperfectly to get a taste of the freedom from perfection: going for a week without making their bed, finding a process-oriented activity or hobby that can't be measured by a standard of perfection, painting their feelings on a canvas, or engaging in activities like learning a new dance that permits them to make and learn from mistakes.

Bibliotherapy

The following readings relate to the content in this chapter:

- ❖ Tara Brach, *Radical Acceptance: Embracing Your Life with the Heart of a Buddha* (New York: Bantam, 2003).
- ❖ James Clear, *Atomic Habits: An Easy and Proven Way to Build Good Habits and Break Bad Ones* (New York: Penguin Random House, 2018).
- ❖ Stephen Guise, *How to Be an Imperfectionist: The New Way to Self-Acceptance, Fearless Living, and Freedom from Perfectionism* (Orlando, FL: Selective Entertainment LLC, 2015).
- ❖ Richard Schwartz, *No Bad Parts: Healing Trauma and Restoring Wholeness with the Internal Family Systems Model* (Boulder, CO: Sounds True, 2021).

Risky Business

Invasion of the Balance Snatchers

It's Been a Hard Day's Night

Work Stress and Job Burnout

I lied and said I was busy.
I was busy;
but not in a way most people understand.
I was busy taking deeper breaths.
I was busy silencing irrational thoughts.
I was busy calming a racing heart.
I was busy telling myself I am okay.
Sometimes, this is my busy—
and I will not apologize for it.
　　　　　　　　　—Brittin Oakman[1]

Arianna Huffington Awakens in a Pool of Blood

On the morning of April 6, 2007, I was lying on the floor of my home office in a pool of blood. On my way down, my head had hit the corner of my desk, cutting my eye and breaking my cheekbone. I had collapsed from exhaustion and lack of sleep. In the wake of my collapse, I found myself going from doctor to doctor, from brain MRI to CAT scan to echocardiogram, to find out if there was any underlying medical problem beyond exhaustion. There wasn't, but doctors' waiting rooms, it turns out, were good places for me to ask myself a lot of questions about the kind of life I was living.

We founded the *Huffington Post* in 2005, and two years in, we were growing at an incredible pace. I was on the cover of magazines and had been chosen by *Time* as one of the world's 100 Most Influential People. But after my fall, I had to ask myself, "Was this what success looked like? Was this the life I wanted?" I was working eighteen hours a day, seven days a week, trying to build a business, expand our coverage, and bring in investors. But my life, I realized, was out of control. In terms of the traditional measures of success, which focus on money and power, I was very successful. But I was not living a successful life by any sane definition of success. I knew something had to radically change. I could not go on that way.

This was the classic wake-up call. Looking back on my life, I had other times when I should have woken up but didn't. This time I really did and made many changes in the way I live my life, including adopting daily practices to keep me on track—and out of doctors' waiting rooms. The result is a more fulfilling life, one that gives me breathing spaces and a deeper perspective.[2]

Invasion of the Balance Snatchers

In the 1956 science fiction horror flick *Invasion of the Body Snatchers*, a small-town doctor learns that alien duplicates are replacing the population of his community. The first time I saw the film, it scared the crap out of me—still does every time I watch it. In the movie, alien plant spores fall from space and grow into large seedpods, each one capable of reproducing a duplicate replacement copy of everyone in town. As each pod reaches full development, it assimilates the physical characteristics, memories, and personalities of each townsperson. Everyone in town is looking over their shoulders, wondering if they'll be duplicated next. The horror movie ends on a pessimistic note: "Where you gonna go, where you gonna hide? Nowhere . . . cause there's no one like you left."

Thankfully, you don't have to guard against body snatchers, but watch out. Balance snatchers are everywhere. They invade your life, lead to work-life imbalance and work addiction, debilitate you, and make you less efficient at your job. In previous chapters, you read about the inherent problems of work addiction and how cunning and baffling it is for workaholics and their families. Part III of this book examines how overworking and work stress can slither into every aspect of your life and create job stress and burnout (as Arianna's story illustrates), if you're not conscious of water-tight boundaries. What about you? Are you stretching your days into the wee hours to juggle more tasks, taking work home, leashing yourself to electronic devices, making yourself available 24/7, giving up much-needed vacation time? Living this way keeps your natural defenses on high alert, marinating you in your stress juices (cortisol and adrenaline), and clobbering you with mental and physical fatigue.

But suppose the body snatcher scenario happened in the reverse in a good way? What if your workaholic brain were snatched and replaced with a duplicate version of you with more work-life balance, less stress, wider perspective of the world, and more positive emotions with time to play and spend with loved ones. What would become of the workaholic you? Where will it go and what will you do? Will there be others like you who understand? And how would it change your life?

Out of her own burnout recovery, Arianna Huffington founded a company, Thrive Global, dedicated to stress reduction, burnout prevention, and well-being. This chapter is about identifying your balance snatchers—those external forces that insinuate themselves into your life, throwing it into turmoil. I will show you how you can enjoy career success while working hard, being kind to and compassionate with yourself, keeping a positive attitude, and maintaining work-life balance.

Thank God It's Monday (TGIM)!

In our technologically driven culture, there are more things to do as life moves faster. And as the line that once protected private hours gets erased, you might feel that your work-life balance is off. Although information technology and the workplace enable work addiction, they are no more to blame than the ABC store is to blame for alcoholism, or the grocery store for food addiction. Workaholics are often lonely wage earners who arrive at their desks before anyone else and are the last to leave. They prefer not to take time off, or if they do, they take their work along with them. Fun and laughter are frivolous wastes of time, and workaholics feel contempt for people who are humorous, carefree, and underproductive, or who keep an even pace in their work lives. The paradox is that work stress and job burnout undermine your health and productivity.

Many workers dread facing a new workweek after a relaxing weekend, but if you're a workaholic, chances are you white-knuckled your way through the down time and cannot wait to get back to the office on Monday. While your coworkers have the Monday-morning blahs, you're revved up and ready to go. You're probably not a team player, and your need for control makes it difficult to work cooperatively and participate in give-and-take situations. You believe your approach and style are best, and you cannot entertain less perfect solutions. When your narrow perspective prevails on the job, spontaneity and creativity are diminished. Back in the day, some management experts went so far as to say that the best advice for any workaholic is to work alone or only with other workaholics.[3]

Could You Be a Shooting Star?

As you can see, workaholics toil on shaky ground. They're not the high-level performers management perceives them to be. Truth be told, workaholics hurt the company because they're addicted not to getting results, but to the process of working. They tend to be motivated more by fear and loss of status than by high-level motivations like the desire to make a creative contribution. And they're more reluctant than optimal performers to take necessary risks in the organization to achieve positive, creative outcomes. Table 9.1 shows the characteristics that distinguish optimal performers from workaholics.

The career trajectories of workaholics tend to follow a predictable trend. Like shooting stars, they burst onto the scene, are viewed as "up and coming," rise quickly based on their initial big splash, and then level off, consumed with managing the details of their careers. The leveling off ordinarily starts at midlife, accompanied by cardiovascular disease, psychosomatic disorders, alcoholism, drug use, and marital problems.

A body of research shows that lengthy work hours lead to job burnout, quickly extinguishing the fever pitch and harming employee mental and physical health.[4] British researchers discovered that workers who put in more than eleven hours a day were 67 percent more likely to have a heart attack, compared to those who put in fewer hours.[5] And a 2017 study found that working over forty-eight hours per week was tied to poorer mental health, higher levels of anxiety and depression, reduced sleep, and more sleep disturbances.[6]

TABLE 9.1.

Profile of Optimal Performers in the Workplace

Optimal Performers Are:	Workaholics Are:
Good collaborators or delegators	Unable to delegate work or work as a team; they work best alone
Socially gregarious	Employees with few or no friends
Employees who enjoy the process and outcome of work	Employees who work for the sake of working
Motivated by intrinsic needs and the desire to make creative contributions	Motivated by fear and loss of status
Efficient; they see the whole picture as well as the details	Inefficient; they get bogged down with details
Creative risk takers who stretch beyond customary bounds	Reluctant to take chances to achieve creative outcomes
Masters of self-correction; when they make mistakes, they learn from them	Unable to tolerate mistakes; they try to avoid them or cover them up

Multitasking: Fueling the Burn

You might consider multitasking to be an essential survival tool in a 24/7 work culture that expects immediate results. But if you think multitasking is the ticket to more productivity, think again. Experts agree that multitasking contributes to burnout and can be hazardous in certain jobs like medicine. Your ability to do things well suffers when you try to complete too many tasks at one. Scientists have found juggling email messages, phone calls, and text messages undermines your ability to focus and produce, fatiguing your brain in the process.[7] University of Michigan researchers report that when you're bouncing between several tasks, you're forcing your brain to keep refocusing with each rebound, reducing productivity by up to 40 percent. They conclude that multitasking undermines productivity, efficiency, quality of life, and results in several half-baked projects that leave workers overwhelmed and stressed out.[8]

Studies from Stanford University confirm that heavy multitaskers have more stress because of trouble focusing and shutting out irrelevant information.[9] In an effort to handle the overload from prolonged multitasking, scientists say, your brain rewires itself, causing fractured thinking and lack of concentration. As a result, if you're a multitasker, you waste more time taking longer to switch among tasks and are less efficient at juggling problems than people who don't multitask.[10]

According to a 2021 WHO study, overwork led to more than 745,000 deaths a year from stroke and heart attack. The study reported that the number of deaths due to long work hours from heart disease increased by 42 percent and from stroke by 19 percent between 2000 and 2016. In South Korea, working long hours was a badge of honor until work pressure slowed labor productivity and played a role in more than five hundred suicides a year, spawning a law that capped workweeks at fifty-two hours.[11]

Even if you're not a workaholic, chances are you're having trouble finding work-life balance. A team of Canadian and American researchers found that nearly half of American workers take work home with them and many of them say work interferes with family, social, and leisure aspects of their lives.[12] People who work more than fifty hours a week have the most interference in their personal lives. A total of 40 percent of people under forty-five say they check their work email after hours or on vacation; one in seven say electronic devices cut into time spent with spouses, and one in ten say these devices cut into time spent with their children.[13]

Research shows that longer hours on the job lead to elevated work stress which, in turn, causes you to be a more disgruntled and less effective worker.[14] Compared to managers putting in fewer hours, those who work longer hours suffer greater anxiety, depression, and burnout and have twice the number of health-related problems. And as I mentioned earlier, British researchers observed that long workweeks in high-pressure jobs contribute to the risk of burnout and heart attack. Workers who put in more than eleven hours a day were 67 percent more likely to have a heart attack than those who had a more balanced work schedule.[15] No job is worth the risk of stroke or heart attack, but it's a risk that many workaholics, like Jonathan Frostick, are willing to take.

What Near Death Taught Jonathan about Balance[16]

On a Sunday afternoon in 2021, Jonathan Frostick suffered a heart attack. But instead of seeing his life flash before his eyes, the HSBC regulatory program manager in the United Kingdom said one of his first thoughts was, "I needed to meet with my manager tomorrow, this isn't convenient." From his hospital bed, Jonathan Frostick posted on *LinkedIn* what his eleven-hour workdays and near death taught him about work/life balance and six changes he vowed to make:

So, I had a heart attack . . . This is not how I planned my Sunday. It was pretty standard up to 4 p.m. Morning coffee, a trip to the local country park, a shopping trip, and a late lunch. I sat down at my desk at 4 p.m. to prep for this week's work. And then I couldn't really breathe. My chest felt constrained, I had what I can only describe as surges in my left arm, my neck, my ears were popping. I didn't get a flash of light or my life racing through my mind. Instead, I had the following thoughts:

1. F— I needed to meet with my manager tomorrow, this isn't convenient.
2. How do I secure the funding for X (work stuff)?
3. S—, I haven't updated my will.
4. I hope my wife doesn't find me dead.

I got to the bedroom so I could lie down and got the attention of my wife, who phoned 999. I've since made the following decisions whilst I've laid here, on the basis I don't die:

1. I'm not spending all day on Zoom anymore.
2. I'm restructuring my approach to work.

3. I'm not going to be putting up with any s#%t at work ever again—life literally is too short.
4. I'm losing 15 kg. (approximately 35 lbs.).
5. I want every day to count for something at work else I'm changing my role.
6. I want to spend more time with my family.

And that, so far, is what near death has taught me. Today is four weeks since my heart attack. I can almost still feel every moment as I walked up our driveway thinking how out of breath I was, getting a coffee, sitting down . . . And then the overwhelming sensation that my heart was in my throat, like indigestion that wouldn't pass, the throbbing in my throat, jawline, my arm. Even then I was wondering what was happening. I'm just grateful to be here, to have the chance to be the best I can now be for my wife and children, and to help others. Thank you all for all of your comments, it's really helped me.

I've Been Working like a Dog

In 1974, Herbert Freudenberger coined the buzzword "burnout."[17] Until recently, burnout was considered a pop psychology term, unrecognized as a legitimate psychological or psychiatric disorder or an official disease, tossed around the office with abandon. As you saw earlier, that changed in 2019 when the WHO reached a milestone, officially classifying burnout as a medical diagnosis and including the condition in the *International Classification of Diseases*, the handbook that guides medical providers in diagnosing diseases. It describes burnout as "a syndrome conceptualized as resulting from chronic workplace stress that has not been successfully managed."[18]

There's a difference between burnout and stress. You can recover from stress with certain management techniques, but burnout is a totally different animal, resulting from cumulative stress that hasn't been managed. Once burnout gets its hooks into you, you can't cure it by taking an extended vacation, slowing down, or working fewer hours. Your system literally shuts down physically, emotionally, mentally, and spiritually. You're out of gas, and you've given up all hope of surmounting your obstacles. When you're suffering from burnout, it's more than just fatigue. You have a deep sense of disillusionment and hopelessness that your efforts have been in vain. Life loses its meaning, and small tasks feel like a hike up Mount Everest. Your interests and motivation dry up, and you fail to meet even the smallest obligations. And you do just enough to get by. The following symptoms can help you recognize it:

- ❖ Mental and physical energy depletion, fatigue, or exhaustion
- ❖ Increased mental distance from your job, or feelings of negativism or cynicism related to your job
- ❖ Reduced professional efficacy
- ❖ Moodiness, impatience, and short-tempered
- ❖ Loss of motivation and a reduced interest in commitments
- ❖ Inability to meet obligations
- ❖ Lowered immunity to illness
- ❖ Emotional detachment from previous involvements
- ❖ Feeling efforts are unappreciated
- ❖ Withdrawal from coworkers and social situations
- ❖ Hopeless, helpless, and depressed outlook
- ❖ Job absenteeism and inefficiency
- ❖ Sleep deprivation
- ❖ Foggy thinking and trouble concentrating

A 2020 Gallup survey reported that most employees—76 percent to be exact—experience job burnout, and 63 percent of burnt-out employees were more likely to take a sick day. And 23 percent tended to visit an emergency room, were 2.6 times as likely to be actively seeking a different job, have 13 percent lower confidence in their performance, and were half as likely to discuss how to approach performance goals with their managers. The burnt-out employees were two times more likely to agree that the amount of time their job takes makes it difficult to fulfill family responsibilities.

As the workplace headed into 2022—the third year of the pandemic—the incidence of job burnout jumped to an all-time high. The American Psychological Association's Work and Well-Being study found that 79 percent of the 1,501 employees surveyed experienced work-related stress in the month before the survey. Three in five workers said work-related stress caused them to have a lack of interest, motivation and energy at work. Plus, 36 percent had cognitive weariness, 32 percent emotional exhaustion, and 44 percent physical fatigue—a 38 percent jump from 2019.[19]

When you're burnt out, your workaholic brain is the major contributor because it never sleeps. It works overtime, always on 24/7 alert for a threat. Constantly on guard—scanning, hyper vigilant, worrying, processing, discerning—and reacting time and again to things you can't control is exhausting. The uncertainties of world events, financial pressures, tight dead-lines, health worries, job loss, performance anxiety, to name a few. Your brain wants you to succeed but only in the safety of its cocoon. It holds you back in its comfort zone because it views the world as dangerous and doesn't want you to get your head blown off.

When you continue to overinvest in your job, fatigue sets in, and errors and accidents increase. You become less efficient than your coworkers who put in fewer hours planning and working toward a job goal. In contrast to you, the workaholic, your optimally performing coworker has warm, outgo-ing relationships and a good collaborative sense, and has mastered the art of delegating.

Burning the Candle at Both Ends

Burning the candle at both ends might start to manifest as the need to be needed, an inability to say no, the need to be in control, or an inability to let go until your workaholic engine burns out, as with Arianna. Or it might surprise you to know that it could be something else much more subtle and, in some cases, even sinister.

While I was conducting research on workaholics and family dynam-ics, Gayle Porter, an organizational psychologist at Rutgers University, was studying the impact of workaholism in the workplace. Porter continued to emphasize that work addiction leads to workplace inefficiency and erodes trust throughout the organization even though corporate America failed to focus on the problems resulting from work addiction—even extolling its virtues.[20]

She described how the amount of effort workaholics put into their jobs eventually exceeds their level of productivity. They overwork even when the work task could be completed in less time:

This is the person who convinces himself that working on Saturday is necessary and spends time carefully lining up tasks that would not be completed without doing so. In comparison, another worker exerts extra effort during the week, asks for help, or finds more efficient ways to approach the task to have the weekend off. Both accomplish the required task. However, the first worker has devoted more of the week to doing so. To some, that person would appear to be more involved in the job, or appear to be the harder worker, but the motive was not to do better, only to keep doing.[21]

Porter also discovered that it's not uncommon for workaholics to generate a crisis and then get attention and praise for resolving it:

> During a crisis, everyone's attention goes to its resolution. Rarely is time taken to reexamine the history of decision points at which the crisis might have been averted, but the cost of meeting crisis conditions is significant. All organization members should be concerned about the possibility that someone in their midst may contribute to or create crisis. Indeed, managers focus on praise for those who function well during that time. The same person could be playing both roles, and this person may be a workaholic.[22]

Burning Out at the Office? Try 'Microcare'

The prefix "micro" means short or extremely small, but there's nothing small about Microcare's big potential to promote your mental health and productivity in a small amount of time. And because of their shortened versions, there are various types of Microcare—*small* micro-adjustments in your work habits that make a *big* boost in your work health and wellness. They are ideal for workers who say they don't have time to take a break from their jobs. *Microbreaks, Microsteps, Microchillers, Microweeks, and Microcations* are versions of how major companies have jumped on the Microcare prevention train to encourage onsite balance and calm down employees' stress and anxiety. During the COVID-19 quarantine beginning in 2020, as the combined merits of mindfulness and remote working showed increases in productivity, more corporate leaders jumped onboard.

Sharat Sharan, CEO, president, and co-founder of ON24, a San Francisco-based marketing technology company, touted the advantages of Micro meditation because, he acknowledged that personal health and energy are passed down to your team. "After the great recession, I started meditating and now begin every day with twelve minutes of meditation," he said. "That routine has helped me stay mindful, pragmatic and put out positive energy. In the midst of a crisis, you need to personally embody the attitude that you want your team and your own business to demonstrate."

Chronic workaholism and job pressures create roadblocks to relaxation, job engagement, and productivity and exacerbate burnout, especially in today's world of remote and hybrid work. A new study from Microsoft's Human Factors Lab found that virtual fatigue is definitely real, but workers can counteract stress accumulation by taking short breaks between meetings during the day.[23]

Microsoft researchers monitored the brain activity of study participants and found that virtual fatigue begins to set in roughly thirty minutes into a meeting. They discovered that the brain works differently when employees take breaks between meetings, stopping cumulative stress from building up, giving our brains a chance to "reset."

In back-to-back meetings for two hours, subjects' brains showed a steady increase of beta waves, which reduces the brain's ability to focus and engage. But when participants took a break between meetings, the beta activity decreased. Even more fascinating, the beta waves remained low even when followed by four additional consecutive virtual meetings. Researchers also found that back-to-back virtual meetings weaken our focus and engagement, but when participants took breaks to reset, engagement held steady. Lastly, the study showed that transitions between virtual meetings, when done with no breaks, can cause significant stress. But when participants took even short breaks in between, beta waves dropped and didn't spike as much at the beginning of the next meeting. As the report sums it up: The antidote to meeting fatigue is simple: taking short breaks.

Scientists at North Carolina State University corroborated Microsoft's findings, showing the value of *Microbreaks* or what I call *Microchillers*—five-minute time outs—throughout the workday. These short breaks are effective energy management strategies and can be as simple as stretching, walking up and down stairs, gazing out a window at nature, snacking or having a five-minute mindful meditation. The researchers conducted two studies. In the first study, on days when full-time employees had poor sleep quality, they experienced higher fatigue the next morning and took Microbreaks more frequently at work. After taking Microbreaks, they had higher work engagement during the day and lower end-of-work fatigue. Study 2 replicated and confirmed Study 1 that poor sleep quality led to morning fatigue. When workers took Microbreaks, work engagement improved, and end-of-work fatigue declined.[24]

CEO Arianna Huffington agrees that *Microsteps* are the big idea too small to fail.[25] By making very small changes, you have the power to change your life. Microsteps are the foundation to Thrive Global's behavior change platform:

At Thrive Global, we've even brought *Reset* into our meetings, beginning each of our All Hands with a different member of our team sharing their Reset with the rest of the company," she said. "Instead of launching straight into updates and announcements, we get an intimate glimpse of our colleagues by being brought into their world—the people, the music, and the quotes they love. And it's amazing how much we can learn about each other in sixty seconds. Reset within a meeting creates a dynamic that helps us all more authentically connect—all the more important when we're not physically together.

Huffington's company also implemented "Thrive Time" to sidestep employee burnout. "It's based on the recognition that, of course, getting results and meeting deadlines often requires putting in extra time and going the extra mile," Huffington said. "And that's certainly true at Thrive. Thrive Time is what allows us to sustain that. It means taking time off to recover and recharge after you've met the deadline, shipped the product, or worked over the weekend. It could be a few hours, a morning, a whole day or even more."

More companies like Microsoft and Kickstarter are implementing *Microweeks* or four-day workweeks. Due to burnout during the "Great Resignation," job seekers are looking for shortened workweeks to alleviate burnout, give them a break from virtual fatigue, and provide a chance to handle personal matters. And if you're one of the 47 percent of Americans who refuse vacations because it's too stressful to plan a big getaway or concerned corporate honchos would frown upon your absence, consider a new trend called *Microcations*— short getaways of fewer than five nights, such as a four-day weekend to attend a wedding or family event. Microcations are designed for workaholics as a baby step in helping them to detach from work to see that their work will survive if they take a bit of time away. Microcations have increased in popularity with workers taking several of them over the course of a year instead of a week or two-week vacation in one fell swoop.

Another way to bring more balance into your life is mindfulness or present moment attention to what you're doing throughout the workday. My research team at the University of North Carolina at Charlotte found that mindless workers had statistically higher burnout rates, were more disconnected from the present, and had less self-insight than mindful workers, who showed more present-moment awareness such as clarity, calmness, and connection.

Blaine Vess Makes Micro-Adjustments to Telepressure

Telepressure is a compulsive need to quickly respond to emails, texts, news alerts, voicemails, and other digital messages. It can seduce workaholics or anyone struggling with boundaries into losing themselves in the bottomless pit of work tasks and electronic devices. Research shows that workers with high levels of telepressure are more likely to report lack of focus on the job, burnout, health-related absenteeism, and sleep problems. Plus, their work-life balance is more negatively impacted.[26] CEO Blaine Vess described how he dealt with telepressure when he was running his company by making *micro-adjustments*:

> When I was running my company, I was on email all day. It interrupted me constantly. I always enjoyed working nights and weekends when other people weren't working or emailing me. My philosophy was to keep things moving. I functioned like a switchboard operator—constantly checking to see what message I received and responding or redirecting the sender appropriately. It took me a long time to realize that functioning like a switchboard operator is not real work when you're trying to run a company. I was determined to change my ways.
>
> I landed on a simple tool called Mailman. Just as in real life, the mail carrier delivers mail, Mailman puts your emails in a hidden folder in your email applications so you can still access it when you want. I initially set it to deliver my email twice per day, at noon and five o'clock. I noticed when noon rolled around, I was on my email like a feeding frenzy, and it disrupted my productivity in the afternoon. I also noticed I didn't like receiving email at five when I was spending more time with my wife. Now, I've landed on receiving email once per day at three p.m. That gives me most of the day to work on real tasks. It's also early enough that I can respond to folks before I finish work around five. There were days where I would glance at Mailman's hidden folder to see how many messages were in there. This made me anxious, and I would click into the folder and start answering emails. So, I found another tool to complement Mailman—a Google Chrome extension called "Click to Remove Element" that allows me to hide the mailman folder. If I glance to see how many messages are in there, I can't see the folder, and I can't start answering emails. This simple method of applying "out of sight, out of mind" has been extremely helpful. I also applied this "out of sight, out of mind" mentally to my phone. I turned off Gmail's notifications and deleted the apps for Facebook and LinkedIn. These changes weren't enough, though. I still had the Gmail app and looked at it constantly, even after I was using Mailman and I knew that I wouldn't have received new messages. Then, a friend in Portugal told me how he'd stopped watching and reading the news. This sounded radical to me at first, but I wanted to see if I could figure out a way to block the news from my life. I dug into my iPhone and saw that it had a way to block websites. I started blocking all the sites that I frequently checked, like cnn.com, facebook.com, linkedin.com, gmail.com, news.google.com, and anything else I might visit to distract myself. I even deleted the Gmail app, which I never thought possible. The key to what's worked for me has been the concept of "out of sight, out of mind." It made apps and websites more difficult or impossible to access. These changes have made me a much more present person in my life.

Draw a Line in the Sand

In the space below, name some balance snatchers that have invaded your life:

1.

2.

3.

4.

5.

Then go down the following list of some tried and true ways to set boundaries and check the ones you can apply so that work doesn't invade every corner of your personal life:

❖ Arrange to power down and clock out at a certain time.

❖ Work after hours only when it's absolutely necessary and an exceptional case.

❖ Master your electronic devices instead of becoming a slave to them. Turn them off on breaks, at lunch, and after hours. Put away your laptop, iPhone, or pager just as you would a hammer or saw after working on a cabinet in the den. Make it a rule: no work tools in bed, at the table, or in the den while watching TV.

❖ Learn to say no when someone asks you to do something you don't have time for.

❖ If you have to add a new task, take another one off your to-do list.

❖ Tell yourself there's a limit to what you can do, put the rest out of the picture, and see this as a strength, not a weakness.

❖ Dial back on overtime to reduce your health risks and follow the adage, "Work smarter, not longer."

❖ Stay fit outside the office and think of your work site as the Olympics, where your physical and mental endurance hinges on being in good shape. Then prime yourself with good nutrition and vigorous exercise, avoid nicotine, and if you drink, use alcohol in moderation.

❖ Make an appointment with yourself and schedule something fun in your time off. Indulge yourself with a hobby, hot bath, manicure, yoga, facial, reading, or meditation. Just fifteen or twenty minutes of personal time can lower your stress and raise your energy level.

Gauging Your Work Stress Needle

Workaholics generate crises because they're so caught up in their own distorted and urgent approach to work, perceiving even minor incidences as a crisis. But balanced workers know there are degrees of work stress that cause us to freak out, adding to cumulative burnout. Your work stress needle helps to self-regulate and map job stressors on a regular basis. I start by asking clients to tell me how stressed they feel in various situations to determine the sources of job stress. I use a 10-point scale where 0 is mild stress and 10 is the highest possible stress:

0 1 2 3	4 5 6 7	8 9 10
Mild Work Stress	*Moderate Work Stress*	*Major Work Stress*

Sometimes asking if a situation is worth losing it gives you a change of perspective, brings your "thinking brain" online, and helps to separate small things from the big kahunas. Not to mention it regulates our lizard brain so we don't react with colleagues in ways we might later regret. On the 10-point scale, everyday setbacks such as a printer paper jam are 0-to-3 level triggers. A coworker talking over you in a meeting might be a 4-to-7. And real life-or-death threats and crises such as a coworker collapsing and rushed to the ER score an 8-to-10.

I often notice, for example, that I react to a printer jam (clearly a 1 on the scale below) as if it's a 9 or 10. The quick assessment of the degree of threat from my prefrontal cortex (see chapter 5) brings instant calm. And over time, due to neuroplasticity, I find myself less likely to sweat the small stuff. The needle helps you map work stress progression and get a clearer indication of what types of job situations trigger you, measure how the stress changes over time, and where and with whom threats reside. It also gives information about the conditions under which you're most and least resilient.

When workaholics can remain chill during mundane 0-to-3 triggers, it's easier for them to keep their cool during a dire 4-to-7 event when being calm is essential. Even in some 8-to-10 life crises, it's possible—and arguably more effective—when we can remain calm. Noting specific situations or people you avoid during the workday can help you figure out what threatens you. Your needle might be at a 3 right now, but it might've been a 7 or 8 last week when you made that presentation at work. In situations where your needle is high, you can employ simple Microchillers (see the appendix) such as deep breathing, yoga, and mindfulness meditation, which can lower it.

Suppose you spill milk on the kitchen counter. You can remind yourself that the fumble is a 1, not a 10. Or the coworker in the cubicle next to you carrying on a loud conversation on his cell phone. You let yourself know that's some-where between a 3 or 4, depending on the unique circumstances but still not a 10. Quantifying each upsetting event helps you self-regulate and activates your prefrontal cortex before your amygdala has a chance to throw it offline. Each time you remember to quantify these upsets, you will become more skilled at staying calm.

On the flipside, suppose you treat the spilled milk as an 8, cursing and slamming the carton on the counter, splashing more milk, and getting angrier. Bingo, double jeopardy! Your unbridled second zinger reaction just made spilled milk worse than it was, turning an original 1 into an 8. In effect, you forfeited your power to your emotional brain that hijacked you, making you a victim instead of master of the circumstance. The goal is for you to oversee your reactions, not for your reactions to be in control of you.

Upsetting situations and thoughts raise your stress temperature making it possible for you to be stressed and not recognize it because you've become so accustomed to it. Taking your stress temperature from time to time makes you more mindful of the conditions that cause your stress and reactions—such as time of day or week or the specific circumstances like financial pressures, global concerns, health problems, or job strain—and help you identify and better manage stressors and set boundaries that promote self-regulation.

What about in this moment? You can take your temperature by asking how stressed you feel right now using the 10-point scale. You can also recall times when you were under stress and compare those to how you feel in the present moment. You can use this measurement to map stress patterns by comparing your ratings as they go up or down from one situation to another or from one part of the day to the next, for example, in the morning compared to later in the day. This measurement tells you if your mood sours as the day drags on and what circumstances trigger the shift. This enables you to identify patterns and themes that give insight into your work stress temperature and what you need to change to be calmer, more engaged, and productive on the job.

Take a Vacation Instead of a Guilt Trip

The talk show host Joy Behar said, "I don't like to relax; it stresses me out." And she's not alone. Many people have trouble sitting still, especially workaholics. You may be among the ranks of those who can't seem to quiet their minds but calming your mind can be one of the best antidotes to work stress. And one of the best ways to do that is taking time off.

Unfortunately, fear and guilt are partly responsible for the slow evaporation of vacation days. During breakfast on a recent business trip to New York City,

I chatted with a young executive from Chicago who had come to the Big Apple for a long weekend vacation. I asked her why she hadn't planned to stay longer. "I wish I could," she said, "but my boss frowns upon us being out of the office for more than a few days. I used to not take any vacations until I discovered short trips and long weekends work best. I don't want management to think I'm a slacker. Lazy feet don't eat."

Sadly, the young executive is not alone. You could be among the thousands of American workers taking a guilt trip instead of a vacation. Years ago, I either didn't take vacations or refused to go without my laptop, cellphone, and mountains of work. Although my old habits have changed, they are typical of today's employees, who either haul tons of work on vacations or no longer take time off at all.

The Economic Policy Institute of Washington, D.C., reported that the average American worker took only two and a half weeks of vacation and holidays in 1990—less than the average worker in any other developed country, including Germany, where workers take six weeks a year. In 2004, Management Recruiters International reported that nearly half of U.S. executives said they wouldn't use all their earned vacation because they were too busy at work[27]. A 2010 CareerBuilder survey found that 37 percent of working Americans did not take all their vacation days, an increase from 35 percent in 2009. And of those who did take all their time off, 30 percent worked while on vacation.[28]

In 2012, the average American worker left 9.2 vacation days on the table—up from 6.2 days in 2011—and most people said they did so because they were stressed out by the extra work they had to do around any vacation: "We have to get ahead of our workload in order to leave, and then we have to catch up to our workload upon our return."[29]

In 2018, American workers left a record number of vacation days on the table—768 million days, up 9 percent from 2017—according to research from the U.S. Travel Association, Oxford Economics, and Ipsos. Of the unused days, 236 million were forfeited completely, equating to $65.5 billion in lost benefits. More than half (55 percent) of workers reported they did not use all their allotted time off. And in 2020, 72 percent of Americans did not take a summer vacation, partly due to the pandemic.[30] A 2021 study found that 62 percent of Americans, like the young executive, were afraid to take time off because they were worried that corporate honchos would judge them or label them as a slacker, that they might get passed over for job promotions, or that someone might be angling for their job.[31]

Increasingly, patients in my clinical practice say they are afraid to take vacation days for fear they will not be perceived as team players. Some even say they are afraid to leave the office for lunch, because if positions were cut, they would be the first to go. This worry has increased nationwide. In 1977, 45 percent of people felt secure in their jobs, according to the Families and Work Institute. That number dropped to only 36 percent in 2006.[32]

To make matters worse during the pandemic, nearly half of American workers experienced mental health issues. Yet, employees said mental health wasn't a valid reason to take paid time off (PTO) and that they had so much PTO anxiety they completely avoided scheduling medical appointments four times a year because they didn't want to have to ask for time off.

Vacations and time off from work are essential to bring balance to hard work. For those who say it's not worth the stress getting ahead of your workload to leave, and then catching up on the workload upon return, it's time to give your guilt a rest. Here are some tips to create a seamless transition to relaxation during your time out of the office so you can return renewed and refreshed:

* Buffer your work exits and reentries. Don't work right up until the moment you leave and head back to work as soon as you get off the plane. Schedule an extra day off before you depart and another when you return, to ease back into work slowly.

* Have a plan. When you're away, limit your connection to the office and don't check your electronic devices more than once or twice a day.

* Choose a point person. In your absence, have someone you trust manage day-to-day tasks and make sure your coworkers know you'll be away. In your out-of-office voicemail and email messages, designate a single person to be contacted on matters you consider important.

* Breathe deeply. Meditating and paced breathing stimulate your parasympathetic nervous system, which works to balance the surges of adrenaline and cortisol from work stress. When your lungs are full of air, your body can't produce adrenaline, so it's your body's way of getting you to relax.

* Balance activities. Alternate your time between staying active and resting. A run on the beach and ten minutes of meditation give you two different kinds of biochemical boosts.

Tips for Clinicians

If you're keeping your work and life well balanced, you'll have a lot to say to clients about how to find and hold that balance. Achieving balance when you're a workaholic requires more than cutting back on hours. It involves getting through the denial of your work addiction, deep personal introspection and insights, and attention to the parts of life that you've neglected.

DENIAL

Work addiction is a disorder that tells you that you don't have it. Many workaholics disassociate themselves from the traits of work addiction. Comments such as "I don't work that much," "I spend lots of time with my family," and "I have lots of friends and hobbies" are part of the denial process.

A closer look shows that workaholics' family lives, vacations, friendships, and hobbies often resemble their jobs in being overly scheduled, rapid-fire, and focused on making money. You can help clients with denial by having them describe the balance in their lives and probe them about the comments that family members or colleagues make regarding their work style. Outsider feedback is often in direct contradiction to the workaholic's assertion. You can use these contradictory reports and comments as evidence with which to confront the denial. Also, spouses, partners, or other loved ones can be invited to attend sessions to give firsthand accounts that might contradict and break through the workaholic's denial. In most cases, someone has penetrated the workaholic's denial before he or she first shows up for counseling.

One of the first comments many workaholics make when they come to therapy is, "Don't tell me I have to quit my job," punctuated by rationalizations such as "I have two kids to support. Are you going to pay my mortgage while I quit work?" or "I love my job." The workaholic's biggest fear is that the only way to recover is to slash work hours or change jobs. The implied belief is: "Either I work, or I don't. There is not an in-between." These statements reflect the rigid all-or-nothing thinking. It reflects their inability to envision a flexible balance between work and leisure or between work and family. It also reflects the driving fear that if they give up their compulsive working, there will be nothing left of their lives and their world will fall apart. This fear comes from having their identity wrapped up solely in work. These beliefs cause workaholics to avoid therapy and, in many cases, to cling more tenaciously to their work for security.

I've found that it's important to be prepared to deal with clients' resistance and to reassure them that the number of working hours has little to do with the kinds of changes necessary, and that they are the architect of the changes in their lives. This can relieve clients, give them a sense of control, and help them focus on the pertinent issues in therapy. Typical clients blame their jobs or their families for their work addiction. Here's where you can explain the enabling process and help them identify their enablers. You can also help them to separate the enablers in their lives from their work addiction, so that they can assume more responsibility for overworking.

Clients often need you to redirect their attention to the source of their pain, which is inside rather than outside. It's not unusual for workaholics to blame their problems on today's lifestyles and pressures. But blaming the company, the recession, or the need for two paychecks only rewards self-destructive behaviors and distracts everyone from the real source of the problem. Blaming fast-paced society and modern technology lets workaholics off the hook. Although they have choices about the way they live, they may be unwittingly choosing to continue their addiction while claiming they have no choices. Having workaholics become aware of their responsibilities, instead of blaming the enablers, helps them become more accountable and empowers them instead of victimizing them. You can consider asking workaholics to do a cost-benefit analysis on paper of the pluses and minuses of their compulsive working. This exercise can help them see their losses more concretely and weigh the advantages against the disadvantages.

SETTING BOUNDARIES AROUND WORK HOURS

In your sessions, be sure to address problems in boundary setting and help clients say no when choices are available to them or when they're already over-committed. The boundaries that workaholics set depend on their unique life-styles. Some clients can limit their work to eight hours a day, with no weekend or holiday work, and can recognize that additional hours are not honorable but a "fix." Others don't have that flexibility. Still others do, but have trouble saying no.

You can challenge clients to set weekly boundaries creatively and to evaluate from week to week their success at maintaining healthy boundaries. Blaine's out-of-sight, out-of-mind strategy can be used in many ways with many different electronic devices. But be prepared to challenge many justifications for a clients' inability to maintain the boundaries they set. The next week then becomes another opportunity for them to practice the skill again without judgment.

Many of the techniques I now use with clients are ones I used myself. I set specific hours for working at home, worked only in my home office, and gave myself fifteen-minute cushions between appointments to give time to stretch or get where I needed to go. I renewed old friendships and developed new ones. And I confronted the fact that I had been hiding from the world since third grade, using work to keep me from close relationships even though I hungered for them. Closeness had felt scary and unpredictable, and I'd worked to keep even Jamey at arm's length. I felt out of control with someone who in an instant could break my heart like a brittle twig.

Change was not easy for me, and there was no specific moment when the light switch came on. Instead, it was more like the subtle changing of the seasons. I started to see Jamey with fresh eyes, watching him care for his orchids

and realizing the wisdom contained in the pleasure he got from simply working in the yard. One weekend I accepted his invitation and tried working with
him, just to do something together. Much to my surprise, I discovered how
much I, too, relished the smell of cut grass, the feel of warm earth, and chats
with neighbors.

MANAGING WORK AND PERSONAL TIME

I have found it helpful to have clients evaluate their time-management effectiveness. I suggest that you discuss the art of prioritizing and delegating and
have clients bring in specific examples of ways they practice these skills. You
can also help them focus on what requires immediate attention and refrain
from imposing unrealistic deadlines; evaluate their ability to ask for help when
they need it; explore reasons why they find asking for help difficult; and pro-
pose how they might be better served by delegating work.

Consider suggesting that clients set aside daily personal time to destress
their lives and create clear-minded thinking. You can recommend ample rest,
regular exercise, and getting three nutritionally balanced meals a day rather
one or two, as well as advising clients to avoid eating on the run, while working, between meals, or while watching television. It's important to investigate
the underlying reasons why workaholic clients inevitably fail at following the
sort of balanced regimen that many other people find simple and easy. Thus,
the underlying reasons for the difficulty and failure become the focus for the
therapeutic session, and you can acknowledge and reward even the smallest
gains that build into larger ones over time.

THE SWEETNESS OF DOING NOTHING

Many clients find, when they examine the balance in their current lives, that
there's no room for leisure, play, or idle moments. I often assign them "homework" that involves doing something fun that produces no product and that
requires spontaneity and flexibility. These activities are usually process oriented like free-form painting, digging in the garden, soaking in a hot bath, or
walking barefoot in a rain shower. The Italians call it *il dolce far niente*, "the
sweetness of doing nothing." It doesn't translate in the United States, where
tasks and schedules define us. The closest equivalent we have is *killing time*.
But *il dolce far niente* demands far more from you: that you intentionally let go
and make being a priority. You can introduce this "foreign" concept to clients
as a lead-in to help them find the sweetness of being alive—spending time
in the present moment without a goal by doing something for just the sheer
pleasure of it.

Another way to help your clients draw a line between work and time off is to have them compose a "to-be list" alongside their "to-do list." For each do item on their list, ask them to put a be item in the column beside it. Examples might include sitting outdoors, listening to nature sounds, and taking a walk, noticing the feel of your feet against the ground and the smells in the air.

You might also consider recommending hobbies, sports, and pastimes that can be done "imperfectly" and that immerse clients in process rather than outcome. Richard, a sixty-two-year-old bank president, took up golf but committed himself not to keep score, not to hurry from hole to hole, and to stay focused on having a good time instead of on winning—the opposite of his behavior at the office. He told me that business associates marveled when, for the first time, they saw his fun, lighthearted, and playful side. Golf, originally a therapy task, became a joy.

PERFORMING OPTIMALLY INSTEAD OF WORKAHOLICALLY IN THE WORKPLACE

Flashy, dramatic bursts of working often draw attention from supervisors and colleagues, but consistency and moderation are the redeeming traits of optimal performers. Like the hare in the fable, workaholics make a big splash, crash, and then burn. If you're an optimal performer, however, you're like the tortoise. You plod along, showing consistent, high-level performance over time. Optimal performing doesn't contain the adrenaline highs, the ups and downs, or the stress of work addiction. The attention comes more slowly to optimal performers, but the delayed gratification pays off in the end.

The following tips can help you as the clinician assist workaholics to learn the benefits of replacing temporary highs now with greater, longer-lasting rewards over their career trajectory:

❖ *Don't let work dominate your life.* When you feel overloaded, don't cancel dinner with a loved one or your afternoon aerobics class. These are the very activities you need to help you maintain balance. Typically, workaholics think that staying at the office for two more hours is the answer to achieving results. But that usually makes them more tired and less clear-headed and often leads to more work overall. Maintaining outside interests and exercising daily brings a clearer perspective to your work and gives you more vitality to get out from under the pile of work. Plan for spare time just as you would an important business meeting. Schedule time for doing things you like to do best.

❖ *Delegate and negotiate.* If you're someone who has trouble turning a project over to someone else, learn to delegate in order to perform optimally. Review your workload and determine what part you can turn over to an assistant or coworker. If deadlines are too tight, negotiate them with your supervisor. Deadlines can almost always be modified, although the workaholic mindset won't let you readily admit that. Develop a plan explaining the need for the extension and suggest a revised time frame. Or come up with a creative alternative. Tina, a production manager for a New York symphony orchestra, found herself working fifteen hours more a week without a pay increase. Instead of spending several hours watching symphony rehearsals, she put a college intern in charge with a cell phone so she could be reached in a pinch. A Merrill Lynch senior biotechnology analyst who was swamped with sixty-hour workweeks found a way around a hiring freeze to get his projects started. He recruited a graduate student from Harvard who helped him two days a week for free.

❖ *Learn the art of prioritizing your work.* Have clear and practical priorities. Don't over-plan. The clearer you are about what you want to accomplish and how you plan to accomplish it, the more focused and efficient and the less stressed you will be. Identify the key aspects of your job. Pay attention to the essentials first and put the nonessentials on the back burner for now or farm them out to another employee.

❖ *Take charge of your technology.* The pandemic caused more people to work from home, in cafes and coffee houses, and on airplanes, making the corporate workspace dead zones of empty cubicles—a ghost town. Don't fall into the trap of using the extra time that your technology provides to do more work instead of taking a leisurely break. Make sure you're in charge of your cell phone or laptop, rather than letting your technology oversee you. You can have time-saving technology without becoming a slave to it. You can check your email twice a day, for example, instead of every time the computer beeps. You can turn off your smart phone at a reasonable hour and put limits on when and where you choose to carry a laptop—declaring off limits your Caribbean cruise or your trek through the Amazon jungle. I suggest that clients leave their laptops in the trunk of the car when they arrive home. Or at the very least, I urge them to put their technological tools away in a drawer after a reasonable day's work—just as you would put away ingredients and utensils after baking or carpentry tools after building shelves in your den.

Bibliotherapy

The following books are topics for further reading relevant to this chapter:

❖ Arianna Huffington, *Thrive: The Third Metric to Redefining Success and Creating a Life of Well-Being, Wisdom, and Wonder* (New York: Harmony Books, 2015).

❖ Marina Khi Khidekel, *Time to Thrive: End Burnout, Increase Well-Being, and Unlock Your Full Potential with the New Science of Microsteps* (New York: Hachette, 2021).

❖ Emily Nagoski and Amelia Nagoski, *Burnout: The Secret to Unlocking the Stress Cycle* (New York: Ballantine Books, 2020).

❖ Bryan Robinson, *# Chill: Turn Off Your Job and Turn On Your Life* (New York: William Morrow, 2019).

10

Companies Behaving Badly, Encouraging Employees to Drink the Kool-Aid

There are way easier places to work,
but nobody ever changed the world
on forty hours a week.
　　　　　　　　—Elon Musk

Jax Feels Pressured to Underreport Work Hours

As a second-year medical resident in a major Northeastern hospital in the United States, I often work over twenty-four hours in a stretch and am fearful to drive home because I'm so tired and worried I might fall asleep at the wheel. Most of the time I call and talk to someone on the phone. The other option is either take a nap at the hospital, but after working over twenty-four hours, I don't want to be there anymore. My program director said to take an Uber if I'm too tired to drive and that cost comes out of my pocket. My grandmother was here for the holidays when I was on call. She said, "I have so much more respect for doctors. I had no idea what they go through to get where they are."

The governing body for residents, the American College of Graduate Medical Education, has guidelines that limit us from working no more than an average of eighty hours per week over four weeks. That rule was put into action after an overworked resident made medical errors that caused a patient's death and resulted in a lawsuit. Residents sign a contract that states the guidelines, and we must report our weekly hours through an online form. Many residents, including me, frequently go over the eighty hours a week, and I often do not have the four required periods of twenty-four hours off in a month. In my first year of residency, I accurately reported my ten hours over the allowed eighty and immediately was caught in an email chain with several of my superiors asking me to explain myself. After that email chain, I realized that reporting the extra ten hours isn't worth the additional work of having to explain myself when historically no changes have been made.

It's a double-edged sword because I want to be honest with my reporting. But if I ask to go home "early," I would be abandoning my patients and leaving their care incomplete, which is poor patient care. Plus, there's a common saying in residency that medicine is a team sport. And I would be abandoning my team, leaving my clinical work for someone else which violates the whole concept of a team. Another catch-22 is if your residency program goes over the limited hours, the consequence could be that it will be shut down, and you would not graduate or become a board-certified physician. The dilemma is if you report your hours, then you in effect abandon your patients and team, get your program in trouble, and don't graduate.

Eighty hours a week is a lot of hours, although in the last month, I worked ninety-two hours one week. But out of fear of backlash, I didn't document the hours because it would require a meeting with my program director who is a physician. I would be questioned about why I didn't work less hours, and the other residents on my team would be reprimanded about why I was overworked. That means if I work the limited eighty hours, another resident on the team would have to burden the load.

As I talk with other residents across the country, they experience similar situations. I can't imagine any resident confident enough to speak out about this because of the backlash they would face. The medical system doesn't directly say not to report your hours accurately, but the indirect message is that you will be blamed for overworking if you do. The medical administration higher-ups are aware of the predicament, but they turn a blind eye. The archaic medical system causes me internal turmoil, but I'm expected not to rock the boat and to take the path of least resistance to keep my head above water.

"Dark" Companies and "Evil Corporations"

Everything you have read about workaholics up until now is about America's obsession with work and the stress and burnout it causes. But the workplace doesn't create work addiction; workaholics often seek out high-stress jobs, bringing their compulsive habits into the office: rigid thinking, familial neglect, overworking, and social isolation—even family of origin issues. But workaholics and work addiction could not survive without the workplace. As long as workplaces have existed, companies have enabled work addiction—sometimes behaving badly. The American workforce has put up with trickle-down fear, intimidation, and uncertainty that undermine job performance and employee wellness. While fear can drive short-term results, it does so at the cost of high employee burnout and turnover that compromises long-term business performance. And it provides atomic fuel for employee abuse.

As Jax documented, not being loyal could mean not becoming a board-certified doctor. Although Jax isn't a workaholic, she is nevertheless caught in an abusive system that sends mixed messages that require her to go above and beyond what she would consider healthy boundaries and risk burnout. In this way, the corporate structure supports and encourages work addiction by perpetuating an archaic work ethic and promoting loyalty to the company at the personal expense of its employees. A global survey by *World Business* revealed that 49 percent of workers said overwork was encouraged and applauded by their company. More than 70 percent said they worked weekends, and 14 percent admitted they'd be proud to be called a workaholic.[1] Workaholics are often attracted, consciously or unconsciously, to these types of work cultures because they are looking for a lot to do. Although, companies do not cause work addiction any more than the ABC store causes alcoholism, they must take some responsibility for enabling and promoting work addiction.

Many businesses exploit employees by putting profit before people and squeezing every ounce of sweat from their workforce. Harassment, bullying, incivility, and ostracism are commonplace in these toxic organizations, and studies show they lead to lower job productivity and higher job burnout— even suicide. After working weeks without a break and pressuring his employees to work twenty-hour days, Lee Han-bit took his own life. He left a note decrying the South Korean work culture that exploited him and required him to pass the exploitation on to his crew: "I, too, was nothing but a laborer," he wrote. "But then," he added, "I was nothing more or less than a manager who squeezed the laborers."[2]

Death from overwork is so common in Japan, they coined a word for it— *karoshi*. And a new buzzword, "*Burakku Kigyo*"—loosely translated as "black companies" or "evil corporations"—is used to describe businesses that take advantage of employees. In 2012, a group of activist journalists and university professors formed a special committee to bestow the "Black Corporations Award" on the firms that treat their employees the worst—"the most evil corporations of the year." This annual award raises awareness of dark company issues and exposes some of the evil abusers of employees.[3]

According to one source, a Japanese company advertised itself as a great place to work. Although company employees left work at 7 p.m. on paper, in one reported case an employee said he was expected to work until late at night almost every day. "Employees were required to sign off at 7 p.m., even if they were still working, and were given iPads so that they could do so even if they were out of the office at meetings. If they didn't sign off, they'd get a call on their cellphones brusquely asking them to sign off immediately but keep working. 'The amount of time you're actually working and the amount of time that is recorded you're working have absolutely no relation to each other.'"[4]

Of course, Asian companies aren't unique in mistreating and overworking employees, as Jax's ninety-hour work weeks demonstrate. In the post-pandemic era of 2022, Elon Musk, founder and CEO of Tesla, was accused of corporate slavery and perpetuating work addiction and job burnout. The world's richest man, who admittedly works over 100 hours a week, was accused of pushing employees to match his hourly pace. While praising Tesla China employees for "burning the three-a.m. oil," he said that Americans are "trying to avoid going to work at all."[5]

Mary also described her experience living with a spouse in a high-pressure job: "My husband is working for an American internet company and is expected to be on call virtually seven days a week. His lack of balance and my hard worker tendencies have put a severe strain on our marriage. We live in this fast-paced high-technology area where one hundred hours a week at Microsoft is the expected work week. All the other dot-com companies use this as the standard. We simply cannot keep up the pace."

Corporate Exploitation and Abuse

Social scientists are concerned with how companies misuse technology to keep a noose around their employees' necks. They fear the combination of information technology and excessive corporate demands carry the risk that companies will exploit workers by tethering them to their electronic devices 24/7.[6] If career advancement depends on 24/7 connectivity, it becomes more difficult to distinguish between a worker's choice to work and an employer's manipulation. The prevalence of information technology raises questions about the future of corporate responsibility.

Many organizations have set expectations so high that addiction-level work involvement is a requirement for jobs. Some people believe employers should be held liable for employees' addictions to information technology. Efforts are afoot to stop companies from violating the personal boundaries of employees after hours. It's already the law in Portugal and France, where employers can be in hot water for contacting employees after work hours, and that includes emails. In 2022, a similar bill to make it illegal to force employees to answer work communications outside of work hours was being debated in New York City.

An example of increasing corporate demands is the disappearance of company picnics, which used to be a family affair. Their replacements are heralded as "power picnics"—the traditional company picnic serving double duty to get more work squeezed in during the annual event. Chicago's Windy City Fieldhouse—which hosts company picnics—reported a 20 percent increase in company events with an added work dimension, such as two-hour brainstorming sessions before the celebration.[7]

Companies are making sure that they get a greater bang for their buck, that every dollar spent contributes to the company's growth. This shift in corporate emphasis has begun to show up in sobering ways: "As PowerPoint presentations replace softball, the guest lists are changing. Business partners, vendors, and potential customers are being invited and families are getting nixed."[8]

Employers foster work addiction by not limiting the hours employees work or the amount of work they take home, discounting the importance of family life, and applauding those who work tirelessly rather than those who have balanced lives. Jax told me the hours she spends on call at home don't count toward the eighty-hour per week limit. Many companies send mixed messages to employees: a workaholic trait. They say they don't want workaholics, but they scrutinize time records or put subtle pressure on employees to log more hours. An alarming 46 percent of professional workers claim they have too much stress and pressure in their jobs.[9] In 2012, job pressures were the second highest cause of stress, after financial worries.[10]

Some companies have been accused of deliberately manipulating the darker sides of workers' consciousnesses for profit. They set tight deadlines that are impossible to meet, hint at nonexistent competitors, and tell employees that clients are dissatisfied when they're not. Such corporate tactics create paranoia, stress, and a prolonged adrenaline rush that leads to burnt out workers. Employees never know which crises are real and which are fabrications. The label "cultures of sacrifice" has been applied to those organizations that manufacture crises as a ploy to keep pressures on employees to produce:

> In a culture of sacrifice, people are driven by feelings of responsibility to the company. This is particularly true for those who link loss of performance with loss of self-esteem. These people become the company workaholics. Workaholics get caught up in a never-ending mission to gain control by devoting more and more time to work to the exclusion of virtually everything

else. If they slow down or relax, they worry they will be seen as slackers or incompetents. In their quest to be "good enough" they draw themselves and others into a working frenzy that focuses on quantity rather than quality, aggressively pushing the company and fellow workers to the point of collapse. . . . Failure is inevitable in this culture. These companies operate on the assumption that the company is more important than its workers, and they are prepared to sacrifice excellent workers to prove the point.[11]

Changing Tires at Eighty Miles per Hour

Many companies operate from top to bottom through a workaholic structure. In contrast to slogans that condemn drug use, like "Just Say No" or "Just Don't Do It," the message that rings loud and clear—sometimes subtle, sometimes direct in the workaholic organization—is, "Don't Leave Work without It." As I travel far and wide and in my clinical practice, I hear more stories of corporate threats. One woman told me the threat was subtle: "Oh yeah, I could take all my earned vacation. But if I do, I won't have a job when I get back. They may say it's okay but believe me it isn't!" Again, this woman wasn't a workaholic but was caught in an organization that fostered work abuse by overworking employees who would prefer to take time away from the office.

Other workers say they're afraid to take lunch breaks for fear of how they'd be perceived by management. There comes a point where these work environments hurt employees, whether they are workaholics or not. Organizations that actively recruit workaholics and promote work addiction tend to attract more workaholic types. Nonworkaholic types, however, do not fare as well in these jobs. During the "Great Resignation" post-pandemic boom in 2022, many employers facing a hiring crisis made a habit of employing four people to do the work of five after 4.5 million employees quit their jobs in the month of November 2021 alone.[12]

The philosophy of one major American bank is: *We expect you to change tires going eighty miles an hour.* An executive at this bank told me that at meetings, six or seven managers typically sit around a table discussing issues, each one constantly checking her cellphone as it goes off. The consensus is that to survive in this culture, employees can no longer afford to just focus on one thing at a time. Multitasking is an essential lifeboat to keep from drowning in a sea of work.

The Abusive Organization

Work addiction cannot exist without an organization that enables it. No wonder so many of us come away from virtual meetings feeling crazy, off balance, and uneasy. Organizational experts charge that many businesses turn a blind eye, encourage the denial of work addiction, and promote it as acceptable to boost the company's bottom line.[13] Some critics claim that corporate America functions like an individual addict by denying, covering up, and rewarding dysfunctional behaviors among its employees. Dysfunctional managers and those in key corporate positions negatively impact the organizational system and its employees by perpetuating work addiction at every level. If you toil in an abusive organization, you're employed by a toxic workplace where the human element is overshadowed by the details of the workload. Experts cite six characteristics that promote work addiction on the production line, in the boardroom, or in sales meetings.[14]

1. *The mission of the organization is denied, ignored, or forgotten.* You're so preoccupied with being productive that you forget why the organization exists. You lose sight of the overall mission of your work because you're pressured by the economics of the business.

2. *Corporate survival reigns supreme.* Corporate survival is the top priority, and you're viewed as a commodity to be used up and then discarded. Stress management is offered to keep you and your coworkers productive. The business survives as employees drop like flies.

3. *Profit is the driving force of the workaholic company.* Your company seeks short-term, immediate gratification instead of deferred, long-range solutions, results, and profit. The integrity and mission of the organization, as well as your mental health and that of other employees, are better served by a long-term focus at the expense of immediate profit.

4. *The workaholic environment is self-centered and has no boundaries or respect.* You're expected to carry your workload home on weekends and glue yourself to your laptop, email, and iPhone on weekends and holidays to perform adequately. With its lack of boundaries, your company doesn't respect and honor your personal life. It's selfish, greedy, and demanding. You're constantly at the disposal of the organization, regardless of your personal or family needs. The workaholic organization makes you dependent on it through perks and benefits. It buys your loyalty, even though you're miserable and officewide morale is low. Quitting isn't a viable option for you.

5. *Crisis management is the norm in workaholic organizations.* Crisis shifts the focus of the organization away from emphasizing your needs and welfare

to solving the crisis. When businesses are organized to respond to problems without forethought, they're perpetually putting out fires. This keeps you and your colleagues hyped up, with your adrenaline flowing, your attention focused on the needs of the organization, and your emotional and mental health needs on the back burner. There's less attention devoted to long-term planning; when it does exist, it's often cursory.

6. *Intimacy does not exist in the workaholic environment.* You feel like a cog in the corporate machine. Your work environment is cold and impersonal. Socializing and close relationships are minimized or even discouraged. Your company operates on the premise that employees are dispensable, like machine parts, and, once used up, you will be replaced by someone else.

Toil Glamour: Has "Balance" Become Uncool?

If you're a workaholic, you're at risk of being attracted to and thriving in a workplace that has any or all of these six characteristics—where balance is a dirty word, overworking is extolled, and burnout indicates you're a hard, dedicated employee. You might even insinuate your way into the ranks of management, encouraging work addiction throughout the company, falling prey to the *hustle culture*—a rebranding of work addiction for Millennials and GenZers—buying into the idea that it's cool to be "always on"—to push yourself to the max each of the 1,440 minutes of the day. You boast about no breaks. No leisure. No weekends off. No vacations. No sleep or exercise. "Gobble, gulp, and go" or skipping meals altogether are badges of honor. You bathe in the same glamorous light that advertisers poured over the cigarette and liquor ads of the 1930s. In movies and commercials back then, it was considered sexy to smoke and drink until they realized it caused cancer, heart disease, and stroke.

When you choose hustle over health, studies show that you cut your career short, destroy your mental and physical health, and harm your relationships. Plus, you may even die at an earlier age than your peers. Yet, it has become a status symbol among some of the country's top CEOs to put in long hours. According to one 2019 source, Elon Musk logged as much as 120 hours a week at Tesla, Google's Marissa Mayer clocked up to 130 weekly hours, and Tim Cook at Apple sent emails at 4:30 a.m.[15]

With leaders setting these extreme examples, a 2019 survey of 2,000 respondents by OnePoll found that nearly half (48 percent) of the American workforce consider themselves to be modern-day workaholics. A total of 58 percent of the respondents said they worry about work on an off day, feel too busy to take a vacation, and check emails immediately after waking up.[16] If you're addicted to work, you could even join the movement afoot in this country to deconstruct the term, "work-life balance"—many eschewing the phrase as a dinosaur of the 1990s. As noted earlier, before exiting his post at Amazon in 2019, Jeff Bezos advised employees to stop aiming for work-life balance because it implies a tradeoff between the two.

Major corporations are batting around the new buzz phrase, "work-life integration." Used properly, the upside of "integration" is that it provides flexibility for workers to have a doctor's appointment in the middle of the day or attend a parent meeting with a child's teacher. The downside, however, is that it's a slippery slope for workaholics, giving them permission to integrate work around the clock. Some advocates of work-life balance believe that the movement creates additional blurred boundaries and burnout such as remote work caused during the pandemic. Skeptics say big companies get a bigger bang for their buck with integration instead of balance and are afraid employees with balance will be less productive. They ask if this is another corporate ploy—as when businesses started providing free electronic devices—to permanently tether workers to 24/7 connectivity, making it impossible to get away from work stressors.

In 2020, an example of this bait and switch tactic came to light when a Chinese tech company distributed "smart cushions"—presumably a health aid that alerted employees' mobile phones to prompt them to stand up and move around after sitting for too long. But once the devices were deployed, an employee was challenged about why she was stepping away from her desk for half an hour every morning—information provided from her smart cushion. The workers were warned that if the cushions detected them taking long, unauthorized breaks, their bonuses would be affected. The employees had never been informed that the cushion would monitor them in such a negative manner.[17]

This incident—along with other exploitive and darker corporate trends discussed earlier—prompts the questions "Does big business provide resources to help employees or to corral them?" and "Are workers being unfairly squeezed to become more productive?"

If you're an active workaholic, you're more likely to get engulfed by the dubious tactics of big business. If you duck out at family dinners when your phone pings, wear your Bluetooth headset while playing catch with your oldest, or answer emails during your daughter's soccer game, you're not integrating; you're opening the door for the invasion of balance snatchers, working at the expense of your personal life. When you're not fully present with loved ones, blurred boundaries cause you to miss out on special times you cannot recapture and send the message that your job is more important than they are. But if you're a balanced worker or in recovery from work addiction, you're less willing to sacrifice your whole life for unreasonable work demands. See the next section to see if your workplace measures up.

Does Your Company Pass the Smell Test?

Are you in a win/lose work culture? Do you work in a job that promotes work addiction, stress, and burnout? Or are you fortunate enough to work in a company that considers human factors, nurtures its employees, and encourages work-life balance? Test your workplace to see how it rates on corporate abuse by answering yes or no to the following questions:

_____ 1. Is your job rapid paced, with little time to casually talk with coworkers or supervisors?

_____ 2. Does your work environment feel cold, sterile, or devoid of the human touch?

_____ 3. Does your work environment thrive on crisis, chaos, and pressure?

_____ 4. Do you work for a company that emphasizes production and profit above the welfare and morale of its employees?

_____ 5. Does success in your company hinge on putting in overtime on weekdays, weekends, or holidays?

_____ 6. Do you think your company fosters work addiction?

_____ 7. Are you constantly in a hurry and racing against the clock on your job?

_____ 8. Is it necessary to juggle many activities or projects at one time in order to keep up at your job?

_____ 9. Does your company put you under the gun with short notice of high-pressure deadlines?

_____ 10. Have you had any stress-related illnesses caused by this job?

_____ 11. Do you work for a company that puts the welfare of its employees above profit and production?

_____ 12. Does your company have a nurturing attitude toward workers who have concerns about family and personal time or who experience stress and burnout?

_____ 13. Is your job environment relaxing, evenly paced, warm, and friendly?

_____ 14. Do you feel like a human being more often than a commodity at your job?

_____ 15. In your job, can you limit the amount of work you bring home and have weekends and holidays for yourself and loved ones?

_____ 16. Do you think your company has a long-term, vested interest in you as a human being, as opposed to a short-term interest?

_____ 17. Does your company promise celebrations—including birthdays and holidays—or other socializing as an integral part of the work schedule?

_____ 18. Do you work with colleagues who are cooperative and supportive and with whom you can communicate?

_____ 19. If you have a problem in your job, can you talk with someone who will listen and offer you support?

_____ 20. Does your job provide personal satisfaction, meaning, or purpose?

SCORING: Start with 60 points. Subtract 2 points for each yes answer to questions 1 through 10. Add 2 points for each no answer to questions 1 through 10. Subtract 2 points for each no answer to questions 11 through 20. Add 2 points for each yes answer to questions 11 through 20.

YOUR JOB'S REPORT CARD:

Scores	Grade	Interpretation
0–59	F	Poor. Consider a healthier workplace. You may already have the signs of stress and burnout or other physical symptoms that lead to bad health.
60–69	D	Below average
70–79	C	Average
80–89	B	Good
90–100	A	Excellent. Stay put. Sounds like you've hit the jackpot of a non-workaholic, healthy workplace.

Making a U-Turn in the Workplace

In the past, the corporate world believed having ranks of workaholic employees would guarantee greater production. The paradox is studies show that toxic workplaces, where harassment and bullying occur, lead to burnout, diminish job productivity, and hurt the company's bottom line.[18] Corporations are finding that they can achieve more creative results and greater revenues from a more balanced workforce. Salespeople who have achieved balance in their lives, for example, are more likely to attract potential clients than obsessed, high-pressure salespeople, who are more likely to turn clients off and drive them away.

How can corporate America take all the problems of work addiction and convert them into dollars and cents? That question is being asked more and more. Many businesses are taking a stand against work addiction and structuring more humane working environments. A former head of Caterpillar was a pioneer in insisting that employees lead balanced lives:

> I don't want workaholics working for me. . . . One of my predecessors called that "living on the square" . . . One side of the square represents our work life, one our family life, one our spiritual life, and one our community life. I believe we're healthier, happier—and more productive—if we live on all sides of that square.
>
> I doubt that such people [workaholics] can be effective managers over a lifetime. I question whether they've learned how to delegate, if they've sought ways to become more efficient, if they've learned how to set priorities.[19]

Nowadays, finding cost-effective ways to help employees balance career with family, recreation, and self-care needs are major concerns for employers. More companies are starting to hire socially balanced employees and to institute work-break aerobics and meditation workshops. In some cases, bosses are telling employees, directly or indirectly, to slow down, and a growing number of companies insist workers use their vacation time. Susan's boss rejected one day she "took off" for vacation because she had left him electronic messages that same day. He told her: "You weren't on vacation because you sent me a message, so take another day of vacation. Get away from the office and forget about work for a while."

ON24's corporate head Sharat Sharan said that black swan events like COVID-19 are the ultimate trials of leadership and business sustainability, suggesting that leaders find outlets to stay calm because their personal health and energy are passed down to the team.

Both Google and Dow Chemical have established onsite mindful meditation classes to reduce workers' stress levels.[20] Some companies have destressed work environments by using natural light, indoor gardens and plants, and relaxation rooms with trickling fountains.[21] Still others have instituted stress reduction policies such as flextime, job sharing, and paid paternity leave.

The chief executive officer of the Energy Project created a business around the concept of "energy renewal," which promotes the idea that energy is finite

Work Cultures of "Unfear"

Fear and uncertainty have been undermining performance and well-being in the workplace for as long as workplaces have existed. And workaholics tend to work from a place of fear and impose it on subordinates and coworkers. Under fear, the human brain focuses on how to avoid the threat instead of engaging with and producing work tasks—blocking success outcomes, according to the authors of *Unfear*.[22] They contend that mismanaged fear is responsible for almost all of the dysfunction that most organizations experience.

While fear can drive short-term results, it does so at the cost of high employee burnout and turnover and undermines long-term business performance. According to the authors, winning organizations aren't fear-free, but they know how to transform negative energy into opportunities for learning and growth. They create resilient cultures of "unfear," according to the authors, with strategies that create cultures of "unfear" by investing in brain capital of psychological safety to enhance performance, greater profits, sustainable growth, and personal rewards. The authors insist that a work culture of unfear reduces stress, boosts well-being, and overcomes blocks that get in the way of success, leading to greater profits, sustainable growth, and personal rewards.

More Fortune 100 companies are realizing work addiction is a major health and safety issue, that it's to their advantage to promote healthy employees and work environments. They are finding that meditation, chanting, and yoga benefit both payroll and personnel. Mark Bertolini, the CEO of health insurance company Aetna, discovered that yoga helped him with lingering pain from a skiing accident. So, he put in place a stress-reducing mindfulness program for Aetna's workers and had Duke University scientists study the results. The findings showed that with one hour of yoga classes a week, there was a 33 percent drop in workplace stress.[23] So far, over three thousand of Aetna's workers have completed the program, saving Aetna $2,000 in annual health care costs for people who moved from the highest-stress group to the lowest-stress one.

but, unlike time, is renewable.[24] The energy that employees bring to their jobs is far more important in terms of the value of their work than is the number of hours they work. By managing energy more skillfully, it's possible to get more done in less time, more sustainably. His ideas have helped organizations such as Coca-Cola, Green Mountain Coffee, Google, the Los Angeles Police Department, Genentech, and the Cleveland Clinic. His company has dedicated space to a "renewal" room in which employees can nap, meditate, or relax. There's a spacious lounge where workers hang out together and snack on healthy foods. The company encourages workers to take renewal breaks throughout the day and to leave the office for lunch. The workday ends at 6:00 p.m., and nobody is expected to answer email messages in the evenings or on weekends. In addition, employees receive four weeks of vacation starting in their first year at the company.

Other companies can raise employee awareness of workaholism and balance by establishing "healthy work" days, in conjunction with Earth Day, with posters and special seminars featuring the components of a healthy work environment. Organizations can present the information by using outside speakers so that all workers learn about the effects of work addiction on the job in a nonthreatening way.

If you're a company administrator, you can assess the degree to which your organization promotes work addiction. Using the six characteristics of the workaholic company and the workplace report card in the section titled "Does Your Company Pass the Smell Test?" as criteria, company officials can objectively evaluate the work environment at their organization to determine what needs changing to improve the welfare of workers first and the profit of the organization second.

The removal of work addiction from the workplace dramatically reduces burnout and stress, health problems, poor communication, and low morale. It saves businesses billions of dollars a year and provides both a better work climate for employees plus a better product for consumers. It's a win-win for employers, employees, and consumers—everybody benefits.

Tips for Clinicians

If you're a clinician, consider asking yourself what type of work environment you have established for yourself and your clients. Is the atmosphere rushed and frenetic, or is it serene and relaxed? Grading your work environment with the test in the "Does Your Company Pass the Smell Test?" section can help you evaluate your workspace to see what kind of example you're setting. It's important to be a positive role model by creating a positive work environment for workaholics and their families.

THRIVING INSTEAD OF SURVIVING IN A WORKAHOLIC COMPANY

You can help workaholics or just plain hard workers who are trying to survive in a workaholic culture. The following tips can even help them thrive instead of just survive:

- *Know where to draw the line.* Don't wait for your company to decide what's reasonable for you. Evaluate your job and life and decide for yourself what's reasonable. How far you are willing to go to meet your boss's unreasonable demands? Be prepared to put your foot down when you believe your employer oversteps those bounds. There are many occasions on the job when you have a choice to stay late or work weekends. You may be reluctant to say no. But feeling overloaded and saying no without feeling guilty or disloyal is a healthy practice.

- *Keep your own balance.* Each of us is responsible for maintaining our work-life balance. Consider taking ten or fifteen minutes in the middle of the day to walk or meditate to release bottled-up stress and become more clear-minded. Take an aerobics class, a meditation workshop, a stress-reduction class, or an exercise program during work breaks to sidestep stress and burnout. Striving for balance in your personal, social, and family life may be a high-wire act, but it ensures greater harmony within yourself, at home, at work, and at play and makes it easier for you to survive in a workaholic company.

TALK TO CLIENTS ABOUT THE BALANCE CONTROVERSY

Whether we decide to stick with "balance," "integration" or simply "life balance," boundaries and a degree of mindfulness of the present moment are necessary to apply twenty-first century neuroscience, prevent burnout, and recover from work addiction. The gas and brakes metaphor (see chapter 5) of the autonomic nervous system is a reminder that we don't have to strive for equal or perfect balance. When we drive our cars, the goal isn't an equal application of gas and brakes. On the highway, you might use more gas than brakes for many miles. Stuck in traffic, you use more brakes than gas. We use both as needed to get to where we need to go while remaining on the road at a safe distance from other cars.

So, we should for present-moment awareness and full engagement in whatever we're doing in the moment. Watch your mind and notice where it goes from moment to moment for the next twenty-four hours. Note the difference when you're present (brakes) and when your mind drifts to the past or future (gas). When your mind wanders, gently bring it back into the present and continue with your workday. As you practice using gas and brakes in collaboration, you cultivate mindful productivity (see chapter 13). Tension subsides, you'll have more calm, clarity, and well-being, and will arrive at your destination in one piece.

Bibliotherapy

For further reading, the following books parallel the topics discussed in this chapter:

❖ Gaurav Bhatnagar and Mark Minukas, *Unfear: Transform Your Organization to Create Breakthrough Performance and Employee Well-Being* (New York: McGraw-Hill, 2022).

❖ Edward E. Lawler, *Treat People Right! How Organizations and Individuals Can Propel Each Other Into a Virtuous Spiral of Success* (San Francisco, CA: Jossey-Bass, 2003).

❖ Chade-Meng Tan, *Search Inside Yourself: The Unexpected Path to Achieving Success, Happiness (and World Peace)* (New York: HarperOne, 2012).

❖ Jeffrey Pfeffer, Dying for a Paycheck: How Modern Management Harms Employee Health and Company Performance—and What We Can Do About It (New York: Harper Business, 2018).

11

"Good Trouble" in Corporate America

Many of us are stuck in jobs we're
not passionate about, compromising
our own identity in order to serve
our fears.
　　　　—MILCK, singer/songwriter

Songwriter Gives Pink Slip to Corporate Structure

I had an opportunity to sit down with singer/songwriter Connie K. Lim, professionally known as MILCK (her name spelled backward, pronounced "Milk") to discuss her views of the revolution among the American work force during the COVID-19 pandemic, accompanied by the "Great Resignation." For many workers, COVID-19 put a focus on the fragility of life, leading them to reevaluate how they want to live their lives, and MILCK was no exception. During the quarantine in the moments of quiet, she pondered that question, ultimately giving a pink slip to corporate America.

> As a daughter of immigrants, I was taught to climb the ladder faster, better, more efficiently and intelligently to earn a seat at the table. I had to work three times harder than everyone else. And that ambition—that's still within me—had me climbing ladders that continued to reinforce oppressive structures for people of color. As a musician, I started asking the kinds of questions business leaders have failed to ask to retain their best and brightest employees from the mass exodus that led to the hiring crisis. I wondered how I could shift the rigid corporate structure and create something that opens curiosity, imagination, and exploration. The industry model is to create the music, do the corporate structure, and then trickle down to causes with the priority on streaming numbers. I wondered what if I follow what I want to do and flip the structure upside down and

put advocacy work at the top. Then I can design my work and projects around that to tell the story, bring attention to these things, and really hold that to my heart.

As a result of my soul searching, I took the risk of leaving a major record label to work independently. Now my projects aim to change the typical ways of the music industry, shifting my focus and rebuilding my team to ensure that the artists I work with are creating music with a purpose and all parties involved are properly represented and compensated. Atlantic Records wanted me to create songs first, then find philanthropic ties for the music afterwards. With my current approach, I'm crafting the music with intent, focusing on the goal first and foremost.

When I walked away from my major label deal, although there were moments when it was scary and I questioned what I had done, at the same time I felt I was taking care of myself. Since I was young, I watched my Asian ancestors doing jobs where they couldn't express themselves and had to keep their heads down and work. I remember thinking I want to be free. I promised myself that when I became an adult, I would do what I needed to do to build a life where I could express my ideas. Regardless of who wins at the top, we the people on the ground will need to keep causing "good trouble" as the late John Lewis said. This is life-long work, and we gotta have reminders to pace ourselves.

"Workjerkery" and Workaholic Bosses

For as long as we've had workplaces, bosses have followed in the footsteps of the bad behavior of their corporate structure. The American workforce has put up with the "bad trouble" trickling down from a dysfunctional corporate structure: job pressures, intimidation, and fear-induced demands from toxic bosses—many of whom are workaholics putting product and profit over people. Toxic workplace cultures hurt workers and company profits. A SHRM study found that bad bosses cost companies $223 billion dollars in turnover between 2014 and 2019.[1]

In "the good old days," business was built on a motto that you live by the book and follow the straight and narrow. If you didn't rock the boat and went along with the corporate culture, you could retire with the proverbial gold watch and live happily ever after. If your workplace was toxic, work demands abusive, manager corrupt—and if you suffered work stress, burnout, or mental health issues at the hands of a toxic boss, you were expected to grin and bear what has been dubbed as "workjerkery."[2]

The number one reason employees complain about work and eventually say, "Take this job and shove it," is because of a toxic boss. Most employees have had or been a bad boss. You probably have a story, too. Does your boss wail at the clock and shake a fist at the heavens because there's never enough time to do everything? Is your boss someone who rushes around moaning about the shortage of time and creating crises for everyone in his or her path? Is your boss the sort who sets short deadlines, overloads you with more to do than is humanly possible, and then breathes down your neck? If so, your boss could be a workaholic.

Having a workaholic boss who is a jerk can be a nightmare, and he or she can have many faces. "Perhaps it involves micromanagement, or neglect, or small acts of soul-crushing criticism, or larger harassment and abuse," according to one expert on "workjerkery." "Perhaps the malevolence was overt. Perhaps it was more subtle, so that if you were to later describe it to friends, it would seem minor and inconsequential, and you might come off as appearing hypersensitive. (This is true of so much workplace conflict; often a jerk is a jerk for a series of small, collective actions, not for one colossally atrocious deed.)"[3]

Andrea worked for a major East Coast newspaper. Her boss, she says, was a workaholic who routinely awakened employees in the middle of the night and on weekends to get an obscure fact from the West Coast for a next-morning deadline. "Naturally everything was closed, so there were times when I ended up calling Tokyo at 3:00 a.m. to get the information he wanted," she said. "It was always one crisis after another!"

Workaholics are often rewarded for their attempts to change and control other people by being promoted into management positions. Although many bosses are blatant in fostering work addiction, some are much more subtle. Their over-responsibility, poor communication skills, and inability to express feelings usually make them ineffective managers. Managers who are out of touch with their emotional lives are likely to be insensitive to the needs and feelings of their subordinates. If they're uncomfortable expressing feelings, they are less likely to provide positive feedback, praise, and appreciation.

RULING WITH AN IRON FIST

Instead of seeking advice, asking for input, or showing humility, workjerkery bosses rule with an iron fist, using intimidation as a defense against their own insecurities and unwittingly undermining—rather than supporting—subordinates to reinforce their own, more powerful position. They tend to pressure employees to match their own inhuman standards of long hours and frantic pace. Employee morale nosedives and burnout skyrockets under

Profile of the Workaholic Boss

❖ Constantly watches over employees' shoulders to monitor their work, while refusing to delegate

❖ Constantly pushes and hurries employees to the point where they feel undue stress and burnout

❖ Makes unreasonable demands in terms of work hours, workloads, and deadlines

❖ Has unpredictable, erratic moods, so employees never know what to expect

❖ Creates a climate of frenzy, urgency, and tension without respect for the feelings or personal lives of employees

❖ Manages time inefficiently because of overscheduling and overcommitting

❖ Judges himself or herself and employees without mercy as they struggle to hit impossible targets

❖ Tends to be overly critical and intolerant of even the most minor employee mistakes

such autocratic control. Countless millions of people become anxious at the thought of facing a new week with a work-addicted manager, supervisor, or employer. See "Profile of the Workaholic Boss."

Alcoholics like nothing better than a drinking buddy. Workaholics feel contempt for slackers, preferring instead to surround themselves with people who can match their crisis-oriented pace. Workaholic supervisors and managers spread work addiction by setting impossible and incredibly high goals and then pushing employees to replicate their own frenetic work patterns, often against the employees' natural work pace: "One of ITT's former presidents set a companywide precedent for work weeks of sixty hours or more and more late-night meetings. Some CPA firms send a memorandum to all their employees just before tax season reminding them that a fifty-hour workweek is considered the minimum. These pressures impose feelings of guilt on all executives who do not work the same number of hours others are working. As a result, employees feel insecure about their jobs unless they spend Saturdays at their desks."[4]

DR. JEKYLL TO MR. HYDE

The management style of the workaholic boss who practices "workjerkery"— overly critical, demanding, and unable to tolerate mistakes—creates roadblocks to employee engagement and quality productivity, causing disharmony, absenteeism, tardiness, mistrust, and conflict. Plus, it lowers morale and destroys team spirit. Judith shared her frustration working under Susan, the district sales manager at a multimillion-dollar computer company:

> Susan's addictive work habits make it unbearable for her sales reps. She's in the office by 7:30 a.m. and doesn't get home until eight or nine o'clock. Her obsession and constant driving leave no time for family life, and her social life includes only people within the company. She won't leave the sales representatives alone to do their jobs. She can't delegate and wait until a task is accomplished and is burning out trying to keep her hands in everything they do. She's always breathing down our necks by phone or email. She's afraid we won't do the job as well as her. The morale of the sales force is rock bottom. They don't function as a team. Their spirits are shattered, and they're constantly frustrated that they're not accomplishing enough in a time frame to satisfy Susan. Some of my fellow workers try to respond to everything she wants, and they're getting as crazy as she is, constantly working. I've seen people come into the office with bloodshot eyes, completely drained. They look as if they haven't slept in three or four days. She's like Jekyll and Hyde—tough to read—constantly flying off the handle and jumping down people's throats. When she notices you're under the pile [of work], instead of offering support, she harps on what you're doing and then jumps you.

If you're an employee, no matter how hard you try to please, you can never satisfy your boss's perfectionist standards. You get little positive feedback for your work efforts, and you end up feeling resentful. As the "workjerkery" moods of a workaholic manager swing from high to low, you try to satisfy him or her by swinging back and forth as well. You're never sure what to say or do, and you waste enormous amounts of energy trying to second-guess your boss.

Willa, an office manager for a prominent attorney, said her boss has giant-size mood swings:

> One day he's happy, the next day he's snappy. He works day and night and hardly ever talks to the other people in the office. He comes in, walks into his office, shuts the door, and stays there all day long. Everybody walks on eggshells and has learned to steer clear of him for fear of becoming the target of his anger. The tension is so thick, you could cut it with a knife. When he's grumpy, I feel like I've done something wrong and spend half the day worrying because maybe it's my fault. Or I try to get him out of his bad mood. Although part of my job is to inform him of problems that need to be addressed for the good of the business. I'm afraid if I tell him some critical things he needs to know, he'll blow up at me. When I do have meetings with

him, I measure each word to make sure I don't use the wrong approach or sound too negative, so I won't set him off.

Workaholic managers are notorious for making and breaking promises and setting unrealistic deadlines that cannot be met. The work climate is unpredictable and inconsistent, just like the tone of an alcoholic's home. Apprehension, fear, and insecurity are normal reactions for employees in these job positions. Instead of benefiting companies, workaholics cost money in terms of personal injury lawsuits and workers' compensation and medical insurance claims—all related to the stress and emotional burnout of work addiction. Job stress and work addiction cost businesses over $160 billion a year in 2006 and $300 billion a year in 2020.[5] These health costs are due to absenteeism, diminished productivity, and stress-related illnesses such as high blood pressure, heart disease, abdominal problems, and a host of mental health problems such as depression and anxiety.

To cope, you might guess at what your boss wants and find yourself making stabs in the dark. Emotionally battered and bruised, you might limp through your career. Poor self-esteem, lack of control over your destiny, poor coping skills, and problems in interpersonal relationships can all result as you try to meet demands from the dysfunctional powers that be. Rather than focusing on quality production, you concentrate your efforts at work on covering your tracks, distorting the truth, and watching your back. Many workers get revenge from passive resistance—a trend that came to be known in 2022 as "quiet quitting." One man said his way of getting back at his boss is to do as little as possible, although his productivity would increase dramatically if he quit to work under someone else.

Take This Job and Shove It

If you're toiling in a dysfunctional environment, there comes a time to decide which is more important—the job or you. Leaving one life path for another can be hard, but when you make the decision from self-care, it can be the best decision of your life. Steve Gorman quit playing drums with the Black Crows in 2001 because the band was dark and deeply dysfunctional. When he said, "I'm done," he said he felt calm and peaceful and more like himself than he had in years.[6] Len Schreiner quit the priesthood because he fell in love, and it helped him go beyond the limitations of the priesthood to a much more extensive consciousness.[7] And Anna Dubenko quit her doctoral studies at Yale. She felt stuck in an academic career, and her heart wasn't in finishing her dissertation. At first it was difficult to conceive of quitting. But once she started asking what she wanted her life to look like and realized she wanted something totally different, she felt an incredible sense of relief.[8]

The moral to these stories is if you toil in a dysfunctional workplace or have a job that doesn't fit with your values or a boss or workaholic manager breathing down your neck, you might be ready to jump ship. But check out important steps to take before calling it quits.

STEPS TO TAKE BEFORE JUMPING SHIP[9]

If you're debating whether to quit or stay-put, before you throw in the towel, make sure your emotions aren't clouding your decision and think it through thoroughly. People spend more time at their job—as much as one third of your days according to some sources—than just about any other place on earth. If you're miserable, it can take a tremendous toll on your life. Of course, all jobs have drawbacks. But if you're an unhappy worker most of the time, you're an unproductive worker much of the time. It doesn't benefit either you or the company to continue down that path. So, what do you do? Take a breath and step back before jumping ship too quickly to make sure you've thought everything through. Your decision will benefit from an objective, bird's-eye view.

1. Make a rational decision. The worst step is to impulsively bail from your present position without thinking it through. You don't want to trade one problem for another. Make sure emotions don't outrun your rational decision and take time to think things through. According to Michelle Wax, "It's important to consider if leaving your job is going to solve your problem—or if it's just a temporary fix that will come up again in the future. It's also important to take stock of what you enjoy currently, and what you'd love to spend your days doing in a perfect world," Wax said.

2. Schedule a meeting with your boss. If your job is intolerable, use it as a talking point when you meet with your manager. Without complaining, talk over your concerns. Make sure your boss understands your point of view, the importance of your personal life and your expectations concerning job demands. Ask if there's another way to divide up work tasks. Align your goals with those of the company and work with your boss to prioritize projects. Ask about company expectations and find out exactly what performance goals you must meet to receive an excellent review.

3. Ask for a raise. Dr. Ebbie Parsons, III, founder of Yardstick Management, suggests asking for a raise. "When it comes to asking for a raise, it's best to first approach your manager openly, backing up your request with real facts, metrics and impact-focused milestones," Parsons said. "If for any

reason you feel you are being compensated unfairly and this is why you're planning to leave your job, the best thing to do is set up a meeting with an HR leader at your company to discuss your concerns and what they can do to ensure better equality. In addition, you should consider asking for a higher percentage to match your 401K because this shows your employer that you're thinking long-term, which is a win-win for both you and them."

4. Request to work from home. "If you are considering quitting your job, something to think about is requesting to work from home a certain number of days each week," Parsons adds. "This will allow you to schedule your meetings on the days you are in office, freeing up larger sections of time to focus on important projects and tasks. Having more focused, dedicated time is also an important factor to express with upper management."

5. Conduct a stress audit to pinpoint your dissatisfaction. Exactly what is it about your job that makes you dissatisfied? Is it the boss from hell? Boredom with tedious work? Not enough money? Long hours? Heavy workload? According to Michelle Wax, putting pen to paper allows all the thoughts to come out of your head, and it's easier for your mind to process and create a rational decision. "A stress audit is fairly simple but requires being completely honest with yourself," she said. "This can be hard to do, especially when you've been in a role or a company for a while and have connections with the people and work you do there," Wax adds. "As you conduct your own stress audit, don't filter or ignore any gut reactions or thoughts that come up." Once you can isolate exactly what the factors are, decide if you can correct them. If not, it might be time to start exploring other options that better fit your personality.

6. Empower yourself. Avoid thinking of yourself as a victim of your job and remind yourself that it's not happening to you; you're making it happen in which case you can make it un-happen, too. Reminding yourself that you're the master, not the slave, empowers you and makes the days more tolerable until you find a more meaningful career.

7. Reach out to coworkers for support. If you feel like your situation is unsustainable and unfair, reach out to colleagues to see if they're having a similar situation and ask how they're managing it. If coworkers are also at the end of their rope, consider establishing support group meetings to deal with intolerable work situations. When possible, enlist your employer as a resource, including him or her in meetings to find constructive solutions to stress-related problems.

The good news is that the pandemic required more companies to realize that work stress is a major health and safety issue and that it's to their advantage to have healthy employees. Happy employees are productive employees. Big corporations are finding unique ways to support employees and de-stress work environments: paid paternity leave, remote and hybrid work, job sharing, flextime and onsite stress-reduction classes. Workers fare well when management communicates praise and encouragement, is clear about workplace expectations, and provides the tools employees need to feel challenged.

"Good Trouble" and a "New Normal" of Work

In 2018, just before the COVID-19 pandemic became rampant, "good trouble" was brewing around workplace mental health reform. "Good trouble"—coined by activist and senator John Lewis for nonviolent protests against unjust situations—was the kind of trouble to be proud of. "Good trouble," as I use it in this context, is a protest against "workjerkery" from head honchos in the workplace.

In the early months of 2020, COVID-19 struck fast and hard, ushering in a movement that would revolutionize the workplace in ways experts could never have predicted. Sharat Sharan, CEO, president, and co-founder of ON24, described it as a tsunami. "While we could see it coming, once it hit, the pandemic changed business overnight. And when a crisis like this happens, the pace of business is totally different. Weeks start to feel like months, and outcomes are impossible to predict."[10]

The workforce hit the ground running to accommodate corporate attitudes and demands. Businesses struggled with mandates to work in the office versus remote and hybrid working. Employees had to learn to use their elbows to punch elevator buttons and to greet coworkers. The debate over mask wearing was a huge controversy as was whether to get vaccinated. Plus, the migration from office to remote work had a profound impact on how people thought about their lives and when and where they wanted to work. After acclimation to working from home, the American workforce started to realize in hindsight how dissatisfied they had been toiling in oppressive office work environments. They got comfortable Zooming in their sweatpants and pajamas and walking into the next room to their workstation instead of commuting for twenty minutes across town.

Business leaders, citing the unexpected benefits of remote and hybrid work, predicted business would not go back to normal but back to a "new normal." According to Meena Krenek, principal and interior design director at an architecture and design firm in Los Angeles, colleagues shared more of their personal lives and got a rare window into who their coworkers were once they left the office—while not wearing corporate attire or makeup and often while simultaneously soothing a fussy child. "We learned new ways of social engagement with coworkers and clients that we could take back to humanize work environments," she said.

> The landscape of the virtual calls entailed unique experiences from coworkers' children participating in our conversations, from cats walking across keyboards as clients were talking, to getting a virtual tour of their new workspace at home . . . I believe we are sharing different sides of ourselves. Our perception of each other seems more genuine, which makes us feel much more connected and is allowing us to be more comfortably vulnerable. We are listening harder on the video calls and developing greater value for empathy. We need to continue to inspire, provide mental safety and support feelings of fulfillment.[11]

The author Daniel Stillman agreed that working from home and collaborating remotely is strangely intimate because we're peering into coworkers' homes and getting a window into their personal lives:

> Working remotely asks us to be more intentional in how we talk and collaborate—in this way, we're better able to design the experience in ways we couldn't before. I hope people will learn to bring some of these insights back into how we communicate 'in real life' . . . once we can do that again. My hope is also that we learn that we don't have to get on a plane and get into the same physical room to have an impactful, human conversation."[12]

Cara Pelletier, director of diversity, equity, and belonging at Ultimate Software added that many of the intimate adaptions we made to remote working could be used to reshape a more humane workplace: "The hope is that as our workforce evolves because of the crisis, we bring more empathy to our everyday connections. If things go back to normal for *most* people, we must lean on our working from home experience to remember that adaptations gave us equal access to participation and productivity. Our eventual transition back to the office presents an opportunity for us to better support one another, anticipate the needs of our teams, and pave the way for a more empathetic and *human* workplace.[13]

Remote workers cozied up to their workstations at home as COVID-19 infections spread rapidly and widely. Companies like Amazon, Google, and Apple—eager to call employees back to the office—delayed reopening offices. Wall Street firms, among the most adamant that employees return to the office, reconsidered return-to-office plans. To make the transition as easy as possible, some companies started suggesting—even requiring—that more employees work from home.

Resistant business leaders argued against remote work, pulling the old hat trick "It's your job to work hard and deal with stress, so grin and bear it." They cited productivity concerns and tactical problems that limited a supervisor's ability to observe and coach employees. As the 2022 post-pandemic remote work trend rose, Elon Musk issued an ultimatum that everyone at Tesla was required to spend a minimum of forty hours in the office per week. He said, "to be super clear," this can't be "some remote pseudo-office" but rather where their actual colleagues are located. "If you don't show up," he demanded, "we will assume you have resigned." Still, a handful of sensitized leaders saw the writing on the wall—that remote and hybrid work were permanent fixtures—and pushed back. They argued that companies could use the "new normal" for good in the new work world order. Josh Feast, CEO of the software company Cognito Corporation, asserted that supervisors could find innovative ways to connect with and manage workers from afar "by ensuring their colleagues feel heard and know they are not alone. Exhibiting heightened sensitivity to emotional intelligence—particularly in a time where physical isolation has become a necessity—is vital. To ensure everyone feels fully supported—emotionally—supervisors must set up alternate methods of oversight. Fortunately, technology is now more human-aware and can aid us in these efforts to remain connected and lead with empathy."[14]

Alice Hricak, managing principal of corporate interiors at Perkins and Will, said working from home showcased new approaches and debunked old ideas that it leads to low productivity, less visibility, and little opportunity for collaboration. David Powell, president of Prodoscore said their data showed that if an employee was highly productive in-office, they'll be productive at home; if an employee slacked off at the office, they'll do the same a home. "After evaluating over 105 million data points from 30,000 U.S.-based Prodoscore users, we discovered a five percent increase in productivity during the pandemic work from home period," he said. "Although, as we know, any variant of the Covid-19 virus is unpredictable, employee productivity is not."[15] Two studies in early 2022 validated positive remote work outcomes, showing that remote and hybrid employees were happier, more productive, and stayed in their jobs longer than when they toiled in the office. Plus, working from home led to better work-life balance and was more beneficial for the physical and mental well-being of employees.[16]

The positive wave led Ragu Bhargava, CEO at Global Upside, to advise business leaders that "the new normal" was a complete transformation in how we work, emphasizing the importance of evolving with the needs of employees. He warned that those who viewed remote work as temporary or unorthodox risked losing staff and no longer being competitive as the workplace evolved around them. "There's this clinging narrative of a 'return to normalcy' that many employers are holding onto, when in fact, the world of work will never truly return to the way it was before," Ragu said. "The pandemic revolutionized the workplace and expedited an already growing need for remote workers. The pandemic served as a massive wake-up call, teaching us not only that work was more than capable of being completed from home, but showing the need for flexibility for employees to take control of their own schedules—a necessity for those with long commutes, pricey childcare arrangements and those who simply wanted to spend more time with their families."[17]

The "Great Resignation"

"Good trouble" continued brewing and global support growing as companies behaving badly came under fire from an awakened, disenfranchised workforce. Workers refused to suck it up, put their heads in the sand, and push through. No longer were employees willing to turn off the lights in their offices and cower behind a potted plant to protect themselves from harmful corporate demands. No longer were they willing to subject themselves to sexual, physical, or mental abuse or trauma. And no longer were they willing to pay the price of burnout as a "normal" side effect of hard work.

"Good trouble" led to the birth of the "Great Resignation," imbuing the labor force with greater decision-making power than ever before. A newly empowered American workforce, with clear expectations of what they wanted, refused to endure corporate exploitation and abuse any longer. Armed with their personal morals and purpose priorities, a record number—4.5 million in November 2021 and another four million in January 2022 alone—left their jobs in droves, dramatically changing the job market as we knew it.[18]

Job hoppers in the red-hot labor market refused to let companies pigeonhole them into narrow, tight roles, force them to draw on their weaknesses or stay within the confines that limited their individual and, ultimately, the company's growth. Some launched their own businesses, some retired earlier than they had planned. Other job seekers searched out organizations with more work options such as better benefits, higher salaries, shorter commutes, and more flexibility. Still others sought positions where they felt appreciated and valued. Job seekers looked for organizations that placed priorities on workplace well-being, safety and sustainability that led with empathy and caring, that encouraged diversity and inventive ideas, and that allowed employees to draw on their strengths and boost the prosperity of the company. The mass exodus unearthed a major shift in public conversations about workplace mental health and wellness, empathy, security, stress, and burnout.

Corporate America and Work Addiction Recovery

One unintended consequence of the pandemic and the "Great Resignation" is that they dragged the abusive organization kicking and screaming into its own recovery from enabling work addiction. Peel away the veneer of most corporate structures from top to bottom, and it's clear that the symptoms parallel those of an abusive organization (described in the previous chapter):

1. The mission is denied, ignored, or forgotten.
2. Survival reigns supreme.
3. Profit is the driving force.
4. The entity is self-centered without boundaries or respect.
5. Crisis management is the norm.
6. Intimacy does not exist.

The abusive corporate message rang loud and clear: in exchange for compensation, you owe us your blood, sweat, and tears. And work stress and burnout are the price you must pay. But silver linings were embedded in the hardships of the pandemic lockdown. Once it became clear that the labor force had the upper hand, companies realized they could not entice workers back into the office with perks like catered breakfasts, ping-pong tables, or happy hours. And they learned that minimizing, covering up, or turning their heads the other way would create a revolving door and difficulty attracting and retaining talented employees who could find other work cultures where empathy and compassion were the norm. More leaders started to change their attitudes and policies and jumped on the "remote and hybrid work bandwagon." Employers were forced to adjust and consider more personal issues than ever to accommodate parents who were homeschooling and provide the tech equipment for teleworking.

The office-to-home transition brought a whole new set of rules that raised the awareness of business leaders. It required them to hone their emotional intelligence (openness, empathy, and connection), to understand that employees were more than a warm body and to realize they bring their whole selves to the workplace, that personal lives must be factored into how organizations manage, and to humanize the workplace in ways that big business had been unwilling or unable to do in the office. "When companies prioritize the well-being of their employees, business health follows," said John Morgan, president of Lee Hecht Harrison. "How leaders view their talent is a big change that has been accelerated by the pandemic. Successful leaders are looking at their talent as a renewable resource and finding new ways to invest in their employees to future-proof talent pipelines. The rise of the coaching culture is part of this trend that will likely have big impacts on employee and company performance."[19]

By early 2022, 62 percent of companies had heeded the call and reworked their policies to comply with the new normal, and 88.9 percent aimed to improve work-life balance for employees.[20] More companies created environments of care, and prioritized well-being throughout their cultures. They made employee mental health and well-being top priority. They committed to creating psychological safety and open communication, and they prioritized self-care with the understanding it goes together with job performance. Bumble and Hootsuite, for example, closed their offices for a week to address burnout and employee mental health. As employees and employers continued to navigate work from home and the fine line of being always available, more companies started prioritizing mental health to avoid burnout and fatigue. MikMak, in partnership with its internal mental health coalition, instituted company-wide office closure from July 5–July 9, 2021, to encourage employees to take care of themselves without the pressure of work in the background.[21]

The Knot Worldwide, a leading global family of brands, gave their employees a "Mental Health Honeymoon" by closing their offices from May 28–June 1, 2021. In addition, the company incorporated various other initiatives and programs to encourage employees to focus on mental health including year round bi-weekly virtual meditations, an EAP Wellness series with Health Advocate and counseling, weekly resources around mental health, balance, and well-being and the launch of Ginger, an on-demand emotional and mental health support app for life challenges through coaching via text-based chats, self-guided activities, and video-based therapy and psychiatry.[22]

Dr. Meisha-Ann Martin, director of people analytics at Workhuman, cited the importance of companies to consider the psychological safety of employees, citing the long-term benefits of frequent check-ins. "Establishing weekly or bi-weekly check-ins allows for higher levels of engagement, increased motivation, innovation, and better performance, which can lead to major breakthroughs," she said. "These are simple short-term acts that can have massive long-term benefits for the employer and employee. To make gratitude a habit, employers and managers should check in with employees more frequently and offer recognition to ensure workers feel heard, valued, and respected in the workplace."[23]

Employers across the country—from Goldman Sachs to Starbucks— began to re-evaluate how they approach employee mental health. "We all owe a debt of gratitude to public figures speaking up about their mental health issues, because they empower everyday people to speak up as well," said Henry Albrecht, co-founder and CEO of Limeade. "We do not know what they have gone through. It's a sign of strength to know when to ask for help."

Ten New Rules of Engagement

Organizations can no longer pay lip service that employees are their biggest asset when very few invest in them. The legacy of the "Great Resignation" of 2021–2022 was that to future-proof employees, companies must lead with more walk than just talk and genuinely consider employees as a renewable resource. More companies started ditching old fashioned management styles and updating them with ten rules of engagement that cultivate *employee-centered* rather than *employer-centered* work cultures and prevent work addiction from the top down. These ten rules of engagement contain the C-words associated with the C-Spot (see "Finding Your C-Spot" in "Recharging Your Batteries" in chapter 12).

1. Curiosity versus judgment. Workaholic cultures harbor blame and judgment. The first new rule of engagement is establishing more interest in curiosity than blame and judgment when work problems emerge. There's less interest in judging coworkers or yourself and more priority on creating a healthy work-life balance and supportive work environment. Curiosity about a work problem, instead of heavy-handed snap judgments, imbues everyone with deeper insights into possibilities and solutions to job problems.

2. Calm versus anxiety. Workaholic bosses who strike fear in the hearts of their employees cultivate a toxic work culture and compromise employee mental health. Threats, coercion, and intimidation—dinosaur management styles from the Industrial Revolution—only backfire. Absence of fear and worry promotes job engagement and productivity as well as the company's bottom line. A calm workplace starts with cool-headed leaders who encourage mindfulness meditation, tai chi, yoga, and calming practices on a regular basis. They advocate for work-life balance, paid time off, vacations and Microcations, and a culture where employees can take Microsteps and practice Microchillers and Microbreaks throughout the workday.

3. Clarity versus confusion. A workaholic company often lacks clarity in communicating goals and expectations and promotes confusion among

its workforce. Employee-centered work environments promote clear-mindedness and direction about company goals and employee job descriptions. Employees see beyond their immediate roles to the bigger picture where solutions and possibilities lie. Companies take a frequent inventory of their strengths and limitations and encourage employees to do the same as a baseline for goal setting and growth. Company leaders are skilled at facilitating clarity within the organization, communicating expectations, and making sure employees know their roles. They follow trending reports and research on why workers are leaving jobs and what recruiting retention measures are needed.

4. Compassion versus cold-heartedness. Workaholic companies lack warmth and caring for workers, placing productivity and profitability above emotional needs. Employee-centered companies encourage emotional intelligence as much as business intelligence and treat employees as humans with care and respect, not as worker bees that churn out work. Top down compassionate and empathetic leadership is the glue that holds a company together. Studies show when employees feel heard and cared about and are treated with respect, they have higher job satisfaction, less turnover and more loyalty to the company.[24] Employees feel safe to be vulnerable and to share their own slip-ups, challenges, and personal feelings, which foster their interest in mentoring and teamwork.

5. Confidence versus intimidation. A workaholic organization undermines the confidence of its workers by exercising tight control to get a bigger bang for its buck. Employee-centered businesses have confidence in employees and provide work autonomy. They acknowledge and reward employees for hard work without unreasonable job demands and deadlines or micromanaging. Studies show employees want to be recognized and appreciated but also want to feel confident in their positions instead of working from past intimidations, rejections and failures, or future fears. Companies that practice this rule of engagement look for the places where employees add value and reward them financially and verbally with abundant positive feedback and affirmations.

6. Connection versus isolation. A major characteristic of a workaholic organization is isolation from corporate honchos and employees from one another. One-sided communication and iron-fisted management styles are the biggest complaints from the American workforce. In an employee-centered work environment, workers enjoy a satisfying connection with colleagues versus isolation from them. Employee-centered communication brings a more personalized and effective approach and puts leaders into the position of listener and facilitator, not talker and intimidator. They

check in with team members to let them know they belong and to keep them in the loop and connected to the company.

7. Courage versus fear. Workaholic companies have a rigid corporate scaffolding that stifles innovation, limits worker potential, and hurts the company's bottom line. In an employee-centered work culture, employees are encouraged to be mold breakers and professional risk takers. They're rewarded for asking what edge they can go to in their careers to create a more productive workplace. What bridge they can jump off to sprout their wings. What limb they can reach to get to the fruit of the tree.

8. Creativity versus stagnation. Workaholic businesses put more emphasis on production than on the process of getting there. This approach leads to a narrow focus and missed opportunities for seeing the big picture and creative possibilities. Employees say the opportunity for growth and autonomy is at the top of their wish list. Employee-centered companies practice "personalization" and "customization" by providing flexible work arrangements—such as hybrid or remote working—to accommodate their employees' personal needs. They foster creativity and brainstorming among staff by asking and answering questions that stimulate critical thinking. And they draw out creative ideas to give employees a deeper understanding of their values, needs, and beliefs. Creative ideas that are solicited and implemented give workers more ownership in the company, plus higher performance, greater productivity, and longer tenure.

9. Comedy versus drama. Work should not make us sick or cause us to burnout. It should be satisfying—even fun. But workaholic organizations consider fun and laughter frivolous wastes of time. They thumb their noses at lightheartedness and the humorous side of life—even though it has the potential to uplift moods and build company morale—a joke, funny things your children do, a silly story that happened over the weekend. Somewhere along the way corporate America has forgotten that work is supposed to be enjoyable—even fun, like the Seven Dwarfs who sang, "Hi Ho, Hi Ho, it's off to work we go." Well, maybe not that lighthearted. But work doesn't have to be grim, humorless determination where we sweat, toil, and burnout before earning the right to enjoy it. Employee-centered businesses consider humor and lightheartedness to be essential ingredients baked into the workday.

10. Celebration versus exasperation. Workaholics forget, ignore, or minimize celebrations such as birthdays, anniversaries, or holidays. Work takes precedence in workaholic businesses where celebrations are considered a frivolous waste of time—even in some cases a distraction from productivity. Discontentment filters down the chain of command, when dis-

satisfied leaders rule from the top, and bleeds into the fiber of workplace relationships. Workers often feel exasperated from such a toxic culture. Employee-centered work cultures celebrate important moments with staff and create get-togethers if for no other reason than for everyone to enjoy each other's company.

Tips for Clinicians

After a year of the pandemic, the remote workforce struggled to disconnect from work and burned the midnight oil. A large number even claimed they became modern-day workaholics—48 percent by one account. Self-described workaholics found their condition exacerbated by the blurring of boundaries between personal space and the professional environment—conditions detrimental to their mental health, productivity, and job satisfaction. Seven out of ten remote workers said they were unable to disconnect from work at night. This led to the "Great Resignation" in which workers quit their jobs in droves due to burnout at epidemic proportions, seeking jobs elsewhere to enjoy more work-life balance. With more clients working from home and more clinicians using telehealth, it's important to create guidelines for a productive workspace for clients and yourself.

GUIDELINES FOR REMOTE WORKING

A burnout prevention plan keeps you from hitting your breaking point long before burnout sets in. If you're a remote or hybrid worker and this scenario occurred in your household, as it did in thousands across the county, there are tips you can share with clients on how to set boundaries during remote working and create optimal productivity.

If you're a remote worker, you're in your personal space, not your usual professional environment. Laundry needs to be done, dishes washed, and the house tidied up. This might even be a good time to clean out the gutters or the basement. Plus, you wanted to see *The View* since you were always at the office when it aired. Or there's a good movie on Netflix you've been longing to watch. The pooch needs walking, and your spouse keeps yelling questions from another room, causing you to keep losing your train of thought. You might as well go for the chocolate cake in the fridge, although you've worried about the "quarantine fifteen," and developing "pandemic posture" from hours spent slumping over your computer screens.

On the flip side, since being at home 24/7, you find yourself toiling into the night, long after you would have called it quits at the office. Your work desk is just in the next room, and you can get a lot off your plate if you burn the midnight oil. You've heard that Zoom burnout is a built-in feature of the quarantine. Yet, you've been glued to your screen all day in back-to-back meetings. And you can tell that your brain's ability to focus and engage is waning, causing you to lose balance between private time and professional tasks.

❖ Establish a designated workspace. Confine your work to a specific area in your home so your job doesn't intrude into the lives of other household members, and you can concentrate. Have a space that you designate as your workstation instead of checking emails, voicemails, or texting in front of TV or spreading work out on the kitchen table. After hours, keep your workspace at arm's length as if it's five miles across town. Resist the temptation to check texts and emails after logging off at the end of the workday. If possible, only go to your designated space when you need to work. After a long workday, make it a practice to put away electronic devices and work tools. Putting work reminders out of sight keeps them out of mind and helps you relax and recharge your batteries.

❖ Resist temptation. Establish water-tight psychological boundaries so you're not constantly reminded of temptations around you. There's chocolate cake in the fridge and your mutt is on his hind legs begging to be picked up. Of course, there are unfinished personal tasks, too—such as dirty laundry, vacuuming, or organizing your spice rack—that otherwise could compromise your productivity. Complete these personal activities outside of work hours as you normally would.

❖ Put limits on distracting sounds. Block the neighbor's barking dog and excess noise from household members or ambient traffic with noise cancelling devices such as headphones, white noise machines, or ear buds. Studies show a delicate blend of soft music combined with soothing nature sounds—such as waterfalls, raindrops, a rushing brook, or ocean waves—activates the calming part of your brain, helps you concentrate and lowers heart rate and blood pressure.

❖ Practice the acronym W.A.I.T. Since being at home 24/7, you might find yourself toiling overtime on the job long after you would have called it quits at the office. If overworking becomes a pattern, use the acronym W.A.I.T., which stands for Why Am I Toiling? The answers could be that you're avoiding facing the home chores that piled up while working. You might be putting yourself under pressure to finish a project. Or perhaps you've bitten off more than you can chew. Regardless of the reason, try to maintain the same hours you log in at the office, so you don't get swallowed up by the workload.

❖ Discourage personal intrusions. If you're a teacher or doctor, friends don't just stop by the office to chat, hang-out or interrupt your work. But sometimes well-intended friends, family members, and neighbors think working at home is different. Interruptions and drop-ins can cause you to lose your focus, procrastinate, or get behind on a deadline. It's important to prevent intrusions into your workspace by informing others that although the location of your job has changed, it is no different from any other profession requiring privacy and concentration. Notify others that during at-home work hours, you're unavailable and cannot be interrupted. And let them know the after-hours when you're available to connect.

❖ Employ your video communications more than you normally would. Now that you're more isolated, make sure you have your company's telecommuting devices—such as Zoom—hooked up and ready to go so you can stay connected with team members or office mates and you're available for video calls and teleconferencing. If you start to feel lonely, consider setting up a support group of friends and colleagues who are also working at home by satellite. Make plans to meet on a regular basis and share creative ways you've adjusted to the new situation.

❖ Avoid cabin fever. Now that you're spending a disproportionate amount of time at home, get outside as much as possible with gardening or walking around the block. Mounting research shows that spending time in nature lowers stress, helps you relax and clears your mind. After work hours, enjoy other areas of your home: watching a good movie, reading a book, or cooking a fun meal. And lead as much of a full social life as possible such as by having COVID-negative friends over for dinner. The new normal is not to limit social devices but to take advantage of them. Use Facetime, Facebook, or Skype with friends and family members so you feel connected to the people in your life that you care about.

❖ Practice self-care. Many of us forfeited our daily self-care routines during the pandemic restrictions. It's important to keep them or put them back in place. Scientists recommend a minimum of thirty minutes of extra light activity per day and five minutes of movement each hour throughout the day to mitigate COVID-19 restrictions and inactivity.[25] After hours of sitting, short breaks—I recommend five minutes or less—are effective energy management strategies and can be as simple as stretching, walking up and down stairs, gazing out a window at nature, snacking, deep breathing, yoga, or having a five-minute mindful meditation.

COPING WITH A WORKAHOLIC BOSS

The boss from hell is the most common reason people quit their jobs. You might have a client who works in an intolerable situation. Workaholic bosses have long arms that stretch through electronic devices into the personal lives of remote workers. Your clients can't fire the boss or restructure the organization, but they can take some action that will benefit them in the long run. Here are some steps to deal with a workaholic boss:

❖ *Avoid anger and impatience.* These are the traits of workaholics who are socially isolated, and task focused. Remain tactful and diplomatic, even when you're frustrated. Talk with your boss and try to see his or her human side. Try to find an idea, pastime, or point of view that gives you common ground to connect with your boss so that you can stay objective and see the problem as bigger than just the two of you.

❖ *Schedule a meeting with your boss to find out what his or her expectations of you are, and the expectations of your boss's boss.* Ask exactly what type of performance is expected for you to receive an excellent review rating. According to some experts, 99 percent of the time work hours are not among the factors.[26] This practice ensures that you won't be downgraded for not putting in extra hours. Make sure your boss understands your point of view, the importance of your personal life, and your expectations concerning job demands. Make priorities, set goals, and schedule your time accordingly.

❖ *Reach out to coworkers who are experiencing similar problems with the boss.* Start support-group meetings before or after work, or during lunch in designated places at the work site. By meeting together and talking about your problems constructively, you can develop a rich support system to draw on in the job setting. When appropriate, schedule a group meeting with the boss and explain your concerns in a constructive way. Ask for feedback or ground rules so that all of you can be productive and avoid future problems.

Many workaholics fall into the all-or-nothing mind trap and believe quitting their job will solve their work addiction (see chapter 4). Clinicians can't tell clients what to do under these circumstances. That's their call. But you can process the pros and cons with them. For example, if their current position is all they can find, even if they're not thrilled with it, you don't want them to trade one problem for another by being unemployed. And if their job is tolerable and pays the bills, they might have to weigh the financial advantages considering the job's negative aspects, plus the other factors such as the people who are dependent on them and their amount of debt.

Bibliotherapy

The following books provide further reading on topics relevant to this chapter:

❖ Daniel Goleman, *Emotional Intelligence: Why It Can Matter More Than IQ, 25th Anniversary Edition* (New York: Bloomsbury Publishing, 2020).

❖ Daniel Stillman, *Good Talk: How to Design Conversations That Matter* (Amsterdam: Management Impact Publishing, 2020).

❖ Tessa West, *Jerks at Work: Toxic Co-Workers and What to Do About Them* (New York: Ebury Edge, 2022).

Recovery from Work Addiction

The Perspective Less Taken

Between stimulus and response,
there is a space. In that space is our
power to choose our response. In
our response lies our growth and
freedom.

— Viktor Frankl

Bryan Is Banned from the Hospital (Oops, Me Again!)

On the third trip to the ER after the hospital had done nothing to fix my spouse's pain, I lost my shit. My tirade was reminiscent of the classic scene from the 1983 film *Terms of Endearment*. When the nurses hesitated to give her daughter a pain shot, Shirley MacLaine's character screamed, "Give her the shot do you understand? Give my daughter the shot!" Shocked, the medical staff quickly complied. I, too, yelled at the top of my lungs, a blood vessel ballooning in my neck—not as clean-cut as MacLaine, "This is the third time we've been here in the middle of the night, and you guys haven't done a god-damn thing!"

The triage staff took notice of my outrage (how could they not?), but so did my spouse, who said, "I want you to leave!" I left the hospital, the medical staff took appropriate action, and Jamey was finally admitted. After a few days, he recovered, and so did I. I'm not ashamed of the outburst. Watching someone I love scared and writhing in pain, felt like a matter of life and death. Still, in hindsight I wish I'd used that space Viktor Frankl mentioned—my C-Spot, as I discuss in this chapter—to handle the situation, but my perspective had other ideas.

Did the situation unmake my day? No, *I unmade my own day.* I wasn't rocking it. The diatribe didn't help matters and only made Jamey's day even more difficult. In hindsight I could have achieved the same (or even better) results if I had spent some time watching and acknowledging my frustration, calming down, and taking a bird's-eye view of the situation. The staff still would've admitted him, and I wouldn't have been banished from the ER by my upset spouse. If only I could've flipped my perspective in the heat of the moment.

In the throes of my work addiction, I spent much of my life in a fight-or-flight state, as a reactive person—outwardly, but mostly inwardly—harboring judgment toward myself and others, simmering with anger when things didn't go my way, people didn't agree with me, or I couldn't control certain situations. I was a chain smoking, workaholic maniac—one big bundle of stress, racing against the clock, shaking my fist at the heavens. I stumbled through life, over-reacting in predictable ways to anything and everything that didn't suit me— clueless that I had choices. It was the only way I knew. Gradually, I learned that changing my perspective, along with my work habits, would arm me with work resiliency and balance.

Flip Your Perspective Instead of Your Lid

Through mindfulness meditation, I came to understand that we don't get to choose how we're going to die or when or how most situations play out. But we can choose how we respond to unpleasant situations and how we want to live in the present moment. Although that's a powerful and awesome feeling when we make the choice, it's not easy to do. Life's curveballs will slam you at lightning speed from all angles, throwing you off your path. The curveballs are a given. The question is, "What are you going to do about it?" This is a question that many of us never stop to *think about*. I know I didn't used to give it a second thought.

Anger and reactivity are hallmarks of work addiction. And even if you're not a workaholic, you've probably had the experience of a situation or a person setting you off. A rude comment, bad news, an unexpected inconvenience, and we lose our mind. It's not because the other person is bad, stupid, or an asshole (although they may be, but that's beside the point). And it's not because you have bad luck or life has a vendetta against you. When someone or something makes you angry, it's because you *allow* them to, not because of them. Anthony de Mello once said, "To recognize that my upsets come from myself is the first step to remedying them."

It's a bitter pill for workaholics to swallow, but peace of mind is up to our willingness to flip our perspective. If you stand in a different place and look at life from another angle, the change in perspective gives you power to change your world. The things you look for have a way of finding you. When you expect a bad outcome, it can turn out that way simply because your thoughts and behaviors fit your expectations. What life throws at you doesn't determine your peace of mind; your perspective does. Your thoughts and actions—and ultimately your serenity—depend on the angle from which you view life. When you stand in just one place, you only get to see the world as you *think* it is, not how it really is.

This principle applies to making *micro-adjustments* and changing long-held habits by simply associating them with a positive experience. To change hard habits, sometimes all you need is a perspective shift. For example, you remind yourself that you get to spend time with the ones you love (spouse or partner and maybe the kids) but only if you choose to leave the laptop and stack of files you brought home in the trunk of your car instead of piling them on the kitchen table.

Another example of a tiny change is to alter our language: "We often talk about everything we *must* do in each day. You must wake up early for work. You have to make another sales call for your business. You must cook dinner for your family. Now imagine changing just one word: You don't 'have to'. You 'get to'. You *get* to wake up early for work. You *get* to make another sales call for your business. You *get* to cook dinner for your family. By simply changing one word, you shift the way you view each event. You transition from seeing these behaviors as burdens and turn them into opportunities—even adventures."[1]

Toxic Positivity and Keeping It Real

It's important to add here that flipping your perspective is about emotional honesty and keeping it real. Flipping your perspective is not the same as *toxic positivity* in which you put your head in the sand and try to convince yourself everything's great when it isn't.[2] You can become just as obsessed with requiring yourself to be happy as you are about your addiction to work. When you do this, you're not honest with your feelings.

Suppose you're upset about losing your job. Instead of validating your feelings and thoughts, you force yourself to look on the bright side without giving the dark side a second thought: "Now I have all the time in the world to do what I want." (This, a happy workaholic will not make.) Or you tell yourself, "Now I don't have to work with that asshole boss." (Truth be told, you always liked your boss up until now.) Or you say, "I'm supposed to find something good in this situation, and I don't see it." (Oops, something must be wrong with me.)

You get where I'm going? You can't have a front without a back, a right without a left, or an upside without a downside. Misery and unhappiness are not caused by the actual event; they're caused by not wanting and resisting the event. In therapy we have an old saying, "Whatever you resist persists." Happiness comes with the balance of accepting both sides of the coin. Flipping your perspective is about emotional honesty and allowing yourself to feel what you feel—to recognize that you're disappointed, frustrated, or scared—which makes the perspective shift authentic. But just as everything has a flip side, it's important not to stay in the negativity, either. That's just as dishonest and unhealthy as camping out only in the positivity.

When the Monks Came to Town

Insidiously and unwittingly, work addiction and loss of life balance created my own emotional prison, burnt out and trapped on autopilot in the negativity of my perspective. Like many workaholics, I came to realize I wasn't in control of my life. It was in control of me, and it sucks when you're bent and swayed by random unpredictability. I grew so accustomed to seeing myself at the mercy of unpleasant situations, that each negative event became another bar on my jail cell. It wasn't until a life-altering event helped me see how my *actions* can be more powerful than my *reactions*, and I realized I already held the key to my own freedom.

This realization hit me like a jackhammer when ten Tibetan monks performed on campus of the University of North Carolina at Charlotte where I was a professor. They spent a few days constructing a breathtaking mandala from multi-colored rice flour, and their work culminated in a campus concert of chanting and dancing. On the night of their performance, a group of angry religious fundamentalists picketed the auditorium, charging that Buddhists worship idols and Buddhism is the devil's work. Circling in protest, they joined hands and sang, "Jesus Loves Me."

I reacted with fury at the picketers (this was before I had an inkling that I could choose how to think or feel). I remember thinking the seemingly innocent religious zealots were stoking the embers of a hate-fueled fire that smoldered inside them. But guess what? So was I, although I didn't realize it. The demonstration was yet another display of hatred towards people different from the protestors, and I'm not proud to say that I hated them back. When the monks heard about the disturbance, they smiled, held the start of the show, and walked outside. They approached the circle, joined hands with the protesters, and sang, "Jesus Loves Me" with deep sincerity and respect. I was gob smacked. Disarmed by the monks" gentle actions, the group quietly disbanded.

Other examples of this kind of action are stories of family members who are able to forgive someone for murdering a loved one. In 2019, Brandt Jean took an extraordinary action toward Amber Guyger, a police officer who accidentally entered his brother's apartment which she thought was hers and killed him in his own home. As the judge handed down a ten-year prison sentence to Guyger for the killing, Brandt Jean asked from the stand, "I don't know if this is possible, but can I give her a hug, please?" As the two shared a tight hug, the courtroom was quiet except for the sounds of sobbing.

Like *When Harry Met Sally*

I read these stories of forgiveness and continued to be deeply moved by them and the *actions* (the non-*reactions*) of the monks and their ability to stay in a centered place of calm, connectivity, and compassion—some of the C-words that compose what I would later term the *C-Spot* (see "Recharging Your Batteries"). Witnessing it with my own two eyes taught me that *action* is more powerful than *reaction*. Once you begin to take conscious control of your actions—instead of allowing your reactions to decide them for you—you're in charge of your mind, behavior, and ultimately your life. By choosing another perspective, you're free.

I remember mentally rehashing the monk's actions and thinking, "I want what they have." It was like the classic scene in *When Harry Met Sally*, when Meg Ryan's character faked an orgasm in the middle of Katz's Deli in New York City and another customer blurted out, "I'll have what she's having." That's how I felt. As I would later discover on my journey, not unlike the female G-Spot, it's tremendously euphoric when you can find and stay in your C-Spot, regardless of challenging circumstances. At the time I witnessed the actions of the monks, I didn't know it was possible for me to change my perspective. But my curiosity at what I'd seen jump-started me on a path of seeking and studying mindful meditation and learning to work mindfully (see chapter 13).

There's a Space for You

In my search, I read the philosophy of Stoicism that says even if you can't control external events, you can choose your responses. While the philosophy was exactly what I was looking for, it still didn't give me a roadmap for how to accomplish it. Then I stumbled upon the awe-inspiring account of neurologist and psychiatrist Viktor Frankl. During his confinement in Auschwitz and other extermination camps during World War II—separated from his wife, starving, and stripped of clothing and human dignity—Frankl endured unspeakable atrocities. Despite experiencing suffering and degradation and witnessing friends and family being tortured and people dropping dead

Finding Your C-Spot

Work addiction crowds our lives and colonizes our hearts, causing us to lose touch with our true selves or center—a place inside I call the *C-Spot*. If you're like most workaholics or stress-immersed laborers, you run roughshod over your C-Spot and don't even realize it's there. My research at the University of North Carolina at Charlotte found that workaholics have higher burnout rates and are more disconnected from their C-Spot. In contrast, nonworkaholics showed more clarity, compassion, calmness, and confidence—traits that they are more in touch with themselves and their C-Spot.[3]

How do you recognize it? Your C-Spot is teeming with numerous "C" states. You know you're in that place when you can sustain one or more of the following: curiosity, calmness, clarity, compassion, confidence, connection, courage, creativity, comedy, and celebration. Although this list isn't exhaustive, all of them describe the C-Spot as a state of openness or connection, as opposed to the workaholic mind's closed protectiveness.

Notice that many of these C-states have the Latin prefix, "con" or "com," which means "with" or "come together," and they convey a sense of openness to "join with"— which is in direct opposition to fighting, beating, or battling. When you connect two objects or people, you link them "with" each other. When people convene at a certain place, they meet "with" others. When people congregate, they flock "with" each other. And when you're in that spot, you're living your best life. But remaining in your C-Spot in the heat of a challenging moment is the starting point on the path to living more fully, which I was eventually able to do (see the story of "The Little Red Car" in chapter 14).

Studies show people with open minds (working and living from their C-Spot) use conjunctions such as "and" or "also," plus, they are less likely to use negative words such as "no" or "not," which are closed-ended words. Now, that might seem irrelevant to you, but not to me. It's a significant indicator that the language we use reflects our openness to connecting with others and that we're less likely to be under the influence of the lizard brain's negativity bias and more immersed in the C-Spot.

Your C-Spot acts as an inner barometer guiding your work life in a peaceful observing awareness of what you think, feel, and do. Over time, the transition into your C-Spot strengthens your ability to *act* instead of *react* and stay calm, cool, and collected regardless of how dire the circumstances. By living from this open state, as opposed to the guardedness of the workaholic mind, you're able to get your lizard brain on board to continue protecting you while living a calmer, happier, and more fulfilling life.

Once in your C-Spot, you connect with your natural body rhythm—the vitality you feel when you're in your best Self and all is right with the world. When you work and live from your C-spot, you have the best capacity for flexibility and adaptability.

around him, he recognized that he still had choices. The Nazis could strip him of outer resources such as food, clothing, and family, but they couldn't rob him of his greatest resources, the ones he carried inside. His will to live and his spirit were his alone to control.

Frankl drew from his *C-Spot* when he said, "Between stimulus and response there is a space. In that space is our power to choose our response. In our response lies our growth and our freedom." Even though the C-Spot exists within everyone, most of us stampede over it in threatening moments. Yet, Frankl was able to find that inner space between the Nazi's mistreatment and his own power to choose his feelings, thoughts, and actions.

By staying in his C-Spot, he was able to choose his way regardless of the outer conditions of his life. Despite being locked inside a concentration camp, he was free—because he *chose* to be. In his classic book on the experience, *Man's Search for Meaning*, Frankl wrote, "When we can no longer change a situation, we are challenged to change ourselves . . . Everything can be taken from a human but one thing: the last of the human freedoms—to choose one's attitude in any given set of circumstances, to choose one's own way." In those wise remarks, Frankl described a strategy to activate the prefrontal cortex to keep from going into orbit long before neuroscience identified the concept of *neuroplasticity* (see chapter 5).[4]

That inner freedom helped Frankl survive the Holocaust, find meaning in his personal tragedy, and empower himself. He chose the response to his circumstances instead of letting the circumstances dictate his choices. And his famous quote helped millions of people—me included—discover the gap, the C-Spot, between circumstances and reactions. In another best-selling account of the Holocaust, Dr. Edith Eger told the story of how, when cannibalism broke out in the death camp, she chose to eat grass instead of the dead flesh of her comrades. She described how all of us can use challenges to avoid being a victim, always make choices, and unlock our mental prisons.[5]

If you're a workaholic, although you're not inside a literal prison, you are nonetheless trapped. The workaholic bars you unwittingly erect from inside out to cope with daily pressures, obstacles, interruptions, delays, rejections, and unrealized expectations negatively affect your mental and physical health and exile you from relationships and the serenity and happiness you seek.

In my own determined search to free myself from the self-imposed workaholic prison, I took charge of the ensuing burnout and focused on work-life balance. I trained in IFS therapy with Richard Schwartz, stumbled onto yoga, started mindfulness meditation, and learned to separate from my workaholic parts (see chapter 14). The practices helped me to recognize the crack in the foundation of my life and to become more aware of how I had unwittingly forfeited my personal power to the addiction. I began my climb out of my work stupors and anger into a saner life that I examined through dispassionate fresh eyes. I read the teachings and spent time in the presence of monks, gurus, and spiritual leaders like His Holiness the Dalai Lama, Pema Chödrön, and Thich Nhat Hanh.

Quiz: How Wide Is Your Work Resiliency Scope?

Is your work perspective narrow and closed or broad and open? The wider your perspective, the closer you are to the onramp of your C-Spot and the more resilient you are. To find out, read the following statements. Write next to each one the number that fits: 1 (strongly disagree), 2 (disagree), 3 (agree), or 4 (strongly agree).

_____ 1. Life is full of problems.

_____ 2. I usually assume people will take advantage of me.

_____ 3. Things never turn out the way I want.

_____ 4. Nothing I do is good enough.

_____ 5. Whatever can go wrong will go wrong.

_____ 6. I'm a born loser.

_____ 7. Trouble follows me wherever I go.

_____ 8. I'm not a worthy person.

_____ 9. I can't change the way things are.

_____ 10. I don't have what it takes to meet most challenges.

_____ Total Score

SCORING: Add up the numbers and put your total score in the blank at the bottom. The lower your score, the more resilient you are. Use the following key to interpret your score: 10–20 means you have a wide scope that makes you work resilient; 21–29 means you have a medium-width scope that you can expand; 30–40 means you have a narrow scope that needs broadening in order for you to become more resilient.

The Three-to-One Ratio

Negativity has a longer shelf life than positivity because of the "negativity bias" that's hard-wired in us for survival (see chapter 4). You're more likely to store a threatening, negative memory than a positive one after just one episode—all in the name of survival. I'll bet you remember where you were, who you were with, and what you were doing on September 11, 2001—that is, assuming you're old enough to have been born. But where were you a few days later at the same time? I'd be surprised if you could tell me, because it wasn't threatening enough to stand out. You're more likely to recall the time you fell out of the tree and broke your arm than all those times you safely climbed the tree. Or that bad-tasting medicine your mom forced down you. You're more apt to remember that than her lemon meringue pie.

Scientists have discovered that it takes three positive thoughts to offset one negative thought. According to Dr. Barbara Fredrickson, positivity researcher at the University of North Carolina, for every heart-wrenching negative emotional experience you endure, you need to experience at least three heartfelt positive emotional experiences that uplift you. Applying the three-to-one ratio, as she calls it, builds a collaborative relationship between your emotional or negative amygdala and your rational or positive thoughts.

Positivity isn't following the cliches of *Grin and bear it* or *Don't worry, be happy*. Positivity takes you deeper into the qualities of your C-Spot. According to Fredrickson, being positive isn't trading bad thoughts for positive ones; it changes the scope of your mind and widens the span of possibilities: "The potential for life-draining negativity lies within you, just as does the potential for life-giving positivity. You have more say than you think about which you feel and when. The treasure for your own positivity is waiting."[6]

WIDENING YOUR MINDSCAPE

As a result of many experiments, scientists know that when you intentionally broaden your scope, your work stress automatically lifts. A positive scope widens your attention, shifts your outlook, expands your world view, and allows you to take more in and see many ways to face work challenges. The more you take in, the more ideas and actions you add to your toolbox.

There's a lot of wisdom behind the adage, "Look on the bright side." Think about it this way: when work stress hangs over you like a cloud, you can't see the sun. But when you can create positive feelings, it helps you part the cloudy thinking and let the sunshine through. As your scope widens, you see the big picture of possible solutions instead of getting mired in the challenging situation. But to say you're not going to worry, that you're just going to be happy, doesn't do justice to the scientific underpinnings of positivity's depth and power as an antidote to work addiction.

Scientists have discovered that positivity stretches your mind open to take in as much as you can, widening your span of possibilities more than negativity or neutrality. When you're dealing with a stressful situation, positivity showcases the range of possibilities. It helps you focus on a positive outcome that negativity hides from view. Simply put, negativity keeps you focused on the problem, whereas positivity helps you find solutions. Positivity acts as a stress buffer when you're mired in work addiction, broadening your mind and range of vision. When you're under the gun with looming deadlines or overloaded with work tasks, your mind is designed to constrict and target the negative threat. If you're searching for a solution to a work crisis, your negative emotions keep you focused on the problem. Without knowing it, you focus on the stressful event and block out the big picture. But positive feelings like lightheartedness, joy, curiosity, gratitude, love, and hope expand your range of vision.

BROADENING YOUR POSITIVITY

Look over the list of ten negative statements in the quiz. As you read down the list, notice the constrictive tone of the statements and how they cloud out possibilities. Notice how you feel as you complete the list. Not so hot, huh?

Now go back and broaden each statement to include possible solutions. For example, you might reword the first statement as, "Life does contain problems, but there are also solutions to problems; I can focus on the possibilities." After you've broadened the statements, notice the difference in tone. Do you notice a difference in how you feel? I'll bet you feel more uplifted.

Now it's your turn. Make a list of three or four negative statements you've had recently. Write them exactly as you hear them in your mind's echo chamber. Then go back and decrease the negativity by adding possibilities. Try to rewrite the statements genuinely in ways that are truthful for you. Pay attention to how you feel as you add more positivity.

STACKING YOUR POSITIVE DECK

It's simple science. When you have positive emotions on a regular basis, they have cumulative benefits that dwarf your negative emotions. Scientists call this strategy the "broaden and build" effect.[7] Here are some broaden-and-build strategies you can use to stack your positivity deck and blunt workaholic habits:

1. Step back from work situations and come up with a wide range of possible solutions.

2. Tell yourself work problems are not personal failures and that nothing is permanent. Every event has a beginning and an ending.

3. Broaden your scope beyond work demands and think of the full range of things that make your life meaningful.

4. Practice self-compassion instead of making negative self-judgments.

5. Dwell on positive subjects and focus on positive aspects of your life where you can make a difference. Avoid high-stress media reports, violent movies, or squabbles in the office.

6. Hang out with positive coworkers. Like negativity, positivity is contagious. When you surround yourself with positive colleagues, positivity rubs off.

7. Give yourself a pat on the back when you reach a milestone or important accomplishment. Tell yourself how awesome you are: "I knew I could do it!"

8. Focus on the solution, not the problem. If there's a problem at work, encourage coworkers to brainstorm and come up with possible ways to fix it instead of getting stuck in the complaints.

9. Reframe gloomy prospects in a positive way. Few situations are 100 percent bad. Tom was upset that he had to pay a half-million dollars in taxes; he had lost sight of the fact that he'd earned five million that same year. He was so caught up in his loss that it eclipsed his gain. Tom was a rich man living an impoverished life—all because of his narrow scope.

UNDERSCORE THE UPSIDE

Negativity can be a knee-jerk reaction that you might not be aware of. A friend of mine loved the warm, long days of summer. One day in June, on the longest day of the year, I said to her, "You must be on cloud nine." She replied, "No, I'm sad because tomorrow the days start getting shorter again." When I pointed out how she was shrinking her joy, she was surprised that her narrow scope had hijacked her. She was able to broaden her outlook, remember how she'd looked forward to this time of year, and savor the warm weather instead of focusing on the cold days to come.

If you're like many workaholics, your mind automatically constricts situations without your realizing it. Perhaps you focus on times you failed, someone who did you wrong five years ago, or goals that you still haven't reached: "Same lousy job, the boring coworkers, the office party that was nothing to write home about."

You build up your negativity deck without realizing it. And that becomes the lens you look through. You can reverse your negative mindset with practice in finding the upside. Don't let positivity slip by without underscoring it. Start taking the pleasant aspects of the world into your mind: "I enjoy conversations with my coworker"; "I love the smell of freshly brewed coffee from the break room"; or "The smell of those flowers at my workstation is wonderful." When you underscore the small things around you that you appreciate, it grows positive feelings and cheers you up.

THE UNDO EFFECT OF POSITIVITY

Studies show that a positive outlook can undo the damage to the mind and body from workaholic stress and negativity, making you more work resilient. Positive events in your life help repair cardiovascular wear and tear caused by the stress response to negative events. Positive emotions send your body a different message than negative emotions, putting the brakes on the stress juices, activating your parasympathetic nervous system, and calming you down.

Positive feelings contain the active ingredients that enable you to escape from debilitating stress and grow stronger. Positive thinkers can cope better with adversity because they can see solutions to stressful problems. Positivity helps you think in terms of "we" instead of "me," to look past imagined threats from people of different races, genders, or ages. In addition, it gives you an appreciation for the common ground you share with others. This broadening automatically draws you closer to friends and family. And you're more likely to feel oneness with strangers, people of different lifestyles and ethnic groups, and cultures around the world.[8]

AN ATTITUDE OF GRATITUDE

Oprah Winfrey said, "If you look at what you have in life, you'll always have more. If you look at what you don't have in life, you'll never have enough." Truer words have never been spoken. Practicing gratitude helps you see the flip side of a narrow mental scope that builds without your awareness. When you count your blessings, you broaden your outlook and get an emotional lift. Try this exercise. Write down as many things as you can think of that you're grateful for, that make your life worth living. Then make a list of the people, places, and things that bring you comfort and joy. Your list can include material items, such as cars, electronic devices, clothes, jewelry, houses, trips, and so on. It can include loving relationships, children, pets, and coworkers. And it can include your health and the health of your loved ones.

After you've made your list, reflect on your appreciation for each item. Practice this exercise regularly until you begin to see more positive aspects of your life. And you'll be more aware of how full it is than of whatever may be lacking.

The Power of Optimism

Scientists say that we focus on a flawed spot rather than an overall shiny surface, which can make success look and feel like failure. In graduate school, Lyn got upset when she got an A- in a course and asked to take the final exam over in hopes of making an A+. To Olympic athletes, a gold medal is great, but a silver or bronze one can be a disappointment.

Organizational research shows that an optimistic disposition pays off in job hunting and promotions, that optimists achieve more career success than pessimists, and that optimism has beneficial effects on physical and psychological well-being.[9] Compared to their sunnier coworkers, disgruntled workers have trouble looking on the bright side, working as team players, thinking outside the box, and finding solutions in problems. Coworkers and managers lack confidence in pessimists, and they don't trust them to lead. Pessimists are shut out of top assignments and their careers are derailed because they get mired in work tasks instead of surmounting them.

No wonder studies show that optimists have lower stress levels and more stable cardiovascular systems. You can also see why blood samples reveal that optimists have stronger immune systems and fewer stress hormones than pessimists.[10] Optimists know and believe in their capabilities and adopt healthier habits. Statistics show that optimists have fewer health complaints, healthier relationships, and live longer than pessimists.[11]

Optimists don't possess some magical joy juice. They're not smiley-faced romantics looking at life through rose-colored glasses. They are realists who take positive steps to cope with stress rather than succumbing to it. Think about it. Being able to see the positive side of a negative situation can arm you with weapons to overcome the obstacles you face.

Practice looking for the silver lining in situations you perceive as negative. Even if your life is stressful, find one or two positive things that you enjoy and look forward to. Surround yourself with optimists instead of pessimists who pull you down. Pay attention to the attitude you bring to work or home and try to keep negativity in check.

In a pinch, your mindset tends to be negative. But you can ask, "Is the glass half empty or half full?" See the gains in your losses, the beginnings contained in your endings. When you hit forty, you can think of the milestone as half a life left or half a life lost. When you enter a rose garden, you can savor the beauty and fragrance of the flowers or feel repelled by the thorns. You can usually find at least a granule of good in anything "bad" when you look for it.

Find Opportunity in Stressful Events

Once you understand that positivity is always present when you're grumpy or negative, you can start to focus your mind more on the positive side and build it up. Try using these steps to shine a different light on your workaholism:

1. Pinpoint the challenge or opportunity contained in work problems.

2. Empower yourself. Ask how a work challenge is happening *for* you instead of *to* you. Remember the personal resources you have at your disposal and how they provide opportunities for you to overcome obstacles and learn more about yourself.

3. Take the viewpoint that mistakes and shortcomings at work are lessons for you to learn (focus on open-ended curiosity), not failures for you to endure (avoid close-ended judgments). Ask yourself what you can learn from the challenge so that you'll be more resilient next time.

4. Turn the stressor around by focusing on the opportunity it contains. Ask yourself: "How can I make this situation work to my advantage?" "Can I find something positive in this negative situation?" or "What can I manage or overcome in this instance?"

PUT ON YOUR WIDE-ANGLE LENS

Like the zoom lens of a camera, the mind tends to zero in on stressful and challenging situations, magnifying problems and hardships and obscuring the big picture. What about you? Do you look at life through a zoom lens or a wide-angle lens?

One way to find out is to identify a problem you have. Perhaps your mutual fund isn't worth as much as it used to be, or you worry you must pull several all-nighters to get caught up at work. Once you recognize a complaint, put on your wide-angle lens by zooming out and looking at the big picture, seeing the complaint in the scheme of your whole life. As you broaden your outlook, how important is the unfavorable judgment you made? If you're like most people, the complaint loses its sting when you put it in a wider context. The philosophical question, "If you're on your deathbed, what do you wish you'd done differently?" automatically activates your wide-angle lens. As you read the following poem, notice how you feel inside:

> THE PERSPECTIVE LESS TAKEN
> Life sucks.
> And don't try to tell me that
> It's all in my perspective
> Because when I'm honest with myself,
> Bad things make the world a scary place.
> Even if
> Positive things happen once in a while
> Negative things outnumber the positive things.

And it's not true that
Resilience is in my mind and heart and how I choose to look at life
Because
I can create my own happiness
Only if life turns out the way I want
It's not true that a happy life exists
I'm sure you can agree that
A positive perspective is beyond my control.
Nobody will ever convince me that
Life doesn't suck and today is an awesome day.[12]

How do you feel? Not so hot, huh? Notice what sensations you're aware of in your body (maybe a heaviness, weighted down, butterflies in your stomach, tightness in your chest). You just experienced a day in the life of your brain's negativity bias. Now, read the poem from the bottom to top. Now, how do you feel? Much better, right? And what sensations are you aware of inside (perhaps a lightness, tingling, loosened muscles, slowed heartrate)? You just reframed your outlook by observing the same situation from your wide-angle perspective. Your body bears the burden of your mind's thoughts whether they're positive or negative. Your perspective is one of the most powerful tools against lizard brain fears and threats.

FAR FROM THE SHALLOW NOW: LOOKING FOR THE GIFT IN A COSMIC SLAP

"Tell me something, girl; tell me something boy, are you stuck in the shallow?" In critical times like the pandemic or if you're in a work addiction haze, Lady Gaga's lyrics "far from the shallow now" come to mind. It's easy to get stuck in a seismic event when it comes at you fast and hard. But when you allow yourself to go deeper, you learn to think of your resilience as ironclad and actions as steadfast.

Surmounting and benefitting from life's earth-shattering events aren't easy but not impossible, either. Arianna Huffington, founder and CEO of Thrive Global, looked at the pandemic as an opportunity to reconnect with some of the essential truths about ourselves that we might have forgotten when she said, "There are two threads running through our lives. One is pulling us into the world to achieve and make things happen, the other is pulling us back from the world to nourish, replenish, and refuel ourselves. If we ignore the second thread, it is much harder, especially during these times, to connect with ourselves and with those around us."[13]

In an interview with Barbara Walters, the actress Elizabeth Taylor said she laughed when doctors told her she had a brain tumor. Walters gasped. But

Taylor wisely added, "What else are you going to do?" Taylor's attitude proves you can do a lot when adversity strikes. The actor and comedian Richard Belzer once said, "Cancer is a cosmic slap in the face. You either get discouraged or ennobled by it." And baseball great, Babe Ruth said, "Every strike brings me closer to the next home run." But if you're not a natural-born optimist, no worries. You can learn active coping skills to face the seismic events in your life.

The main skill is to discover the gift in adversity. Then focus on how that gift changes your life for the better. In referring to the motorcycle accident that paralyzed him, Sean said, "It was probably the greatest thing that ever happened to me." The accident changed Sean in ways that otherwise would not have been possible. Recovering workaholics and alcoholics often say hitting bottom is their greatest blessing because it wakes them up to a brand-new way of living. After going through the heartache of a broken relationship, for example, many workaholics say they find healthier, more meaningful relationships and work-life balance.

Studies on what is known as posttraumatic growth show that the meaning in cosmic slaps can enrich your life if you're willing to look for that meaning.[14] Research on trauma survivors shows that adversity can have the following benefits:

- Help you see you're stronger than you thought
- Bring new meaning to your life
- Take you deeper into your spirituality
- Deepen the closeness you feel to yourself and others

An amputee from the Ukraine War counsels other disabled soldiers wounded by Russian forces. A person recovering from COVID-19 volunteers to help raise money for the mental health needs of frontline workers. Adversity's biggest gift when navigating work addiction—to borrow a line from my friend Arianna Huffington—isn't just about looking out; it's about looking in where you discover inner fortitude and the ability to find richer meaning that you might have otherwise overlooked.

Driven: Working from Outside In

When I interviewed actress and *Dancing with The Stars* champion Julianne Hough, she told me, "I've been a dancer my whole life and went through a lot of trauma—mental depression and anxiety. Things happened in my childhood that drove me to become very successful and a champion. But at about twenty-five I realized I was so empty inside . . . I decided there's got to be more." Hough realized that the "more" she was searching for was on the inside, not the outside. She was able to explore beyond her comfort zone. "That's when I got into this cognitive therapeutic mindset of figuring out what really happened and what drove me to prove myself," she told me. In her journey, Hough gained a lot of knowledge and awareness of how to be more mindful and positive. For many like her, the seeds of burnout, planted in childhood, overthrow the nervous system and rules in overwhelming situations that threaten adult survival. Work addiction's autocratic rule overextends us, forcing us to bite off more than we can manage to survive.

When you're driven, the biggest obstacle lies between your own two eyes. Those of us who are workaholics crowd our lives so much that we lose touch with our center. In chapter 5, I used the metaphor of a car—all gas (fight-or-flight response) and no brakes (rest-and-digest response). If you're a workaholic, you unwittingly relinquish the steering wheel to the workaholic voice and pressures of demanding people and situations. The workaholic part of you steers your life, and it doesn't relinquish the steering wheel even when you're fully grown and out of the threatening situation. You're so accustomed to autopilot that you're not attuned to your surroundings or yourself. You hit the ground hurrying and rushing from the moment you wake up, shaking your fist at the clock because there aren't enough hours in the day. As you frantically and mindlessly toil on a task—concerned the boss won't like the finished product or you won't meet the deadline—you're out of your present mind, stuck in future worries or past regrets.

As I discussed earlier, you bludgeon yourself with a long list of oppressive mandates such as "musts," and "shoulds," and "have tos": "I must win that contract"; "I have to get that promotion"; "I should be a better colleague"; "People must do as I say"; "Management must see my point of view"; "I should have performed better on my team"; "Life must be easier than this." These external and internal pressures backfire, undermine your abilities, and create unnecessary stress. After years and years of workaholic rule and years and years of "too much for too long"—your engine eventually burns out. Like a hard-driven car, the human body wasn't designed to be driven; it was designed to be drawn. Our lives are shaped from the inside out. If we lose our inner connection, in small ways and big, our lives and the world unravel.

Drawn: Working from Your C-Spot Inside Out

The key to burnout prevention, job performance, and career success is to be *drawn*, not *driven*. Finding the onramp to your C-Spot starts in small, sometimes imperceptible, ways. Just before I stepped into ABC studios to film a segment of 20/20, a booming voice in my head said, "Your delivery *must* be perfect," followed by a wave of anxiety. Little did I realize I was caught in a mind trap I discussed in chapter 4—what psychologist Albert Ellis called "musturbation"—allowing that relentless workaholic voice to *drive* my mind and career. Under constant pressure to perform, your career can easily become the dominant force in your life. But the workaholic voice doesn't have to dominate for you to be on top of your game. In fact, the opposite is true.

Each of us has an inner compass that serves our lives in the highest way and knows when it's time to reclaim our voice. The ABC interview went off without a hitch because I was able to draw from my kind, compassionate C-Spot, which centered and calmed me. When work stress hijacks you and you access your C-Spot, you can scale any obstacle, no matter how dire the circumstances. When you're drawn, you substitute curiosity and compassion for judgment to see the threat with more clarity and feel more at ease dealing with it. The curiosity and clarity from your C-Spot gives you the ability to accept obstacles, difficulties, and disappointments with calmness, giving you agency to scale them.

Whether you realize it yet or not, you *are* powerful enough to choose how you respond to unwelcome moments. Think back on some of your meltdowns, when your workaholic mind snatched control and hijacked you. Did losing your shit really make things better? After circling the parking lot a few times and not getting the closest spot to the mall entrance, is it worth flipping your lid? Does it actually matter if you don't score the best restaurant table by the window? Or if you barely miss getting the last seat in first class, I mean, seriously? Do you really have to shoot the finger to the motorist who cuts you off on your morning commute?

Once you realize the driving voice isn't you and you don't have to live up to its demands, you can take a breath, step back, and become more resilient and self-assured. When you're drawn, you're master instead of slave to the work addicted voice. Toiling from your C-Spot puts you in charge of your busy mind, so you don't succumb to external or internal pressures. Attuned to yourself and your surroundings in a calm, nonjudgmental way, you're anchored in the present moment and focus on what's happening right now. You value *being* in the process as you work through to task completion, not simply *doing* a work task to produce an outcome. You're a master of self-correction and work from integrity, admitting mistakes and fixing them. You focus on the opportunity nested in a career obstacle instead of the difficulty. Regardless of the circumstances, your self-talk is compassionate, calm, and confident.

When I interviewed musical artist and four-time Grammy winner India.Arie, she spoke about how many of us run from our loud demanding voice by letting it drive us instead of taking time out to get quiet, become acquainted with our C-Spot, and become drawn by it:

I feel like when we live busy lives, a lot of times we're not only engaging our responsibilities, but we're running from our feelings, pain, or fear. Or whatever that stuff is inside—that loud voice. I think there was something symbolic about the pandemic mandate to stay inside our homes. It felt like an opportunity to go inside ourselves. It doesn't have to be esoteric where you're meditating for an hour. Just to go to a place and look at all the stuff you're afraid of because when you look at your shadow, it dissipates more quickly than we think it will. And inside that place where you're able to look at yourself, your fear, and often answers come up. You must become acquainted with that part of yourself. It's hard at first to be quiet when you've never been quiet because that's where all the scary stuff is when you're quiet. But it's not as scary as you think once you look at it. The answers are inside for all of us. And there are certain things nobody can tell you but *you*. Now that the stakes are so high in our country, you've got to find a way to hear yourself.[15]

Tips for Clinicians

Positivity, optimism, and self-compassion are effective tools to use in helping clients find their work resilient zone and recover from work stress, burnout, and workaholism.

CONSIDER TEACHING RESILIENT TOOLS

The good news is that resilient tools can be taught to people who lack them. Researchers at Stanford University developed a training strategy to give people the skills to open to others' suffering. Called Compassion Cultivation Training, the nine-week program shows promise in teaching participants how to nourish their own compassionate instincts and how to feel another's pain without being engulfed by it.[16] Emory University has a similar program that teaches compassionate meditation and studies its influence on participants. Experts say that self-compassion is not natural for everyone, and in fact taking an eight-week course in it has been found to be highly effective.[17]

You can use the following factors to assess your workaholic clients' resilient zone and their ability to maintain it:

❖ The strain of having others dependent on you

❖ The number and frequency of traumatic events you've faced

❖ Outside pressures and self-imposed pressures

❖ The degree of your responsibilities and commitments

❖ Strong supportive relationships

❖ Your ability to take care of yourself

❖ Your overall physical health

❖ A positive outlook

Workaholics can control only some of these factors. But you can help them focus on their resources instead of their losses. Explore how they can find their resilient zone by assessing where they are with these practices: staying healthy, getting ample sleep, exercising, eating well, drawing on their optimism, broadening their narrow work scope, establishing strong social contacts, noticing, and shifting their internal reactions, and limiting outside and self-imposed pressures.

RESILIENCY AND TAKING RISKS

On the flip side, the route to the resilient zone is through stepping into unfamiliar territory and the unexpected. I realize this sounds contradictory, but it's one of life's paradoxes: you build resilience by having a degree of control while embracing novelty. Workaholics are more likely to find their resilient zone if they stick their necks out than if they settle into "safe" ruts and routines.

You can encourage them to broaden themselves by facing new challenges, meeting different people, developing a new skill or hobby, spending more time being instead of doing, learning a new game, or traveling to new places.

FLIPPING STRATEGIES TO BREAK THE STRESS CODE

As I mentioned earlier, you can't have a front without a back, a top without a bottom, or a right without a left. The global work culture's language reflects the pervasive acceleration, turbulence, sickness and burnout in today's job environments: *deadlines, sick days, rise and grind, workload, side hustle* ("hustle" is defined as "force someone to move hurriedly"), *driven, to-do list, shortcomings.*

That language reflects how we treat ourselves during a workday. An essential tool to break the stress code is for workaholics to develop the habit of flipping a thought (or reframing) and reversing the way they use words related to work. When you flip the narrow, oppressive words, it frees you up to understand how you can reset the imbalance in your life. Consider sharing the following list with clients to illustrate what a healthy, balanced life with both gas and brakes might look like:

❖ Create a *to-be list*—watch a sunset or a bird nesting—alongside your *to-do* list.

❖ Make your list of *tallcomings*—your positive qualities—equal to or longer than your *shortcomings*.

❖ Have *lifelines*—pauses to smell the roses—on the way to your *deadlines*.

❖ Take *health days* in addition to *sick days*.

❖ *Rise and shine* instead of *rise and grind*.

❖ Put on your *wide-angle lens* when your *zoom lens* eclipses the big picture.

❖ Place as much emphasis on being in the *present* moment as thinking about the *future*.

❖ Tell yourself, "Don't just *do* something, *sit* there."

❖ Get outside in nature for *green time* after prolonged periods of *screen time*.

❖ Find things you *can control* instead of ruminating over what you *can't control*.

❖ Stack *cans* instead of *cannots*.

❖ Let yourself be *drawn with passion* instead of *driven by pressure*.

Encourage clients to become aware of the language they use to describe daily experiences as they go through the workweek. You might even suggest that they think of negative words or phrases they can flip to develop the muscle memory and make it more second nature. This tool can help them see that their stress needle is tilted in a negative direction and when they flip it, they break the stress code to a more positive frame of mind and a balanced life.

CHARTING YOUR C-SPOT

You can show clients how to chart the qualities that they're aware of in their C-Spot. You can try it on first before using it with clients. Choose any of the "C" words *most* present in your life today. Above that "C" word draw a vertical line, which will be the highest line in the graph. Next consider the "C" word that is *least* present in your life today. Above that word, draw a vertical line that will be the lowest line. Then fill in the remaining lines that are present in your life today in proportion to the highest and lowest. The final profile gives you a picture of which of the C-states you can cultivate to broaden your C-spot.

244 The Perspective Less Taken

Bibliotherapy

If the human spirit can choose life over death in the direst of circumstances, these stories and strategies give workaholics hope and inspiration that they, too, can choose their perspective from their C-Spot to overcome work addiction—no matter how challenging the situation. The books I mentioned in this chapter are excellent sources to help clients learn that their power comes from inside out instead of outside in:

❖ James Clear, *Atomic Habits: Tiny Changes, Remarkable Results* (New York: Avery Books, 2018).

❖ Edith Eger, *The Gift: 12 Lessons to Save Your Life* (New York: Scribner, 2020).

❖ Barbara Fredrickson, *Positivity: Top-Notch Research Reveals the 3-to-1 Ratio That Will Change Your Life* (Three Rivers Press, 2009).

❖ Viktor Frankl, *Man's Search for Meaning* (Beacon Press, 2006).

❖ Whitney Goodman, *Toxic Positivity: Keeping It Real in a World Obsessed with Being Happy* (New York: TarcherPerigee, 2022).

❖ Richard Tedeschi et al., *Posttraumatic Growth: Theory, Research, and Applications* (New York: Routledge, 2018).

13

Mindful Working

Do not lose yourself in the past. Do not lose yourself in the future. Do not get caught in your anger, worries, or fear. Come back to the present moment. This is mindfulness.
—Thich Nhat Hanh

Singer Jewel Stumbles into Mindfulness Healing

Growing up with no running water on an Alaskan homestead where she was indoors for eight months out of the year, singer/songwriter Jewel knows about isolation. Her parents had a show in hotels for tourists, and she grew up singing cover songs in bars. "When I started having high anxiety around eight or nine, I saw people in bars drinking, trying to outrun their pain," Jewel told me. "And I saw it never worked and made a promise to myself to learn to handle the pain as it came." After moving out of an abusive household at fifteen, Jewel was homeless by age eighteen, hitchhiking across the country and learning to play the guitar so she could street sing along the way, learning to shoplift to handle stress, anxiety, and trauma.[1]

How did the anxious teenage shoplifter, suffering from debilitating panic attacks and agoraphobia, transition into an award winning, multi-platinum recording artist with one of the best-selling debuts of all time? And then on to become an advocate for mental health in the modern workplace? "Statistically, kids like me end up repeating the cycle of abuse, and I didn't want to be a statistic," she said. "But there was nowhere I could learn a new emotional language. In school I learned math and English, but at home I learned an emotional way of relating to the world." She set off on a mission to understand how *not* to be a statistic and what to do with her pain.

Jewel noticed when she was journaling, it helped her anxiety go down. Looking back, she realized it was a great mindfulness tool because it caused her to be curious in the present. She told me she couldn't figure out what she was thinking because of her anxiety. "Our hands are the servants of our thoughts," the singer said. "So, I came up with an exercise to watch my hands during the day, and that was the first time I discovered that my anxiety disappeared when I was present." Her song "Hands"—which later became a big hit—was about the moment she stumbled into being consciously present. "I was very prolific at shoplifting, so I learned to write whenever I had the urge to steal to become prolific at writing because I was trying to stop being prolific at stealing," Jewel said.

She almost didn't sign her record deal because she had just started learning how to be happy in that year of being homeless. "When you suffer with agoraphobia and panic attacks and start getting relief from those pain points, it's like gold. That's worth all the money in the world. And you take somebody with my fragile emotional baggage background—and God forbid I get famous—that's like becoming another statistic. The odds were really high that I would tank, so I made myself a promise. I remember being on the beach in San Diego saying that my number one job was learning to be a happy, whole human. My number two job was to be a musician."

The recording artist said she had to come up with a plan that was just as strategic for her happiness as it was strategic for her music career. "At forty-seven, I'm very proud to sit here and say I've never let that promise down," she said. She began to develop a set of tools to rewire her brain and create new emotional patterns that were later validated by neuroscientists. After learning meditation and discovering and innovating her own mindfulness practices, Jewel was able to heal her depression symptoms. "When you're consciously present, you make better decisions, and there are exercises that build the muscle ability to be consciously present for longer periods of time like basic meditation or mindful walking—mindfulness in motion—that creates new neural networks."

Today, the musician is working to help employers invest in their human capital in a more meaningful way by solving pain points for employees. "Traditionally our work culture is perk driven," she said. "Companies have been offering everything from dry cleaning to dog sitting. But what if your employer could help you solve your pain points in your life outside of work?" Jewel got in on the act of detoxifying toxic work cultures when she partnered with SaksWorks to launch a first in-person work culture curriculum that offers deeper engagement and loyalty while also creating greater productivity. "Employees will show up at work with more bandwidth, more creativity, and more courage—as well as more loyalty," she added.

Our work shouldn't make us sick. That isn't to say we can't be productive. Those things aren't antithetical. In fact, we're learning that when we help people soften their anxiety and trauma, they become more productive, but it's not about working more, it's about working smarter. We're learning that by helping people clear up their stress, anxiety, and trauma, it expands their emotional bandwidth, and they're showing up to work much more functional and productive without having extra work hours.

Workplaces lost an estimated one trillion dollars in a year due to depression and anxiety alone. It behooves employers to get involved and help solve this for their employees because we have to. Traditionally, would it be an employer's job to start thinking about these things? No, but you have humans in your workplace, and you have to handle the fact that these humans are struggling. There are simple solutions to make that pain point go down. We're realizing emotional health affects our physical health and then improves productivity and reduces turnover. We must find a way to create a wholistic system that benefits productivity. Connection cures so much. If you could create a highly connected work environment and show leaders why it's a win-win, it should increase their bottom line.[2]

Work Addicts Out of Their Present Minds

Before I talk more about healthy mindful working, it's important to describe what I call workaholic mindless working. The harried workaholic rushing to the office to "get ahead of the game" is a typical example of "mindless working." Workaholics are in fast-forward speed much of the time, trying to get to the good stuff—heading for the nirvana of pleasure and skipping over what's happening now. You know what I mean. You must get through the traffic jam to your appointment instead of *being* in the traffic jam. You must hop in and out of the shower to get to work instead of *being* in the shower. You must rush through lunch so you can complete the project on your desk instead of *being* present with each bite. The workaholic habit of mindless working often leads to heart or other physical problems.

Is your mind like Grand Central Station, with so many thoughts coming and going that you don't have a chance to pause and catch your breath? Do you frantically work on projects, focused on the next item on the agenda without regard to what it's doing to you mentally and physically? Are you worried about whether the boss will like the finished product or thinking about what you'll be doing this weekend? These out-of-the-moment episodes create loads of stress and disconnect you from yourself and your surroundings. Before you know it, you're mired in your own stress juices.

Your mind could be wandering right now. You could be thinking about what you ate for lunch and what you "should" have eaten. You could be worried about unpaid bills or about an unfinished project, wondering how you'll meet the deadline. Or you might be replaying in your head an argument you had with your spouse. When your mind wanders too much, it could be stressing you out or at the very least preventing you from actualizing your full potential at work.

WHEN YOU STRAY, YOU PAY

Harvard University researchers have found that the human mind wanders 47 percent of the time, and that when you stray, you pay. When your mind wanders, you're more stressed out and unhappy than when you stay in the here and now. The Harvard researchers found that people were happier—no matter what they were doing, even working overtime, vacuuming the house, or sitting in traffic—if they were focused on the activity instead of thinking about something else.[3]

I have referred to these out-of-the moment episodes as *brownouts*—workaholic blackouts when you tune out the here and now, have memory lapses during conversations, or momentary forgetfulness because you're out of your present mind.[4] But you don't have to let a mental fog eclipse your self-attunement and submerge you in your own stress juices. Your presence of mind gives you the power to flip the pattern around, landing you in the driver's seat, putting you back in charge. When you pay attention and fully engage in each moment, you discover your daily world in a completely different way. And your life takes on a fresh glow. That's what this chapter is about: how to work mindfully and productively in an alert, active, calm manner.

HOW YOU USE YOUR MIND AT WORK MAKES A DIFFERENCE

Neuroscientists say the way you use your mind can determine how much work stress or work productivity you have. Keeping your focus on the present instead of ruminating about what already happened (which you can't change anyway) or about what might happen (which you can't control anyway) keeps your stress level down, makes you more effective at work, and makes for a happier life. When you get swallowed up by job pressures or career disillusionments, you end up paying the price at some point. If you're like most people, you have to work—whether you're caught in the drudgery of a dead-end job, worrying about losing your job, trying to turn a passion into a career, or supporting a family by whatever means necessary. Given that reality, it's common that workaholics don't do more to improve their working lives.

Although you've probably heard the Jewel's adage "work smarter, not longer," it's not easy to translate that philosophy into everyday work schedules.

But that's what mindful working can help you do: bridge that gap. Burgeoning evidence-based studies demonstrate that a mindful approach to work has dramatic payoffs for employees, the workplace, and corporate America. As a result, companies such as Google, Yahoo, Time Warner, and Apple, as well as the U.S. military, have begun to integrate mindfulness principles into the training of their workers. For example, a Google engineer designed a mindfulness course called "Search inside Yourself" to enrich and maximize the work productivity and personal fulfillment of Google's employees, giving them a better way of coping with work stress.[5]

Mindfulness: Hippie Nonsense or Neuroscience?

Mindfulness meditation is the ability to pay compassionate, nonjudgmental attention to what you're thinking and feeling and to what's happening inside your body and around you in the present moment. Once considered an occult Eastern spiritual practice, mindfulness has achieved respectability in the United States as a viable clinical technique. Jon Kabat Zinn's evidence-based research program called mindfulness-based stress reduction at the University of Massachusetts Medical Center has brought mindfulness into mainstream medical treatment, and it has special significance for treating workaholism.[6]

Although the ancient practice of mindful meditation has been around for thousands of years, it is estimated that only 14 percent of people meditate. Some people still think of the 1970s stigma when it first came to the United States. Cynics scoffed at the idea of fringe mystical practices involving gurus, weird chants, burning incense, sitting lotus style on a cushion, or drugged out people looking for ways to zone out. But not anymore. Modern neuroscience has revived meditation to bring about change from inside out and has become a medical mainstay to deal with job stress, anxiety, and burnout.

The goal of mindfulness is not to zone out, empty your thoughts, withdraw from the world, or get high on life. It's not a religious practice, nor does it require you to change your beliefs or commit to a particular religious doctrine. It's a tool to notice the habitual workings of your mind, watch how your thoughts routinely create stress and how you can get them to relax. A large body of research shows meditation is good medicine for mind and body. When your workaholic mind hijacks you into worry, stress, or depression, it eventually compromises your mental and physical health—shrinking your contentment, well-being, and work performance.

As you practice this technique, you turn inward to manage your moods and begin to put your self-care above work and other people that would otherwise create stress, burnout, and physical illness. You train your mind to do what it doesn't do instinctively: to come back to the present, to enjoy the moment, and to appreciate your life instead of focusing on survival worries ("What if I get laid off?" or "Can I measure up?"). With practice, mindfulness moves you to a state where your mind is relaxed and alert at the same time.[7] A growing body of scientific evidence attests to the link between mindfulness and well-being.[8]

Dr. Vivek Murthy, the U.S. surgeon general during the Obama and Biden administrations, asserts that loneliness on the job is a public health crisis.[9] He is a proponent of mindfulness meditation to mitigate the loneliness that solitary workers—especially workaholics—experience, enabling us to connect with ourselves. "Meditation can settle your mind and allow you to reflect and experience peace and solitude which we often don't get when we're constantly surrounded by information streaming from our devices," he told me.

> When it comes to loneliness, the foundation for connecting with others is a strong connection with ourselves. We must be comfortable with ourselves and confident that we have value and a sense of worth. One thing that helps is to spend time with ourselves and become comfortable with solitude. Solitude and meditation are times when the mind connects the dots with what's happening in our lives, part of processing the world. When we don't have reflective time for ourselves, we bury a lot of the challenging issues and don't deal with them. It can detract from our emotional well-being when we don't spend enough time in solitude.[10]

Practicing Mindfulness Exercises

Mindfulness practices aren't as easy as I make them sound, but they're not all that difficult either. Even though you're not aware of it, you're judging yourself and your experience of others much of the time. And your mind might be miles away from your body, caught up in streams of thoughts about future or past judgments.

Take time right now to notice your thoughts. In a relaxed position, put yourself fully into the present moment. Try watching the thoughts streaming through your mind with a nonjudgmental attitude. You don't have to do anything but pay attention to them. Don't try to change or fix them. Just be aware of them. Are the thoughts centered on the future or the past, or are they focused in the present? Are they calm and serene, or worried and anxious? You'll probably notice that they're preparing you to react to situations with more stress than necessary. Or they might be replaying a negative situation that you could have handled differently. This type of paying attention to your mind is an example of mindful awareness.

Sidestepping Your Mental Fogs

Mindfulness techniques are powerful antidotes for dodging mental fogs. In four simple steps, you can harness the social circuitry of your brain, enabling you to be attuned to your own mind:

1. Keep your focus in the present moment.
2. Move at a steady, calm pace.
3. Be attuned to yourself and your surroundings.
4. Accept without judgment whatever you're aware of that arises in each moment.

Kayakers say the best way to escape when you're trapped in a hydraulic—a turbulent, funnel-shaped current—is to relax, and it will spit you out. But the natural tendency is to fight against the current. And that can keep you stuck, even drown you. Similarly, the way to get unstuck from a torrent of survival thoughts streaming through your mind is to welcome them and watch them with curiosity. Let them come and go without personalizing, judging, resisting, or identifying with them. And eventually they will float away.

Now let's do another exercise that takes your attention to your body:

❖ Turn your attention to your fingers and focus there for a minute.

❖ Wiggle your fingers and notice how this sensory experience feels. Focus on how the wiggling looks and sounds. Do you hear any crackling in your joints or sounds of skin against skin? What else are you aware of?

❖ Notice if you judge yourself or the exercise, or if you have trouble staying focused.

❖ Now ask yourself if this exercise gave you an immediate connection to the present moment. Or did your judgment interfere with your being fully engaged? If you were fully engaged during the exercise, you might have noticed that previous worries or stressful thoughts were absent.

Mindful Working: Rx for Work Addiction

Most solutions to job stress, workaholism, and workplace problems impose change from the outside in. Sometimes this works, but more often it doesn't. When applied to work addiction, the practice of mindfulness brings about change from the inside out, regardless of workplace circumstances or the nature of job problems. I call this simple solution to an epidemic problem facing the American workforce *mindful working*—the intentional, moment-to-moment awareness of what's happening inside you and immediately around you accompanied by self-attuned, compassionate interest during your daily work schedules and routines.

Working mindfully is meditation in motion. You keep your attention on the stream of the process, instead of just focusing on completion of the task. You're able to bring curious, nonjudgmental attention to your work and notice moment-to-moment body sensations, mental processes, and feelings that arise while you're working or thinking about your job during the best of times and the worst of times. In addition, you master schedules, difficult work relationships, and new technologies instead of becoming slaves to them. Instead of beating yourself up when things fall apart, you can use self-compassionate attunement to ease yourself through work stress, business failures, job loss, or worry and anxiety about career goals.

MINDLESS WORKING AND SURVIVAL SUFFERING

In a given day, how many people do you notice (yourself included) who drive while texting, stroll in the park on a beautiful day with a cell phone glued to their ear, or simultaneously eat lunch, type a memo, and talk on the phone? We have become a nation of multitaskers, blind to the present moment. If the workday continues to invade personal time, life becomes an endless series of intrusions that can swallow you up, disconnecting you from yourself and others. If you don't take time for self-reflection, it's easy to get caught in a race that leaves you hurried and harried.

If you're like most workaholics, you toil around the clock at a survival level. Your mind creates stress even when none is present for one reason: survival. When your body perceives a threat, worry causes you to respond as though the threat is real even when it's just imaginary. Stress or depression over a downturn in the economy, loss of a promotion, a faltering relationship with a boss or colleague, or fear of an upcoming job challenge creates survival suffering (or high arousal in your nervous system). When you're in survival suffering mode, you're working mindlessly. You lose your attunement, and your mind begins to use you. Your worry and stress feed dread and uncertainty. Then your mind imagines the worst (for example, "I'll probably fall flat on my face"), and the worry and dread become the real problem, eclipsing the original situation. You become hijacked by the internal suffering—a magnification of the original problem. When you practice mindful working, you use present-moment awareness to flip the survival suffering around. Then you calmly navigate workplace woes with clarity, self-compassion, courage, and creativity. And you're more efficient and productive at work.

SELF-REGULATION AND MINDFUL RECOVERY

If you're an active workaholic, chances are that you're disconnected from yourself, and you view working as a safe place from life's threats and challenges. Faced with such "reptilian threats" as tight deadlines, a challenging presentation at work, relentless pressures from a difficult boss, threat of job loss or unemployment—all activate your fight-or-flight response. This primitive mechanism pumps out a flood of adrenaline and cortisol, priming the body for action. These stress hormones raise your heart and respiration rates, tense your muscles, and slow your digestion. Constant workaholic pressures cause your inner alarm system to stay on alert mode, raising the risk of high blood pressure, heart attack, type 2 diabetes, chronic pain, and a weakened immune system. In many situations, the workaholic body on red alert experiences panic even though the workaholic isn't consciously aware of any stress—an example of mindless working.

In mindful recovery, you learn balance and self-regulation. You keep close watch on your personal life, moving at a reasonable pace and staying attuned to your inner world and your interactions with others in an alert, compassionate way. Your self-attunement activates the parasympathetic nervous system, creating a soothing, calmer approach to work tasks. With present-moment awareness, you know when to close your laptop, mentally switch gears, and be fully present in the moment—when your teenager agonizes over her first crush, or your partner or spouse reflects on the details of the day. But your insatiable workaholic appetite keeps you on autopilot and eclipses your awareness of yourself, others, and your physical surroundings, allowing work tasks to dominate every aspect of your life.

Your relationship with work becomes the central connection of your life— the place where life really takes place, the secret repository of drama and emotion, as compelling as the place other addicts experience with booze or cocaine. You're preoccupied with work no matter where you are—walking hand in hand at the seashore or hiking with a friend. Family and friends, or any kind of inner awareness, are little more than a vague, if pleasant, backdrop.

In mindful recovery, however, you're as emotionally present in off-work times as you are during work hours. You learn to turn off your work appetite and to appreciate the wonderful mystery of being alive without the need for work highs or numbing yourself with multitasking and busyness. Jon Kabat-Zinn described the advantages of that inner mindful connection: "Mindfulness provides a simple but powerful route for getting ourselves unstuck, back in touch with our own wisdom and vitality. It is a way to take charge of the direction and quality of our own lives, including our relationships within the family, our relationship to work and to the larger world and planet, and most fundamentally, our relationship with ourself as a person."[11]

The Pause That Refreshes

Scientists have discovered that the way to reclaim your work life and personal life is through mindfulness. People who meditate have less stress, fewer health problems, improved relationships, and longer lives.[12]

Some people get so used to living with stress and chaos that it becomes a habit, and they add stress to their lives even when they don't mean to. Does that sound like you? Ask yourself how often you race through the day without pausing to consider who you really want to be. Mindful investment of your energy, not time management, is the key to work happiness and success. Experts argue that you can manage your energy by taking breaks, getting ample sleep, paying attention to who you are, what you're doing, and where you're going from moment to moment. These actions create optimal work conditions, high performance, health, work success, and personal renewal.[13]

HITTING YOUR PAUSE BUTTON

If performance energy or lack of it begins on the inside, doesn't it make sense that to harness it you would start there, too? To begin this process, look inside where your performance energy resides—inside your skin, where you live, think, and feel. Start by considering the ways you can slow down the pace and rhythm of your life, bringing gentle awareness to your thoughts and feelings. Treat yourself with kindness on the inside instead of cracking the whip. Think about whether you're master or slave to your crammed schedules and electronic devices. Set aside times to eat slower instead of what one mindfulness expert called "the three G's": "gobble, gulp, and go."[14] And avoid eating while standing, walking, driving, working, or otherwise being on the run.

To create mindful conditions at work, say no to new projects when you're already overcommitted. Or you might give yourself time cushions when setting important deadlines and do just one activity at a time, devoting your conscious attention to it. You might delegate work tasks (if you are able to do so) or prioritize them, eliminating or setting aside for now those that are the least important or unnecessary. Or you might give yourself extra driving time to arrive at your destination and extra time between appointments so you can have a conversation with a colleague. The examples are endless, and you'll have to tailor your strategies to the unique rhythm and style of your job and personal life.

KEEP A MINDFUL WORK DIARY

A mindful work diary can help you document progress in using your mind instead of letting it use you. You can record your success in avoiding the workaholic highs and lows and become more mindful of your unwitting work habits and the perspective you have on your job. A work diary can help you pinpoint situations that detour you from a mindful approach to work. It can trigger changes you'd like to make in dealing with work challenges and become more efficient and satisfied in your job. The diary becomes a road map of your journey from mindless to mindful working as you apply the practices in this chapter and describe the outcomes.

According to Thich Nhat Hanh, the mindfulness with which we walk the line between a turbulent work world and our inner steadiness determines our happiness: "When we are able to take one step peacefully and happily, we are working for the cause of peace and happiness for the whole of humankind. . . . We can do it only if we do not think of the future or the past, if we know that life can only be found in the present moment."[15]

Types of Mindfulness Practices

Meditation expert Tara Brach likens mindfulness meditation as exercise for a healthy mind just as physical exercise is what we need for a healthy body: "Meditation is a mental training that gives us access to the resources we like the most like mental clarity, creativity, compassion, and empathy."[16] The equivalent in building an exercise regimen would be working out on a Stairmaster or going to the gym for an aerobics class three times a week. You can practice mindfulness in several different ways and to varying degrees. If you have the time, dedication, and interest, you can practice *focused attention mindfulness meditation*. You set aside time in the day to sit down in a quiet place and focus your attention on your breathing, a mantra, or another object of concentration.

If you want to go hog wild, you can attend an intensive event at a mindfulness workshop or retreat center. Mindfulness intensives are held in a specific place with a group of people, often in silence, for an extended period. The exercise equivalent would be biking in the Tuscan countryside for a week or going to a weight-loss spa for several days. There are many excellent retreat centers across the United States. But if meditation is new territory for you, a good entry into mindfulness is *open awareness meditation*. You can practice it with a minimum of time and dedication by simply being mindful during activities such as eating, cooking, walking, and working that are already built into your day.

OPEN AWARENESS DURING YOUR WORKDAY

You could even practice open awareness right now. As you read on, you might find your mind wandering from time to time. Just be aware of your wandering mind, accept that wandering, and gently bring your mind back to the words on the printed page. An open awareness exercise can be any brief activity that makes you aware of what's happening as it's happening in the flow of your daily routines. Earlier in this chapter, I gave you an open awareness exercise that asked you to be mindful of your thoughts. Then I gave you a second one that asked you to be aware of your hands. A third type of open awareness exercise takes you beyond yourself with moments of mindful awareness that pertain to any activity you're deliberately paying attention to in the present.

You intentionally walk with present-moment awareness by bringing your attention to the sensations of your feet against the ground, or by noting the feel of the air, sights, and sounds around you as you walk. When you weed the garden, you can pay attention to the plants' resistance against your hands as you tug on them, and the sound of stubborn roots and smells of fresh soil as you unearth the weeds from their home. When you clean the toilet bowl, brush your teeth, drive your car, or cook a pot of soup, you can step out of your thought stream and make yourself fully present in the activity. While waiting in the doctor's office, you can practice mindful listening. In line at the grocery store, you might tune in to your body sensations. Stuck in traffic, you can practice mindful deep breathing.

You can do the following brief mindfulness exercises during your workday:

❖ Take off your socks and shoes and feel your toes in the carpet. Pay close attention to how the carpet feels against your feet. If you have an open window, focus on the sounds of chirping birds or inhale the fragrance of a flower.

❖ During lunch, sit down and give food your full attention, being present with each bite. Pause before starting a meal, noticing the colors and textures while inhaling the smells of the food. Eat your lunch slowly and deliberately. Chew food two or three more times than you usually do to taste it fully, paying attention to each ingredient and savoring each morsel. You will taste your food in a completely different way; for example, instead of tasting tuna salad, discover the flavor of celery as it crushes against your teeth, the bursting tartness of pickles, and the blending of the tuna and green lettuce. Take a sip of a beverage and be with the sensation against your tongue and stay with the felt sense as it slides down the back of your throat.

❖ After eating, stand and stretch your body. Let yourself fully feel the stretch, noticing where tension is held and released. Shake the part of your body where you sense tension. As you continue to stretch, bring your attention to each part of your body that has remained tightened. Bend over and touch your toes and feel that stretch, visualizing the tension in your body evaporating.

A MINDFUL WORKING EXERCISE

The following open awareness exercise can help you slow down and pay closer attention to your body, mind, and spirit during your workday:

The next time you go to your work site, imagine you have entered your workplace for the first time. Notice the entranceway, the architecture of the outside and inside of the building, and the people at their workstations. Look at your coworkers as if you've never seen them before, seeing and appreciating them with renewed interest. Notice what hangs on the walls and the textures and colors of the walls, ceiling, and floor. Smell the flowers on someone's desk. Be aware of how your colleagues are dressed and the colors of a blouse or jacket a colleague is wearing. Pay attention to who conforms to rules and who marches to the beat of their own drum. What sounds do you hear, and what smells (such as cologne or freshly brewed coffee from the break room) permeate the air?

Be mindful of your coworkers' faces. Look into the eyes of a business associate, subordinate, or boss. Then look beyond their facial expressions and into their hearts, where their true selves reside, noticing what's imprinted there. Do they look happy or sad? Ready to embrace the day or wishing they were back home in bed? Are they smiling or frowning? Who has wrinkles and worry lines, and whose face is stress-free? Do people in this work environment touch each other or keep their distance? Do they affirm one another or put each other down with sarcasm and cutting remarks? Are they pulling together as a team or working against one another, coming apart at the seams?

Notice what you're thinking and feeling as you mindfully examine your workplace. If you notice yourself making judgments, try not to judge yourself for judging. Instead, see if you can substitute curiosity and compassion for the people or situations you're judging.

The New Science of Microchillers: Meditating on the Fly

Never again can you say you don't have time to meditate or that you don't have time to learn how. If you're like most workaholics, you're unwilling to take the time out of your workday to stop what you're doing, find a place to calm your mind, and practice mindfulness meditation for twenty minutes. That's why I developed Microchillers—small five-minute doses of mindfulness in motion. You can practice them throughout your workday without stopping simply by turning inward to manage your moods.

Microchillers inoculate you against cumulative stress and burnout. They distill the main elements of meditation, allowing you to bring mindfulness to bear on your ancient circuitry's threat reactions in a matter of minutes without stopping workday routines. Meditating on the fly with these simple, easy-to-apply exercises step you out of a stressful thought stream, bring instant calm and keep you fully engaged in the present moment so you can continue business as usual. Here are a few examples, and you can find a Microchiller sampler in the appendix.

RESOURCING

When you're under work pressure, it helps to have a Microchiller in your mind's hip pocket that you can retrieve as you move from appointment to appointment. A resource is something that brings you comfort, joy, or serenity—something you like about yourself, a positive memory, or experience, or a person, place, pet, or spiritual guide. One of my resources is the memory of sipping morning coffee on the screened porch of a rented beach house, watching a shrimp boat—with sea gulls swooping over the bow—putter across the backdrop of a huge red-ball sunrise. When I retrieve that memory, I notice my shoulders loosen and my heart rate slows down. Now, your turn. Bring a resource to mind. Describe to yourself all the details that sustain or nurture you, imaging them vividly in your mind's eye. Direct your attention to your body sensations and notice where in your body you feel the pleasing sensations. Bring awareness to your breathing, heart rate, and muscle tension, noticing any changes. Chances are that your breathing is slower or your muscles more relaxed. Spend time savoring any changes in your body. Finally, bring your attention to your whole body, noting all the changes that have occurred and soak them in.

BREATHING

Right under your nose is a valuable Microchiller when job stress steals your breath. While working in front of your screen or moving through your work-day, take a deep abdominal breath through your nose. Hold it while you count to six. Then purse your lips and exhale slowly through them. Do this six times. Your body can't maintain the same level of stress with the extra oxygen you get in your bloodstream when you breathe from your abdomen.

H.A.L.T.

When work stress takes hold as you move through the workday, ask yourself if you're hungry, angry, lonely, or tired. The HALT Microchiller is an alert sig-nal that brings you back into the present moment. If one or a combination of the four states is present, slow down your pace, take a few breaths and chill. If you're hungry, take time to eat healthy. If you're angry, address your anger in a health manner. If you're lonely, reach out to someone you trust. And if you're tired, take a rest.

GROUNDING

After a reaction to an upsetting event, you might feel out of your body or ungrounded in some way. This Microchiller helps you feel anchored in your body and brings your prefrontal cortex back online. You can practice this exer-cise while driving if you keep your eyes open or sitting at your workstation in a chair with a back to it. Sitting up straight, notice how the back of the seat is supporting your back. Bring your full attention to that area of support and focus there for one minute. Then bring your attention to your feet resting on the floor. Pay attention to the bottom of your feet and the support of the ground or floor underneath. Focus on that area of support for one minute. Next, bring your attention to your bottom on the seat. Focus on the support of the chair underneath your seat for one minute. Then, take another minute to notice the sensations of your breathing, heart rate, and muscle tone. Most people say they feel more relaxed, more in their bodies, and that their breath-ing and heart rates slow down, and their muscles loosen.

PAST RECALL

When faced with a challenging situation, your mind is hard-wired to automat-ically go to the negative. But when you recall a situation that you mastered, this Microchiller moves you into your C-Spot where you feel calm, courage, and confidence. Research shows that reflecting on past victories shifts your outlook and helps you scale obstacles. The first step is to remember the event in vivid detail and what you felt. Then redirect your attention to the accompanying pleasant or calming sensations and hold them in your mind's eye for a minute. Notice your slowed breath, heart rate, and muscle tension.

The beauty of Microchillers is that you can practice them anywhere, anytime because they're quick, easy, portable, and cost-free. You can blend them into your daily routines without added time—sitting in front of your screen, making your way from the parking garage to your office, driving from one appointment to the next, waiting in a grocery store line, or stuck in traffic. When you're fully engaged in a Microchiller, you notice that previous stressful work thoughts are absent. You might notice that your heart and respiration rates drop, and tight muscles loosen.

As you move through your workday, start to watch your mind and notice where it goes from moment to moment. Note the difference between when you're in the here and now and when your mind drifts to the past (the boss who did you wrong) or the future (what if your job is on the chopping block?). Once you find your mind wandering, gently bring it back into the present and go back to the work task you were doing. When stress overtakes you, catch five minutes or less to focus on your breath or notice all the different colors within eyesight. When you continue to practice Microchillers, tension starts to subside. You feel more relaxed and confident, and your mindful productivity and career success soar. (See the appendix for a sampling of more Microchillers.)

Tara Brach is an advocate of short five-minute meditations. "In fact, we know that if somebody puts in five or ten minutes a day, there's a growing momentum of a pathway back home again," she told me. "We're working with neural pathways, changing the habitual neural pathways that leave us anxious and reactive and finding pathways that let us access the more recently evolved part of the brain where we have more capacity for mindfulness, clarity, and compassion. So, it doesn't have to take long; it's an intentional training, not woo-woo. And it has science behind it."[17]

Former ABC News anchor Dan Harris said meditation changed his life after a bout with cocaine and a panic attack on live television in 2004 on *Good Morning America*. He vouches for grabbing the brief times to meditate and told me he agrees with the five-minute Microchillers:

> One is to take a cursory glance at the science, which strongly suggests that small doses of daily meditation can lower your blood pressure, boost your immune system, and literally rewire key parts of the brain that have to do with self-awareness, focus, stress, and compassion. It's very compelling. The other thing I'd say is it doesn't require a massive time commitment. I tell

people one-minute counts. I'd rather see people do five to ten minutes a day, but I'm quite familiar with the diabolical difficulty of habit formation. So, I like to use two little slogans: "one-minute counts" and "daily-ish."[18]

Neuroscientists back up what meditation practitioners describe: that mindfulness helps to lower stress and reduce addictive behaviors by reducing the activity in the amygdala. Studies show that meditating just once makes you less error prone. Your mind wanders less, and you focus better on completing work more efficiently. Plus, you're more aware of other people's emotions and sentiments and less likely to dive into situations that add to your stress.[19] With 1,440 minutes in one day, studies show that those five-minute daily doses of Microchillers can benefit you mentally and physically. Not bad! You have better sleep, increased immunity, lower blood pressure, improved digestion, and heightened well-being. And you still have 1,435 minutes left over to live calmer, healthier, and happier.

Tips for Clinicians

If we clinicians were to read early Buddhist texts, we would be convinced that the Buddha was essentially a psychologist. It's possible to practice Buddhist-derived meditation and ascribe its aspects to the psychological view of the mind while maintaining your own beliefs in other religious traditions. The combination of brain science, mindfulness, and therapeutic techniques has become enormously popular and highly effective in twenty-first-century psychotherapy. This unique blend has been applied to many diverse problems, such as anxiety, depression, addictions, and bad eating and spending habits.

MINDFULNESS BENEFITS BOTH CLIENTS AND CLINICIANS

Mindfulness techniques have relevance for workaholics, who seem especially vulnerable to the evolutionary pressures of working from the "reptilian brain." By using mindfulness techniques, you can help workaholics develop an internal locus of control that helps them feel more empowered over their internal and external work demands. Michael Yapko described the value of using mindfulness in psychotherapy: "It [mindfulness] teaches people that they can find resources inside themselves they didn't know they had and change their self-definition as a result."[20]

Research also shows that clinicians who practice mindfulness bring the benefits to their sessions. Mindful counselors have heightened self-awareness and greater empathy and compassion toward clients. Plus, mindfulness develops the clinician's ability to experience and communicate a felt sense of the client's inner experiences, be more present to client suffering, and help clients express their body sensations and feelings.[21]

THE TURTLE WON THE RACE

Mindful working offers simple ways to avoid future-focused working in which workaholics are hurrying, rushing, and juggling too many projects with jangled nerves. The purpose of meditation is to quiet the mind so the individual can hear what is already there, which enables workaholics to accomplish more, do a better job, and gain self-respect and admiration from coworkers.

Scientific research shows that meditation slows down heart rates and changes brain-wave patterns. It has a positive effect on the immune system, increasing the production of certain life-sustaining hormones. You can suggest many types of meditation that help workaholics unwind from work highs and manage stress, including progressive relaxation exercises, yoga, quiet reflection, daily inspirational readings, prayer, and mindfulness meditation.[22]

In clinical settings, we observe that when clients intentionally slow down certain body movements related to stress, the process brings up emotions, giving the nervous system time to regulate itself, time to develop new habits so the parasympathetic nervous system can put the brakes on the sympathetic nervous system. This allows recovering workaholics to approach work demands in a calmer, more balanced, and relaxed way.

Another approach with workaholic clients is to help them become more aware of their preoccupation with the future to the exclusion of the present. Encourage them to take virtual workshops to develop tools to mitigate chronic work stress, anxiety, and mild depression, and teach the four basic steps of mindfulness:

1. Keep your focus in the present moment.
2. Move at a steady, calm pace.
3. Stay attuned to yourself and your surroundings
4. Accept without judgment whatever you're aware of that arises in each moment.

You can help clients make a conscious effort to slow down the pace of their daily lives by intentionally eating, talking, walking, and driving slower. You can help them explore ways to prevent rushing by building time cushions between appointments and scheduling extra time to get to destinations. You might suggest that they steer clear of "grabbing, gulping, and going"—eating while standing, driving, being on the run, or while watching TV. They could consider treating mealtime as a singular activity with value. Sitting down, eating slowly, and chewing a few extra times before swallowing, as well as appreciating the food's textures, aromas, and tastes, will help them relax and enjoy the meal as well as aid in digestion. Here are examples of mindfulness exercises you can use with clients to help them slow down before getting caught up in a work tornado:

❖ Try a mindful exercise during your morning shower. Pay attention to the sounds and feel of thousands of beads of splashing water popping against your skin. Hear the rushing sounds against your shower curtain and smacks of water against the tub. As you lather your body, be aware of the smell and feel of the slippery soap gliding over your naked skin, and the soap bubbles swelling and popping on your neck, arms, and chest. Notice how the water feels rolling down your body, the fresh fragrance of shampoo and its cleansing sensation against your scalp. As you dry off, feel the fabric of the towel against your naked skin. Continue your present-moment awareness while brushing your teeth and going through the rest of your morning routine.

❖ Prepare a meal mindfully—as if you're cooking it for the first time. Pay close attention as you assemble the ingredients. Notice the unique character of each vegetable, fruit, or piece of meat—the myriad colors, diverse smells, and varied textures of foods. Even the sounds vary as you chop, slice, cut, grind, and pound. You might pop an ingredient into your mouth, noting its texture against your tongue and its unique taste before you blend it into a final dish. As you combine the different ingredients, notice the visual transformation as they become one. As you're cooking, observe the chemical changes when the separate items morph into a collected whole. Inhale the aroma, seeing if you can still identify the unique individual smells or simply one succulent blend. When you sit down to eat, take in the smells and colors of the meal before you dig in.

After clients complete a few of these exercises, ask them to consider the following questions to deepen their mindfulness experience:

1. As you looked at your usual routines in a new way, what did you notice?

2. Were you aware that there's more happening around you and inside you than you realized?

3. Did your thoughts kick into gear and try to rush you through the activity?

4. Were your old stressors along for the ride, or did they stay behind?

5. As you notice where your mind is from moment to moment, do you feel more connected to yourself? Does your life seem more vivid?

Bibliotherapy

You can use bibliotherapy with workaholic clients around a number of topics discussed in this chapter.

❖ Karlyn Borysenko, *Zen Your Work: Create Your Ideal Work Experience Through Mindful Self-Mastery* (New York: TarcherPerigee Books, 2018). Know yourself, own your perspective, and find your balance at work.

❖ Jewel's memoir, *Never Broken: Songs Are Only Half the Story* (Blue Rider Press, 2016) is an inspiration story about how she overcame early struggles to become an internationally known singer/songwriter.

❖ Vivek Murthy, *Together: The Healing Power of Human Connection in a Sometimes Lonely World* (Harper Wave, 2020). The U.S. surgeon general under presidents Barack Obama and Joe Biden describes how his own childhood experience of loneliness affected him and how loneliness has become an epidemic in the modern workplace.

❖ Tara Brach, *Trusting the Gold: Uncovering Your Natural Goodness* (Boulder: Sounds True, 2021). A beautifully written narrative about how mindfulness can free us.

❖ Sharon Salzberg, *Real Happiness at Work: Meditations for Accomplishment, Achievement, and Peace* (New York: Workman Publishing, 2014). How to cultivate real happiness at work with mindfulness meditation.

❖ The Dalai Lama, *The Art of Happiness at Work* (New York: Riverhead, 2003).

❖ Bryan Robinson, *#Chill: Turn Off Your Job and Turn On Your Life* (William Morrow, 2019). A meditation book for workaholics divided into twelve months of the year that parallel the Twelve Steps in Workaholics Anonymous, along with 365 short Microchillers—one for each day of the year.

14

Untangling from the Workaholic Part of You

The voice in my head is an asshole.
                                    —Dan Harris

My Conversation with Hannibal Lecter

Many years ago, I was fortunate to learn about parts work and to have my first experience with Richard Schwartz, the creator of Internal Family Systems therapy (IFS for short).[1] I knew nothing about IFS but had colleagues in training at the time. They invited me as "fresh meat"—someone who knew nothing about the therapy—to sit in the middle of the training circle and allow Dick to perform his magic on me. Little did I know that I would perform it on myself.

We started the session with a casual conversation about why I had moved from my hometown to Asheville, North Carolina. Before I knew it, I was aware of the part of me that wanted more free time to play that brought me to the mountain town, polarized with the workaholic part that wanted me to keep working day and night. The workaholic part took on the image of cannibalistic serial killer, Hannibal Lecter from the movie "The Silence of the Lambs," wiggling his tongue at me. I was terrified of this part of me and hated him for how he had ruled my life, consuming me and nearly destroying my health, marriage, and friendships. And I had succumbed to him.

Before I could interact with Hannibal, Dick led me through an IFS process in which I had to put a mask on the monster and put him behind bars. Once my internal system felt safe, I was able to talk with and understand him—even to appreciate him for how he had protected me and all he had done for me in my life. As I untangled from him (Dick uses the word "unblended"), I felt my real Self (or C-Spot as I came to call it) emerge from its sleepy eclipse as if the sun suddenly broke through the clouds. It was organic, palpable, and euphoric. That experience of untangling from my workaholic part set me free on a path of personal insight that I now use to treat my own clients, after going through the extensive IFS training.

Your Silent Conversations with Yourself

You, too, have silent conversation with yourself. Paying attention to them provides a window into what makes you tick and what drives your life. When the popular singer/songwriter and heartthrob, Shawn Mendes, steps on stage in front of sold-out arenas, an ego voice in his head often takes over to try to help him perform. But it inevitably causes him to slip up, that is, until he lets it go and brings the house down. In the documentary "In Wonder," Mendes described how lightning fast his ego shows up and gets in his way:

> You first get on the stage, and ego comes rushing in. And it goes, "Don't mess up because you're the man. Everyone's saying you're the man, so don't mess up." So, then you get to the mic and your first note's flat. Always. And then thirty seconds in, you go, "Ah, yeah I'm just a guy, and I love music." And your whole-body releases. And I just let go, and I look around and I'm just like, "Just do this. Drop the ego. Time to surrender."

All of us are on some type of stage in our lives—singer or sanitation worker, judge or janitor, teacher or technician, physician or pilot, accountant, or author—and Mother Nature hardwired us with ego parts for survival. Not unlike your rib cage that protects your vital organs, your parts protect your psychological vulnerabilities. They're always trying to shield you from humiliation, failure, or danger—even though they can keep you trapped in a life of misery. Parts are always trying to protect and help you, but their efforts often backfire and cause you to mess up as they did with Mendes and me for much of my career. As former ABC anchor Dan Harris told me, "Seeing the cacophony is the point because the better your visibility, the less likely you are to be owned by the malevolent upper tier of your ego."

The "I" in the Workaholic Storm

You and I have a running monologue in our heads with the intention to control ourselves whether it's to stop from blowing up at the injustice you see in news feeds, eating another slice of pizza, or blurting out at a colleague who talks over you in a virtual meeting. But if you think of how many times you have said or done something you wish you could take back, you can blame your impulsive, immersed, non-thinking ego parts. When threatened, our parts are lightning fast, circling like a school of sharks, ready to attack and take over in a nanosecond. In emergency situations—if your house is on fire, you're in a car wreck, or someone pursues you in a dark parking deck—you need the breakneck speed of your parts to protect you from harm.

Your ego parts are responsible for road rage when someone cuts you off in traffic, fury when your love interest cheats on you, or professional worry and uncertainty after missteps at work, putting your job on the line. Their job is to protect you from harm at all costs, and when out of control, they can be dangerous, even deadly as we have seen played out on the national and global stages with racial unrest and police killings, mayhem and deaths during the domestic terrorism and insurrection on the Capitol of the United States on January 6, 2021, and global fears of the Coronavirus threats from 2020 into 2022.

But under ordinary circumstances they *overestimate* threats and *underestimate* our ability to handle them and engulf us even when we don't need them, often adding insult to injury. When parts engulf you—like my hurry, frustration, and urgency—chances are you think the voices are you because you hear them in your silent conversations. And you get used to thinking of them as you, which keeps you entangled. Many of us consider ourselves to be distorted, imperfect, or inadequate because our parts have wiped the floor with us for so long. But you're not the worry, impatience, urgency, anger, perfectionism, criticism, shame, procrastination, judgment, and control that take over without your say-so. These are *subpersonalities* or *parts* of you, residing in your emotional brain.

I had learned to believe that my hurry, frustration, and anger *were* me. If you're like most people, you, too, think of and refer to yourself in ways that reflect these parts of your personality with which adults labeled you or with which you identified since you were young. These messages freeze-frame and become aspects of you—interpretations of the past that carry memories and superimpose them on present situations.

So that begs the question, "Are you an "i" or an "I"? That might sound like a silly question, but it isn't. You might be thinking, "What a relief to learn that I'm not all these parts, but then who am I, really?" You're the uppercase "Self" with a capital "S"—the one who hears and sees the lowercase parts of "self"— the one who speaks back to them when they pop up. So, how do you liberate yourself from the parts and live more in your C-Spot?

The good news is you don't have to declare open season on your workaholic parts. The key isn't to stop talking to them, steamroll over them, or try to silence them. The key is to communicate with them in a way that benefits you and moves you into a calmer, clearer, and more compassionate place— befriending and engaging them from a distance with curiosity. Once you become clearheaded and regret what you said or did, you have shifted into your reflective, self-distanced C-Spot. But what if you could *act* more from your C-Spot (and *react* less from your parts) in the first place? IFS clinicians and neuroscientists have found that self-distancing from your parts regulates your emotions and provides impulse control.[2]

As you become mindful of the workaholic parts that give rise to your entanglement, you develop agency to detach from them. Psychologists call this process "self-distancing"—a detached perspective that separates your subpersonality parts from your upper-case Self. Once you start to find the gap, it has the potential to put you on the on-ramp to your C-Spot.[3] The distancing allows you to step back from your usual perspective and gain a wider picture and clearer understanding of what's going on inside. In other words, most of us don't see the water we're swimming in daily. But when we step back and sit on the riverbank, we gain the insights of a third-party observer.

"And once the storm is over," in the words of Haruki Murakami, "you won't remember how you made it through, how you managed to survive. You won't even be sure, whether the storm is really over. But one thing is certain. When you come out of the storm, you won't be the same person who walked in. That's what this storm's all about."

Workaholic Illusions and Untangling

You create this long-distance relationship through a process of emotional detachment I call untangling. The first step is to separate or untangle from the parts that create your reactivity (e.g., criticism, anger, frustration, anxiety, worry, judgment, control) to get better acquainted with them. This action involves dis-identifying with the incessant thought stream of your mind—most of it repetitive and pointless.

Suppose you have your eye on a certain job for which you're qualified, or you're attracted to a person but don't feel confident enough to go after the job or the person. That, too, happens because your parts have entangled you, blocking your confidence. Parts of you might be holding irrational judgments that you're completely unaware of, such as: *They're bound to dislike me; I've felt like a failure all my life, and I can't bear to fail again;* or *I'll never be good enough for them.* These judgments reverberate in your mental echo chamber that you can untangle from. After all, there's no objective evidence for any of these beliefs. You haven't taken the first step yet to apply for the job or speak to the person you find attractive. Untangling helps you see the truth about yourself—that the negativity you perceive in yourself is an illusion—a distortion caused by your brain zooming in on what it perceives to be a threat, which entangles and eclipses your C-Spot in the heat of the moment.

Zooming out helps you see that your past isn't real any more; it's merely the mind's illusion of you that parts carry from the past and impose on the present. The lingering perception about an experience creates your emotional reactions, not the new experience itself. So, when you're emotionally aroused by the past, you experience memories of the upsetting event, not the actual event. Your emotional brain might judge you as selfish, mean, shy; or it might call you names such as control freak, worry wart, sad sack, penny pincher, workaholic, alcoholic, or pessimist. The list is endless. Even if you are a control freak, what you call yourself only describes a part or side of you, not all of you.

Whether you're taking a test, making a pitch to clients, starting a new job, or struggling as a new parent, self-doubt (a part of you) can eclipse your confidence and flood you. Your inner voice says, *You can't do this. You might as well give up*—is the lowercase "self" or a part of you. If I think of myself as a control freak, the narrow identity eclipses my C-Spot where confidence resides. If I think of myself as an angry person, it's difficult for me to know the rest of me. If I identify myself as a selfish person, I probably won't like myself very much because I'm not able to see the bigger picture where my positive qualities reside.

However, if I think of my controlling nature, anger, or selfishness as parts of me, it allows me to untangle from them and start to experience my uppercase "Self" or my C-Spot. The separation makes room for positivity, happiness, and deeper insight into the rest of me. The tool of untangling from your workaholic illusions helps you live more from that centered state that Richard Schwartz calls Self Leadership, and I call the C-Spot because it's the place inside all of us teeming with qualities such as calmness, curiosity, compassion, clarity, contentment, celebration, courageousness, connectedness, creativity, consciousness, competence, confidence, comedy, and cool-headedness. This list is not exhaustive, but you get the point.

Check out the dots in the figure below. Which one of the center dots is bigger? The one surrounded by a circle of large dots or the one surrounded by a circle of tiny dots?

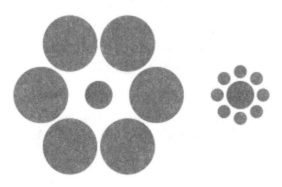

The answer is they're both the same. Imagine your C-Spot is the dot in the center. And the surrounding dots represent your lower-case parts. Although your parts defy your size in both cases, you're the exact same size in each figure. In other words, when your parts entangle you, it's a distortion or perceptual illusion of who you are—the lower-case self with which you have identified for most of your life. So, the process of untangling allows you to experience your upper-case Self more often on a regular basis.

Let's say, for example, you call yourself a worrywart. Your worry is not you. It's just a surrounding dot—a perceptual illusion that has tangled up with you like a ball of yarn, making it seem as if it *is* you. If it was you, you'd worry 24/7, and no one worries every second of the day. Your C-Spot (the dot in the center) exists apart from your worry, apart from your judgment, apart from your doubt, apart from your anger—all of which reside in your surrounding survive mind. Still, you've been conditioned to define yourself by these parts and to look outside yourself to course correct, instead of finding solutions on the inside where they exist.

Now check out the square superimposed over the concentric circles below. The sides of the square look wobbly and misshapen. This, too, is a perceptual illusion. Consider for a moment that your upper-case Self or C-Spot is the "misshapen" square, and the concentric circles in the backdrop represent your entangled lower-case parts that constantly talk to you. When you remove the square from its background, you see that it's perfectly square and not wobbly at all. This is another example of how your C-Spot (the square) is who you are at your core, not the things your parts have told you or the untrue stories they make up that you believe.

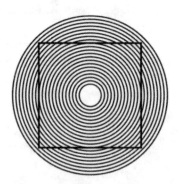

When the parts make quick assessments and draw automatic conclusions, they eclipse your C-Spot and distort threats. They make false associations on a regular basis that seem more horrendous than they are. A frowning colleague doesn't like you. A twig becomes a snake. The foam in your morning coffee is a scowl. No-shows at your event mean they never really liked you that much.

A forgetful spouse on your birthday means you're unloved. A family member accidentally trips the house alarm, and your automatic worry part tells you it's a break-in. I could go on and on, but you get the picture. Psychologists call these examples projections in which we interpret the objective world through our negative and subjective, deep-seated parts.

Your workaholic parts will continue to do their thing, trying to protect you. Left to their own devices, they will continue to take you down one dead end after another. But when you learn to separate from them, you begin to recognize you need them as much as your brain, heart, or stomach to function. This realization brings about a major shift—more serenity and comfort inside your own skin. But sometimes parts overprotect like a helicopter parent by entangling you, refusing to budge, and insisting on protecting you in the present just as they did when you were six or seven years old—unless you're able to intuitively sidestep the illusions, which is exactly what environmental advocate Erin Brockovich was able to do.

The Erin Brockovich Success Story

Erin Brockovich grew up with dyslexia. Before it was diagnosed, she had trouble in school and was labeled in a negative way. She told me that her parents gave her the power to believe in herself. They talked to her about stick-to-itiveness. She looked it up in the dictionary and discovered that it's a real word. "This is a very powerful word—the propensity to follow through in a determined manner, dogged persistence born of obligation and stubbornness," she said. "And I took that to heart and applied it to everything I did. You've got to tap into who you are and rise from that place."

With the support of her parents and her own fortitude, she broke out of the negative messages, holding her hostage, telling her she was incapable. She started to believe in herself, applied her pit-bull, stick-to-itiveness to every obstacle. As a single unemployed mother, she connected to the courage in her C-Spot and stuck her neck out, helping residents of Hinkley, California, win a massive arbitration against the Pacific Gas and Electric Company. The company was found liable for dumping chromium-6—a carcinogen used to suppress rust formation at the Hinkley gas compressor station—into an unlined pond in the 1950s and 1960s. The chemical seeped into the town's groundwater. The company hid the problem and misled the community on the effects of that specific type of chromium and its link to local health problems.

But her success story doesn't end there. For her efforts, she was extolled in the 2000 biographical film aptly titled *Erin Brockovich*, for which Julia Roberts won an Oscar dramatizing Brockovich's true story. Since the film, her name has become a household word—even a verb. "To Erin Brockovich something" means to investigate and advocate for a cause without giving up. Today, Hinkley is known as the "Erin Brockovich town."

To this day, Brockovich told me that negative part still pipes up occasionally (as it does with most of us): "When I hear that negative voice, I acknowledge it and say, 'Yep. Nope, not today. Buzz off,'" she said. "I can almost feel that gear in my head click. And I decide I'm not listening to that, and I'm going to hear what my gut's saying to me. I'm going to follow that little voice that says, 'Hmm, I think you should look into this further.' And then you're going to get the other voice that says, 'Oh, you're crazy. You can't look into that. You don't know what you're doing.'" She intuitively learned to separate from the naysayer parts that tried to keep her from sticking her neck out. Acting from her C-Spot brought success and ultimately fame and gratitude from a town and a nation.

Your Internal Boardroom

It's the workaholic parts we carry around on the inside that often cause us to feel confused and misguided. The key to finding your own strength and personal empowerment starts with learning to distinguish your C-Spot from your workaholic parts. One tool to achieve this distinction is to imagine you have an internal boardroom where all life decisions are made. Let's take my internal boardroom to show what I mean. I'm the CEO of my organization known as Bryan Robinson. I imagine that I sit at the head of my conference room table. In any given situation, I have certain parts that show up table-ready for action in a split second to help me cope with life. These parts are stockholders in my organization, and each one wants a say-so in how I, the CEO, run my life. A random thought or feeling or an upsetting situation can trigger parts to take over the internal organization and hijack me, the CEO.

One afternoon I'd just finished seeing clients and came out of my office. I noticed a neat stack of papers, a book, and a check on a desk in the waiting room. It had been the first session for the bright, corporate executive, suffering from stress and burnout. I had given her a book to read and some forms to complete for the next session. When I saw the stack, my judgment part hijacked me and I thought she obviously wasn't impressed with my recommendations and wanted to show it by leaving the neat stack, along with payment for the session, as if to say, "Thanks, but no thanks!"

All week I wondered what had gone wrong. During dinner, driving to and from work, and out with friends, my parts rehashed the session in my mind and agonized over how I'd misjudged what I thought to be a great session. Although we had made another appointment for the next week, my parts figured the client wouldn't show. To my surprise she did show. Standing in my office doorway with a sheepish frown, she said, "I've dreaded this appointment all week. I'm afraid you're going to think I'm a bad patient. But I must confess I misplaced the forms and book you gave me, and I haven't done my homework."

I chuckled inside. My judgment part had eclipsed my CEO and hers, too. This happens to all of us, kicking us out of our respective chairs at the head of the table, putting us through needless mental torture, making us miserable. Through the eyes of my judgment, I'd been incompetent, while my client's judgment told her she was unreliable. Neither judgment was true because both came from our parts, not from the objective facts of the situation (the CEO).

Once the judgment took over my organization, other parts—such as *worry*, *frustration*, and *another form of judgment*—showed up at the boardroom table, freaking out over my "incompetence." Sometimes when we're frantic in this way, other parts emerge that might want us to drink several glasses of wine or eat compulsively to soothe the worry and frustration. After an upsetting situation, our internal boardroom could be in complete disarray for an entire week, because our judgment (which says, *I'm incompetent*) had taken over. Thank goodness I was aware my client's judgment part and mine were kicking both of us in the pants—calling her *a bad patient* and me *an incompetent therapist*— because Judgment wanted both of us to sharpen our respective saws. While ridiculing us, making us feel badly, the judgment's goal was to keep us from feeling ridiculed. The paradox is that it did exactly to us what it didn't want outside forces to do: judge us in the safety and confines of our mind. Plus, the whole scenario was an illusion to begin with. She wasn't thinking what I attributed to her, and I wasn't thinking what she attributed to me. Our parts had highjacked us and eclipsed our C-Spots where calm, clarity, and confidence reside.

Self-Talk and the Language of Separation

A workaholic client told me, "I have this annoying voice in the back of my head. It says I haven't earned the right to relax. 'Unwinding is a waste of time,' it says, 'and you have nothing to show for it. Now, stop being a loser and get busy doing something productive.'"

Back in the day, people who talked to themselves were considered "crazy." Now, experts consider self-talk to be one of the most effective tools to thrive in just about anything we do. Next time you hear the harsh workaholic voice flashing in your mind like a blinking neon sign, consider that debating, ignoring, or waging war with it will only raise your stress needle. But listening to it as a separate part of you, instead of as you, gives you distance from it and helps you appreciate that it's trying to help in its own way.

Former ABC anchor Dan Harris realized his relationship towards his parts changed when he started meditating: "I've noticed my attitude is warmer. Just as you say, it's not bad. It's trying to serve you, to protect you, however, unskillfully often," he said. "Instead of meeting the aggression with more aggression, I blow it a kiss and say, 'I get it. I salute you. Welcome to the party.' There is this idea in Western culture that we're going to slay our dragons, but I think it's hugging the dragon that is the key."

Scientists and mental health experts have found the best approach is to respond to your workaholic voice as if it's another person. First, you have to remember the voice isn't *you*. It's a sneaky *part* of you, not *all* of you (I realize I'm repeating myself, but this isn't an easy concept to grasp). Imagine someone scolds you on your cell phone, and you hold it away from your ear, listening from afar without reacting. Similarly, once you're aware of an inner arousal that is about to sweep you up in an emotional loop, acknowledge your knee-jerk urge to react, hold it at arm's length, and observe it with dispassionate curiosity. After a period of observing, you notice your critical entangled voice blinking like a neon sign, bludgeoning you with its ire.

The language of separation allows you to process an internal event as if it's happening to someone else. The key is to avoid talking to yourself with the pronoun "I" because it keeps you entangled with your parts, clouding your C-Spot, and preventing you from present-moment awareness. First-name self-talk (using your name), referring to yourself as "you," or referencing yourself as "he" or "she" shifts focus away from your part's inherent egocentricism. So, the story a part tells you isn't the only story in your mind. And your C-Spot has a chance to shed a different light on the scenario.

Self-distancing brings your C-Spot to bear on threatening situations. This psychological distance flips the switch in your emotional brain, moving you away from your parts, landing you at the onramp to your C-Spot. You're calm, think clearly, feel compassion, perform competently, and have more confidence and courage. Some people find giving a name—sometimes even a gender—to the workaholic voice helps to separate from it. Dan Harris told me his inner planner has a name, and his anger has a name: "When they come up in meditation, I say, 'Welcome to the party, Robert.'" Arianna Huffington calls her negative voice, "The Obnoxious Roommate." Erin Brockovich told me she calls hers, "Negative Nancy."

The science of self-talk has shown time and again that how we use our inner voice makes a big difference in the degree to which we thrive in our lives. Negative self-talk from parts can lead to anxiety and depression. Positive self-talk from your C-Spot mitigates dysfunctional mental states and cultivates healthier states of mind.

The language of separation helps you separate from that relentless workaholic voice that says nothing you do is good enough, and we need to do more. And it takes us out of our subjective, egocentric perspective, landing us in a bird's-eye view as an outside observer. As a rule, we act impulsively when we can't use our C-Spot to talk to ourselves as we're performing tasks. Your C-Spot can give you the self-control to avoid making impulsive decisions versus rumination and re-experiencing the same repetitive emotions. Without being able to verbalize messages to yourself, it's difficult to have the same amount of self-control as when you can talk yourself through the process. Using the following checklist enables you to address yourself with the language of separation, promote self-distancing, and live more from your C-Spot as a detached observer of your own life:

❖ Call yourself by name to reduce a part's egocentrism and untangle from it. "I know you have a to-do list, Bryan, but we're taking it easy today."

❖ Replace the first-person pronoun *I* with a non-first-person pronoun, *you* or *he/she* in silent self-talk when speaking to a part. "What's up, Anger. I see *you're* active today." Or "My Worry is active today, and I plan to talk *him* off the ledge."

❖ Employ a curious and compassionate perspective when speaking to your parts to activate the C-Spot. "I see you're feeling urgency about my finishing that project today, and I appreciate that you're looking out for me. But I still have time, and today is a holiday that I want to enjoy. What about you stepping back and relaxing, too?"

❖ Send positive self-affirmations using your own name to establish a third-party perspective and bolster your confidence. Instead of thinking, "I really spoke my truth today about racial injustice," substitute, "Bryan, you really rocked the way you spoke your truth about injustice in the world." Self-affirmations serve as "cognitive expanders," allowing you to talk to yourself the way you might speak to someone you care about so the self-judgment voice isn't the only story you tell yourself.

❖ Take the perspective of the narrator, instead of the actor, of your thoughts and feelings when you're amidst a disturbing situation. Scientists have shown that narrative expressive writing creates a self-distanced versus a self-immersed perspective and helps you overcome the egocentric impulses of your parts and apply wise reasoning from your C-Spot.

❖ Employ story editing when a part makes up a scenario without evidence and revise a negative perspective. "The frowning person in the front row obviously didn't like my presentation" becomes "The frowning person in the front row could be bothered for many reasons: from not feeling well to disparaging himself for not practicing what I was suggesting."

Triple-A Practice: Aware, Acknowledge, Allow

If someone told you something you're doing is adding to your unhappiness and possibly even harming your relationships and career, you'd probably stop doing that thing. Right? After working with author and psychotherapist Richard Schwartz and practicing Internal Family Systems (IFS) therapy for over twelve years, I developed a Triple-A practice I use to varying degrees with practically every client I treat. It's based on the assumption that there's no such thing as "bad feelings" or "bad parts of ourselves" as Schwartz eloquently explains in his book, *No Bad Parts*.[5]

I have a poster in my office that says, "All parts are welcome"—a saying I got from my mentor and friend Schwartz which means it's okay to feel anger, sadness, hurt, frustration, fear, disappointment. And it's important to welcome those parts, spend time with them, and get to know them like you would a new friend. In her book *Welcoming the Unwelcome* the writer, meditation expert, and monk Pema Chödrön expressed this sentiment in a similar way: instead of accepting only the things we want in our lives, we must learn to accept the things we don't want to be happy.[6] We don't skip over unpleasant thoughts and feelings; we befriend them. Again, we can't have an upside without a downside, and embracing both takes us from workaholic madness to a place of serenity.

In my practice, I teach clients three-steps in the Triple-A practice. Step One is to become *aware* of unpleasant feelings (such as worry, anxiety, or anger). Step Two is to *acknowledge* them inwardly, talking to them as you would a friend or family member with something like, "Hey Worry, I see you're stirred up today." I show clients how to have silent conversations by talking to their parts and referring to them in the third person as "you." This practice brings psychological distance and zooms out your perspective, so you see the big picture, as if it's happening to someone else, allowing you to see possibilities beyond the restrictive aspects of a part's zoom lens. Step Three is to *allow* all aspects of yourself to be present—even the unpleasant ones.

Workaholic Mind Chatter

You've got a challenging job interview coming up, you're making a pitch to a group of colleagues, or you have lingering thoughts about what your boss thinks of you after the way he squinted at you in the meeting. The chatter in your head keeps circling like a school of sharks. You're stuck, adding insult to injury and don't know what to do. To the rescue, Dr. Ethan Kross, psychologist and professor at the University of Michigan, who has been conducting studies on the value of first-name self-talk to mitigate what he calls chatter to disable social anxiety before and after a stressful event when we ruminate about our performance.

In one study, Kross and his research team gave 89 participants five minutes to prepare a speech.[4] Half were told to use only pronouns to refer to themselves while the other half were told to use their names. The pronoun group had greater anxiety with such comments as, "How can I possibly prepare a speech in five minutes?" while the name group had less anxiety and expressed confidence using self-talk such as, "Bryan, you can do this." The name group was also rated higher in performance by independent evaluators and were less likely to ruminate after the speech. Other studies also show that first-name self-talk is more likely to empower you and increase the likelihood that, compared to someone using first-person pronoun self-talk, you see a challenge (C-Spot perspective) instead of a threat (survival parts perspective).

The psychologist explains that self-talk comes in different forms, and chatter is the harmful, toxic self-talk that runs on auto-play over and over in your head. "If all our attention is on chatter, it doesn't leave anything over to do the thing we need to do at work," he told me when we sat down to talk. "Chatter causes us to overthink things, have paralysis-by-analysis and under perform at work. Even things we're good at such as presenting before colleagues or performing a complex procedure, we start thinking, 'Are we doing it well?' Once we start zooming in too much, our capabilities unravel."

If you're like most workaholics, you have mind chatter that rules your life. It kicks you around and keeps you focused on your flaws, so you constantly feel as if you're struggling internally. The workaholic's solution? Work longer and harder. Of course, that's not the real solution. Immersing yourself in work mires you deeper in the problem because it'll never be enough. That's why we call it work addiction. The real solution is using the concept of distance—a unique feature of the human mind—the opposite from being immersed, Kross said. "When chatter zooms us in narrowly, distancing enables us to take a step back to think about our circumstances more objectively." Kross and his research team have shown that enlarging your perspective is one of the best distancing tools. And talking to yourself in the third person using your name is the best tool of all.

"We're much better at giving advice than taking it ourselves," the psychologist said. "So, we use language to overcome this bias. When you refer to yourself using words we typically use to talk to other people, it switches your perspective. Use your name to give yourself advice. Think of what you'd say to a close friend. It gives you that distance that lets you come up with a smart plan to addressing your circumstances." Kross explained that when we get immersed in chatter, our mind makes everything bigger than it actually is. Self-talk enables you to step back from the immersion and develop more self-kindness to balance your self-judgment. And research suggests that encouragement and self-support can be a game changer. The more self-compassion you have, the greater your emotional well-being.

By now, you have probably realized this practice is counterintuitive, but it's also simple science. As I mentioned in the previous chapter, the best way to escape when you're trapped in a turbulent, funnel-shaped current known as a hydraulic, is to relax, and the hydraulic will spit you out. If you fight against the current, it can keep you stuck, even drown you. This same principle holds true to *flowing*, instead of *fighting*, when you're caught in a riptide or leaning into a curve, instead of away from it, when you're on a motorcycle so you don't flip over. And it even applies in natural childbirth where, instead of tightening the body and resisting labor pains, mothers-to-be accept and *go with* the labor pains, *not against* them, which reduces both maternal pain and obstetrical problems during birth. Let's look more closely at each step.

AWARE

When you first become aware of the harsh workaholic voice, it might be so unpleasant that your first impulse is to debate, ignore, get angry, steamroll, or try to get rid of it. Back in the day (and even today), some "experts" used words like *fight, tame, battle, conquer, combat*—even *quiet*—to describe strategies to oppose our parts. But you wouldn't combat a fever or a scab on your hand—both of which are protecting you—so why would you combat your anger, frustration, or worry when they're trying to protect you from harm? That's like attacking the fire department when your house is on fire.

When you oppose your parts, you trap yourself into the very negative loop you're trying to avoid. But as you begin to look underneath the surface at their intent, instead of identifying with them, you appreciate that they're trying to help. You wouldn't change lanes on the interstate before checking your rearview mirror. And you wouldn't shoot a gun and then aim at the target (I hope). You would take time to check out your surroundings and then act. Hence, the collaborative relationship with your parts and your C-Spot.

I realize when your parts take over in the blink of an eye, it doesn't always feel warm and fuzzy, and it's natural to doubt a part's motives. In many cases, the fast and forceful reactions are self-defeating and cause more distress than they prevent. Suppose you're in the middle of a threatening situation, and a part starts calling you names, cursing you, or trying to keep you from sticking your neck out. Naturally, you might ask, "How could a part protect me when it's so harsh and unrelenting?" To that I say sometimes it operates much like the kick-ass drill sergeant who doesn't want you to get your head blown off in combat or an observant parent who smacks her child's bottom because she doesn't want him to play in traffic.

After you're aware of your internal reaction, let yourself grow curious about its purpose or even how it's trying to protect you from what it registers as a threat. Instead of judging its reactions to threats as harmful, consider them as protection. And when you practice this perspective enough, muscle memory will eventually perceive your parts as helpful instead of harmful. When you become aware of the choice between *reacting* and *acting* and resist the urge to blow your top, it creates neuroplasticity that eventually widens your C-Spot.

ACKNOWLEDGE

Once you're *aware* of your workaholic part, try to *acknowledge* it with genuine interest as a separate part of you and see if you can figure out how it's trying to help or protect you in the way I was able to do with my "Hannibal Lecter part." This is where you talk to your workaholic part just as if it's a person inside you with as much compassion as possible. You might say something like, "What's up Workaholic? I see you're on a roll today." Or you could try to feel appreciation for its protection with, "I see you're upset that I've been chilling today. I realize you're trying to protect me in your own way. What do you need to calm down?" Or perhaps a simple friendly greeting: "Hello Workaholic, I notice you're white-knuckling it today" or "I see you, Workaholic and that you're biting at the bit to get something done."

Acknowledgment includes stretching to understand why your workaholic part is reactive then validating and empathizing with it. You might say something like, "I see you're anxious that we won't make the deadline. You're not alone. I'm with you every step of the way." Or "I know you're anxious about tomorrow's presentation, and we'll get through this together." These simple acknowledgments and validations throw the switch in your prefrontal cortex—the more recently evolved thinking part of the brain—allow access to your rational mind and heart, ushering in compassion, calming you down, and unlocking the door to your C-Spot.

Let's look at another example of how the acknowledgment shift works. A client of mine named Brad was having trouble concentrating on his golf game and his guitar lessons. When he stepped up to tee off, a part of him rushed in to overthink his strategy, much like in the earlier case of singer Shawn Mendes. The same thing happened with his guitar lessons, causing him to fail miserably and feel badly about himself. When I asked him to look curiously inside and identify what part or parts were at his boardroom table, he replied that an inner voice kept saying *I'm gonna screw up* and another was saying *What are people gonna think of your bad performance?*

I suggested that he acknowledge the concerns of the parts before he performed to develop an understanding of their motives. He learned that the parts were trying to prepare him for the inevitable failure that they expected.

Employing the practice of untangling, he talked to his parts reassuring them with, "I know you're concerned, but I've got this." He was able to get them to relax, and he shot the best golf game ever. Plus, his guitar playing improved by leaps and bounds.

Performance in many arenas can be enhanced when you give all parts at the boardroom table a voice, instead of trying to ignore, fight, or stifle them. Once they've had their say and feel heard as a stockholder by you, they're usually willing to settle down and let you, the CEO run the show. When you're able to hear the voice as a part of you instead of as you—without wasting energy being frustrated or angry with it or trying to get rid of it—you have more room to lead from your C-Spot. You know you're at the helm (the "I" in the storm) when you're in any of the "C" states that compose your C-Spot. One of the most significant changes that can ever happen to you is set in motion as you begin the process of untangling from your parts.

ALLOW

The third step, and perhaps the hardest to grasp, is to allow your workaholic parts to be present exactly as they are without trying to change, battle, tame, or fix them. As I said earlier, this is counterintuitive, but it's extremely important. You're not accepting that it feels good or bad or that you want to prolong or grow the unpleasant feeling. You're allowing the fact that it's there to protect you in its own way. You're simply leaning into it, giving it space, and trying to understand how it's protecting you.

An important aspect of allowing is spending time *noticing and savoring* in present-moment time how different your *action* is from your usual *reaction*— how much calmer and clearer you are. This type of noticing forms new neural connections in your brain known as *neuroplasticity* (which I discussed in chapter 5) and makes them stick. It deepens your understanding of the part and strengthens the likelihood that you will have a similar response the next time the part is triggered.

I'm reminded of a time when I had a low-grade fever that made me sluggish and concentrating difficult. I had trouble working and took frequent naps. I underwent every test known to humankind, and all the results were negative. I started to resent my fever because it kept me from being on top of my game. Finally, it dawned on me that the fever was protecting me—defending my immune system from foreign agents—and I was attacking it. That *awareness* led to *acknowledgment* when I questioned my resentment with curiosity: "Why are you attacking the fever when it's protecting us?" The self-talk enlarged my perspective and led me to course correct my actions by *allowing* the fever to do its magic. I closed my eyes and sat with the fever as I might provide bedside company for a sick friend. I showered it with compassion and support for how hard it was working to take care of me. The next day it was completely gone. Befriending an unpleasant part—psychological or physical—with the Triple-A action helps it relax and calm down. When you fight or resist, as I had been doing, it's like tossing gasoline on a fire that swells with stronger opposition and reactivity.

Much like my fever, it can feel like parts are working against you when, in fact, they're working hard to protect you from threat to obtain what they believe you need to survive. In trying to help, they eclipse you because they think they know more than you about what's best for your survival. So, the allowing is your effort to work *with* your hard-wired parts, instead of *against* them, much like I was finally able to accept my fever that made me feel miserable but was waging war with foreign invaders to my immune system. The paradox is when you can cultivate a heartfelt allowing of an activated part, it segues you into your C-Spot and a calm descends over you.

Once you're freed from or avoid the hydraulic, it's possible for two more A-words to automatically emerge, allowing you to develop a deeper Appreciation and finally Acceptance for how the part has been protecting you for a long time. When you appreciate and accept the earnest intent of your parts and develop a collaborative relationship with them—versus identifying with them—it expands what neuroscientists call your resilient zone and makes it more likely that the next time a part of you gets triggered, you will have an easier time remaining in your C-Spot. Over time using this befriending process creates muscle memory that responds to parts as helpful instead of harmful. When you sit for a few minutes and contemplate with appreciation every time parts rushed in to protect you (even when they added insult to injury), you might notice a shift inside. That shift softens you, helps you overlook a part's harsh protection, and accept it. Acceptance takes you deeper into self-compassion and transitions you into your C-Spot.

The Little Red Car

One autumn Sunday afternoon my feeble attempts at separating from my parts finally paid off as I exited the freeway in Asheville, North Carolina. When I gazed to my left, the woman in a little red car who had been in front of me smirked and shot me the finger. A flash of anger rose up inside me. I watched my anger part coming toward me to take charge, demanding that I return the ugly gesture. But instead of focusing on the woman in the car, my observation of him gave me a dispassionate, bird's-eye view of his reaction (Notice I use the language of separation and refer to my anger in the third person). Speaking to him from my C-Spot with empathy, I was able to talk him off the ledge with, "I know you're pissed off and want me to act out, but that's not how I want to be in the world." As my anger relaxed, I suddenly felt an ease into my C-Spot. I felt calm, cool, and collected along with an incredible high as if I'd scored a touchdown or hit a home run because I was able to self-regulate and stay centered. The little red car chugged angrily off into the distance, and I continued doddering down the road, a smile on my face, peacefully enjoying the beautiful autumn afternoon.

After the woman flipped me the bird, my anger emerged and tried to take over to save the day. But having already cultivated a long-distance relationship with him, I remained in my C-Spot or at the helm of my inner boardroom. Once *aware* of this part, I *acknowledged* him, just as I would speak to another person. I let him know I understood he was upset and that I could handle the situation. Instead of fighting or trying to get rid of him, I talked him off the ledge with empathy and simply *allowed* him to be present, encouraged him to stay in his seat, and he relaxed when I didn't oppose him. As the anger rescinded into his place at the table, the space he had occupied filled with calm, clarity, and cool-headedness from my C-Spot. That experience led me to create the acronym WAIT, a quick and easy shortcut, to bring the Triple-A practice to bear on your parts, mitigate the amygdala, and strengthen your C-Spot.

WAIT, There's a Shortcut

How many times have you been in the middle of an important task requiring your full concentration when someone interrupts you? Maybe you were irritated. According to neuroscientists, you have a ninety-second cushion to recognize the difference between the interruption and your irritation—that space between the stimulus and your response where you have a choice on how to respond. As you develop a sharper awareness of that space, you discover you don't have to take the entanglement bait.

> Watch what's going on inside and be *aware* when you're triggered by workaholic thoughts or situations.
> *Acknowledge* the workaholic part by stepping back and observing it from afar. Then silently speak to it with something like, "I see you're here with me and stirred up."
> Invite the part to calm down and *allow* it to be there exactly as it is, continuing to talk to it with compassion.
> Tell the part in a compassionate mental whisper, "I'm here, too, and I've got this." Soak in any feelings or body sensations from your C-Spot.

With practice and the development of muscle memory, this acronym plays a starring role in helping you untangle from your reactions. You'll notice your heart rate drop, breathing slow, and muscles loosen and that you feel calmer, clearer, and more centered. It's available when you remember that action isn't the absence of upset or adversity but the willingness to embrace it all. Once you start welcoming your parts, you don't have to suffer the unpleasant effects of them. And with each episode, you become more mindful of that gap between the triggering situation and a part's quick reaction that neurologist Viktor Frankl described (see chapter 12), and you're more successful choosing your actions from your C-Spot.

Tips for Clinicians

TEACHING CLIENTS THE TRIPLE-A EXERCISE

You can teach clients to use the Triple-A practice while they walk from the parking garage to the office, cook dinner, or sit at their desk. Here's an example of how you or your client can use it during a workday. I recommend that you practice the steps first before demoing to clients. Suppose you're facing a stressful event: a tight deadline, a presentation to your colleagues, or a performance review. And you hear a voice in your head (we all have one) say, "You're going to screw up." You can use the Triple-A (Aware, Acknowledge, and Allow), before, during, or after the triggering event.

Once you're *aware* of the workaholic part, you simply focus on it then observe it for a few seconds—much like you would inspect a blemish on your hand. Then *acknowledge* it by silently speaking to it inside with something like, "Hello Workaholic, I see you're stirred up today." Continue a dialogue with the part until you can *allow* it to be there without fighting, debating, ignoring, or steamrolling over it. Most clients start to feel separation from a part when they practice the Triple-A as they move throughout their workday, and they notice an automatic transport into their C-Spot where they feel calmer, centered, and more clear-minded. You can even teach clients to notice the accompanying body sensations such as loosened body muscles, slowed breathing, and reduced heart rate. You can even point out that once they're fully engaged in the present moment in this way, they're not regretting something in the past or worrying about the future, nor are they battling the workaholic voice.

I have used the Triple-A practice successfully with numerous workaholics and other clients struggling with a variety of issues. You can use it with clients, too, especially when someone gets triggered in a challenging session. I treated a client named Diane with Internal Family Systems therapy when one of her parts felt threatened. All of a sudden, she leaned forward and squinted her eyes, and her tone went from soft spoken to harsh. "I can destroy you," she said. Then I instinctively went into the Triple A. I was *aware* that a part of her had eclipsed her C-Spot to protect her. I *acknowledged* the part and spoke directly to it. "I know you could, and I'm glad you're here to protect Diane." My non-combative validation of the protector part caused it to feel safe because I *allowed* it to be there. I could actually see in her facial expression and physical demeanor the protective part untangle and retreat. She smiled and sunk back into the cushions of the sofa. The Triple-A paved the way for her protective parts to relax, deepened her trust in me, and opened her up to therapy. Years later, I still hear from Diane through shared texts and emails thanking me for how our time together continues to change her life for the better.

After dedicated practice, clients are often amazed at how the Triple-A muscle memory enables them to respond instead of react to their triggered parts, no matter how dire the circumstances. A long-term client named Sarah, who suffered from Fibromyalgia, wrote about her experience using the Triple-A practice and gave me permission to use her account. As she walks you through the befriending process, you will notice that after the first three Triple-A steps, the three A's start to deepen in a non-linear, circling fashion until she arrives at two other A-words: *appreciation* and *acceptance*—the onramp to the C-Spot. The parentheses are mine.

SARAH FACES A GIANT SPIDER SITTING ON TOP OF HER HEAD

I'd been using the Triple-A practice under Bryan Robinson's care for a while when fatigue and a variety of pain symptoms encroached on my life. My physician and I had been chasing a number of pain symptoms to no avail for several years at this point when the fatigue and pain skyrocketed. Though not bed ridden, I stopped exercising and quit participating in my normal activities as I tried to lower the increasing pain and fatigue. There was no position I could sit, stand, or lie in that didn't hurt. The amount of pain I felt upon waking each morning brought tears of grief and despair.

At one point I was bringing my physical pain issues to counseling as much as any mental, emotional, or relationship issue. In one session Bryan realized my collection of symptoms sounded like Fibromyalgia. I'd wondered the same and so, the next time I saw my physician, I asked what he thought of my symptoms. That was the day chasing each individual symptom came to an end, and I received the official diagnosis. My doctor had a medicine he prescribed for me and supplements for me to take but none of it helped. In the meantime, Bryan and I got busy practicing the Triple-A along with parts work from Internal Family Systems therapy to my Fibromyalgia.

(*Aware*) When I first met with Fibromyalgia as a part, I saw in my imagination the image of a giant spider sitting on top of my head with its long legs wrapped all around me. It was as if the spider's brain connected to my brain while its legs applied pain all over my body. There were neither feelings nor words from the spider. Even though the spider's legs seemed to be the cause of my pain, she was without affect—just there doing her job. I welcomed (*Acknowledge*) her and updated her as to how old I was and what my life was like. I told her I was no longer a small defenseless child needing protection from parts but was a grown adult with a Self that could provide all the leadership and protection I needed.

During the week, between sessions, as I periodically tuned into Fibromyalgia as this spider, it changed. It became an octopus and, as with the spider, her head rested on top of my head as her arms covered my body. But as an octopus, it felt friendlier than the spider. Also, rather than being indifferent, it felt as if the octopus cared about me. But even with the octopus, there were no words. She wouldn't talk to me. I decided to hang in there with Fibromyalgia as an invested but silent partner in the form of an octopus (*Allow*).

By this point I recognized there were days the symptoms were much worse. I began to tally up everything that brought on Fibromyalgia flares— when the pain was truly debilitating. My list included a poor night's sleep, changes in the weather, receiving bad news, feeling dejected, put-upon, or despairing, and eating anything that challenged my gut. Much of that list I had little control over. There was one other curious situation that brought on major flares. Whenever I said yes to anything or anyone when I should have said no, I'd get a really bad flare with a severe increase in pain and fatigue. In other words, for me there was a direct correlation between Fibromyalgia and codependency (*Aware*).

Out of desperation I decided I didn't care that the Fibromyalgia part, the octopus, wouldn't speak to me (*Allow*). I got in the habit of "communing" with her whenever I had a bad flare (*Acknowledge*). She might not want to talk to me but I was content to hang out in her energy (*Allow*). That's when I began to notice (*Aware*) another change. The octopus's interest in me was growing. I felt growing compassion from her. And her arms now moved in a stroking, soothing manner as if she meant to give me comfort, not pain. I began putting words in the octopus's mouth, so to speak (*Acknowledge*).

"It feels as though you really care about me. I know that other parts try to protect me. I think you're trying to protect me too. Is that right?"

The octopus's eyes blinked, focusing more intently on me as her arms stroked my skin. That felt like an affirmation. Days went by like this, the two of us "communing" whenever I wanted her company. I appreciated knowing that all the pain and fatigue were somehow meant to protect me (*Appreciation*). And I put that to use. With the information I'd gained using this approach with Fibromyalgia, I was inspired to get on top of the codependency. The practice of saying no when I needed to say no began to make a difference in my pain, lessening it. Then one night there was a startling change. Suffering from a flare I went inside my imagination looking to commune with the octopus when a teenage boy, nineteen maybe, showed up in her place! He was smiling at me, looking like he owned me, proud as a peacock. I laughed out loud! "Are you fibromyalgia? Have you taken the place of the octopus?"

Smiling at me with twinkling eyes, he nodded yes.

'Do you know who I am? That I'm no longer a defenseless child but a grown woman with a life of my own?

He gave me more smiles, more twinkling eyes and nodded at me (*Aware*).

'Well, you are welcome here with me! Why have you shown up as a teenage boy?

This expression of Fibromyalgia as a part, like the spider and octopus, wasn't speaking. He's never actually spoken to me. He smiles, winks, nods with enthusiasm. Sometimes, not often, he puts his forefinger to his lips while he studies me with rapt concentration, shaking his head to indicate I'm missing the mark. When I figure out how to get back on track, he smiles at me with pride then disappears! He behaves like a teenage boyfriend, all over me (like the octopus's arms or spider's legs), overprotective, willing to make a fool out of himself to take care of me. But he never annoys me. He's enchanting and helpful beyond measure! I call him Timothy (*Appreciation*).

Even though Fibromyalgia as Timothy still doesn't speak to me, he engages me directly and even independently regarding why I have Fibromyalgia flares. The merest thought of him brings him into focus and sometimes he shows up independent of my thoughts just because a flare's coming on. Between the two of us, I always figure out exactly why I'm having a specific flare (*Aware*). In the beginning he seemed to give me this information so that I'd behave differently in the future—not do the things that brought on flares.

One day, though, I could not help the fact I'd had a bad night's sleep and could not take the time to rest during the day. So, toward the end of the day and in a world of hurt, I stopped and said, "Timothy, I know I need to slow down, but I can't. Some days are like this and today was justifiably so. I promise I can have a restful day tomorrow. I have not gone ninety miles an hour today unaware of what I'm doing. It's been purposeful and necessary. Bedtime comes soon and tomorrow will be a better day" (*Acknowledge*). I felt better immediately. The next day I had a restful day, and the flare was over. That was a turning point in my gaining control over how much or little pain I experienced in any given flare.

As time has gone by and my relationship with this part has grown, here is what I've noticed (*Aware*). I no longer have flares that last for days. Whenever I notice I'm having a flare (increased pain in my body and legs that makes climbing stairs nearly unbearable and/or an increase in fatigue that threatens to knock me off my feet), I acknowledge what brought it on (*Acknowledge*). Timothy usually shows up, smiling reassuringly, at which point the flare begins to fade or Timothy's affirmation makes me feel resilient and that resilience causes the flare to subside (*Allow*). And these days I wake up achy after a good night's sleep but not with debilitating pain.

In the beginning, I thought Fibromyalgia and everything associated with it was some form of punishment. Persistent, sometimes constant, pain is easily interpreted that way. But getting to know Fibromyalgia as a part I realized that, as with any protective part that got birthed in my childhood, it's done its best to serve me as a protector with limited information and primal instincts (*Acceptance*). And Fibromyalgia did get birthed in my childhood. Intertwined with the anxiety of my childhood and youth and with the intensity of the Fibromyalgia turned down low, I tolerated it well. It was in place by the time I was twelve. Four years ago, after a series of losses, the intensity of it got turned up so high I couldn't ignore it any longer. And now the Triple-A cycle has helped me turn down the pain and other symptoms of Fibromyalgia like nothing else I've tried. It consistently works for me and gets better with practice.

Bibliotherapy

The following resources are recommended for further reading to gain a thorough understanding of self-distancing self-talk and how to communicate with your parts:

- ❖ Pema Chödrön, *Welcoming the Unwelcome: Wholehearted Living in a Brokenhearted World* (Boulder, CO: Shambhala, 2019).
- ❖ Tom Holmes, *Parts Work: An Illustrated Guide to Your Inner Life* (Kalamazoo MI: Winged Heart Press, 2011).

❖ Ethan Kross, *Chatter: The Voice in Our Head, Why It Matters, and How to Harness It* (New York: Penguin Random House, 2021).

❖ Richard Schwartz, *Introduction to the Internal Family Systems Model* (Chicago; Trailhead Press, 2001).

❖ Richard Schwartz, *No Bad Parts: Healing Trauma and Restoring Wholeness with the Internal Family Systems Model* (Boulder, CO: Sounds True, 2021).

❖ Timothy Wilson, *Redirect: Changing the Stories We Live By* (New York: Back Bay Books, 2011).

15

Radical Self-Care and Fierce Self-Compassion

*The difference between successful
people and really successful people is
that really successful people say no
to almost everything.*
—Warren Buffett

CNN Anchor Alisyn Camerota on Radical Self-Care

Alisyn Camerota is a journalist, author, and anchor at CNN. And she has a powerful message about radical self-care and how she protects her mental health in the face of what she calls "a breathless, fever pitch calorie-burner pace." Obviously, Camerota is no slacker, but she's not a workaholic, either, and she knows how to prioritize work-life balance. During her successful career climb, she has mastered something most of us continue to strive for: a formula of radical self-care that keeps her career soaring and her mental well-being on an even keel.

When I asked Camerota about this, she said sometimes when you're at the end of your rope, you must do something drastic to grab people's attention. "I hear a lot from women who are juggling families, homes, marriages, and careers and reaching overload. They say, 'Oh, I could never get my husband to take the kids to soccer practice.' And I say, 'Okay, here's my advice. Get in bed and don't get out. Somebody has to pick up the slack.'"

But does she practice what she preaches? She told me she has never been "cursed" with perfectionism or to have to get it all right.

I hear women say, "It's so hard to be a working parent because you can't give one hundred percent to everything." And I say, "So what. Who cares?" I'm a big proponent of the *Good Enough School of Parenting* and the *Good Enough School of Journalism*. I try hard and do well enough, but I don't strive for perfection. I do well at balancing and knowing my limitations, and I've never felt guilty about it. My kids know this about me. They know I'm doing my best and that I have flaws. I lower the standards for everybody and that has worked for me because I don't want them to expect me to be at every game and be available for every homework assignment.

Camerota told me she takes her work health very seriously, too, but also knows her limits. "There's a relentlessness to the breathless, calorie burner pace of my job," she said.

We report on pandemics, hurricanes, death and destruction, a building collapsing, wars and so on. I've always been able to compartmentalize the losses and not carry them home. But I'm also aware that on some unknown level it takes its toll. One thing I always say is I need to be out of motion. So, when I get home and my husband and kids say, "Okay, you ready to go out to dinner?" I say, "I need to be out of motion." And I lie down in my bed and stare out the window at the leaves gently rustling in the wind. I can easily get myself into that alpha state because my body doesn't like to be at that fever pitch. I dial it back, write in my journal, or stare out the window at the leaves.

Camerota said she knows the signs when she's pushing too hard or is too stressed and believes there's no upside to not addressing it. "Working doesn't have to be nose-to-the-grindstone misery. You get more productivity out of well-rested, healthy employees. It's a skill—an art—to know your limits," she advises. "Don't be embarrassed to hold your limits. Step into them and feel free to let people know what they are. Carve out time you need for yourself. Some people decompress with exercise, some people take a walk in the park, some read. You know your bliss. You know yourself well enough and what you need, and it doesn't serve anybody—yourself or loved ones—if you get too overwhelmed and stressed."

Holding a Knife to the Throat of Self-Care

Workaholics and others who struggle with work-life balance unwittingly hold a knife to the throat of self-care, relegating it to the bottom of the priority list. This leads to work abuse and escalates physical illness and mental health problems. One in five people will be affected by mental illness over the course of a lifetime, often because they put everything before their own well-being. Mentally healthy employees are productive employees who practice self-care and ultimately boost the organization's bottom line. If you have a history of slaving in a toxic work culture, you have the power to prevent yourself from mistreatment. No matter where you work and no matter how demanding it is, you don't have to overwork or continue to toil in a workplace that doesn't value you as a human being.

Many of us have been taught that self-sacrifice is the nobler ticket to job performance and success and that self-care is selfish, narcissistic, or a New Age fad—even cheesy. During the 1990s, comedians mocked the notion of self-care and self-affirmations with tongue-in-cheek phrases such as, "I'm smart enough" or "I'm good enough." Al Franken created and performed the fictional character Stuart Smalley on *Saturday Night Live* in a mock self-help show called *Daily Affirmations.*

Years since, otherwise willing participants have steered away from the off-putting idea of building yourself up. And mental health clinicians have struggled to reverse this mindset. You undoubtedly have heard the airplane metaphor, "When the oxygen mask deploys, put yours on before trying to help others around you." Self-care is a pervasive message in the work of psychotherapist, Holocaust survivor, and author Dr. Edith Eva Eger, who said, "I beg of you when you get up in the morning, please say, *I love me; I honor me.* Self-love is self-care. It's not narcissistic, and there will never, ever be another you." But in the workplace, that wise advice often falls on deaf ears.

In disavowing self-care, workaholics find more comfort in brutalizing themselves for job missteps and shortcomings such as a missed deadline. If you're a workaholic, you have a deep belief that harsh treatment will boost your productivity. Or you worry that too much leeway might turn you into a slacker. Research shows nothing could be further from the truth. Negative self-judgment increases work addiction and decreases productivity. Coming down hard on yourself after a setback adds insult to injury and reduces your chances of rebounding and ultimate success. Self-condemnation after a setback is the real career blocker, not the setback. Truth be told, when you take care of yourself before anything else, it pays off. You're a better spouse, parent, and worker.

Of course, it's impossible to give one hundred percent to everything, as Alisyn Camerota acknowledged earlier. And full-time workers, especially women, face this struggle daily when balancing work and family. During her 2022 confirmation hearings to the Supreme Court, Ketanji Brown Jackson spoke to her two daughters: "Girls, I know it has not been easy as I've tried to navigate the challenges of juggling my career and motherhood. And I fully admit, I did not always get the balance right. But I hope that you've seen that with hard work, determination, and love it can be done."

As a working mom, actress and singer/songwriter Rhonda Ross—daughter of icons singer Diana Ross and record producer Barry Gordy—told me about her biggest challenge in finding balance with her son. "There's a balance in how much is my work to give him and how much he's come to this planet with and how much is his to work out," she said. "I feel that more is for him to work out than I give him space to do. The next challenge is with my husband and finding my own personal power. When do I put the airplane oxygen mask on myself and when do I put it on my son, my husband, my mother, or my siblings?"

Work Addiction Veiled in Noble Intentions

Self-sacrifice is nowhere more honorable and self-neglect more rampant than in the helping and mental health professions—bulging at the seams with grown-up parentified children. In these workplaces, workaholics bring their needs to caretake, fix, make peace, and carry the burdens of others.

As you saw in chapter 1, work addiction is often veiled in noble intentions. If you're a careaholic, you might not sit behind a desk or in front of a computer. It's more likely that you're a frontline worker—tending to the sick, caring for the young, advocating for the needy, or saving the souls of the lost. You try to give one hundred percent to everything, have difficulty asking for help, and forfeit your own self-care and emotional well-being in favor of others. You have a strong need to be needed and use caring and helping in the same way alcoholics use booze to self-medicate pain or cope with stress. You overload yourself with other people's problems as a distraction from your own worries and stresses. Caring is counterproductive when helping others becomes a means to avoid or self-medicate your own pain. If you're focused on taking care of someone else, you don't have to think about your own burdens. And if you have unfinished business of your own, you're not likely to let someone else struggle with theirs.

The psychologist John Bowlby explained why this pattern occurs: "The person showing it [careaholism] may engage in many close relationships but always in the role of giving care, never that of receiving it . . . the person who develops in this way has found that the only affectional bond available is one in which he must always be the caregiver and that the only care he can ever receive is the care he gives himself."[1]

When Stephanie took her first-ever vacation from her husband, kids, and job to visit her sister, she made sure everyone would be taken care of in her absence. She cooked, labeled, and froze meals for each day she would be gone. She washed their clothes, cleaned the house, and arranged for her children's carpool. At work where she was a staff supervisor, she delegated her responsibilities and assigned tasks to be completed while she was gone. Natural actions of a loving mother and caring colleague, right?

Hold on. There's more to the story. During her "vacation," Stephanie worried that her family and coworkers couldn't manage without her. She found it hard to relax and enjoy her sister's company because she felt guilty for being away. Upon her return, much to her chagrin, she discovered that everyone had done quite well in her absence. She felt badly that her coworkers and family hadn't needed her more and felt guilty for feeling that way. On a deeper level, she recognized that a part of her would have rather things go wrong than run smoothly so the people in her life would lean on her, satisfying her need to feel important.

Stephanie is a careaholic. The word, "careaholic" might sound odd. And you might even ask, "How can you care too much?" William Shakespeare once said, "Care is no cure, but rather corrosive, for things that are not to be remedied." There is a flip side to the critical workaholic—the workaholic at the opposite extreme whose work is veiled in noble intentions who cares too much. Don't get me wrong. Helping others is a wonderful thing that makes the world-go-round. But there's a difference between compassionate caring and corrosive careaholism.

If you take pride in anticipating the needs of others and meeting them before they ask, or if you insist on helping someone—even if they don't want, ask for, or need your help—you might be taking more than you're giving. You might be feeding your own needs instead of practicing selfless compassion. You know you're genuinely caring when you have an unselfish desire to give without making others overly dependent on you or taking away their ability to care for themselves. You give only as much help as is needed. And sometimes you even let people fall down without rescuing them because success is built on failure. That's radical self-care and it's the antidote to careaholism. Does your work addiction masquerade as careaholism? Take the test and find out.

Preventing Emotional Bankruptcy

When you're a careaholic, burning the candle at both ends, you could be headed for emotional bankruptcy or *compassion burnout*—the physical exhaustion and depletion of emotional energy brought on by the stress of caring for and helping others at the expense of taking care of yourself.

As Stephanie's case illustrates, the inability to focus on yourself eventually works against you. If you feel emotionally depleted when you give to others, ask yourself if you've taken time to give to yourself first. Your inability to say no and put yourself last takes its toll. And, if you're a careaholic, when you don't have anyone needing you, you start to feel empty and lack purpose. As the stress cycle kicks in, the relief (over-caring) eventually becomes the problem.

When Careaholism Masks Work Addiction

Read the following twenty-five statements and grade how much each one pertains to you, using the following scale: 1 (never true), 2 (sometimes true), 3 (often true) or 4 (always true). When you're finished, add the numbers in the blanks for your total score.

_____ 1. I get overly involved by taking on other people's problems.

_____ 2. I feel overly responsible when bad things happen and feel that it is my role to make them better.

_____ 3. I overidentify with others by feeling their emotions as if they were my own.

_____ 4. I have an ongoing urge to take care of other people.

_____ 5. I neglect my own needs in favor of caring for the needs of others.

_____ 6. I take life too seriously and find it hard to play and have fun.

_____ 7. I have a need to solve people's problems for them.

_____ 8. I have not dealt with a lot of painful feelings from my past.

_____ 9. I feel unworthy of love.

_____ 10. I never seem to have enough time for myself.

_____ 11. I criticize myself too much.

_____ 12. I am afraid of being abandoned by those I love.

_____ 13. My life always seems to be in crisis.

_____ 14. I don't feel good about myself if I'm not doing something for someone else.

_____ 15. I don't know what to do if I'm not caring for someone.

_____ 16. Whatever I do never seems to be enough.

_____ 17. I have dedicated my life to helping others.

_____ 18. I get high from helping people with their problems.

_____ 19. I have a need to take charge of most situations.

_____ 20. I spend more time caretaking than I do socializing with friends, on hobbies, or on leisure activities.

_____ 21. It is hard for me to relax when I'm not caring for others.

_____ 22. I experience emotional fatigue and compassion burnout.

_____ 23. It is hard for me to keep emotional boundaries by saying no when someone wants to tell me about a problem.

_____ 24. I have developed health or physical problems from stress, worry, or burnout.

_____ 25. I seek approval and affirmation from others through people pleasing and by overcommitting myself.

SCORING: The higher your score, the more of a careaholic you are. Use the following key to interpret your score: 25–49 means you are not a careaholic; 50–69 means you are mildly careaholic; and 70–100 means you are highly careaholic, and chances are that you were parentified as a child.

Careaholics hit bottom from compassion burnout which shows up in a variety of ways: depletion of emotional energy and physical fatigue, gastrointestinal irritations, insomnia, despair, hypertension, lack of purpose, or depression.

Fortunately, self-care can recharge your batteries if you're facing burnout. Think of yourself as a bank account. When overworking or caretaking is withdrawing more than self-care, it's time to make some deposits toward your well-being. Practice setting limits on the demands placed on you, leaving elbow room to stretch and breathe, as well as time to look out the window or take a walk around the block. Set aside fifteen minutes to an hour each day to get in tune with yourself. Relax with a book, soak in a hot bath, exercise, meditate, get a facial, massage or manicure, practice deep breathing, or just watch the grass grow. Get ample sleep, avoid "gobble, gulp, and go," and eat nutritious foods instead of fast food on the run.

Then look inside yourself and examine your motivations for helping others. Do you believe fixing others will fulfill a greater need in you than in them? Respect other people's refusal of your help. If you end up helping someone, make sure you're in the habit of showing them how to fish instead of feeding fish to them. Sometimes the best way to care for others is to care for yourself first. So before embarking on a helping campaign, help yourself in the same ways you tell others to care for themselves.

Think of these practices as building investments so that your daily deposits equal the withdrawals that work makes from your personal account. Ask yourself if you made a "to-be list" alongside of your "to-do list," what you would put on it. One item on mine is sitting outdoors looking at the Blue Ridge Mountains and listening to the sounds of nature.

"Me Time"

Some people—especially workaholics—sneer at the phrase "me time" as self-serving and egocentric. A 2021 study of 2,000 Americans by OnePoll found that nearly a third are so caught up with work, life, and kids that they go more than three months without "me time"—time to relax alone. And, although people agree that self-care should be practiced four days a week, 67 percent can't stick to that, according to the study. "Self-care is just as much about your emotional well-being as it is about your physical health and the health of your environment, such as your home, your community, or the world at large," said Janelle Shiplett, vice president of marketing at Saje Natural Wellness. "Prioritizing each of these three dimensions of wellness every day is critical to making sure you are setup with resources and practices to deal with stress when it inevitably comes around."

When you're struggling with stress and burnout, brain scientist, Dr. Jill Bolte Taylor, insists that when it comes to "me time," the most essential self-care is sleep. She describes the brain cells as constantly working by communicating with our muscles to enable every ability we have whether it's walking, talking, or eating. "The brain cells eat, and they create waste, so sleep is the optimal time for the waste to be cleared out between the cells so they can actually function," she said. "I compare it to when the garbage collectors go on strike, we know how congested the streets become. That's the same thing going on with brain cells. If you wake up to an alarm before your system is ready to wake up, you have cut part of sleep off that your brain wanted."[2]

Many Americans follow the advice of the late comedian Joan Rivers, who said, "I don't exercise. If God had wanted me to bend over, He would've put diamonds on the floor." As many as 40 percent of us spend an average of ten hours a day sitting on their duff in a car, at a desk, or in front of a screen—workaholics perhaps even longer. But your body wasn't designed to be desk-bound for long periods of time. Prolonged sitting reduces blood and oxygen flow, causes weight gain, and leads to type 2 diabetes, and puts you at 80 percent greater risk of dying from heart disease. Simple "me time" practices such as work breaks and short, five-minute strolls outside the office or up and down a flight of stairs in inclement weather can offset these physical problems.

Getting outdoors in nature during the workday is one of the best forms of "me time." A 2020 groundbreaking study in Scientific Reports found that spending a minimum of two hours a week in nature (such as parks, woodlands, or beaches) promotes physical and mental health and well-being and gives you a bigger perspective of your life. It doesn't matter how you spend the two hours. It can be done in one block or spread out over the entire week to get the benefit. It doesn't seem to matter what activity you're involved in, either, if you're outdoors: sailing, biking, kayaking, walking, or playing tennis.[3] Plus, living in greener urban areas is linked to lower incidences of heart disease, obesity, diabetes, asthma, mental distress, and mortality rates. If you're stumped for a solution at work, stressed out or overwhelmed with a project or hit a wall, spending time with Mother Nature gives you a creativity surge or ah-ha moments for a workable problem.

Taking "awe walks"—strolls in which you intentionally shift your attention outward to the natural environment instead of inward where you could be thinking of unfinished work raises and sustains your energy level and re-calibrates a fatigued brain. Research shows that "awe walks" mitigate many of the effects of prolonged sitting, chronic screen time, and virtual fatigue. And you go back to your desk with batteries recharged, energy renewed, and head cleared.[4]

Elements of Radical Self-Care[5]

1. Radical prioritization of your own well-being—the airplane analogy with the deployed oxygen mask—over the well-being of others
2. Radical boundary management between work and life
3. Radical selection of your friends and support network (energy creators versus energy suckers)
4. Radical awareness of emotions and triggers and ability to nip strong reactions and escalations in the bud
5. Radical commitment to proactive mental and physical health (mindfulness, exercise, breaks, hobbies, and eating habits)
6. Radical ability to ditch your concern of disappointing others
7. Willingness to go against popular opinion
8. Radical ability to say no even when it's not easy and inconvenient for someone you care about
9. Radical awareness to choose your heart over your head when your mind says yes and your heart says no
10. Radical acceptance that it's impossible to give one hundred percent to everything

Radical Self-Care

Many business leaders still practice old hat tricks from the dark ages. They believe self-sacrifice, iron-fisted leadership, and criticism build the organization and the company's bottom line. And they believe when the company requires employees to work longer and harder, it gets a bigger bang for its buck. I spoke to a CEO of a major corporation who said he was glad his employees were not taking all their vacation days because it saved the company money. What he failed to see was that hiring employees who give themselves tender loving care contributes to growing a business and the company's bottom line. Science shows that self-care and self-compassion reduce job stress and fuel job performance and achievement.

The outdated, punitive trend of self-sacrifice to sustain your job has received a backlash of its own.

Sometimes we must go to extremes and take radical steps to protect our mental health to get people's attention. In the face of extreme work challenges, radical self-care requires going against popular opinion or refusing to appease others, even when they call us selfish or weak. What would happen, for example, if you took Alisyn Camerota's advice and went to bed instead of taking your kids to soccer practice? Radical self-care is caring as much about how you treat yourself or allow yourself to be treated as you do about the expectations of others and being willing to take the necessary steps—going to unpopular extremes if necessary—to take care of yourself and protect your mental and physical well-being at all costs.

Tennis champion Naomi Osaka defeated Serena Williams in the U.S. Open finals. The crowd booed her, forcing her to cover her head in humiliation. Three years later at the 2021 French Open, Osaka was suffering from anxiety and depression. After openly sharing her vulnerability with the powers-that-be, the tennis great refused to talk to the media. The head honchos at Grand Slam Tournaments (GST) demanded she face the media or be disqualified.

Refusing to comply and further traumatize herself, the tennis champ did a courageous thing. She put her foot down, and the GST fined her $15,000. Amid scathing public criticism, she pulled out of a job she deeply loved instead of sacrificing her mental health. The backlash was swift and fierce with some calling her spoiled, weak, and selfish. The media reactions showed that workplace mental health continues to be a divisive topic that doesn't get the same billing as a broken arm or sprained ankle. Osaka's treatment wasn't just about the mental health of sports figures. It has implications for all workplace conditions for all of us everywhere facing these kinds of punitive demands that run counter to our workplace well-being. Plus, it's a wakeup call for workaholics who unwittingly succumb to a toxic work culture in the throes of their work addiction instead of taking care of their mental health.

When Osaka openly shared her anxiety and depression, she received support from Olympic swimmer Michael Phelps, who has struggled with his own mental health challenges. By putting her self-care at the top of the list, Osaka changed what sports figures are willing to put up with. Simone Biles followed in the tennis champ's footsteps. After saying she had the weight of the world on her shoulders, the gymnast pulled out of most of the Tokyo 2020 Olympics (except for the balance beam finals) and was vilified for prioritizing her mental health and physical well-being over pleasing her critics. And Prince Harry, who has struggled with depression, left the British royal family, despite public criticism, to protect his mental health and the well-being of his family.

When the spotlight is on highly accomplished people, we often perceive them as superhuman—immune from the everyday struggles most of us face. But fame and fortune don't inoculate celebrities from mental health challenges.

Their stories show that mental health issues are universal and that speaking out is a strength, not a weakness. Most of us are not international sports figures or royalty, but we all have a responsibility to protect our mental health, including workaholics toiling in an exploitive work culture.

As a workaholic and tenured professor at the University of North Carolina at Charlotte, I was challenged to put my integrity and self-care over administrative pressures when I didn't participate in the corporate political diatribe. The then-vice chancellor of the university held a faculty meeting with tenured professors, expecting each of us to take a turn to vilify the then-dean of our college. When the vice chancellor nodded for me to speak, I said I had nothing to add. Anger flashed in his beet-red face. Later that evening after an on-campus musical performance, I ran into the vice chancellor and his wife in the lobby. When I reached out to shake his hand, he turned his back without a word and walked away. His wife offered a wimpy smile and shrug then followed him out the door. On the heels of that meeting, the vice-chancellor fired the dean (I never understood why), and he never spoke to me again.

Although I was tenured, after many internal conversations, I knew my first commitment was to maintain my moral compass, and I left my cozy position. I no longer wanted to participate in an archaic system that put employees in a stranglehold of pressure and fear. And I didn't want to sacrifice my integrity and values to an institution that dismissed people's right to choose their responses. When you're true to yourself, you have a huge unburdening, and you take that truth with you. This was a time before I knew about the C-Spot, but I unwittingly made the difficult decision from that place—as you assuredly have done as well. I felt an incredible sense of freedom that launched me into so many more rewarding adventures—after a departure I never regretted.

Practicing Radical Self-Care

❖ Make your mental wellness a top priority and take steps to protect it daily, even if your company doesn't. Throw people-pleasing out the window and please your mental health first. What Osaka did wasn't selfish; it was self-care. She's the only person on the planet who knows what actions to take to protect and sustain her own emotional well-being.

❖ Maintain control over your career. Speak up if you feel mistreated at work, and don't make career decisions that compromise your mental health. Advocate for your wellness, no matter the pressure from your employer, and don't back down when your mental health is at stake.

❖ Set healthy boundaries. Follow Naomi Osaka's example of being willing to say no when companies make unreasonable demands that run against the grain of your mental health. Saying no more than you say yes is a trait of healthy and successful people.

❖ Avoid self-shaming. You are not weak or selfish when you refuse to subject yourself to unhealthy workplace demands. You're a normal person responding to an abnormal situation. Some employees are born with pit-bull determination, while others are more vulnerable to the slings and arrows of workplace pressures.

❖ Maintain a close, strong support system. Enlist family, friends, and coworkers you can lean on in times of turmoil. Serena Williams and Michael Phelps came to Osaka's defense and supported her decision to take care of herself.

❖ Exhibit a professional attitude. Tennis champ Naomi Osaka released a statement expressing the hope that both parties can find solutions to this controversial ordeal in the future.

❖ Consider leaving the job. No one can tell you to quit your job without knowing the intimate details of your work and personal life. It might be worthwhile to consult with HR or a counselor to weigh pros and cons of leaving a job that doesn't provide meaning and purpose or that requires you to sacrifice your mental health and well-being.

Put Down Your Gavel

One night I got caught in a harrowing blizzard in a remote area of the North Carolina Mountains without snow tires or four-wheel drive. I couldn't stop or pull off the road, and my car was skidding on ice. Clutching the steering wheel, I had to drive another thirty miles winding up steep treacherous mountain curves. At first, I heard my judgment's reprimands, "I hope you're satisfied, dummy. You've done it now." Before the harshness escalated, I was aware that my judgment had tangled up with me like a ball of yarn. I took a deep breath, moved into my C-Spot, and coached myself with kindness, "Okay Bryan, easy does it. You've got this. You're going to be just fine. Just breathe. That's right, Bryan, just keep it on the road. Awesome job!" Obviously, I made it home safely because I'm here to tell the story, but I attribute my survival to how I spoke to myself.

After sharing a life-threatening situation, Richard Schwartz said, "Even in the face of real danger, it's possible to hold your parts. Sure, it's difficult. I've had years of experience showing my parts that things go better when they separate and let me handle things, so they trusted me enough to do that. But any measure of Self-leadership is helpful in dire circumstances."[6]

The way we treat ourselves inside our skin also determines how well we handle daily aspects of our lives such as work stress and professional and personal balance. If you're like most workaholics, you're hard on yourself, making it difficult to bounce back after a setback. And you're more prone to anxiety and depression, which can sabotage your work performance. But when you replace self-judgment with self-compassion—the kind, supportive treatment you give yourself in the face of challenges, obstacles, and setbacks—you recover quicker. It's natural to want to get rid of judgment and make it go away. But you need your judgment part. That's how you make sense of the world around you. But when your overworked judgment entangles you and overestimates threats, it raises your stress level—telling you how worthless, selfish, dumb, or bad you are—ultimately adding insult to injury and sabotaging your success. Befriending your uninvited mental guests—in this case judgment—with kindness brings you the peace of mind you seek.

FIRST AND SECOND ZINGERS

The Buddha referred to two arrows of life—the first arrow is life's unpleasant curve balls. The second arrow is the one that wounds us. When you judge yourself over the nagging emails from your boss or a racing deadline, what's actually causing your misery? Not the nagging emails or approaching deadline (the *first zingers*) but the *second zinger*—in this case the judgment you impale yourself with in reaction to work pressure—is the wounding source causing your misery.

Sometimes your judgment creates distress by imagining a first zinger when there is none. Suppose even before you begin a presentation to colleagues you have a sinking feeling that it will go south. If you stop to think about it, the distress (second zinger) comes from your judgment predicting you'll mess up. It's the self-judgment that distresses you; there is no first zinger.

When you fail at something, make a mistake, or have a setback, judging yourself creates a second layer of stress that makes you more likely to give up. Self-judgment throws you into a cycle of setbacks. For example, "I ate a piece of carrot cake" spirals into, "I've already blown my diet, so I might as well eat a second piece" which turns into, "I'm such a loser; I'll never get this weight off." The second zinger (the stress of the judgment you put yourself through) makes you feel bad, not eating the cake. The bad feelings throw you into a cycle of seeking comfort in the very behavior you're trying to conquer.

If you're like most workaholics—most people in fact—you get immersed in your stream of thoughts and identify with second zingers, thinking it's your

The Self-Care Trap

In this chapter, you have seen how both careaholics and workaholics are challenged with self-care, which they forfeit in favor of caretaking and work. It's clear that the inability to give or receive care and the one-sidedness of giving to others without the ability to receive are traps. Turns out that the over-emphasis on self-care without a mutual connection to others might not be all it's cracked up to be, either, especially for workaholics. The one-sidedness of self-care can trap workaholics in their disconnection from others, keeping them focused on themselves.

According to Dr. Yael Baldwin, clinical psychologist and Mars Hill University professor, self-care is an essential component of our well-being, but it can be a trap for some. In her book, *Mutual-Care: Let's Break Free from the Self-Care Trap Together,* she identifies *mutual-care* as the link to the full connection that's missing for many of us, especially careaholics and workaholics. In the following account, Baldwin illuminates the importance of mutual-care as a connection in which two people intentionally cultivate and sustain each other's psychological richness and flourishing in a reciprocal manner:

> As a recovering self-care addict, I spent the past decades believing I could solve my woes with self-care (my Kindle is loaded with self-care books—read and marked—my iPhone is filled to the brim with affirmation apps and self-care podcasts I listened to while stretching and working out). All the while I thought if I just got good enough and did self-care right, I'd feel fantastic *and* be a better person for the people I love and those I work alongside. I thought all this self-care would also give me work-life balance and keep job burnout at bay. But it turns out that all the self-care in the world wasn't going to land me on the shores of true joy and meaning that ultimately comes from caring, reciprocal connections. What I've discovered, personally and professionally, is we fare better with a greater focus on *mutual-care,* and we need it today for work-life balance more than ever. My life shifted for the better once I realized self-care alone wasn't going to cut it.
>
> When work has us feeling down, anxious, depleted, or overwhelmed—which we all inevitably do at times—the self-care movement tells us to ask, 'Have I done enough self-care lately?' There's no doubt a certain level of self-care is required to function well. But self-care has limitations that we can't ignore—from the illusion that we can give ourselves all that we ever need, including and especially care, and that we should rely only on ourselves to do so. Therein lies the trap. Providing yourself all the self-care in the world won't give you what you want, workaholic or not, if you seek a life in which your collective well-being matters.

As an antidote to the disconnection and loneliness many of us feel in and outside the workplace—and that all the self-care in the world cannot alleviate—a dedication to mutual care can combat the deleterious effects of workaholism. When you're exhausted from work, connecting with a mutual-care partner who knows and willingly provides what you need—whether it's a home-cooked meal, an ear to listen with a cup of tea on the couch, or a walk and talk—it can help you feel calmer, clearer, *and* connected. Receiving and giving, especially when it's reciprocated, is a double-reward hit. You both feel better, and it usually helps your relationship more than if you did something for yourself, by yourself.

Having a mutual-care partner at work is also a win-win. I was in a zoom meeting with a CPA consultant when suddenly, a big smile came over her face. A colleague had surreptitiously placed something on her desk. She gleefully raised a hot fudge sundae into the zoom frame, saying, "I mentioned to my colleague that on this gray, rainy Friday, ending the day with a hot fudge sundae would be in order. And look at what just appeared. I have the best colleagues. It makes this a great place to work."

Studies show that many people feel lonely in the workplace, and workplace friendships are on a steady decline. Research shows that having at least one mutual-care partner at work—someone you can ask for help and advice and who will do the same—helps you feel that you belong. Just as loneliness hurts us, care and connection promote healing and well-being. Smart companies know this and foster connections. Jeff Weiner, former CEO of LinkedIn has said his company's mission is connection. He found focusing on mutual connection gave his company an "incredible competitive advantage." And yet too often we're taught that we must first cultivate our own well-being (via self-care) in order to have good connections. But the other direction works, too. The difference between illness and wellness is found in the pronouns when we move from the "I" to the "we." Let's face it, we forget in our "I-centered" culture that there's no "I" without a "we" first. That's the starting point.

Although self-care says we should care for ourselves, mutual-care spreads the message that we're in this together. It's as okay to receive as to give, and you'll thrive more and suffer less when you give and receive what you need and want to and from each other, reciprocally. As a workaholic, when you transition from self-care to mutual-care, you move in a more balanced direction. During those inevitable moments when you feel down, dissatisfied, or overwhelmed at work, home, or play, it pays to ask, "Have I given and received enough mutual-care?"

only choice. The Triple-A practice (see chapter 14) helps you manage your zingers. Once you develop an *awareness* and observe the difference between first and second zingers, the distinction slows your urge to react. When you *acknowledge* them with curiosity, instead of judgment, you recognize the real stressor—the second zinger—more clearly, feel separation from it, and an ease in managing it. And when you *allow* the second zinger, you feel disappointment without heartache, frustration without exploding, and pain without suffering. As you develop the skill to see them as separate, you realize you don't have to react every time you get zinged. This distinction is good medicine because it softens your reactions, and you're able to greet your second zinger reactions with kindness instead of reacting to them. And you're back in your C-Spot.

Next time a situation or random judgmental thought (A) zings you, notice you're in an unpleasant emotional state. Hold the feelings (B) at arm's length and observe them impartially as a separate part of you. Instead of pushing away, ignoring, or steamrolling over them, the key is to acknowledge them with something like, *Hello frustration, I see you're active today.* This simple recognition gets second zingers (B) to calm down (C) so you can face the real challenge—the first zinger (A)—with more clarity and ease.

Comforting self-talk from your C-Spot cushions such stressful situations as a job interview, a presentation to colleagues, a job loss, racing against a deadline, your boss raking you over the coals, or a coworker talking over you in a meeting. Self-compassion can soothe the stressors associated with work addiction, not because you replace negative feelings with positive affirmations, but because as you embrace your negative feelings, new positive emotions rise within you from the C-Spot. When you're kinder to yourself and accept your shortcomings and limitations with compassion, you're better able to deal with the stressful situation, not the added negative feelings from self-judgment.

The Science of Self-Compassion

Scientists are discovering that if you don't like yourself, you won't be motivated to accomplish as much as possible. Self-judgment, self-criticism, and self-loathing build barriers (such as performance anxiety and self-sabotage) to job engagement, motivation, and career advancement. The science of self-compassion shows that only as you cultivate the right attitude toward yourself will you have the right attitude toward your job, workaholism, and work moderation. Studies show that employers who express empathy are more likely to retain employees, increase engagement, amp up productivity, and create a sense of belonging in the company.[7]

If you're a workaholic who doesn't have self-compassion, you can cultivate it, according to research.[8] And it's well worth the effort for the mental and physical health benefits. After an eight-week program of mindfulness-based stress reduction (composed of yoga, meditation, and relaxation exercises), 90 percent of the participants increased their self-compassion.[9] Another study found that under threat, self-affirmations give you a broader perspective, reduce defensiveness, and lessen worry and rumination. Kind words serve as "cognitive expanders" that allow you to talk to yourself the way you might speak to someone else so that the judgment voice isn't the only story you tell yourself.[10]

Scientists have even found that self-compassion affects your body and overall physical health. One study showed that people who practice self-compassion have lower risk of developing cardiovascular disease. Research participants who practiced self-compassion had thinner carotid artery walls and less plaque buildup than those with low self-compassion.[11] These indicators were linked to lower risk of heart attacks and strokes—years later. The positive results persisted even when the researchers controlled for behaviors and other psychological factors that might influence cardiovascular disease outcomes such as physical activity, smoking, and depressive symptoms.

These research findings underscore the importance of practicing kindness and compassion, particularly towards yourself. If self-compassion is powerful enough to mitigate heart disease, stroke, stress, irritability, and depression, plus boost job engagement and performance, it only follows that business leaders would want to create a compassionate workplace to foster these mental and physical health advantages. After all, studies show that the American workforce has been calling for empathy and caring from higher-ups and corporate honchos. Sadly, that message hasn't thoroughly filtered up the chain, as I discussed in earlier chapters.

Self-compassion expert Dr. Kristin Neff finds it ironic that many business leaders fail to see that fierce self-compassion pays off for the company more than self-criticism. They think self-compassion will undermine employee motivation when, in fact, studies show it boosts the company's bottom line. "The more we can accept ourselves, the more able we are to change and take risks and the less anxious we are about failure," Neff told me. "Self-criticism adds to performance anxiety, undermines your ability to do your best, and causes you to procrastinate. It prevents you from learning from your mistakes—missed learning opportunities. If we don't have self-compassion, we pull the rug out from under ourselves and make it so much harder than it needs to be."[12]

Two Sides of Self-Compassion

Self-compassion is a tool for career success *and* failure, according to Kristin Neff. "It helps us gain success, and it helps us deal with failure, which helps us succeed," she told me. "The way you grow and learn is by dealing productively with failure. If you go into shame mode after failure, it disallows you to look at and learn from your failures. It's not going to allow you to grow or take risks. You can be vulnerable, learn and grow if you have your own back with self-compassion: 'If I blow it and people ridicule me, I'll be okay because the bottom line is I'll be there for myself.'"

Neff points to two types of self-compassion—the fierce and the tender—both relevant for everyone and essential to function optimally in our careers and lives.[13] She describes *tender self-compassion* as what most people think about as self-accepting and self-understanding for emotional healing. You need the tender self-compassion if you've been a victim of workplace oppression. If you've been oppressed in the workplace (by corporate higher-ups, a toxic boss, or coworker), you need *fierce self-compassion* to commit to be courageous and try to change it.

From the point of view of the oppressor, you need tender self-compassion to hold the shame as being part of a group that oppressed others. But you also need fierce self-compassion to commit to not continue the oppression. Neff believes we've gendered these two life force energies, and we value one more than the other, which hurts both men and women.

> We give all the power to the fierceness and belittle the tenderness because one is considered more powerful and valued than the other. But we need both sides—the fierceness and the tenderness—and they need to be integrated. For example, some people—men in particular—believe self-compassion is a female thing; therefore, it's weak and less valuable. That belief comes from our patriarchal society.
>
> On the other hand, women have remained silent because they have been afraid to speak up, although more women are saying, "We aren't going to take this anymore." That's fierce self-compassion. Women don't have to be afraid or ashamed of their anger. It's a gift. We don't want to be out of control or let it loose. We need to be mindful with it, but it's something to be proud of because of the incredible energy it gives us. It has enabled us to be accomplished and break new ground. Both types of self-compassion go to the same place: how women can be fiercer and men, more tender."

Neff also had advice for dark organizations that exploit workers (see chapter 10). "It's no longer okay to dominate people. It's important to learn to develop meaningful connection with employees, to listen and relate in a way that com-municates care," she said. "We know compassionate leaders are more respected by their employees. When we use both sides of self-compassion, we are more likely to excel. The tender allows us to accept ourselves just as we are. It's okay to be imperfect. But the fierce side encourages us like a good coach:'I really care about you, so how can we grow and change and learn and do better next time?'"

Neff insists these are more than just good ideas. They are good skills to learn and grow as a leader and take whatever risks you need to take. These are tools that can be learned and developed. Corporate leaders often confuse being supportive with being complacent. "Complacency isn't self-compassionate," she said. "And it doesn't alleviate suffering. Kind, supportive, encouraging, clear-sighted, open-minded compassion does help motivation. Imagine how much more people can achieve if they're more supportive of themselves."

Maslow's Hierarchy of Self-Care

Psychologist Abraham Maslow created a motivational framework called Maslow's Hierarchy of Needs. Comprised of a five-tier pyramid, the lad-der demonstrates the connection between career motivation, productivity, and self-care needs. You can use it to assess where you fall on the hierarchy, keep your head above work addiction tidal waves, and set career goals to move up the rungs of success. To reach the top, you must meet all five levels of basic needs at each rung from the bottom up: (1) Physiological Needs (2) Safety and Security (3) Compassion and Belonging (4) Self-Esteem and (5) Self-Actualization.

1. MEETING BASIC PHYSIOLOGICAL NEEDS

At the bottom level is the foundation for job performance and success. It includes the basic self-care needs you can't live without such as food, water, restorative rest, sleep, and oxygen. You can't meet a pressured deadline or be happy and productive if you're hungry, thirsty, tired, or exhausted. Unfortu-nately, many companies send mixed messages to their workers. They extol them for working excessive hours, cite overwork as exemplary in hiring prac-tices, and reward workaholics with larger salaries and promotions. Yet HR personnel and mental health professionals stress the importance of time off, vacations, and work/life balance for career success. To offset this contradiction, strive for work/life balance. Take lunch breaks, vacations, and time off to incu-bate and hatch creative ideas and recharge their batteries with renewed energy to perform at your highest potential.

2. ADDRESSING SAFETY AND SECURITY NEEDS

To perform optimally at work, you must feel physically and psychologically safe and have financial job security, free from distractions or threats. When lighting is too low, temperature too cold or hot or offices too noisy, it's more difficult to knock out that project or meet a short deadline. A Korn Ferry Survey revealed that in 2019, 70 percent of professionals were more guarded at work than five years before, and 58 percent believed teamwork and comradery suffered because of increased guardedness. Consider advocating for a company workplace safety plan or an environmental, safety, and health policy statement that protects you from injury or work-related illness, shields you from threats and intimidation, and ensures offices are secure from intruders.[14]

3. FINDING EMPATHY AND BELONGING

In meeting your needs at this level, you send a message that you want to be cared about as a human being, not just a worker bee and help create an atmosphere of openness, comradery, and teamwork that boosts job satisfaction, morale, and productivity. A sense of belonging is central to who we are as human beings. Empathy is a pivotal leadership tool in today's global market. Studies show that workplace empathy ramps up productivity and motivation, reduces turnover, and creates a sense of belonging in the organization. Progression at this rung requires the use of compassionate directness and emotional honesty. Research also shows that your own self-compassion moves you up the ladder faster and farther.

4. BUILDING SELF-ESTEEM NEEDS

Your self-esteem is vital to your success and the organization's bottom line. If you're an employee who feels good about yourself, you're able to focus better, need less time off, and have better interpersonal relationships with coworkers. The attitude clients bring to the office—positive or negative—is contagious and spreads to others. When employees sense that higher-ups believe in them, it helps them believe in themselves. And employees who believe in themselves can accomplish more for the organization.

5. ACHIEVING SELF-ACTUALIZATION IN YOUR CAREER

At the highest rung on the pyramid, you can actualize your skills and career goals and reach your full potential. If you're a self-actualized employee, you manage your career with a *growth mindset*—lifelong learning and resilience, accept failure and success equally, and remain confident in your pursuits after a letdown. You adopt and share the mindset that setbacks happen *for* you, not *to* you. You're a creative risk taker, willing to stretch beyond customary bounds and stick your neck outside your comfort zone. You welcome shortcomings and mistakes—no matter how painful, frustrating, big or small—and envision them as lessons from which to learn. You're a master of self-correction, good problem solver, solution focused, and lead with integrity.

Tips for Clinicians

There are numerous tools clinicians can use to inform clients about how to take care of themselves beyond the basics of nutrition, sleep, and exercise. The appendix contains a sampling of self-care tools, and here are a few you can share with clients.

HELPING CLIENTS CONNECT WITH THEMSELVES

Exploring and learning to validate the existential, authentic self becomes an important therapeutic task for workaholics in recovery. Clinicians can confront clients with questions about how they honestly feel about themselves and their lives, what they value, what their sources of validation are, and whom and what activities they have been neglecting because of their work addiction. You may find opportunities to explore ego-threatening feelings such as loneliness, ennui, insecurity, and hopelessness.

As you help clients reframe how they think about themselves, you'll notice that their feelings and behaviors automatically start to shift. The shift starts as they redefine themselves, not by what they have or do but by who they are on the inside. This shift takes them from an external, quantifiable focus to an internal, quality-based, process-oriented focus: they become beings, not just doers. When you can help clients connect with their emotional selves this way, they learn flexibility and how to live in the process rather than exclusively quantifying their lives through products that they can point to with pride.

Breaking out of the self-destructive cycle of work addiction comes with time for renewal, rest, pampering, contemplation, a time where workaholics intimately connect with that deeper personal part of themselves. You can share the following tips with clients so that they can develop an internal relationship with themselves based on self-compassion instead of self-judgment and help them cultivate "cognitive expanders":

❖ *Change how you think about yourself.* Good health and self-esteem are part of a state of mind. Henry Ford once said, "If you think you can or you can't, you're right." The starting point is to realize how exaggerated, addictive thinking undermines your health and self-esteem and how an optimistic outlook can change that. See yourself honestly by recognizing your accomplishments along with your defeats, your strengths as well as your faults. The more you look for the positives, the better you will feel about yourself.

❖ *Learn to identify your feelings and to accept the fact that you're angry or frustrated.* Listen to yourself. Pay attention to your thoughts and feelings. Attune yourself to your feelings and get in the habit of writing them down in a journal. Ask yourself what you're using your activities to escape from. What are you afraid of facing? What resentments or hurts are unresolved? Face your feelings and feel them completely. Ask yourself where the voice came from that tells you that nothing you do is ever good enough. Is it your voice, or is it the voice of a critical parent or another adult figure from your past? Learn to stand up to the critical voice and take charge of it, instead of letting it take charge of you.

❖ *Give yourself pep talks.* Replace the critical voice with one that nurtures and encourages you. Whether you're asking for a raise, making an important presentation, starting a new job, or struggling with parenthood, doubt and lack of confidence can flood your mind. When addictive thoughts pop up like burned toast, ask, "What would I say to my best friend or child if she thought she couldn't do something?" You wouldn't say, "Of course you can't do it. You might as well give up." Your confidence in her ability would lead you to encourage her. Value yourself enough to be your own best friend by giving yourself the same encouragement that you give to others. Pep talks bring self-reassurance and ultimate success. Tell yourself, "Yes, I can do this, and I can do it well." Use a mirror as you send yourself positive, encouraging messages. Imagine the best of outcomes, instead of the worst, before you get into a situation. Encourage yourself just as you would your best friend. Tell yourself, "You can do anything you set your mind to, and you can do it well."

❖ *Please yourself instead of pleasing others.* When you trim yourself to suit everybody else, you whittle yourself away until there's nothing left. Learn to let go of other people's opinions and form your own. Develop solid values and beliefs and stand up for them instead of being a chameleon. Keep company with people you respect who mirror your positive worth.

❖ *Learn to accept your human limitations without feeling flawed.* Learn to admit and accept your shortcomings, to value yourself in spite of them. Your ability to acknowledge and accept your limitations is strength of character, not a flaw. Treat yourself as a human being with emotional needs instead of a machine that can be driven nonstop. Make a mental shift and begin seeing your limitations as normal instead of as a drawback. Acknowledge those human limitations and value them, instead of trying to push yourself beyond them. Make it a goal to stay away from relationships that drain you, instead surrounding yourself with people who support, love, and affirm you.

❖ *Recognize that less is more.* Lower your standards, simplify your life, and be more realistic about what's possible. You can relax your standards and still do a stellar job. Instead of asking yourself what additional commitment you can make, ask yourself what obligations or chores you can eliminate. Instead of taking on more work tasks, decide which ones you can delegate, sell, or give away. Instead of juggling three or four tasks at once, choose to do only one at a time and focus on it.

❖ *Work smarter, not longer.* Make your schedule work for you, instead of working for it. Avoid overscheduling your life and leave gaps in your calendar for something spontaneous and unexpected to happen. Consider assigning errands and chores to others whenever you can, at home, work, or play. Rely on outside help to get the windows washed, the lawn mowed, the house painted, and rooms cleaned. Tell yourself you don't have to do it all. Get up earlier or go to bed later to have extra time for yourself and loved ones. Remember, it's your life. You can oversee it, instead of letting it be in charge of you.

TEACH CLIENTS TO HIGH-FIVE THEIR "TALLCOMINGS"

When our thoughts constantly focus on our shortcomings, we become blind to our strengths and talents. To offset this imbalance, you can capitalize yourself by learning to high-five your "tallcomings" alongside your shortcomings. There's a reason the word "shortcomings" is in Webster's but "tallcomings" isn't. There's no such word. I made it up. Having been hijacked by our critical voice on a regular basis, we get in the habit of ignoring our positive attributes and clobbering ourselves with negatives, creating a flawed view of who we are. It's important to have a critical eye, accept constructive feedback, and recognize our strengths and limitations without dropping our head in your hands. Encourage clients to make it a habit to throw modesty out the window and name as many accomplishments as they can—what they're good at, the skills and talents they possess, and what they've achieved that their negativity bias has constantly overshadowed.

SIX STEPS FOR HEALTHY ON-THE-JOB CARING

1. Be realistic about what is humanly possible for you to do. Remind yourself you cannot save the world and make sure you save yourself first before

trying to help coworkers. When you're already overloaded and need time for yourself, let that be a sign that you're not in a position to take on more emotional commitments. Every time you say "yes" when you want to say "no," you do colleagues and yourself an injustice.

2. Examine your motivation for helping. Do you believe fixing others will fulfill a greater need in you than in them? If the answer is yes, you could be taking more than you're giving. Sometimes the best way to care is *not* to get involved with someone's problems and *not* to help them if it robs them of learning and standing on their own two feet.

3. Respect another employee's refusal for your help. It's important to let a coworker know you would like to help. If they say no, it's important to honor their request instead of pressuring them because you see something that needs fixing.

4. If you end up helping someone, make sure you're in the habit of showing them how to fish instead of feeding them fish. In other words, if the help you give makes a colleague or friend dependent on you, you could be holding them back when they might be ready to fly.

5. Set emotional boundaries. Encourage colleagues and loved ones to become emotionally independent. Avoid over-identifying with their feelings and don't take other people's problems home with you. By leaving problems with their rightful owners, you allow them to grow by finding their own solutions. Some of our best lessons come from learning from our mistakes.

6. Practice what you preach. Before you embark on a helping campaign, help yourself first. Let others benefit from cleaning up their side of the street while you tend to the potholes in your own neglected side. Examine unmet needs in your life that you might've avoided. Take time out for yourself in the same ways you tell others to care for themselves: positive self-talk, meditate, bathe in nature, and learn to enjoy your own company.

Bibliotherapy

The following books are great resources for further reading on how to balance self-care and self-compassion with career success without going overboard:

- Yael Baldwin, *Mutual-Care: Let's Break Free from the Self-Care Trap Together.*
- Tara Brach, *Radical Compassion: Learning to Love Yourself and Your World with the Practice of RAIN* (New York: Penguin Books, 2019).

❖ Christopher Germer, *The Mindful Path to Self-Compassion* (New York: Guilford, 2009).

❖ Ethan Kross, *Chatter: The Voice in Our Head, Why It Matters, and How to Harness It* (New York: Penguin Random House, 2021).

❖ Kristin Neff, *Self-Compassion: How to Stop Beating Yourself Up and Leave Insecurity Behind* (New York, HarperCollins, 2011).

❖ Kristin Neff, *Fierce Self-Compassion: How Women Can Harness Kindness to Speak Up, Claim Their Power, and Thrive* (New York: Harper Wave, 2021).

Acknowledgments

It's hard to believe that the *Chained to the Desk* books have been selling for nearly twenty-five years and this is the fourth iteration. I have many people to thank for its continued success. First and foremost, I want to extend my appreciation to New York University Press for their sustained belief in me and their support of this project over the long term. In particular, I want to give a shout out to my editor Jennifer Hammer, who has been on this journey providing her astute and wise guidance from the get-go and more recently to Veronica Knutson for her tireless support.

My deepest appreciation goes to the anonymous individuals and those not-so-anonymous people who contributed content or case material about their courageous struggles with work addiction and how it damaged their lives, as well as their inspiring stories of recovery. Special thanks to Dr. Yael Baldwin, Erin Brockovich, Alisyn Camerota, Dr. Tara Brach, Dr. Kristin Neff, Dr. Vivek Murthy, Blaine Vess, Rhonda Ross, India.Arie, Sarah Elizabeth Malinak, Camille Sluder, Dr. Nancy Chase, Brittin Oakman, Julianne Hough, Alanis Morissette, Jewel Kilcher, Connie K. Lim (a.k.a. MILCK), Arianna Huffington, Dan Harris, Annie O'Grady, Art Campbell, Stephanie Wilder, Daffie Matthews, George Raftelis, Annemarie Russell, Gloria Steinem, Roger Catlin, Dr. Matthew Baldwin, Jamey McCullers, and Tom Dybro. In addition, my special thanks for their contributions go to my agent Dean Krystek, my personal assistant Nick Powers, and Charlie Covington, my tech expert whose expertise I couldn't do without.

And to my professional colleagues and friends who have been so supportive of me over the years, I thank you. I am deeply indebted to the following very busy people who took their valuable time to read the manuscript and write a blurb: Alanis Morissette, Dr. Amit Sood, Dr. Richard Schwartz, Dr. Joy Miller, Arianna Huffington, Dr. Tara Brach, Dr. Kristin Neff, Dr. Ethan Kross, Dr. Harville Hendrix, and Dr. Helen Hunt. And I cannot forget to mention my dear co-founder friends and special colleagues at ComfortZ-ones Digital—helping workers with situational intelligence in that stressful moment, in that stressful situation—CEO Steve Glaser, Chief Client Officer Gina Cruse, Chief Operating Officer Jim Bailey, and more recently the incredible Eva Condron-Wells, who joined our team. Knowing all of you has enriched my life tremendously.

Last, but certainly not least, my heartfelt thanks go to the thousands of readers who have called and emailed me, searching for help in their battle with work addiction. It has always been my wish that my books would give hope, courage, and comfort to workaholics waging an inner battle against themselves, as well as to their loved ones who also suffer from this best-dressed problem of the twenty-first century. If you're searching for answers, I hope this book helps you find the peace and serenity that you're seeking.

Appendix

Managing Work Addiction and Work-Life Balance in a Hybrid World

You are not the pain that broke you.
You are who it made you become.
—Najwa Zebian, Sparks of Phoenix

Workaholics Anonymous, Work-Life Balance, and the Twelve Steps[1]

The first chapter of Workaholics Anonymous was started on the East Coast in April 1983 by a New York corporate financial planner and a schoolteacher who had been "hopeless" workaholics, as they described themselves. They founded WA to help others who suffered from the disease of workaholism and to stop working compulsively themselves. They were joined in their first meeting by the spouse of the planner who started WorkAnon, a program of recovery for those in relationships with workaholics. At about the same time, a nurse who was suffering from burnout in her high-stress job began one of the first chapters on the West Coast. Other chapters sprang up spontaneously and autonomously throughout the United States and in other countries. In March 1990, representatives from various chapters in four U.S. states got together for the first time and officially formed the World Service Organization for Workaholics Anonymous.

Twelve-Step programs have worked for millions of people with a variety of addictions, including those addicted to alcohol and other drugs, food, gambling, shopping, and certain types of relationships. The Twelve Steps also help those who are committed to a program of spiritual recovery from a life of compulsive, uncontrollable, and harmful work habits. The Steps of Workaholics Anonymous are vehicles for healing work compulsions and establishing a more meaningful and fulfilling lifestyle:

1. We admitted that we were powerless over work—that our lives had become unmanageable.

2. We came to believe that a Power greater than ourselves could restore us to sanity.

3. We made a decision to turn our will and our lives over to the care of God as we understood God.

4. We made a searching and fearless moral inventory of ourselves.

5. We admitted to God, to ourselves, and to another human being the exact nature of our wrongs.

6. We became entirely ready to have God remove all these defects of character.

7. We humbly asked God to remove our shortcomings.

8. We made a list of all persons we had harmed and became willing to make amends to them all.

9. We made direct amends to such people wherever possible, except when to do so would injure them or others.

10. We continued to take personal inventory and when we were wrong promptly admitted it.

11. We sought through prayer and meditation to improve our conscious contact with God as we understood God, praying only for knowledge of God's will for us and the power to carry that out.

12. Having had a spiritual awakening as the result of these steps, we tried to carry this message to workaholics and to practice these principles in all our affairs.

The only requirement for membership in Workaholics Anonymous is a desire to stop working compulsively. There are no dues or other fees for WA membership; the organization is supported by member contributions. WA is not allied with any sect, denomination, political group, organization, or other institution; does not wish to engage in any controversy; and neither endorses nor opposes any causes. The organization's primary purpose is to help members stop working compulsively and to carry the message of recovery to workaholics who are still suffering.

ComfortZones Digital

Introducing ComfortZones Digital (www.comfortzonesdigital.com). As the company describes itself on its website, it is an innovative company focused on "situational intelligence" to manage work stress. Helping workers. In that stressful moment. In that stressful situation. When you're overworking. Overwhelmed. Stressed out. Have too much to do. Not enough time.

According to their website, "You are not alone and no longer have to remain silent about your struggles. ComfortZones Digital is here to prevent burnout, turnover, mental and physical health problems, and low engagement. Our team's personal journeys with work stress have drawn us together. To create what we all wish we had thirty years ago, what we want our family and friends to have, and what every worker deserves to have."

ComfortZones Digital describes what they offer employees dealing with work stress and work addiction. "Our team has combined its expertise and experiences across multiple disciplines to provide you, the employee, with just what you need, when you need it, and where you need it. This is enabled by our mobile app and extensive library of audio content, serving as a digital companion for every stressful work situation."

ComfortZones is here to help:

❖ When you are triggered by an event or interaction during the workday.

❖ When you have ongoing situations that are impacting you every day.

❖ When work stress is spilling over into your personal life.

ComfortZones Digital is defined by:

❖ People who care and have been there.

❖ Experts in the management of stressful work situations.

❖ A combination of the "Best of the Best" techniques from every discipline.

❖ A digital companion for every stressful situation.

The Psychometric Properties of the Work Addiction Risk Test

The Work Addiction Risk Test (WART) has been used clinically and in scientific research. It has been tested for reliability and validity and is currently used around the world by researchers, graduate students, clinicians, and the public to assess the prevalence of work addiction. Scientists in the Netherlands and Spain tested and borrowed items from the WART for their research.[2]

RELIABILITY OF THE WART

The test-retest reliability of the instrument is 0.83, and the coefficient alpha for the individual items is 0.85.[3] An internal consistency estimate of reliability

(Cronbach's alpha) of 0.88 was obtained for the twenty-five WART items,[4] and the split-half reliability of the inventory with 442 respondents was 0.85.[5]

VALIDITY OF THE WART

Face validity and content validity were established for the instrument with five major subscales emerging: overdoing, self-worth, control-perfectionism, intimacy, and mental preoccupations/future reference.[6] Twenty psychotherapists, randomly selected from a state list, critically examined the twenty-five items on the WART for content validity. They were asked to identify twenty-five items from a list of thirty-five that most accurately measured work addiction. Selected test items had generally high content validity, with an average score of 89 out of a possible 100, and 90 percent of the psychotherapists scored 72 or higher.[7]

Concurrent validity was established on the WART in a study with 363 respondents.[8] Scores on the WART were correlated at 0.40 with generalized anxiety on the State-Trait Anxiety Inventory[9] and 0.37 with the Type A Self-Report Inventory.[10] Correlations with moderate to low significance were obtained on the four scales of the Jenkins Activity Survey, the most commonly used measure of Type A behavior: 0.50 on the Type A scale, 0.50 on the speed and impatience scale, 0.39 on the hard-driving and competitive scale, and 0.20 on the job involvement scale.[11]

Concurrent validity also was demonstrated between the WART and the thinking/feeling scale on the Myers-Briggs Indicator in a study with ninety participants.[12] A regression analysis revealed that WART scores correlated more with the T end of the Myers-Briggs scale than with the F end. In addition, WART scores were significantly higher for respondents who worked more than forty hours a week than for those who worked fewer than forty-one hours per week.

AROUND THE WORLD WITH THE WART

A Dutch version of a work addiction scale (called the DUWAS) was constructed, taking nine of its seventeen items from the WART, and a short version of the DUWAS used six of the original items from the WART.[13] The results of the study showed internal validity of the tests using items from the WART. In addition, negative correlations in the study confirmed that workaholism is a negative construct, as my studies have suggested over the years.

A study at Central Queensland University in Australia reported that scores on the WART were correlated with scores on the Smartphone Problematic Use Questionnaire, which measures the negative impact of smart-phone use such as euphoria (as in addictive highs), withdrawal symptoms, interpersonal conflict, and problems in the workplace.[14]

All physicians at a French University hospital were invited to complete the WART as a survey and 13 percent were found to be highly work addicted.[15] A total of 126 Polish academic workers were asked to complete both the WART and the general health questionnaire. Sixty-six percent of the subjects were classified as having a moderate to high risk of workaholism and the study suggested workaholism is associated with poorer mental health.[16]

The full version of the WART was assessed using a nationally representative sample of Hungary (n = 2,710). To increase validity, the analyses were conducted among individuals who worked at least 40 h a week (n = 1,286, 43% women, mean age = 38.9 years, SD = 10.8). The study concluded that the WART is suitable for use as an indicator of work addiction in Hungary, based on clinically relevant symptom dimensions.[17]

Research studies using the WART are currently being conducted in the following countries: Belgium, Hungary, India, the Philippines, Poland, Slovenia, and Turkey. The WART has been translated into Spanish, Dutch, Polish, and Slovenian.

A Sampler of Microchillers

The following brief exercises bring attention to the presence of natural relaxation, eclipsed by work addiction. In five minutes or less, these practices serve as the onramp to your *C-Spot* by putting the brakes on your sympathetic nervous system and activating your parasympathetic nervous system (see chapter 5).

THE PENDULUM

The pendulum here refers to the natural swing of your nervous system between sensations of well-being and stress or tension. With your eyes closed, notice a place in your body where you feel stress. It can show up as pain, tension, an ache, or a sense of constriction. Then swing your attention to a place inside where you feel less stress or no stress. Focus there on the absence of stress, noticing your bodily sensations: steady heartbeat, slowed breathing, warm skin, softened jaw, relaxed muscles. Remain focused there and note the sensation. Then imagine that sensation spreading to other parts of your body.

Now shift back to the place where you originally felt stress. If the tension has decreased, focus on the reduction of tension for a minute or so. Continue moving your attention back and forth between what is left of the tension and the places in your body where you feel comfortable or relaxed. As you shift from one to the other, note where the tension is lessening and spend some time paying attention to the lessening so that it can spread to other parts of your body. If you notice that you feel calmer and more peaceful, you have just activated your parasympathetic nervous system.

Sounds

Sit in a comfortable place with eyes open or shut for one minute. With curiosity, focus on all the different sounds around you, and see how many you can identify. You might notice the heating or air conditioning system, traffic off in the distance, a siren, voices from other areas in the building, an airplane, the ticking of a clock, or your own gurgling stomach. Research shows that present-moment awareness for sixty seconds helps you unwind, clear your head, and raise your energy level. After one minute, instead of trying to remember the sounds, bring your attention inside and notice if you're not calmer and more clearheaded.

The Ninety-Second Rule

Next time you feel yourself triggered, look at the second hand on a watch. As soon as you look at it, you're now observing yourself having this physiological response instead of engaging with it. It will take less than ninety seconds, and you will feel better. Of course, you can always go back to thinking those thoughts that re-stimulate the loop. There's probably a thought somewhere in your brain of somebody who did you wrong twenty years ago. Every time you think of that person it still starts that circuit. The ninety second rule has been used to educate the public about the anger circuitry. When things are getting hot and you're getting hot headed, look at your watch. It takes ninety seconds to dissipate that anger response.

Your "To-Be List"

The compulsion for constant doing defends you from feeling unpleasant emotions and gives you safety and security even if the task itself is satisfying. When you commit to a less stressful life, you notice you can just be without requiring yourself to constantly do. Make a *"to-be list"* to accompany your *"to-do"* list. Watch a sunset or a bird build its nest, listen to nature sounds around you or feel a breeze against your face. These activities recharge your batteries and contribute to your well-being.

The Wide-Angle Lens

Identify a complaint. Perhaps your communication has dwindled or you worry that you have to pull several all-nighters to get caught up at work and your partner will hit the roof. Once you have the complaint, put on your wide-angle lens, pull up the big picture, and see the complaint in the larger scheme of your relationship. As you broaden your outlook, ask yourself how important the judgment is you made by complaining. If you're like most people, the complaint loses its sting once you put it in a wider context because you realize your relationship has a higher priority than you had given it.

THE BUTTERFLY HUG

Think of a small worry, problem or concern that has been bothering you, not a big kahuna. After you've chosen something small, cross your arms over your chest and flap your hands against your shoulders. Turn your attention to the right and find something to focus on. It doesn't matter what it is. It could be a wall, painting, carpet, or some aspect of nature. As you focus on the object pay attention to it in detail for about twenty seconds. Notice the shape, size, colors and see it as vividly in your mind's eye as you can. Then turn to your left and focus your attention on something else for another twenty seconds. Take in as much of the detail of the object as you can. Keep flapping your butterfly wings as you continue the exercise. Now, turn to your right again and focus on another object and pay attention to all of the details: shape, colors, size, and so forth. Then turn again to your left and repeat your focus on another object for about twenty seconds.

After you've finished the exercise, recall the worry or concern. At first, you might have difficulty remembering the original concern, or it might take you some time to remember it. And once you do recall, chances are the original concern will have lost much of its power. Why? The exercise of present-moment awareness activated your parasympathetic nervous system and put the brakes on your lizard brain concern. Once the red alert gets turned off, you have more access to your C-Spot, where you feel calm, clarity, and cool-headedness.

RAPID RESET. After a jolting incident at work or before a stressful encounter, Rapid Reset grounds you and calms you down. Sitting in the chair you use at your workstation, grab the bottom of the seat with both hands and pull up while pushing down with your bottom at the same time. In a fight-or-flight situation, this type of grounding quickly centers you, activates your parasympathetic nervous system, and brings you back into the present moment. Soak in the calming, pleasant body sensations.

CHAIR YOGA

Sitting in the chair at your desk (as long as it has a back), inhale and raise your arms toward the ceiling. Let your shoulder blades slide down your back as you reach upward with your fingertips. Anchor your sit bones in your seat and reach up from there. Place your left hand over on your right knee. Place your right arm on the back of the chair. Stretch lightly for sixty seconds with eyes open or closed. Notice the stretch and what happens inside. After 60 seconds, bring your body back to center. Then reverse the stretch. Place your right hand over your left knee. Put your left arm on the back of the chair for another sixty seconds. Stretch lightly again with eyes open or closed. Pay attention to the stretch and notice the shift in body sensations. After three to five minutes of repeating this exercise, you will notice better breathing, a renewed energy, and improved mental clarity.

Notes

Introduction

1 Richard Friedman, "Is Burnout Real? The World Health Organization Says So. But It's in Danger of Medicalizing Everyday Stress," *New York Times*, June 3, 2019. https://www. nytimes.com.

2 Arianna Huffington, "Yes, Burnout is Real, And We Can Address It Much Better When We Call It What It Is," *Thrive Global*, June 7, 2019.

3 Marilyn Machlowitz, *Workaholics: Living with Them* (Reading, MA: Addison-Wesley, 1985).

4. Daniel Seligman, "The Curse of Work," *Fortune*, March 7, 1994, 133.

5. Bryan Robinson, "Why 'Work-Life Balance' Has Become a Career Dinosaur," *Forbes.com*, March 12, 2021, https://forbes.com.

6. Quoted in Chris Wright, "The Truth about Workaholism," *The Fix: Addiction and Recovery, Straight Up*, September 24, 2012, www.thefix.com.

7. Quoted in Loren Stein, "Workaholism: It's No Longer Seen as a Respectable Vice," *A Healthy Me*, March 25, 2006, 2.

8. Quoted in Emilie Filou, "Death in the Office," *World Business*, July–August 2006, 19–22.

9. American Psychiatric Association, "Current Procedural Terminology (CPT) Code Changes for 2013," www.psychiatry.org.

10. Wright, "The Truth about Workaholism."

11. See, for example, Christina Guthier et al., "Reciprocal Effects Between Job Stressors and Burnout: A Continuous Time Meta-Analysis of Longitudinal Studies," *Psychological Bulletin* (2020), DOI: 10.1037/bul0000304; Tassia Oswald et al., "Psychological Impacts of 'Screen Time' and 'Green Time' for Children and Adolescents: A Systematic Scoping Review," *PLOS ONE* 15 (2020), DOI: 10.1371/journal.pone.0237725; Maricarmen Vizcaino, et al., "From TVs to Tablets: The Relation Between Device-Specific Screen Time and Health-Related Behaviors and Characteristics," *BMC Public Health* 20 (2020): 1–10, DOI: 10.1186/s12889-020-09410-0.

12. Gallup, "State of the Global Workplace: 2021 Report," https://commsweek.ragan.com/wp-content/uploads/2021/07/state-of-the-global-workplace-2021-download.pdf.

13. Visier, "The Burnout Epidemic Report 2021," https://visier.com; Heather Berrigan, "Is the Workplace the Real American Idol?" *Living Church Foundation*, November 30, 2003, 1.

14. Berrigan, "Is the Workplace the Real American Idol?"
15. Wright, "The Truth about Workaholism."
16. American Psychological Association, "APA's 2021 Work and Well-Being Survey Results, accessed December 5, 2021, https://www.apa.org.
17. Richard Schwartz, *No Bad Parts: Healing Trauma and Restoring Wholeness with the Internal Family Systems Model* (Boulder, CO: Sounds True, 2021).

1. The Making of a Workaholic

1. A version of my Alanis Morissette interview, "'I Used to Think I Was Invincible': Alanis Morissette Talks Burnout Prevention and Her Journey to Work-Life Balance," appeared on *Forbes.com*, November 1, 2019, www.forbes.com.
2. Gloria Steinem, foreword to Bryan Robinson, *Overdoing It: How to Slow Down and Take Care of Yourself* (Deerfield Beach, FL: HCI Books, 1992), ix–xii. Used with permission.
3. See, for example, Diane Fassel, *Working Ourselves to Death* (San Francisco: Harper and Row, 2000); Bryan Robinson, "The Workaholic Family: A Clinical Perspective," *American Journal of Family Therapy* 26 (1998): 63–73; Bryan Robinson and Phyllis Post, "Work Addiction as a Function of Family of Origin and Its Influence on Current Family Functioning," *Family Journal* 3 (1995): 200–206; Bryan Robinson and Phyllis Post, "Risk of Addiction to Work and Family Functioning," *Psychological Reports* 81 (1997): 91–95; Amy Nuttall et al., "Maternal History of Parentification, Maternal Warm Responsiveness, and Children's Externalizing Behavior," *Journal of Family Psychology* 5 (2012): 767–75.
4. Elaine Miller-Karas, *Building Resilience to Trauma* (New York: Routledge, 2023).
5. Adwait Vaishnavi et al., "Anger & Hostility; Traits of Type A & Type B Personality and Its Association with Cardiovascular Diseases," *The International Journal of Indian Psychology* 9 (2021): 711–720.
6. Gloria Steinem, *Revolution from Within: A Book on Self-Esteem* (New York: Little, Brown, 1992).
7. Judyta Borchet et al., "The Relations Among Types of Parentification, School Achievement, and Quality of Life in Early Adolescence: An Exploratory Study," *Frontiers in Psychology* 12 (2021), DOI: 10.3389/fpsyg.2021.635171.
8. For an excellent discussion of emotional incest, see Patricia Love, *The Emotional Incest Syndrome: What to Do When a Parent's Love Rules Your Life* (New York: Dutton, 1990).
9. Rebecca Jones and Marolyn Wells, "An Empirical Study of Parentification and Personality," *American Journal of Family Therapy* 24 (1996): 150.
10. Jones and Wells, 150.
11. Malcolm West and Adrienne Keller, "Parentification of the Child: A Case Study of Bowlby's Compulsive Care-Giving Attachment Pattern," *American Journal of Psychotherapy* 155 (1991): 425–31.
12. West and Keller, 426.
13. In her book *On Death and Dying* (New York: Macmillan, 1969), Dr. Elisabeth Kübler-Ross identified five stages of grief that the dying and their loved ones typically go through: shock, denial, bargaining, anger, and acceptance.

14. For a comprehensive examination of family-of-origin roles, see Bryan Robinson and Lyn Rhoden, *Working with Children of Alcoholics: The Practitioner's Handbook* (Thousand Oaks, CA: Sage Publications, 1998) and Hanna Zagefka et. al, "Family Roles, Family Dysfunction, and Depressive Symptoms," *The Family Journal: Counseling and Therapy for Couples and Families* 29 (2021): 346–53.

2. Who, Me? A Workaholic—Seriously?

1. Skynova, "Burning the Midnight Oil During Covid-19, July 8, 2021, https://www.skynova.com.
2. Wayne Oates, *Confessions of a Workaholic* (New York: World, 1971).
3. See, for example, Sandra Haymon, "The Relationship of Work Addiction and Depression, Anxiety, and Anger in College Males," PhD diss., Florida State University, 1992; Bryan Robinson, Claudia Flowers, and Chris Burris, "An Empirical Study of the Relationship between Self-Leadership and Workaholism 'Firefighter' Behaviors," *Journal of Self-Leadership* 2 (2005): 22–36; Janet Spence and Ann Robbins, "Workaholics: Definitions, Measurement, and Preliminary Results," *Journal of Personality Assessment* 58 (1992): 160–78.
4. Ishu Ishiyama and Akio Kitayama, "Overwork and Career-Centered Self-Validation among the Japanese: Psychosocial Issues and Counselling Implications." *International Journal for the Advancement of Counselling* 17 (1994): 167–82.
5. Parul Sharma and Jyoti Sharma, "Work Addiction: A Poison by Slow Motion," *Journal of Economics and Behavioral Studies* 2 (2011): 86–91.
6. Consult the appendix for a more detailed explanation of the psychometric properties of the WART, or refer to the following research studies: Claudia Flowers and Bryan Robinson, "A Structural and Discriminant Analysis of the Work Addiction Risk Test," *Educational and Psychological Measurement* 62 (2002): 517–26; Bryan Robinson, "Concurrent Validity of the Work Addiction Risk Test as a Measure of Workaholism," *Psychological Reports* 79 (1996): 1313–14; Bryan Robinson and Bruce Phillips, "Measuring Workaholism: Content Validity of the Work Addiction Risk Test," *Psychological Reports* 77 (1995): 657–58; Bryan Robinson and Phyllis Post, "Validity of the Work Addiction Risk Test," *Perceptual and Motor Skills* 78 (1994): 337–38; Bryan Robinson and Phyllis Post, "Split-Half Reliability of the Work Addiction Risk Test: Development of a Measure of Workaholism," *Psychological Reports* 76 (1995): 1226; Bryan Robinson, Phyllis Post, and Judith Khakee, "Test-Retest Reliability of the Work Addiction Risk Test," *Perceptual and Motor Skills* 74 (1992): 926; Sandra Swary, "Myers-Briggs Type and Workaholism," honors thesis, Georgia State University, 1996.

3. How to Spot Work Addiction

1. See, for example, Bryan Robinson, Claudia Flowers, and Chris Burris, "An Empirical Study of the Relationship between Self-Leadership and Workaholism 'Firefighter' Behavior," *Journal of Self-Leadership* 2 (2005): 22–36; Benedicte Langseth-Eide, "It's Been a Hard Day's Night, and I've Been Working like a Dog: Workaholism and Work Engagement," *Frontiers in Psychology* 10 (2019): 1444–1447; Cristian Balducci, Lorenzo

Avanzi, and Franco Fraccaroli, "The Individual 'Costs' of Workaholism: An Analysis Based on Multisources and Prospective Data," *Journal of Management* 44 (2018): 2961–2986; Monika Bartczak and Nina Oginska-Bulik, "Workaholism and Mental Health Among Polish Academic Workers," *International Journal of Occupational Safety and Ergonomics* 18 (2012): 3–13; Cecille Andreassen et al., "The Relationships between Workaholism and Symptoms of Psychiatric Disorders: A Large-Scale Cross-Sectional Study," PLoS ONE 11(5): e0152978; Xue Yang, et al., "The Mediation Role of Work-Life Balance, Stress, and Chronic Fatigue in the Relationship Between Workaholism and Depression Among Chinese Male Workers in Hong Kong," *Journal of Behavioral Addictions* 9 (2020): 483–490.

2. Bryan Robinson, *Work Addiction* (Deerfield Beach, FL: HCI, 1989).

3. Oates, *Confessions of a Workaholic*.

4. Diane Fassel describes work anorexics in *Working Ourselves to Death* (San Francisco: Harper and Row, 2000).

5. Gayle Porter, "Organizational Impact of Workaholism: Suggestions for Researching the Negative Outcomes of Excessive Work," *Journal of Occupational Health Psychology* 1 (1996): 70–84.

6. Fassel, *Working Ourselves to Death*, 82.

7. For a more detailed explanation of the psychometric properties of the WART, see the appendix.

8. Wayne Sotile and Mary Sotile, *The Medical Marriage: Sustaining Healthy Relationships for Physicians and Their Families* (Chicago: American Medical Association, 2000).

9. Edward Hallowell and John Ratey, *Driven to Distraction: Recognizing and Coping with Attention Deficit Disorder from Childhood through Adulthood* (New York: Anchor Books, 2011), 182.

10. To augment the work moderation plan, see Bryan Robinson, *#Chill: Turn Off Your Job and Turn On Your Life* (New York: William Morrow, 2019).

4. Inside the Workaholic Mind

1. Diane Fassel and Anne Wilson Schaef, "A Feminist Perspective on Work Addiction," in *Feminist Perspectives on Addictions*, edited by Nan Van Den Bergh (New York: Springer, 1991), 199–211.

2. Rick Hanson and Richard Mendius, *Buddha's Brain: The Practical Neuroscience of Happiness, Love, and Wisdom* (Oakland, CA: New Harbinger Publications, 2009).

3. Diane Fassel and Anne Wilson Schaef, "A Feminist Perspective on Work Addiction," 208.

4. Gayle Porter, "Organizational Impact of Workaholism: Suggestions for Researching the Negative Outcomes of Excessive Work," *Journal of Occupational Health Psychology* 1 (1996): 74.

5. Quoted in Annmarie L. Geddes, "The Pitfalls of Being Addicted to Work," *Cleveland's Small Business News*, June 1995, 57.

6. Porter, "Organizational Impact of Workaholism," 75.

7. David H. Hubel and Torsten N. Wiesel. "Effects of Mononulcear Deprivation in Kittens," *Naunyn-Schmiedebergs Archiv for Experimentelle Pathologie und Pharmakologie* 248 (1964): 492–7.

8. See, for example, Judith Beck, *Cognitive Behavior Therapy: Basics and Beyond*. 3rd ed. (New York: Guilford, 2021); David Burns, *Feeling Good: The New Mood Therapy* (New York: HarperCollins, 2017); Albert Ellis and Windy Dryden, *The Practice of Rational Emotive Behavior Therapy*, 3rd edition (New York: Routledge, 2021).
9. Clayton Critcher and David Dunning, "Self-Affirmations Provide a Broader Perspective on Self-Threat," *Personality and Social Psychology Bulletin* 41 (2014): 3–18.

5. The "Off Duty" Workaholic Brain

1. Ruth van Holst, William Van den Brink, Dick Veltman, and Anna Goudriaan, "Brain Imaging Studies in Pathological Gambling," *Current Psychiatry Report* 12 (2010): 418–25; Luke Clark, et al., "Pathological Choice: The Neuroscience of Gambling and Gambling Addiction," *The Journal of Neuroscience* 33 (2013): 17617–17623.
2. For more information on the stress response, see Christy Matta, *The Stress Response* (Oakland, CA: New Harbinger, 2012); Ronald Siegel, *The Mindful Solution: Everyday Practices for Everyday Problems* (New York: The Guilford Press, 2010); Ronald Siegel and Michael Yapko, "Has Mindfulness Been Oversold?" *Psychotherapy Networker*, March–April 2012, 44.
3. Bronwyn Fryer, "Are You Working Too Hard?" *Harvard Business Review*, November 2005, 90–96.
4. See, for example, Richard Davidson and Sharon Begley, *The Emotional Life of Your Brain* (New York: Hudson Street, 2012); Daniel Amen, *Change Your Brain, Change Your Body* (New York: Three Rivers, 2010); Norman Doidge, *The Brain That Changes Itself* (New York: Penguin, 2007); Richard Hanson and Richard Mendius, *Buddha's Brain: The Practical Neuroscience of Happiness, Love, and Wisdom* (Oakland, CA: New Harbinger, 2009); Martin Rossman, *The Worry Solution: Using Breakthrough Brain Science to Turn Stress and Anxiety into Confidence and Happiness* (New York: Crown, 2010).
5. Davidson and Begley, *The Emotional Life of Your Brain*; Chade-Meng Tan, *Search Inside Yourself: The Unexpected Path to Achieving Success, Happiness (and World Peace)* (New York: HarperOne, 2012).
6. Andrew Newberg and Mark Waldman, *How God Changes Your Brain* (New York: Ballantine, 2010).
7. Roy Baumeister and John Tierney, *Willpower: Rediscovering the Greatest Human Strength* (New York: HarperOne, 2011).
8. For step-by-step exercises to activate your parasympathetic nervous system, see Bryan Robinson, *#Chill: Turn Off Your Job and Turn On Your Life* (New York: William Morrow, 2019).
9. Newberg and Waldman, *How God Changes Your Brain*.
10. Robinson, *#Chill: Turn Off Your Job and Turn On Your Life*.
11. Sara Lazar, "Meditation Experience Is Associated with Increased Cortical Thickness," *Neuroreport* 16 (2005): 1893–97.
12. Hanson and Mendius, *Buddha's Brain*.
13. Cynthia Adams, "Stressed Out? Think Tennis Shoes, Not Tranquilizers." *University of Georgia Graduate School Magazine*, May 2012, 17–21.

6. Wedded to Work Is a Family Affair

1. See, for example, Bryan Robinson, "6 Reasons Hiring Workaholics Causes More Drain than Gain," *Forbes.com*, December 5, 2021; Bryan Robinson, "Adult Children of Workaholics: Clinical and Empirical Research with Implications for Family Therapists," *Journal of Family Psychotherapy* 11 (2000): 15–26; Bryan Robinson, "Workaholism and Family Functioning: A Profile of Familial Relationships, Psychological Outcomes, and Research Considerations," *Contemporary Family Research* 23 (2001): 123–35; Jane Carroll and Bryan Robinson, "Depression and Parentification among Adults as Related to Parental Workaholism and Alcoholism," *Family Journal* 8 (2000): 360–67.

2. Quoted in Marilyn Machlowitz, "Workaholics Enjoy Themselves, an Expert Says: It's Their Family and Friends Who Pay," *Psychology Today*, June 1980, 79.

3. Bryan Robinson, "The Workaholic Family: A Clinical Perspective," *American Journal of Family Therapy* 26 (1998): 63–73.

4. Anthony Pietropinto, "The Workaholic Spouse," *Medical Aspects of Human Sexuality* 20 (1986): 89–96.

5. Barbara Killinger, *Workaholics: The Respectable Addicts* (New York: Fireside, 1992).

6. Robert Klaft and Brian Kleiner, "Understanding Workaholics," *Business* 38 (1988): 37.

7. Quoted in Terri Finch Hamilton, "Women Susceptible to Working Whirl," *Grand Rapids Press*, June 27, 1991.

8. See, for example, Judyta Borchet et al., "The Relationship Among Types of Parentification, School Achievement, and Quality of Life in Early Adolescence: An Exploratory Study," *Frontiers in Psychology*, 12 (2021): 1–10; Nancy Chase, *The Parentified Child: Theory, Research, and Treatment* (Thousand Oaks, CA: Sage, 1998); Jennifer Engelhardt, "The Developmental Implications of Parentification," *Graduate Student Journal of Psychology* 14 (2012): 45–52.

9. Ishu Ishiyama and Akio Kitayama, "Overwork and Career-Centered Self-Validation among the Japanese: Psychosocial Issues and Counselling Implications," *International Journal for the Advancement of Counselling* 17 (1994): 168.

10. Reports of the first research study can be found in these two sources: Bryan Robinson and Phyllis Post, "Work Addiction as a Function of Family of Origin and Its Influence on Current Family Functioning," *Family Journal* 3 (1995): 200–206; Bryan Robinson and Phyllis Post, "Risk of Addiction to Work and Family Functioning," *Psychological Reports* 81 (1997): 91–95.

11. Bryan Robinson and Lisa Kelley, "Adult Children of Workaholics: Self-Concept, Anxiety, Depression, and Locus of Control," *American Journal of Family Therapy* 26 (1998): 223–38.

12. Robinson, "Workaholism and Family Functioning."

13. Akihito Shimazu et al., "Workaholism, Work Engagement and Child Well-Being: A Test of the Spillover-Crossover Model." *International Journal of Environmental Research and Public Health* 17 (2020): 1–16.

7. Spouses and Partners of Workaholics

1. Bryan Robinson, Jane Carroll, and Claudia Flowers, "Marital Estrangement, Positive Affect, and Locus of Control among Spouses of Workaholics and Spouses of Nonworkaholics: A National Study," *American Journal of Family Therapy* 29 (2001): 397–410.

2. Bryan Robinson, Claudia Flowers, and Kok-Mun Ng, "The Relationship between Workaholism and Marital Disaffection: Husbands' Perspective," *Family Journal* 14 (2006): 213–20; Daniele Levy, "Workaholism and Marital Satisfaction Among Female Professionals," *The Family Journal: Counseling and Therapy for Couples and Families* 23 (2015): 330–335; Steffen Torp, Linda Lysfjord, and Hilde Hovda-Midje, "Workaholism and Work-Family Conflict Among University Academics," *Higher Education*, March 10, 2018, https://doi.org/10.1007/s10734-018-0247-0.

3. Cited in Edward Walsh, "Workaholism: No Life for the Leisurelorn?" *Parks and Recreation*, January 1987, 82.

4. Anthony Pietropinto, "The Workaholic Spouse," *Medical Aspects of Human Sexuality* 20 (1986): 89–96.

5. Daniel Weeks, "Cooling Off Your Office Affair," *Northwest Airlines World Traveler Magazine*, June 1995, 59–62.

6. Ann Herbst, "Married to the Job," *McCall's*, November 1996, 130–34.

7. Harville Hendrix and Helen Hunt, *Getting the Love You Want: A Guide for Couples Revised* (New York: St. Martin's Griffin, 2019).

8. Paul Deluca, *The Solo Partner: Repairing Your Relationship on Your Own* (Point Roberts, WA: Hartley and Marks, 2002).

9. Ishu Ishiyama and Akio Kitayama, "Overwork and Career-Centered Self-Validation among the Japanese: Psychosocial Issues and Counselling Implications," *International Journal for the Advancement of Counselling* 17 (1994): 178.

10. Bryan Robinson, *Work Addiction* (Deerfield Beach, FL: HCI, 1989).

11. Studs Terkel, *Working* (New York: Pantheon, 1974).

12. Ann Bailey, "He Puts Work Ahead of the Family," *First for Women*, August 2003, 91.

13. Terry Gaspard, *The Remarriage Manual: How to Make Everything Work Better the Second Time Around* (Boulder, CO: Sounds True, 2020).

14. Gaspard, *The Remarriage Manual.*

15. Stephen Betchen, "Parentified Pursuers and Childlike Distancers in Marital Therapy," *Family Journal* 4 (1996): 100–108; Stephen Betchen, *Intrusive Partners-Elusive Mates: The Pursuer-Distancer Dynamic in Couples* (New York: Routledge, 2005).

16. Betchen, "Parentified Pursuers and Childlike Distancers in Marital Therapy," 103.

17. Thomas Fogarty, "The Distancer and the Pursuer," *Family* 7 (1979): 11–16; Thomas Fogarty, "Marital Crisis," in *Family Therapy: Theory and Practice*, edited by Paul Guerin (New York: Gardner, 1976), 325–34.

18. Bryan Robinson and Phyllis Post, "Work Addiction as a Function of Family of Origin and Its Influence on Current Family Functioning," *Family Journal* 3 (1995): 200–206.

19. Hendrix and Hunt, *Getting the Love You Want: A Guide for Couples*; Harville Hendrix and Helen Hunt, *Getting the Love You Want: A Couples Workshop Manual* (New York: Institute for Relationship Therapy, 2003).

8. The Legacy of Children of Workaholics

1. See, for example, Virginia Kelly and Jane Myers, "Parental Alcoholism and Coping: A Comparison of Female Children of Alcoholics with Female Children of Nonalcoholics,"

Journal of Counseling and Development 74 (1996): 501–4; Phyllis Post and Bryan Robinson, "A Comparison of School-Age Children of Alcoholic and Nonalcoholic Parents on Anxiety, Self-Esteem, and Locus of Control," *Professional School Counselor* 1 (1998): 36–42; Phyllis Post, Wanda Webb, and Bryan Robinson, "Relationship between Self-Concept, Anxiety, and Knowledge of Alcoholism by Gender and Age among Adult Children of Alcoholics," *Alcoholism Treatment Quarterly* 8 (1991): 91–95; Bryan Robinson and Lyn Rhoden, *Working with Children of Alcoholics* (Thousand Oaks, CA: Sage Publications, 1998); Sandra Tweed and Cynthia Ryff, "Adult Children of Alcoholics: Profiles of Wellness amid Distress," *Journal of Studies on Alcohol* 52 (1991): 133–41; Wanda Webb et al., "Self-Concept, Anxiety, and Knowledge Exhibited by Adult Children of Alcoholics and Adult Children of Nonalcoholics," *Journal of Drug Education* 20 (1992): 106–14.

2. Anthony Pietropinto, "The Workaholic Spouse," *Medical Aspects of Human Sexuality* 20 (1986): 89–96; Bryan Robinson, *#Chill: Turn Off Your Job and Turn On Your Life* (New York: William Morrow, 2019); Gerald Spruell, "Work Fever," *Training and Development Journal* 41 (1987): 41–45.

3. See, for example, Bryan Robinson, "Children of Workaholics: What Practitioners Need to Know," *Journal of Child and Youth Care* 12 (1998): 3–10; Bryan Robinson and Jane Carroll, "Assessing the Offspring of Workaholics: The Children of Workaholics Screening Test," *Perceptual and Motor Skills* 88 (1999): 1127–34; Bryan Robinson, "Adult Children of Workaholics: Clinical and Empirical Research with Implications for Family Therapists," *Journal of Family Psychotherapy* 11 (2000): 15–26; Bryan Robinson, "Workaholism and Family Functioning: A Profile of Familial Relationships, Psychological Outcomes, and Research Considerations," *Contemporary Family Research* 23 (2001): 123–35.

4. Bryan Robinson and Lisa Kelley, "Adult Children of Workaholics: Self-Concept, Anxiety, Depression, and Locus of Control," *American Journal of Family Therapy* 26 (1998): 223–38.

5. See, for example, Kelly and Myers, "Parental Alcoholism and Coping"; Robinson and Rhoden, *Working with Children of Alcoholics*; Webb et al., "Self-Concept, Anxiety, and Knowledge Exhibited by Adult Children of Alcoholics and Adult Children of Nonalcoholics."

6. Sheri Navarrete, "An Empirical Study of Adult Children of Workaholics: Psychological Functioning and Intergenerational Transmission," PhD diss., California Graduate Institute, 1998; Elaine Searcy, "Adult Children of Workaholics: Anxiety, Depression, Family Relationships and Risk for Work Addiction," master's thesis, University of South Australia, 2000.

7. Christine Chamberlin and Naijian Zhang, "Workaholism, Health, and Self-Acceptance," *Journal of Counseling and Development* 87 (2009): 159–169; Akihito Shimazu et al., "Workaholism, Work Engagement and Child Well-Being: A Test of the Spillover-Crossover Model." *International Journal of Environmental Research and Public Health* 17 (2020): 1–16.

8. Jane Carroll and Bryan Robinson, "Depression and Parentification among Adults as Related to Parental Workaholism and Alcoholism," *Family Journal* 8 (2000): 360–67.

9. Oates, *Confessions of a Workaholic*; Bryan Robinson, *Overdoing It: How to Slow Down and Take Care of Yourself* (Deerfield Beach, FL: HCI, 1992); Bryan Robinson, "Relationship

between Work Addiction and Family Functioning: Clinical Implications for Marriage and Family Therapists," *Journal of Family Psychotherapy* 7 (1996): 13–29.

10. Quoted in Marilyn Machlowitz, "Workaholics Enjoy Themselves, an Expert Says: It's Their Family and Friends Who Pay," *Psychology Today*, June 1980, 79.

11. Oates, *Confessions of a Workaholic.*

12. Tina Harralson and Kathleen Lawler, "The Relationship of Parenting Styles and Social Competency to Type A Behavior in Children," *Journal of Psychosomatic Research* 36 (1992): 625–34; Patti Watkins et al., "The Type A Belief System: Relationships to Hostility, Social Support, and Life Stress," *Behavioral Medicine* 18 (1992): 27–32.

13. Karen Woodall and Karen Matthews, "Familial Environment Associated with Type A Behaviors and Psychophysiological Responses to Stress in Children," *Health Psychology* 8 (1989): 403–26.

14. Pietropinto, "The Workaholic Spouse."

15. Bryan Robinson, *The Art of Confident Living* (Deerfield Beach, FL: HCI, 2009).

16. Quoted in Daniel Weeks, "Cooling Off Your Office Affair," *Northwest Airlines World Traveler Magazine*, June 1995, 62.

17. For a further discussion of subpersonalities, see Richard Schwartz, *No Bad Parts: Healing Trauma and Restoring Wholeness with the Internal Family Systems Model.*

18. See, for example, Marina Khidekel, *Your Time to Thrive: End Burnout, Increase Well-Being, and Unlock Your Full Potential with the New Science of Microsteps* (New York: Hachette, 2021); Sooyeol Kim, Seonghee Cho, and YoungAh Park, "Daily Microbreaks in a Self-Regulatory Resources Lens: Perceived Health Climate as a Contextual Moderator Via Microbreak Autonomy," *Journal of Applied Psychology* 103 (2021): 772–786; Bryan Robinson, *#Chill: Turn Off Your Job and Turn On Your Life* (New York, William Morrow, 2019); Bryan Robinson, "5 Ways 'Microcare' Promotes Employee Mental Health and the Company's Bottom Line," *Forbes.com*, December 6, 2021, https://forbes.com.

9. It's Been a Hard Day's Night: Work Stress And Job Burnout

1. Brittin Oakman, "Anxiety Doesn't Knock First." Used with the writer's permission.

2. Arianna Huffington, *Thrive: The Third Metric to Redefining Success and Creating a Life of Well-Being, Wisdom, and Wonder* (New York: Harmony Books, 2015), 1–2. Used with the author's permission.

3. Robert Klaft and Brian Kleiner, "Understanding Workaholics," *Business* 38 (1988): 37–40.

4. Ben Wigert, "Employee Burnout: The Biggest Myth," *Gallup* March 13, 2020; Ben Wigert and Sangeeta Agrawal, "Employee Burnout, Part 1: The 5 Main Causes," *Gallup Workplace*, July 12, 2018, https://www.gallup.com; Ashley Abramson, "Burnout and Stress are Everywhere," *Monitor on Psychology*, 53 (2022): 72.

5. Kapo Wong, Alan H. S. Chan, and S. C. Ngan, "The Effect of Long Working Hours and Overtime on Occupational Health: A Meta-Analysis of Evidence from 1998 to 2018," *International Journal of Environmental Research and Public Health* (June 13, 2019), DOI: 10.3390/ijerph16122102.

6. Marianna Virtanen et al., "Overtime Work and Incident Coronary Heart Disease: The White II Prospective Cohort Study," *European Heart Journal* 31 (2010): 1737–44.

7. Christine Rosen, "The Myth of Multitasking," *New Atlantis* (Spring 2008), 105–10.

8. Joshua Rubinstein, David Meyer, and Jeffrey Evans, "Executive Control of Cognitive Processes in Task Switching," *Journal of Experimental Psychology: Human Perception and Performance*, 4 (2001): 763–97.

9. Adam Gorlick, "Media Multitaskers Pay Mental Price, Stanford Study Shows," *Stanford Report*, August 24, 2009, 3–5.

10. See, for example, Kevin Madore and Anthony Wagner, "Multicosts of Multitasking," *Cerebrum* April 5, 2019, https://www.dana.org; Wisnu Wiradhany and Janneke Koerts, "Everyday Functioning-Related Cognitive Correlates of Media Multitasking: A Mini Metanalysis," *Media Psychology* 24 (2021): 276–303, DOI:10.1080/15213269.2019.1685 393.

11. P. Afonso, M. Fonseca, and J. F. Pires, "Impact of Working Hours on Sleep and Mental Health," *Occupational Medicine* 67 (2017): 377–382; Frank Pega et al., "Global, Regional, and National Burdens of Ischemic Heart Disease and Stroke Attributable to Exposure to Long Working Hours for 194 Countries, 2000–2016," *Environment International* 154 (2021): 1–15; Su-Hyun Lee and Tiffany May, "Go Home, South Korea Tells Workers, as Stress Takes Its Toll," *The New York Times*, July 28, 2018, February 5, 2022, https://www.nytimes.com.

12. Erin Kelly, Phyllis Moen, and Eric Tranby, "Changing Workplaces to Reduce Work-Family Conflict: Schedule Control in a White-Collar Organization," *American Sociological Review* 76 (2011): 1047–61.

13. Bryan Robinson, *#Chill: Turn Off Your Job and Turn On Your Life* (New York: William Morrow, 2019).

14. Gayle Porter, "Workaholic Tendencies and the High Potential for Stress among Coworkers," *International Journal of Stress Management* 8 (2001): 147–64; Jungsun Park, Yunjeong Yi, and Yangho Kim, "Weekly Work Hours and Stress Complaints of Workers in Korea," *American Journal of Industrial Medicine* 53 (2010): 1135–1142.

15. Marianna Virtanen et al., "Overtime Work and Incident Coronary Heart Disease: The White II Prospective Cohort Study."

16. Jonathan Frostick, "What Near Death Taught Me," *LinkedIn*, April 21, 2021, https://www.linkedin.com. Used with the author's permission.

17. Herbert Freudenberger, "Staff Burn-Out," *Journal of Social Issues* 30 (1973): 159–165.

18. World Health Organization, "Burnout-out an 'Occupational Phenomenon': International Classification of Diseases," 2019, https://www.who.org.

19. Ashley Abramson, "Burnout and Stress Are Everywhere," *American Psychological Association 2022 Trends Report* 53 (2022): 72.

20. Gayle Porter, "Workaholics as High-Performance Employees: The Intersection of Workplace and Family Relationship Problems," in *High-Performing Families: Causes, Consequences, and Clinical Solutions*, edited by Bryan Robinson and Nancy Chase (Washington: American Counseling Association, 2001), 43–69; Gayle Porter, "Work, Work Ethic, Work Excess," *Journal of Organizational Change Management* 17 (2004): 424–39; Gayle Porter, "Profiles of Workaholism among High-Tech Managers," *Career Development-International* 11 (2006): 440–62; Gayle Porter and Nada Kakabadse, "HRM Perspectives on Addiction to Technology and Work," *Journal of Management Development* 25 (2006): 535–60.

21. Gayle Porter, "Organizational Impact of Workaholism: Suggestions for Researching the Negative Outcomes of Excessive Work," *Journal of Occupational Health Psychology* 1 (1996): 71.
22. Porter, "Organizational Impact of Workaholism," 82.
23. Microsoft Human Factors Lab, "Research Proves Your Brain Needs Breaks," *WTI Pulse Report*, April 20, 2021, https://www.microsoft.com.
24. Sooyeol Kim et al., "Daily Microbreaks in a Self-Regulatory Resources Lens: Perceived Health Climate as a Contextual Moderator Via Microbreak Autonomy" *Journal of Applied Psychology* 3, March 2021, DOI: 10.1037/apl0000891.
25. Arianna Huffington, "Microsteps: The Big Idea That's Too Small to Fail," *Thrive Global*, February 27, 2019, https://thriveglobal.com.
26. See, for example, Larissa Barber and Alecia Santuzzi, "Please Respond ASAP: Workplace Telepressure and Employee Recovery," *Journal of Occupational Health Psychology* 20 (2015): 172–189; Larissa Barber, Amanda Conlin, and Alecia Santuzzi, "Workplace Telepressure and Work-Life Balance Outcomes: The Role of Work Recovery Experiences," *Stress Health* 35 (2019):350–362; Matthew Grawitch et al., "Self-Imposed Pressure or Organizational Norms? Further Examination of the Construct of Workplace Telepressure," *Stress Health* 34 (2018): 306–19.
27. Neil Chesanow, "Vacation for the Health of It," *Endless Vacation*, January–February 2005, 31–32.
28. CareerBuilder, "One-in-Four Workers Can't Afford to Take a Vacation," *Career-Builder Survey*, May 25, 2011.
29. Hugo Martin, "Survey Finds Lots of Unused Vacation Time," *Los Angeles Times*, November 25, 2012.
30. Tamara E. Holmes, "72% of Americans Did Not Take a Summer Vacation This Year," *ValuePenguin*, September 2, 2020, https://www.valuepenguin.com.
31. SWNS staff, "More than Half of Americans Fear Their Employer Would Think Less of Them if They Requested Time off for Mental Health," *SWNS Digital*, September 6, 2021, https://swnsdigital.com.
32. Stephanie Rosenbloom, "Please Don't Make Me Go on Vacation," *New York Times*, August 10, 2006.

10. Companies Behaving Badly, Encouraging Employees to Drink the Kool-Aid

1. Emilie Filou, "Death in the Office," *World Business*, July–August 2006, 19–22.
2. Su-Hyun Lee and Tiffany May, "Go Home, South Korea Tells Workers, as Stress Takes Its Toll," *New York Times*, July 28, 2018, https://www.nytimes.com.
3. Mami Suzuki, "How Japanese Black Companies Oppress Workers and Ruin Lives," *Tofugu*, April 25, 2014, https://www.tofugu.com.
4. Alana Semuels, "The Mystery of Why Japanese People Are Having Few Babies," *The Atlantic*, July 20, 2017, 3.
5. Bryan Robinson, "Why Critics Say Elon Musk's Return-to-Office Ultimatum is Dangerous," Forbes.com, June 3, 2022. https://www.forbes.com/sites/bryanrobinson/2022/06/03/why-critics-say-elon-musks-recent-return-to-office-ultimatum-is-dangerous/?sh=36eefde3351a).

6. Nada Kakabadse, Gayle Porter, and David Vance, "Employer Liability for Addiction to Information and Communication Technology," unpublished paper, 2006.

7. Ellen Gamerman, "The New Power Picnics," *Wall Street Journal*, August 12, 2006.

8. Gamerman, "The New Power Picnics."

9. Lesley Alderman, "How to Tell the Boss You're Getting Worked to Death—Without Killing Your Career," *Money*, May 1995, 41.

10. Sue Shellenbarger, "To Cut Office Stress, Try Butterflies and Meditation?" *Wall Street Journal*, October 9, 2012.

11. Leslie Wright and Marti Smye, *Corporate Abuse: How "Lean and Mean" Robs People and Profits* (New York: Macmillan, 1996), 82.

12. U.S. Department of Labor, "Job Openings and Labor Turnover Summary," October 2021, https://www.bls.gov/news.release/pdf/jolts.pdf.

13. Anne Wilson Schaef and Diane Fassel, *The Addictive Organization* (San Francisco: Harper, 1988).

14. Diane Fassel and Anne Wilson Schaef, "A Feminist Perspective on Work Addiction," in *Feminist Perspectives on Addictions*, edited by Nan Van Den Bergh (New York: Springer, 1991), 199–211.

15. Nicole Pesce, "The Average Worker Checks Their Email before They Even Get Out of Bed in the Morning," *MarketWatch*, February 9, 2019, https://www.marketwatch.com.

16. Sheila McClear, "Half of Americans Consider Themselves Workaholics," *Ladders*, February 8, 2019, https://www.theladders.com.

17. HSBC, "Chained to Their Desks: Controversy Over a Cushion That Tracks the Work Rate of Office Staff," *Week in China*, January 15, 2021, https://www.weekinchina.com.

18. Amna Anjum et al., "An Empirical Study Analyzing Job Productivity in Toxic Workplace Environments," *International Journal of Environmental Research and Public Health* 15 (2018): 1–15.

19. John Sheridan, "Workin' Too Hard," *Industry Week*, January 18, 1988, 31–36.

20. Chade-Meng Tan, *Search inside Yourself: The Unexpected Path to Achieving Success, Happiness (and World Peace)* (New York: HarperOne, 2012).

21. Shellenbarger, "To Cut Office Stress, Try Butterflies and Meditation?"

22. Gaurav Bhatnagar and Mark Minukas, *Unfear: Transform Your Organization to Create Breakthrough Performance and Employee Well-Being* (New York: McGraw Hill, 2021).

23. Kaitlin Quistgaard, "Stress Buster," *Yoga Journal*, August 2012, 26.

24. Tony Schwartz, "Relax! You'll Be More Productive," *New York Times*, February 9, 2013; Tony Schwartz, *Be Excellent at Anything* (New York: Free Press, 2010).

11. "Good Trouble" in Corporate America

1 Beth Mirza, "Toxic Workplace Cultures Hurt Workers and Company Profits," *SHRM* 25 September 25, 2019, https://www.shrm.org.

2. Alex Moshakis, "Micromanagement, Credit Stealing, Bullying: Are You a Jerk at Work?" *The Guardian*, January 30, 2022, https://www.theguardian.com; Tessa West, *Jerks at Work: Toxic Co-Workers and What to Do About Them* (New York: Ebury Edge, 2022).

3. West, *Jerks at Work*.

4. Scott Reeves, "Workaholics Anonymous," *Forbes*, April 20, 2006, 1–3.

5. Daily Editor, "Employees Reveal How Stress Affects Their Jobs," *Business News Daily*, May 31, 2020, https://www.businessnewsdaily.com.

6. Steven Kurutz, "I Quit a Famous Rock Band," *Self-Care: Follow Your Passions, Build Healthy Habits, and Embrace Optimism* (New York: New York Times, 2020), 19.

7. Danya Issawi, "I Quit the Priesthood," *Self-Care: Follow Your Passions, Build Healthy Habits, and Embrace Optimism* (New York: New York Times, 2020) 19–20.

8. Anna Dubenko, "I Quit Yale," *Self-Care: Follow Your Passions, Build Healthy Habits, and Embrace Optimism* (New York: New York Times, 2020), 20–21.

9. Reprinted from Bryan Robinson, "Before You Quit Your Job, Take These Seven Steps First," *Forbes.com*, October 18, 2021, https://www.forbes.com. Used with permission.

10. Bryan Robinson, "How Remote Working is Reshaping a Future New World of Work," *Forbes.com*, May 4, 2020, https://www.forbes.com.

11. Robinson, "How Remote Working is Reshaping a Future New World of Work."

12. Daniel Stillman, *Good Talk: How to Design Conversations That Matter* (Amsterdam: Management Impact Publishing, 2020).

13. Bryan Robinson, "How Remote Working is Reshaping a Future New World of Work."

14. Bryan Robinson, "Why Critics Say Elon Musk's Return-to-Office Ultimatum is Dangerous." Robinson, "How Remote Working is Reshaping a Future New World of Work."

15. Bryan Robinson, "Déjà Vu: Delta Variant Requires Companies to Rethink Return-to-the Office Plans," *Forbes.com*, August 15, 2021, https://www.forbes.com.

16. Owl Labs, "State of Remote Work, 2021," *Owl Labs*, January 15, 2022, https://owllabs.com; Vanson Bourne, "The Evolving Office: How Employee Wellness and Health are Changing Post Covid-19," *Ergotron*, January 25, 2022, http://www.ergotron.com.

17. Bryan Robinson, "Remote Work Is Here to Stay and Will Increase into 2023, Experts Say," *Forbes.com*, February 1, 2022.

18. U.S. Bureau of Labor Statistics, "Job Openings and Labor Turnover Survey," *Economic News Release*, January 4, 2022, https://www.bls.gov.

19. Bryan Robinson, "Debunking the Myth We Must Be Superhuman for Career Success," *Forbes.com*, August 1, 2021, https://www.forbes.com.

20. "Rearchitect Work for an Altered World," *Upraise*, January 2022, https://upraise.io.

21. Bryan Robinson, "Debunking the Myth We Must Be Superhuman for Career Success."

22. Robinson, "Debunking the Myth."

23. Robinson, "Debunking the Myth."

24. Ernst and Young, "2021 EY Empathy in Business Survey," October 14, 2021, https://www.prnewswire.com.

25. Sarah Roberts-Lewis, et al., "Covid-19 Lockdown Impact on the Physical Activity of Adults with Progressive Muscle Diseases," *BMJ Neurology Open* 3 (2021): 1–3, DOI: doi:10.1136/bmjno-2021–000140.

26. Robert Klaft and Brian Kleiner, "Understanding Workaholics," *Business* 38 (1988): 39.

12. The Perspective Less Taken

1. James Clear, *Atomic Habits: Tiny Changes, Remarkable Results* (New York: Avery Books, 2018).
2. Whitney Goodman, *Toxic Positivity: Keeping It Real in a World Obsessed with Being Happy* (New York: TarcherPerigee, 2022).
3. Bryan Robinson, Claudia Flowers, and Chris Burris, "An Empirical Study of the Relationship between Self-Leadership and Workaholism 'Firefighter' Behavior," *Journal of Self-Leadership* 2 (2005): 22–36.
4. Viktor Frankl, *Man's Search for Meaning* (Boston: Beacon, 2006).
5. Edith Eger, *The Gift: 12 Lessons to Save Your Life* (New York: Scribner, 2020).
6. Barbara Fredrickson, *Positivity: Top-Notch Research Reveals the 3-to-1 Ratio That Will Change Your Life* (New York: Three Rivers, 2009).
7. Fredrickson, *Positivity*.
8. Fredrickson, *Positivity*.
9. See, for example, Ron Kaniel, Cade Massey, and David Robinson, "Optimism and Economic Crisis," working paper, July 15, 2010; Suzanne Segerstrom, *Breaking Murphy's Law: How Optimists Get What They Want from Life—and Pessimists Can Too* (New York: Guilford, 2007); Darrin Donnelly, *Relentless Optimism: How a Commitment to Positive Thinking Changes Everything* (New York: Shamrock New Media, 2017); Martin Seligman, *Learned Optimism: How to Change Your Mind and Your Life* (New York: Random House, 2006); Suzanne Segerstrom, "Dispositional Optimism, Psychophysiology, and Health," in *The Oxford Handbook of Health Psychology* (New York: Oxford University Press, 2011).
10. Segerstrom, *Breaking Murphy's Law*.
11. Kaori Kato et al., "Positive Attitude towards Life and Emotional Expression as Personality Phenotypes for Centenarians," *Aging* 4 (2012): 359–367.
12. This poem was inspired by the poem, "The Worst Day Ever," by Chanie Gorkin.
13. Bryan Robinson, "How Adversity Can Empower You in Your Career," *Forbes.com*, April 11, 2020, https://www.forbes.com.
14. Richard Tedeschi, "Growth After Trauma," *Harvard Business Review*, July-August 2020; Richard Tedeschi et al., *Posttraumatic Growth: Theory, Research, and Applications* (New York: Routledge, 2018).
15. Bryan Robinson, "How Soulbird India.Arie is Helping Calm the Nation During These Turbulent Times," *Forbes.com*, June 5, 2020, https://www.forbes.com.
16. Catherine Price and Carmel Wroth, "Compassion Remains a Gift of the Spirit," *Yoga Journal*, August 2012, 78–81, 100.
17. Kristin Neff, *Self-Compassion: The Proven Power of Being Kind to Yourself* (New York: HarperCollins, 2011).

13. Mindful Working

1. For more on Jewel's incredible story, see Jewel Kilcher, *Never Broken* (New York: Blue Rider Press, 2015).
2. Bryan Robinson, "From Abuse to Homelessness to Fame, Singer Jewel Now Supports Workplace Mental Health," *Forbes.com*, November 16, 2021, https://www.forbes.com.

3. Matthew Killingsworth and Daniel Gilbert, "A Wandering Mind Is an Unhappy Mind," *Science*, November 12, 2010, 932.

4. See Bryan Robinson, *Work Addiction* (Deerfield Beach, FL: Health Communications, 1989) in which I first described brownouts as more frequent and severe in workaholics and similar to alcoholic blackouts, which are characterized by memory losses of interactions and events.

5. Chade-Meng Tan, *Search Inside Yourself: The Unexpected Path to Achieving Success, Happiness (and World Peace)* (New York: Harper One, 2012).

6. See, for example, Thomas Bien and Beverly Bien, *Mindful Recovery: A Spiritual Path to Healing from Addiction* (New York: Wiley, 2002); Thomas Bien, *Mindful Therapy: A Guide for Therapists and Helping Professionals* (New York: Wisdom, 2006); Richard Davidson et al., "Alterations in Brain and Immune Function Produced by Mindfulness Meditation," *Psychomatic Medicine* 65 (2003): 564–70; the Dalai Lama and Howard Cutler, *The Art of Happiness at Work: The Conversation Continues about Job, Career, and Calling* (New York: Riverhead, 2003); Jon Kabat-Zinn, *Coming to Our Senses: Healing Ourselves and the World through Mindfulness* (New York: Hyperion, 2005); Daniel Siegel, *The Mindful Therapist: A Clinician's Guide to Mindsight and Neural Integration* (New York: Norton, 2010); Daniel Siegel, *Mindsight: The New Science of Personal Transformation* (New York: Bantam, 2010).

7. Tan, *Search Inside Yourself*.

8. See, for example, Daniel Siegel, *Mindsight: The New Science of Personal Transformation* (New York: Bantam, 2010); Daniel Siegel, *The Mindful Brain: Reflection and Attunement in the Cultivation of Well-Being* (New York: Norton, 2007); Richard Hanson and Richard Mendius, *Buddha's Brain: Practical Neuroscience of Happiness, Love, and Wisdom* (Oakland, CA: New Harbinger, 2009).

9. For more about Dr. Murthy's stand on the importance of connection, see Vivek Murthy, *Together: The Healing Power of Human Connection in a Sometimes Lonely World* (New York: Harper Wave, 2020).

10. Bryan Robinson, "Loneliness on the Job Is a Public Health Crisis: Former Surgeon General Reveals What This Means for You," *Forbes.com*, January 3, 2020, https://www.forbes.com.

11. Jon Kabat-Zinn, *Wherever You Go, There You Are: Mindfulness Meditation in Everyday Life* (New York: Hachette, 2005), 5.

12. See, for example, Hanson and Mendius, *Buddha's Brain*; Martin Rossman, *The Worry Solution: Breakthrough Science to Turn Stress and Anxiety into Confidence and Happiness* (New York: Crown, 2010); Daniel Siegel, *The Mindful Brain* (New York: Norton, 2007); Ronald Siegel, *The Mindful Solution: Everyday Practices for Everyday Problems* (New York: Guilford, 2010).

13. Jim Loehr and Tony Schwartz, *The Power of Full Engagement: Managing Energy, Not Time, Is the Key to High Performance and Personal Renewal* (New York: Free Press, 2005).

14. Jan Chozen Bays, *Mindful Eating: A Guide to Rediscovering a Healthy and Joyful Relationship with Food* (Boston: Shambhala, 2009), 5.

15. Thich Nhat Hanh, *Peace in Every Step: The Path of Mindfulness in Everyday Life* (New York: Bantam, 1991).

16. Bryan Robinson, "Tara Brach on How Meditation Brings Healing to Workplace Fears During Turbulent Times," *Forbes.com*, June 15, 2020, https://www.forbes.com.

17. Robinson, "Tara Brach on How Meditation Brings Healing to Workplace Fears During Turbulent Times."

18. Bryan Robinson, "ABC News Anchor Dan Harris on How Meditation Changed His Personal Life and Built a New Business," *Forbes.com*, November 4, 2020, https://www.forbes.com.

19. See, for example, Deniz Vatansever, Shouyan Wang, and Barbara Sahakian, "Covid-19 and Promising Solutions to Combat Symptoms of Stress, Anxiety and Depression," *Neuropsychopharmacology*, 46 (2021): 217–218; Yanli Lin, et al., "On Variation in Mindfulness Training: A Multimodal Study of Brief Open Monitoring Meditation on Error Monitoring," *Brain Sciences* 9 (2019): 226, DOI: 10.3390/brainsci9090226; Lynley Turkelson and Quintino Mano, "The Current State of Mind: A Systematic Review of the Relationship Between Mindfulness and Mind-Wandering," *Journal of Cognitive Enhancement*, November 25, 2021, DOI: 10,1007/s41465-021-00231-6.

20. Ron Seigel and Michael Yapko, "Has Mindfulness Been Oversold?" *Psychotherapy Networker*, March–April 2012, 55.

21. Daphne Davis and Jeffrey Hayes, "What Are the Benefits of Mindfulness? A Practice Review of Psychotherapy-Related Research," *Psychotherapy* 48 (2011): 198–208.

22. See Bryan Robinson, *#Chill: Turn Off Your Job and Turn On Your Life* (New York: William Morrow, 2019), for details on various strategies for managing stress.

14. Untangling from the Workaholic Part of You

1. Richard Schwartz, *No Bad Parts: Healing Trauma & Restoring Wholeness with the Internal Family Systems Model* (Boulder, CO: 2021).

2. See for example, Ethan Kross, *Chatter: The Voice in Our Head, Why It Matters, and How to Harness It* (New York: Crown, 2021); Ethan Kross, et al., "Self-Talk as a Regulatory Mechanism: How You Do It Matters," *Journal of Personality and Social Psychology* (2014): 106: 304–24; Clayton Critcher and David Dunning, "Self-Affirmations Provide a Broader Perspective on Self-Threat," *Personality and Social Psychology Bulletin* 41 (2014): 3–18.

3. Ethan Kross, *Chatter*.

4. Ethan Kross, et al., "Self-Talk as a Regulatory Mechanism: How You Do It Matters."

5. Richard Schwartz, *No Bad Parts: Healing Trauma and Restoring Wholeness with the Internal Family Systems Model*.

6. Pema Chödrön, *Welcoming the Unwelcome: Wholehearted Living in a Brokenhearted World* (Boulder, CO: Shambhala, 2019).

15. Radical Self-Care and Fierce Self-Compassion

1. John Bowlby, "The Making and Breaking of Affectional Bonds," *British Journal of Psychiatry* 130 (1977): 201–10.

2. Bryan Robinson, "Brain Scientist Witnesses Her Own Stroke, Shares Tips on Life and Career," *Forbes.com*, March 7, 2020, https://www.forbes.com.

3. Mathew White et al., "Spending at Least 120 Minutes a Week in Nature is Associated with Good Health and Wellbeing," *Scientific Reports* 9 (2019): 11, DOI: 10.1038/s41598-019-44097-4.

4. Virginia Sturm, et al., "Big Smile, Small Self: Awe Walks Promote Prosocial Positive Emotions in Older Adults," *Emotion*, September 21, 2020, DOI: 10.1037/emo0000876.

5. My appreciation to Steve Glaser, CEO of ComfortZones Digital for contributing to this list.

6. Richard Schwartz, *No Bad Parts: Healing Trauma and Restoring Wholeness with the Internal Family Systems Model* (Boulder, Colorado: Sounds True, 2021), 127.

7. Tara Van Bommel, "The Power of Empathy in Times of Crisis and Beyond," *Catalyst* September 2021, https://www.catalyst.org.

8. Antoine Lutz et. al, "Regulation of the Neural Circuitry of Emotion by Compassion Meditation: Effects of Meditative Expertise," *PLoS One* 3 (2008): 1897, DOI: 10.1371/journal.pone.0001897.

9. Kristin Neff, *Fierce Self-Compassion: How Women Can Harness Kindness to Speak Up, Claim Their Power, and Thrive* (New York: Harper Wave, 2021); Kristin Neff, *Self-Compassion* (New York: HarperCollins, 2011); Christopher Germer, *The Mindful Path to Self-Compassion* (New York: Guilford, 2009).

10. Clayton Critcher and David Dunning, "Self-Affirmations Provide a Broader Perspective on Self-Threat," *Personality and Social Psychology Bulletin*, 41 (2015): 3–18.

11. Rebecca Thurston et al., "Self-Compassion and Subclinical Cardiovascular Disease among Midlife Women," *Health Psychology* 40 (2021): 747–753.

12. Bryan Robinson, "Self-Compassion is an Essential Tool to Excel in Your Career, Expert Says," *Forbes.com*, June 3, 2021, https://www.forbes.com.

13. Neff, *Self-Compassion* and *Fierce Self-Compassion: How Women can Harness Kindness to Speak Up, Claim Their Power, and Thrive.*

14. Bryan Robinson, "Great Leadership: 5 Steps to Move Employees up the Career Ladder," *Forbes.com*, July 11, 2019, https://www.forbes.com.

Appendix

1. Information on Workaholics Anonymous ("The Steps of Workaholics Anonymous" and the "History of Workaholics Anonymous") is reprinted by permission of Workaholics Anonymous World Service Organization, Copyright 1991 WA World Services, Inc.

2. Mario del Llorens, Marisa Salanova, and Wilmar Schaufeli, "Validity of a Brief Workaholism Scale," *Psicothema* 22 (2010): 143–50.

3. Bryan Robinson, Phyllis Post, and Judith Khakee, "Test-Retest Reliability of the Work Addiction Risk Test," *Perceptual and Motor Skills* 74 (1992): 926.

4. Bryan Robinson, "The Work Addiction Risk Test: Development of a Self-Report Measure of Workaholism," *Perceptual and Motor Skills* 88 (1999): 199–210.

5. Bryan Robinson and Phyllis Post, "Split-Half Reliability of the Work Addiction Risk Test: Development of a Measure of Workaholism," *Psychological Reports* 76 (1995): 1226.

6. Bryan Robinson and Phyllis Post, "Validity of the Work Addiction Risk Test," *Perceptual and Motor Skills* 78 (1994): 337–38.

7. Bryan Robinson and Bruce Phillips, "Measuring Workaholism: Content Validity of the Work Addiction Risk Test," *Psychological Reports* 77 (1995): 657–58.

8. Bryan Robinson, "Concurrent Validity of the Work Addiction Risk Test as a Measure of Workaholism," *Psychological Reports* 79 (1996): 1313–14.

9. Charles Spielberger, *Self-Evaluation Questionnaire (STAI Form X-2)* (Palo Alto, CA: Consulting Psychologists, 1968).

10. James Blumenthal et al., "Development of a Brief Self-Report Measure of the Type A (Coronary Prone) Behavior Pattern," *Journal of Psychosomatic Research* 29 (1985): 265–74.

11. David Jenkins, Ray Rosenman, and Meyer Friedman, "Development of an Objective Psychological Test for the Determination of the Coronary-Prone Behavior Pattern in Employed Men," *Journal of Chronic Disease* 20 (1967): 371–79.

12. Sandra Swary, "Myers-Briggs Type and Workaholism," honors thesis, Georgia State University, 1996.

13. Del Llorens, Salanova, and Schaufeli, "Validity of a Brief Workaholism Scale."

14. Samantha Rush, "Problematic Use of Smartphones in the Workplace: An Introductory Study," PhD diss., Central Queensland University, 2011.

15. A. Rezvani, "Workaholism: Are Physicians at Risk?" *Occupational Medicine* 64 (2016): 410–16.

16. Monika Bartczak and Oginska-Bulik, "Workaholism and Mental Health Among Polish Academic Workers," *International Journal of Occupational Safety and Ergonomics* 18 (2012): 3–13.

17. Robert Urban, "A Four-Factor Model of Work Addiction: The Development of the Work Addiction Risk Test Revised," *European Addiction Research* 25 (2019): 145–160.

Index

Page numbers in *italics* indicate Figures and Tables.

About the Author

Bryan E. Robinson, PhD, is co-founder and Chief Architect Officer of ComfortZones Digital, Inc., Professor Emeritus at the University of North Carolina at Charlotte, and a licensed psychotherapist in private practice in Asheville, North Carolina. He is the author of over forty self-help and academic books and a regular contributor to *Forbes.com* and *Thrive Global.* He co-hosts an annual live international webinar, the Resiliency Forum.

Robinson has published his research in over a hundred scholarly journals. He received the American Counseling Association's Research Award and the University of North Carolina at Charlotte's First Citizen Scholars Medal for his pioneering research on the negative consequences of workaholism. He hosted the PBS documentary *Overdoing It: When Work Becomes Your Life* and has been featured on numerous television programs, including ABC's 20/20, *Good Morning America, World News Tonight,* the NBC *Nightly News,* the CBS *Early Show, The Doctors,* and the PBS show *The Marketplace.*

Robinson's debut novel, a murder mystery about a workaholic titled *Limestone Gumption,* was published in 2014 and was made into a pilot for a television series in 2022. For more information, you can visit his website at www.bryanrobinsonbooks.com or email him at bryan.robinson@comfortzonesdigital.com.

10/2023
$21.95

LONGWOOD PUBLIC LIBRARY
800 Middle Country Road
Middle Island, NY 11953
(631) 924-6400
longwoodlibrary.org

LIBRARY HOURS

Monday-Friday	9:30 a.m. - 9:00 p.m.
Saturday	9:30 a.m. - 5:00 p.m.
Sunday (Sept-June)	1:00 p.m. - 5:00 p.m.